Humana Festival 2009
The Complete Plays

Humana Inc., headquartered in Louisville, Kentucky, is one of the nation's largest publicly traded health and supplemental benefits companies, with approximately 11.5 million medical members. Humana is a full-service benefits solutions company, offering a wide array of health and supplementary benefit plans for employer groups, government programs and individuals.

The Humana Foundation was established in 1981 as the philanthropic arm of Humana Inc. It is a private foundation that supports and nurtures charitable activities that promote healthy lives and healthy communities.

Humana Festival 2009
The Complete Plays

Edited by
Adrien-Alice Hansel and Amy Wegener

Playscripts, Inc.

New York, NY

Published by Playscripts, Inc.
450 Seventh Avenue, Suite 809
New York, New York, 10123
www.playscripts.com

Cover Design by Matt Dobson
Cover Image by Julien Pacaud
Text Design and Layout by Jason Pizzarello

First Edition: April 2010
10 9 8 7 6 5 4 3 2 1

LCCN: 95650734
ISSN: 1935-4452

ISBN-13: 978-0-9819099-3-6

Contents

Acknowledgments

The editors wish to thank the following persons for their invaluable assistance in compiling this volume:

Jennifer Bielstein
Zach Chotzen-Freund
Cathy Colliver
Sean Daniels
Matt Dobson
Julie Felise Dubiner
Emily Feldman
Leslie Hankins
Morgan Jenness
Kory Kelly
Rachel Lerner-Ley
Sarah Lunnie
Marc Masterson
Brendan Pelsue
Jeff Rodgers
Sarah Rowan
Emily Ruddock
Zan Sawyer-Dailey
Kyle Shepherd
Wanda Snyder
Stephanie Spalding

William Craver
Joyce Ketay
Carl Mulert
Elsa Neuwald
Mark Orsini
Bruce Ostler
Thomas Pearson
Jessica Sarbo
Jack Shoemaker
Maura Teitelbaum
Derek Zasky

Actors Theatre of Louisville Staff
Humana Festival 2009

Artistic Director . . . . Marc Masterson
Managing Director . . . . .Jennifer Bielstein

ADMINISTRATION

Budget and Management
General Manager . . . . Jeffrey S. Rodgers
Human Resources Coordinator . . . . .Cora Brown
Systems Manager . . . . .Dottie Krebs
Executive Secretary . . . . Wanda Snyder
Administrative Services Coordinator . . . . Alan Meyer

Marketing
Director . . . . .Kory P. Kelly
Manager . . . . Cathy Colliver
Communications Coordinator . . . . Leslie Hankins
Community Relations Coordinator . . . . Babs W. Freibert
Media & Publicity Coordinator . . . . .Kyle Shepherd
Graphics Coordinator . . . . .Matt Dobson
Festival/Events Manager . . . . Stephanie Spalding
Festival Coordinator . . . . Sarah Rowan
Group Sales Manager . . . . .Sarah Peters
Group Sales Assistant Manager . . . . J. Stephen Smith
Outbound Sales Manager . . . . Lynda Sylvester
Outbound Sales Assistant Manager . . . . Jordan Kelsh

Development
Director . . . . Schuyler Heuser
Manager of Patron Relations . . . . .Trish Pugh Jones
Manager of Foundation and Government Relations . . . . . . Mike Brooks
Manager of Corporate Relations . . . . Terra Leavell
Manager of Annual Fund . . . . Heather Franklin
Coordinator of Patron Relations . . . . Gretchen Abrahamsen
Coordinator . . . . .Andy Nusz

Finance
Director . . . . .Peggy Shake
Accounting Coordinator . . . . Erin Bukowski
Accounting Assistant . . . . Brunhilda Williams-Curington

Operations

Director .... Mike Schüssler-Williams
Assistant Manager .... Barry Witt
Maintenance .... Alan Reed
Maintenance Electrician .... Chris Clark
Receptionist .... Chris Bryant
Housekeeping .... Jessica Brooks, Robert Bryant,
Pat Duncan, Robert Herron, Jessica Parker,
Donna Sanders, Sharon Sloan

AUDIENCE SERVICES

Ticket Sales

Director .... Kim McKercher
Senior Box Office Manager .... Saundra Blakeney
Training Manager .... Steve Clark
Subscriptions Manager .... Julie Gallegos
Senior Customer Service .... Kristy Kannapell
Customer Service .... Cheryl Anderson, Christie Baugher,
Alicia Dossett, Christa Kreimendahl,
Carol Niehaus

Volunteer and Audience Relations

Director .... Allison Hammons
House Managers .... Adela Chipe, Dana Cooley,
Elizabeth Cooley, Stephanie Lawson,
Kyle Sawyer-Dailey, Cory Vaughn
Coat Check Attendants .... Tanisha Johnson,
Rachel Lerner-Ley, Lila Neugebauer,
Brendan Pelsue, Thomas Peter

ARTISTIC

Associate Artistic Director .... Sean Daniels
Associate Director .... Zan Sawyer-Dailey
Artistic Manager .... Emily Ruddock
Company Manager .... Dot King

Literary

Director of New Play Development .... Adrien-Alice Hansel
Literary Manager .... Amy Wegener
Resident Dramaturg .... Julie Felise Dubiner
Literary Fellow .... Sarah Lunnie

Resident Designers

Scenic Designer . . . . Paul Owen
Costume Designer . . . . Lorraine Venberg
Properties Director . . . . Mark Walston
Lighting Designer . . . . Brian J. Lilienthal
Sound Designer . . . . Matt Callahan

Education

Director . . . . Steven Rahe
Coordinator . . . . Jacob Stoebel
New Voices Playwriting Coordinator . . . . Lee Look
Teaching Artists . . . . Liz Fentress, Jessica Leader

PRODUCTION

Production Manager . . . . Kathleen Kronauer
Assistant Production Manager . . . . Paul Werner
Production Stage Manager . . . . Paul Mills Holmes
Resident Stage Manager . . . . Debra Anne Gasper

Scenic

Technical Director . . . . Michael J. Bowen
Assistant Technical Directors . . . . Justin Hagovsky,
Alexis Tucker
Technical Production Assistant . . . . Rebecca Price-Sanders
Shop Foreman . . . . Marshall Spratt
Carpenters . . . . Charles Ames, Braden Blauser,
Noah Johnson, Javan Roy-Bachman, Pierre Vendette
Stage Operations Supervisor . . . . Emily Meyer
Deck Carpenter . . . . Seth Holder
Design Assistant . . . . Brenda Ellis
Scenic Charge . . . . Kieran Wathen
Scenic Artist . . . . Ron Temple
Journeyman . . . . Ryan Harvey

Costume

Shop Manager . . . . Margret Fenske
Assistant to Designer . . . . Emily Ganfield
Crafts . . . . Shari Cochran
Drapers . . . . Kelly Gassert, Shana Lincoln
First Hand . . . . Karen Merrill
Technicians . . . . Christi Johnson,
Bonnie Jonus, Mary Lee Younger
Wig Master/Designer . . . . Heather Fleming

Pamela Brown Wardrobe Mistress . . . . Angela Marie Logsdon
Bingham Theatre Wardrobe Mistress . . . . Cristy Smith
Victor Jory Wardrobe Mistress . . . . Jade Biviano
Journeyman . . . . Lindsay Chamberlin
Wardrobe Technician . . . . Lisa Snee

Lighting
Supervisor. . . . . Paul Werner
Associate Supervisor . . . . Nick Dent
Assistant Master Electrician . . . . Lauren Scattolini
Deck Electrician . . . . Rob Brodersen
Board Operators/Swing Electricians . . . . Danielle Clifford,
Alexandra Manuel, Derek Miller

Sound
Associate Designer . . . . Benjamin Marcum
Engineer. . . . . Paul Doyle
Technicians. . . . . Jessica Collins, Mareth Griffith, Jacob Rosene

Properties
Masters . . . . Doc Manning, Alice Baldwin
Carpenter . . . . Joe Cunningham
Artisans . . . . William Griffith, Scott Rygalski
Soft Goods Artisan . . . . Heather Jakubisin
Journeymen. . . . . Elliot Cornett, Taj Whitesell

Video
Media Technologist . . . . Phillip Allgeier

APPRENTICE/INTERN COMPANY
Director . . . . Michael Legg
Assistant Director . . . . Amy Attaway

Apprentices
Matthew Baldiga, Julia Bentz, David Michael Brown, Alison Clayton,
Michael Dalto, Eric Eteuati, Ami Jhaveri, Anna Kull, Aaron Matteson,
Katharine Moeller, Chris Moore, Allison Moy, Claudine Mboligikpelani
Nako, Andy Nogasky, Nancy Noto, LaKeisha Randle, Steven Rausch,
Daniel Reyes, Jon Riddleberger, Anne Veal, Jacob Wilhelmi

Interns
Artistic Management. . . . . Stephanie Lawson
Marketing. . . . . Yinka Oyekunle, Thomas Peter
Directing . . . . Nathan Green, Lila Neugebauer
Literary . . . . Rachel Lerner-Ley, Brendan Pelsue

Education . . . . Julie Mercurio, Jeffrey Mosser
Production Management . . . . Jillian Spencer
Stage Management . . . . Leslie Cobb,
Kelsey Daye Lutz, Cadi Thomas
Costume . . . . Nicole Bukowski,
Evan Prizant, Vanessa Streeter
Lighting . . . . .JohnBen Lacy
Sound . . . . Stowe Nelson
Properties . . . . Jessie Combest

Foreword

Now more than ever, America needs its theatre. As we face an uncertain future, the theatre offers a public space for people to come together to ask questions, to be absorbed, engaged and opened up to new stories, or sometimes just to share a laugh. Each year, Actors Theatre of Louisville enjoys the distinct privilege—and unique challenge—of launching a diverse body of new work into America's theatrical landscape. The 33rd Humana Festival of New American Plays offered a broad cross section of styles and voices. Hundreds of artists and technicians worked behind the scenes and on stage to bring these stories to life. The result is a richly varied program that embraces an array of subjects and aesthetics, shared in this volume in printed form.

We thank The Humana Foundation for its generous and ongoing support, without which our work would not be possible. Its longstanding commitment to nurturing the arts is inspiring, and ensures that the festival will continue to thrive in the years to come. We salute the nineteen innovative playwrights who, with singular vision and stirring voices, are the true architects of the festival. And now, we welcome you, the reader. Your imagination continues a journey that began with words on paper, and that finds its next incarnation in your hands.

—*Marc Masterson*
Artistic Director
Actors Theatre of Louisville

Editors' Note

Why is this story important
Why is any story about anybody important
Why is right and wrong important
Important to know how others live
Even if you don't live that way
Even if you don't know them
——*Ameriville*, UNIVERSES

> It's…it's about the family. This family. The Webers. And me. It'll be fictionalized, of course, but that's my inspiration. The family dynamics: fathers and sons, competition, survival. And how…sometimes the things we do for love make us unworthy of love. There'll be my history too——my mother. (*Beat.*) What do you think? Is there a book there?
> ——*Absalom*, Zoe Kazan

But this is not the story of a life.
It is the story of lives, knit together,
overlapping in succession, rising
again from grave after grave.
——*Wild Blessings: A Celebration of Wendell Berry*

> DID YOU EVER STOP TO THINK THAT MAYBE WE NEED SOME DIFFERENT STORIES?!?!
> ——*Slasher*, Allison Moore

Storytelling is thriving in the American theatre, in a wondrous array of forms. As witnessed in the 2009 Humana Festival of New American Plays, playwrights continue to find fresh stories to tell, to revitalize classic storytelling techniques and play with genre, and to imagine new ways that an audience can be taken on a journey that unfolds in space and time, body and voice. Any way they package their tales——whether through linear narrative, collage, verse or song——listening to these writers in concert gives a sense of the endless possibility of this living art form, and a glimpse of a culture's preoccupations. Collectively, the multifaceted assortment of plays in this volume offer provocative insights about families, communities, and the enormous power of the stories we tell ourselves and one another while (to echo Charles L. Mee) we "make and remake" our past and the future.

Every year, we at Actors Theatre of Louisville read and consider around seven hundred full-length plays. Our process of reading and falling in love with playwrights' work, then discussing and winnowing the many scripts that intrigue us, ultimately shapes the bill of seven full-length plays and trio of short pieces that we produce as the Humana Festival. Every year, we seek to balance the tone and scope of these pieces, hoping to land on a combination that showcases the current landscape of American playwriting in all its adventure, insight and vibrancy, whether these writers are exploring a family's legacy or a culture's.

The playwrights of the 33rd Humana Festival included a mix of familiar faces and new voices, marking Charles L. Mee and Anne Bogart's third collaboration at Actors Theatre (as well as his fifth and her seventh Festival, and her fourteenth production in Louisville), as well as Zoe Kazan's playwriting debut. Some of the plays took a narrative approach to their subject matter: the web of history and fiction that connects and constricts the literary family in Kazan's *Absalom*; the sharp satire of *Slasher*, Allison Moore's comedy that pits feminist fury against the fleshy, bloody excesses of popular horror flicks; the haunting desperation of Naomi Wallace's intimately connected strangers in *The Hard Weather Boating Party*, pushed to an act of violence of which none imagined himself capable. The other half of the Humana Festival's full-length offerings featured less traditional approaches to character and plot—from *Ameriville*'s multivalent exploration of the vulnerabilities of a post-Hurricane Katrina United States, to Charles L. Mee's fever dream collage of the American Fifties and contemporary society in *Under Construction*, to the interplay of poetry, image and music in Marc Masterson and Adrien-Alice Hansel's *Wild Blessings*, their adaptation of Kentucky author Wendell Berry's poetry for the stage.

The varied possibilities of the short form were on display as well. Mixing the thoughtful and the absurd, *Brink!* is an energetic investigation of rites of passage, threshold-crossing experiences explored in twenty short scenes by Lydia R. Diamond, Kristoffer Diaz, Greg Kotis, Deborah Zoe Laufer, Peter Sinn Nachtrieb and Deborah Stein. The ten-minute plays of the 2009 Humana Festival were likewise a mix of the ridiculous and sublime: there was Alex Dremann's spy vs. spy, mother vs. daughter, twist-a-minute comedy *On The Porch One Crisp Spring Morning*, as well as Michael Lew and Matt Schatz's play-with-song *Roanoke*, which follows the high-stakes world of hardcore historical re-enactors at the Lost Colony of Roanoke. The ten-minute play lineup was rounded out by Marco Ramirez's Heideman Award-winning *3:59am: a drag race for two actors*, whose behind-the-wheel encounter between two men on the edge fuses lyrical beauty and percussive heat in a pulse-pounding drag race.

It's a pleasure, now, to bring the work of these playwrights to a wider audience. What you hold are the blueprints for performances brought briefly, brightly to life in March 2009 through the work of numerous artists and technical wizards (we commend you to the list of Actors Theatre staff members, as well as the production teams for each of these shows). These scripts also stand as vibrant and diverse new experiments born of the ancient impulse to make sense of our world by rethinking, retelling, de- and re-constructing the stories of our culture and our lives. May these plays bring new connections, delight and understanding.

—Amy Wegener and Adrien-Alice Hansel

ON THE PORCH
ONE CRISP SPRING MORNING

by Alex Dremann

Playscripts, Inc.
website: www.playscripts.com
email: info@playscripts.com
phone: 1-866-NEW-PLAY (639-7529)

BIOGRAPHY

Alex Dremann studied playwriting at the University of Southern California and New York University. His full-length plays include *Split Pea Pod, Postcoital Variations, Henchpeople, The :nv:s:ble Play,* and *Demon Pigs Squealing at the Moon.* His short plays include *Hypothermia, Emma of Sandusky, Cannibals Gone Bad, Dead Wong, The Cheever Tapes,* and *Sally Sock.* He got his start with *Wet Paper Bag* at Theatre Neo in Los Angeles, and since then his plays have been performed at Philadelphia Theatre Workshop, Killing My Lobster, and Provincetown Theater Playwrights Festival, among others. Alex currently lives and writes in Philadelphia, where he is the producing artistic director of Secret Room Theatre.

ACKNOWLEDGMENTS

On The Porch One Crisp Spring Morning premiered at the Humana Festival of New American Plays in March 2009. It was directed by Sean Daniels with the following cast:

MOTHER	Katie Kreisler
DAUGHTER	Nancy Noto

and the following production staff:

Scenic Designer	Paul Owen
Costume Designer	Emily Ganfield
Lighting Designer	Nick Dent
Sound Designer	Benjamin Marcum
Properties Designer	Mark Walston
Stage Manager	Paul Mills Holmes
Assistant Stage Manager	Debra Anne Gasper
Dramaturg	Julie Felise Dubiner
Assistant Dramaturg	Rachel Lerner-Ley

CAST OF CHARACTERS
MOTHER
DAUGHTER

SETTING
A porch.

TIME
Present Day.

Special thanks to Jose Aviles, Anne Gundersheimer, Colleen Hughes, Lindsay Harris & Elle McComsey.

3

Nancy Noto and Katie Kreisler
in *On The Porch One Crisp Spring Morning*

33rd Annual Humana Festival of New American Plays
Actors Theatre of Louisville, 2009
Photo by Harlan Taylor

4

ON THE PORCH
ONE CRISP SPRING MORNING

A MOTHER *and* DAUGHTER *sit on a porch on an early spring morning sipping General Foods International Coffee. Both inhale coffee aroma in unison with much satisfaction.*

DAUGHTER. Good coffee, Mother.

MOTHER. Reminds me of that time in Rome.

DAUGHTER. Antoine, our strapping young waiter.

MOTHER. Ah yes, Antoine.

(*Both inhale their coffee aroma and exhale in unison with fond remembrance.*)

DAUGHTER. Mother?

MOTHER. Yes, Darling?

DAUGHTER. I'm not feeling quite so...fresh.

MOTHER. I too sometimes have those not-so-fresh days, Dear.

DAUGHTER. No, I mean mentally, spiritually.

MOTHER. I see. Is there something troubling you?

DAUGHTER. You could say that, I suppose.

MOTHER. You know you can talk to me about anything, Dear. Everything. I'm here for you.

DAUGHTER. That's good to hear, Mother.

(DAUGHTER *sips her coffee.*)

MOTHER. Meaning I'm here for you now.

DAUGHTER. Right. OK, so this is the deal, Mother.

MOTHER. Yes, sweet-pleat?

DAUGHTER. I'm in kind of a bind.

MOTHER. I know.

DAUGHTER. You know?

MOTHER. I've read your file.

DAUGHTER. My file?

MOTHER. Of course. I'm an agent for the CIA.

DAUGHTER. Oh, I see.

(MOTHER *sips her coffee.*)

MOTHER. This really is good coffee.

DAUGHTER. You know *everything*-everything, or just everything?

MOTHER. I know you're a trained assassin and you were hired by Lenape to kill me and now you're not feeling quite so fresh mentally, spiritually or (*Whispers.*) vaginally (*Normal again.*) because the one person you'd even consider going to for advice on such a tricky moral dilemma would be your loving mother—the same woman you were hired to kill.

(MOTHER *sips her coffee. Beat.*)

DAUGHTER. I've poisoned your General Foods International Coffee.

(MOTHER *puts her cup down.* DAUGHTER *sips her coffee.*)

MOTHER. That's unfortunate, because I too have poisoned your General Foods International Coffee.

(DAUGHTER *puts her cup down.*)

DAUGHTER. Well, this is rather awkward.

MOTHER. Indeed.

DAUGHTER. Three or four minutes, you reckon?

MOTHER. If we're lucky.

(*Beat.*)

DAUGHTER. Well, it is good coffee…

(*They both pick up their coffee again and inhale.*)

MOTHER. Is that a hint of almond?

DAUGHTER. That's the strychnine.

MOTHER. Ah.

(*They both inhale the coffee aroma deeply, then sip.*)

I suppose I should tell you that I love you.

DAUGHTER. I suppose I should tell you that I am, in fact, a double-agent for a top secret special-ops division of the CIA, posing undercover as a trained assassin for Mr. Lenape. I work under CIA agent Raymond Wilma.

MOTHER. Oh. I see.

DAUGHTER. I thought that name might sound familiar.

MOTHER. Then you know the truth about Agent Wilma.

DAUGHTER. I want you to say it.

MOTHER. Raymond Wilma and I have been having an affair for many years.

DAUGHTER. And?

MOTHER. And what?

DAUGHTER. And Raymond Wilma hired Mr. Lenape to kill you.

MOTHER. Yes, but I convinced Raymond Wilma to hire you through Mr. Lenape to kill me.

DAUGHTER. That doesn't make any sense.

MOTHER. It was the only way I could expose you and your double-agency—which I have long suspected but have been unable to prove until this very moment. And I knew you would never poison your own mother's General Foods International Coffee without bringing the antidote. Your moral fiber would not allow it. Hence your lack of freshness. I'm guessing there's a vial in your coat pocket as we speak. Hand it over.

DAUGHTER. You have banked your life on my moral fiber?

MOTHER. I have raised a classy young double agent with both ethics and aplomb.

DAUGHTER. The question is, do *you* have the antidote to the poison in *my* coffee?

MOTHER. No.

DAUGHTER. No?

MOTHER. You betrayed me by actually going through with poisoning my coffee, and for that you must pay.

DAUGHTER. I think you're bluffing. I think you do have the antidote.

MOTHER. Perhaps that's what I want you to think.

DAUGHTER. Well, kudos Mother, for successfully exposing my double-agency, but what you don't know is that I am in fact a triple agent, working for Mr. Lenape, posing as a CIA agent, working undercover for Mr. Lenape. It was my plan all along to make you think I had secretly joined the CIA to please you and your moral fiber, but in fact it was to *kill you*, Mother. You see, I've known all about your affair with Raymond Wilma since the third grade when I was first learning how to wiretap and I vowed then and there to exact my revenge on you for betraying Dad. So there is no antidote.

(DAUGHTER *takes a languorous sip of her coffee.*)

MOTHER. You're adopted.

(DAUGHTER *barely avoids the obligatory spit-take.*)

DAUGHTER. W-what?

MOTHER. It's time you knew.

DAUGHTER. I—

MOTHER. But you are my biological daughter.

DAUGHTER. The poison has begun to feed at your brain, Mother.

MOTHER. I was in Tokyo on assignment and my yen for the sake is legendary. When I found out I was pregnant, I spent months trying to hide it—

DAUGHTER. But—

MOTHER. —baggy clothing, standing strategically behind large ferns, the whole thing. Your "father" was oblivious. Toward the end, I had Agent Wilma put me on a long-term assignment in Holland, where I gave birth and put you up for adoption. I came home and four months later your still-oblivious father and I adopted you. So you're both my biological daughter and my adopted daughter, but your father is not your father.

DAUGHTER. I'm…Japanese?

MOTHER. Technically Dutch.

DAUGHTER. You're bluffing. You're bluffing about all of it! My father is my father, and you do have the antidote to the poison you put in my coffee. Your "moral fiber" wouldn't allow otherwise.

MOTHER. Of course I don't.

DAUGHTER. That's because you didn't poison my coffee at all.

(DAUGHTER *takes a big gulping swig of coffee.*)

DAUGHTER. Sweet Jesus, that's good coffee.

(*Alarmed,* MOTHER *takes a vial from her coat pocket and slaps it to the table.*)

MOTHER. All right. A trade.

DAUGHTER. I knew it.

MOTHER. Antidote for antidote.

DAUGHTER. The difference here is that I want you dead and you still love me.

MOTHER. Just because I love you doesn't mean I don't want you dead.

DAUGHTER. And just because I want you dead doesn't mean I don't love you.

MOTHER. As I suspected.

DAUGHTER. And I do need to live long enough to kill you…

MOTHER. I propose we both live to kill again.

(DAUGHTER *reluctantly takes a vial from her coat pocket.*)

Ah, that's my girl. Triple-agent or no, you do have a moral fiber after all.

DAUGHTER. Who'd have thought it would come to this, Mother?

MOTHER. On three, we exchange vials. One.

(*They each roll the vials part way across the table toward the other.*)

DAUGHTER. Where is my father now?

MOTHER. Inside, reading the paper, I'd imagine. Two.

(*They roll the vials closer toward each other.*)

DAUGHTER. Not my father, my *father.*

MOTHER. Bethesda.

DAUGHTER. Bethesda?

MOTHER. Does that alarm you?

DAUGHTER. Should it?

MOTHER. Does it?

DAUGHTER. Lenape is in Bethesda.

MOTHER. Perhaps that's a coincidence. Three.

(*Neither move.*)

I said three.

DAUGHTER. Mr. Lenape is my father?

MOTHER. I didn't say that.

DAUGHTER. Are *you* a double agent?

MOTHER. I didn't say that either.

DAUGHTER. Has Lenape ever been to Tokyo?

MOTHER. Yes.

DAUGHTER. Oh my God.

(*Without moving their vial hands, they both take a sip of coffee. Then, in one fluid jolt, both women snap back their vials, stand, and pull guns on each other.*)

MOTHER. Honey, please, the vial. We're running out of time.

DAUGHTER. My father is an assassin?

MOTHER. *You* are an assassin.

DAUGHTER. An assassin with moral fiber.

MOTHER. Then hand over the vial, dear.

DAUGHTER. You work for Lenape too, don't you?

MOTHER. Yes and no.

DAUGHTER. What do you mean?

MOTHER. I work for your father.

DAUGHTER. Agent Wilma is my father?

MOTHER. Yes.

DAUGHTER. But Lenape was the one in Tokyo?

MOTHER. Yes.

DAUGHTER. Then Lenape and Agent Wilma are…

MOTHER. Yes.

DAUGHTER. The same man.

MOTHER. I'm sorry.

DAUGHTER. But that means—

(DAUGHTER *sits back down.* MOTHER *keeps gun pointed at* DAUGHTER.)

DAUGHTER. He orchestrated this whole thing, didn't he?

MOTHER. Orchestrated what whole thing?

DAUGHTER. He wants us to kill each other.

MOTHER. How so?

DAUGHTER. As Wilma, he probably tricked you into convincing him to hire himself as Lenape to kill you to expose my double-agency. Don't you see?

MOTHER. No.

DAUGHTER. And then he hired me to kill you, knowing my moral fiber would prevent me from killing you without bringing the antidote, which I did, but knowing that, he switched this antidote—and *that* antidote—for poison.

MOTHER. But.

DAUGHTER. He wants us both dead.

MOTHER. Agent Wilma is not that smart.

DAUGHTER. But *Lenape* is.

MOTHER. WHAT?

DAUGHTER. Mother, we have to work together. We have to form an alliance that will bring down Lenape-slash-Wilma. And he mustn't know that we know. I think we should exchange antidotes.

MOTHER. But you said your antidote is more poison.

DAUGHTER. Of course! If I actually do kill you, he will never know I'm on to him. It's perfect. Here, drink this.

MOTHER. But—

DAUGHTER. You'll be dead, but you'll be *in on it*, so it's OK.

MOTHER. I don't believe you. I don't believe my Raymond wants me dead, but I do believe that he wants you to think he switched the antidote for poison so it wouldn't raise suspicion when I actually died. So I'll take it and *pretend* to die.

DAUGHTER. OK then.

MOTHER. OK.

    (*They cautiously put their guns on the table. They cautiously hold out their vials.*)

DAUGHTER. On three. One.

MOTHER. Two.

DAUGHTER & MOTHER. (*In unison.*) Three.

    (*They exchange vials and uncork them.*)

MOTHER. On three. One.

DAUGHTER. Two.

MOTHER & DAUGHTER. (*In unison.*) Three.

    (*They drink. They look at each other. Beat. Beat. They collapse dead, instantaneously and simultaneously. BLACKOUT.*)

End of Play.

ABSALOM
A PLAY IN FOUR SCENES

by Zoe Kazan

BIOGRAPHY

Zoe Kazan is an actor and writer, born in Santa Monica, California and currently residing in Brooklyn, New York. As an actor, her Broadway credits include *The Seagull* and *Come Back, Little Sheba*. Off-Broadway she appeared in *Things We Want*, *100 Saints You Should Know* and *The Prime of Miss Jean Brodie*. Ms. Kazan was a recipient of the Clarence Derwent Award in the 2007-2008 Season. This play, her first, was workshopped at Lincoln Center Theater LAB and had readings at The Vineyard Playhouse, The Ensemble Studio Theatre and Yale University.

ACKNOWLEDGMENTS

Absalom premiered at the Humana Festival of New American Plays in March 2009. It was directed by Giovanna Sardelli with the following cast:

ADAM WEBER	Todd Weeks
TEDDY WEBER	Ben Huber
SOPHIA WEBER	Katie Kreisler
JULIA GRIMES WEBER	Stephanie Janssen
SAUL WEBER	Peter Michael Goetz
COLE MADDOX	J. Anthony Crane

and the following production staff:

Scenic Designer	Michael B. Raiford
Costume Designer	Lorraine Venberg
Lighting Designer	Brian J. Lilienthal
Original Music/Sound Designer	Benjamin Marcum
Properties Designer	Mark Walston
Fight Director	k. Jenny Jones
Stage Manager	Debra Anne Gasper
Assistant Stage Manager	Paul Mills Holmes
Dramaturg	Amy Wegener
Assistant Dramaturg	Rachel Lerner-Ley
Casting	David Caparelliotis, Mel Cap Casting
Directing Assistant	Mike Brooks

Absalom was originally developed at Yale University's 2004 Young Playwrights Festival. Workshop presentation by Lincoln Center Theater LAB, 2008.

CHARACTERS

SOLOMON (SAUL) WEBER, seventy, self-made man
ADAM WEBER, forty-two, eldest son
SOPHIA WEBER, thirty-seven, only daughter
THEODORE (TEDDY) WEBER, thirty-two, youngest son
JULIA GRIMES WEBER, twenty-eight, wife to Teddy
COLE MADDOX, forty-one, writer

A NOTE ABOUT CASTING

There is no need for Sophia to be ugly, Julia to be heavy from childbirth, Cole to be handsome, etc. The important thing is that the characters perceive each other or themselves this way. It is, however, necessary that Julia be charismatic/attractive/charming in a more obvious way than Sophia. Cole also may be superior in these qualities; he even may be one of these "pretty aristocratic" men whom Saul mentions. Saul should be a vital seventy.

A NOTE ABOUT COSTUMING/SET DESIGN

Although this play is set in 1986, it should not feel like a period piece. No Madonna costumes, no David Bowie tunes. The aesthetic sense of this family is more classical than current, more intellectual than pop cultural.

A NOTE ABOUT LANGUAGE

This family is comfortable with words if not with each other. When I have written "pause" or "silence," there should be a pause or silence. Where I have written "beat," I mean for there to be a change in internal direction or action; there need not be an aural or physical pause. Where no pauses are indicated, the play should move.

ABOUT ABSALOM

Absalom was the third and most beautiful of King David's sons. After his half-brother raped his sister, Absalom killed the brother and left the kingdom in a self-imposed exile. Eventually, David cajoled him to return. Some years later, Absalom led a rebellion against his father. David fought back in kind. During the battle, Absalom's long hair got caught in the branches of a tree, and he hung there, helpless. Although David had asked his men to be gentle with his son, David's general fatally ran Absalom through three times with his spear. When David saw his son's body, he grieved, and declared that stones should be piled where the body had fallen.

"The past is not dead. It is not even past."
—William Faulkner

"Since you would have none of me, I bury some of you."
—John Donne

"Absalom in his lifetime had taken and set up for himself a pillar...for he said 'I have no son to keep my name in remembrance'; he called the pillar by his own name."
—2 Samuel, 18.18

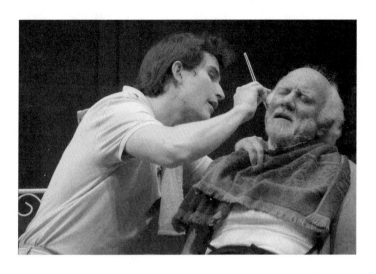

Ben Huber and Peter Michael Goetz
in *Absalom*

33rd Annual Humana Festival of New American Plays
Actors Theatre of Louisville, 2009
Photo by Harlan Taylor

ABSALOM

Scene 1

We are in the Berkshires, on the raised porch of SAUL WEBER's *country house. To the right of the porch, a path leads to a gravel driveway, which winds around a cottage and a cultivated wood to the road. Below the lip of the porch, a lawn spreads to the edge of the stage; this grassy slope bleeds into a little woods, which shelter "the lake:" an acre-square mill pond, a seasonal haven for Canadian geese, water snakes, and the occasional beaver.*

On the porch are a large dining room table with assorted chairs, some potted plants, and one large defunct chaise lounge, a book open over its arm. Behind this tableau is the bulk of the house, low, modern and sterile. The only quaint or idyllic aspect of the scene is the large apple tree that shades the left side of the porch. Its branches are improbably heavy with fruit, and its trunk is scarred with five sets of initials, carved in crude childish letters: "A.W." "C.M.W." "S.J.W." "T.W." and, newer, "T.R.W."

It is Friday, a late June afternoon, 1986. ADAM *is at the picnic table, polishing champagne flutes, china, and silver. A breeze. The porch door slams open:* TEDDY.

TEDDY. Soph thought you might need a hand.

ADAM. Thoughtful.

TEDDY. Do you?

ADAM. Do I look like I do?

> (TEDDY *goes. Beat.* TEDDY *comes out again.*)

TEDDY. She says don't send me back.

ADAM. Tell her I don't need help.

TEDDY. Tell her yourself.

ADAM. SOPH I DON'T NEED HELP.

TEDDY. Give me half, it'll go faster.

ADAM. I've got it.

> (*The tone in his voice ends the discussion.* TEDDY *walks down to the edge of the porch.*)

TEDDY. You've been keeping it nicely. Lawn hasn't looked this good since Ma.

ADAM. Dad's paying. Thousands of dollars on horse manure.

TEDDY. He's shelling out more than that for this shindig. What do you think? Rough estimate.

ADAM. You're the moneyman.

TEDDY. I'm just saying: caterers, valets.

ADAM. It's not like you're paying.

TEDDY. We offered.

ADAM. We?

TEDDY. Knopf. We. Offered. But Saul…. "Do it the old way."

ADAM. Yeah, well, "the old way" Mom was doing it. Soph's been killing herself out here for weeks.

TEDDY. Come on, she lives for this shit.

ADAM. I don't think our sister's willingness to do for our father was ever the problem.

(*Pause.*)

TEDDY. I should get going, Saul will be at the station soon. Need anything from the store?

ADAM. Julia's getting him. She left twenty minutes ago.

TEDDY. Did she take the baby?

ADAM. How should I know, I'm not the father.

TEDDY. Adam. Did she take the baby or not?

ADAM. Go check. If you're so concerned.

(*Beat.*)

TEDDY. SOPHIE, IS THE BABY IN THERE?

(*Silence.*)

I'm sure Julia wouldn't leave her without telling me—

(SOPHIA *comes to the door carrying a mixing bowl and wearing an apron.*)

SOPHIA. The baby's in the study and she's sleeping so don't yell. D.W. called; he wants to know how many copies Daddy needs for tonight?

TEDDY. I'll call him back. Come sit with us.

SOPHIA. Chicken's on the stove.

ADAM. Live a little Soph.

SOPHIA. Grow up a little Ad.

(*She goes back in the house.* ADAM *begins to pour gin into the punch bowl.*)

ADAM. So, have you read it?

TEDDY. Read what?

ADAM. "Read what?" This autobiography, this little thing I like to call "Our Last Vestige of Privacy."

TEDDY. He has the right to tell his story.

ADAM. Have you read it?

TEDDY. Have you?

ADAM. Are you kidding? The thing's better guarded than Gorbachev. I just thought you might have used your inside edge. Snuck a peak. See what kind of shit he wrote about us. You know. The usual.

(SOPHIA *comes out of the house again; she is carrying a basket.*)

SOPHIA. Ted? Liv woke up, and I think she needs changing.

TEDDY. Sure that would be great.

SOPHIA. Ted? Your kid's diaper needs changing.

(TED *rises.*)

TEDDY. Isn't it great to have a woman around the house? To do these kinds of things?

SOPHIA. I mean, I can do it—

TEDDY. Sophie: I'm kidding.

(TED *goes into the house.* ADAM *chuckles.*)

ADAM. Ladies and gentleman, Theodore Weber, the pussy-whipped wonder!

SOPHIA. Don't be grotesque.

ADAM. *Grotesque?*

SOPHIA. Leave him alone.

ADAM. The kid's got a beautiful wife, new house, just made editor. If we aren't hard on him—

SOPHIA. Give him some credit.

(*She picks up the book off the arm of the chaise lounge, starts flipping through it.*)

ADAM. I give him credit. It takes a lot to get ahead in that business.

SOPHIA. He works hard, Adam. (*Re: the book.*) Heart's Needle. What is this, poetry?

(ADAM *sees what she's doing.*)

ADAM. Don't read that.

SOPHIA. I'm not, I just saw it—

ADAM. It's mine.

SOPHIA. I'm not trying to steal it. You left it on the chair.

ADAM. Just give it to me please?

SOPHIA. I don't even like poetry.

(ADAM *takes the book inside.* SOPHIA *climbs the tree, starts picking apples, throwing them in the basket on the table. After a second,* ADAM *comes back to the door.*)

ADAM. What are you doing?

SOPHIA. What does it look like I'm doing?

ADAM. You throw them like that, they'll bruise.

(She doesn't respond. After a moment, ADAM *walks down and holds the basket up for her. She hands him apples. A little quiet.)*

Pie?

SOPHIA. Applesauce. To go with the pierogies.

ADAM. The glories of the shtetl…

SOPHIA. He wants to honor his roots.

ADAM. In that case why don't we dig a hole in the ground and let him piss in it?

SOPHIA. Adam.

ADAM. *Self Made Man.* It's quite a title.

SOPHIA. Please. One night.

ADAM. I think he's making a fool of himself, is all. Sitting up on his throne, doling out the caviar, schilling a book that totes him as the poor orphan from the Old Country. I mean, I assume. Frankly, I think it's been pretty stupid of him to keep it from us, considering we could have at least kept him from completely humiliating himself.

SOPHIA. I don't think he humiliates himself.

ADAM. You've read it.

SOPHIA. No. The publishers. They say it's good.

ADAM. Yeah? Anything good about me? Anything juicy?

SOPHIA. I don't know, Adam. I'm sure it will be fine.

(Beat. SOPHIE *very delicately broaches a new subject.)*

When I drive Daddy back to the city Monday, do you want me to take Theo's things with me?

ADAM. They're fine here.

SOPHIA. You don't think you might feel better…if they weren't around?

ADAM. Sophie, you put them in boxes, you put them in the cottage. I don't sit around holding them. They're fine where they are.

(Beat.)

SOPHIA. Do you think Kathy might want something of his?

ADAM. If I want to talk to my ex-wife, I will call her. Okay?

(Beat.)

SOPHIA. You've been looking a little pale.

ADAM. I'm fine.

SOPHIA. You never told me what remedy the homeopath put you on.

ADAM. I forget.

SOPHIA. You aren't taking it?

ADAM. I take it twice a day orally. There's a little label, in Latin. What does it matter what it is?

SOPHIA. The next time you see the homeopath—

ADAM. Sophie, can we not? Ted's right inside.

(*Beat.*)

SOPHIA. The next time you see him, you should ask him to recommend a diet.

ADAM. Yeah, I'm really hoping to slim down with this cancer treatment.

SOPHIA. Homeopathy can't kill the tumors, it can only help your body heal. If you want to beat this, you need to do the rest. Eat right, sleep well, no alcohol, no stress. You're always welcome to stay with Daddy and me.

ADAM. Yeah, that would be completely unstressful.

SOPHIA. If you aren't going to take care of yourself, you need to call Dr. Derounian and start chemo now. Okay? Okay?

(ADAM *looks at her, laughs.*)

I'm serious, Adam.

ADAM. Up there, you look like a very serious twelve-year-old.

SOPHIA. I do not.

ADAM. Any moment you'll be rolling up your skirt and spying on my friends.

SOPHIA. Shut up.

ADAM. Drawing hearts on your sneakers, hiding *Seventeen* magazine from Daddy.

(*She throws an apple at him.*)

SOPHIA. Shut up!

ADAM. Sneaking into the pantry with the phone. "Oooo, Cole's *so* dreamy."

SOPHIA. I never said that.

ADAM. Yes you did.

SOPHIA. He was like our brother.

ADAM. Not technically.

(*He holds up the basket for her to drop her apples into. She doesn't hand them down.*)

SOPHIA. He called last week.

ADAM. Who?

SOPHIA. Cole.

ADAM. He called?

SOPHIA. Wanted to know if he could come.

ADAM. What did he say?

SOPHIA. His assistant.

ADAM. Didn't have the balls to call himself.

SOPHIA. I'm sure he's busy Adam. That show is really successful, and he runs the whole thing himself.

ADAM. I'm sure.

SOPHIA. He sent a present.

> (ADAM *follows her gesture to a large box. He opens it and pulls out a huge vase.*)

ADAM. He sent an urn?

SOPHIA. It's a vase.

ADAM. It looks like an urn.

SOPHIA. It's a really nice vase.

ADAM. (*Picking up the card.*) And this: this is some official fucking stationary. "For Saul, with respect and in absentia…" He's not coming?

SOPHIA. Daddy told me only to invite the people on his list.

ADAM. You said no to him?

SOPHIA. Daddy said—

ADAM. Yes I'm sure Daddy said. Sophie. Twelve years. Twelve years without a *word*, and suddenly he wants to come here, to see us, and you don't even bother to find out what he *wanted*? How could you? How could you refuse?

SOPHIA. This is Daddy's day, he shouldn't have to be reminded of—all that.

ADAM. That's right. Poor helpless Saul really needs your protection. You win the gold star.

> (SOPHIA *gets down from the tree.*)

Don't be like that. I'm just trying to talk. Don't be mad.

SOPHIA. I'm not mad.

ADAM. It's okay to be angry Sophie.

SOPHIA. Thank you, Adam. I happen to have about a dozen chickens on the stove?

ADAM. And as many caterers in there watching them.

SOPHIA. When you're done, bring that stuff inside.

ADAM. Pussy.

> (SOPHIA *stops and turns.*)

SOPHIA. You really shouldn't worry about what the book says. Ted thinks the whole thing is benign.

ADAM. Ted's read it?

SOPHIA. He edited it. (*Silence.* SOPHIA *falters.*) It's not a big deal. Dad didn't like the direction Jeff Kominsky was taking, Ted was available. Apparently there wasn't much for him to do. His name isn't even on it.

ADAM. Why volunteer if he wasn't going to get credit?

SOPHIA. It was just a favor.

ADAM. He should have told Knopf he's not their housekeeper.

(*An odd silence.* SOPHIA *picks at a stain on her apron. The penny drops for* ADAM.)

Knopf didn't ask him.

SOPHIA. I mean, I don't know exactly what happened—

ADAM. Of course. Who else could Pop trust?

SOPHIA. Ted works for the publisher—

ADAM. No, it makes perfect sense. Pop asked him. Why shouldn't he? And that's why Ted was made editor. Right.

(*A beat as* SOPHIA *gauges her brother's affect. He seems perfectly calm.*)

SOPHIA. I knew you'd understand.

ADAM. Then why didn't you tell me?

SOPHIA. I don't know.

ADAM. You thought I couldn't handle it?

SOPHIA. No—

ADAM. What, given my current...?

SOPHIA. I don't know. I just kept waiting for him to show it to you.

ADAM. He showed it to *you*?

SOPHIA. No.

ADAM. He showed it to you.

SOPHIA. Parts of it. To fact check.

ADAM. Fact check.

SOPHIA. I'm sure he would have asked you if you weren't so busy.

ADAM. Busy.

SOPHIA. With your novel.

ADAM. Do you know the last time I wrote, Soph?

SOPHIA. You've been preoccupied.

ADAM. July first 1984, two years ago next week. Since then, I've been pretty much free if not a little preoccupied. So what did Ted's editing consist of, exactly? More fact checking?

SOPHIA. ...Some content. I think.

ADAM. Ah. "Content." So not only is half of New York coming out here to laud a bunch of crap, it's a bunch of crap written by his dearest son.

SOPHIA. Ted's only doing for him what Daddy did for—for so many.

ADAM. ...Just say it.

SOPHIA. No. What?

ADAM. Go ahead. You've got the moral upper-hand. I didn't starve to prove that—what—that I'm independent?

SOPHIA. I wasn't trying to prove anything, I just didn't want to rely on him to edit my novel!

ADAM. Well, you're relying on him now, living in his house.

SOPHIA. I'm taking care of him! What about you?

ADAM. What *about* me?

SOPHIA. Nothing, I didn't mean that.

ADAM. For Christ's sake, stick to your guns!

SOPHIA. I'm glad you're here. I'm happy you can be near us while—

ADAM. Let's not, okay?

SOPHIA. While he's getting older. (*Beat.*) Do you know why he's retiring? Pop? His knee is giving out. Nothing serious, but he'd have to walk with a cane and he doesn't want the world to see him like that. So every morning for the past two months I've had to walk him down to the car so he can use me for a crutch. He would never admit he needs help. If he asked you—a best-selling author, if I may remind you—

ADAM. Best-selling fifteen years ago—

SOPHIA. He would've looked like an old man. Asking Ted, he could pass it off as a favor, bring him up the ranks—

(TEDDY *comes barreling out of the house, carrying a huge portable phone.*)

TEDDY. They're leaving the station now, should be here in ten. Julia says Saul had trouble on the stairs, almost fell. Should he be seeing a doctor?

(ADAM *picks up a knife and begins to peel the apples.*)

SOPHIA. If you can get him within a hundred feet of a stethoscope, keep me posted.

TEDDY. (*Picking up the apple slice* ADAM *just peeled and eating it.*) The caterers want to know are you done with the kitchen.

SOPHIA. This is the last time I hire someone to cook. (*She starts to head inside, then turns.*) When Julia gets here tell her I've started the cake.

(*She's gone.* TEDDY *crunches another apple slice.* ADAM *peels.*)

TEDDY. I'm concerned about *parking.* You think we can put people out by the squash court?

ADAM. I highly doubt that parking lots of literati are going to trek all the way out here, in Friday traffic, to watch a has-been editor rehash his glory days and disappear into senility.

TEDDY. They'll come. Remember the parties Mom used to throw? I'd sneak down here in my pajamas, sit up in the tree to watch the people dancing. And you and Cole would be down there. Stealing drinks. Scamming on the ladies.

ADAM. Sophie says Cole called her.

(*A beat.*)

TEDDY. Yeah, she mentioned. Crazy, right? After, what, ten years?

ADAM. Twelve. (*He clears his throat.*) May 1974, Theo's fifth birthday. That was the last time we were all together. That'd be twelve years. And Sophie turned him away.

TEDDY. Well, he deserves it. All he wants is Saul's money.

ADAM. You don't know that.

TEDDY. I do, actually. D.W. told me Cole's lawyers have been calling Saul's office for weeks.

ADAM. About what?

TEDDY. It seems that Cole's got the idea that Saul's going to hand him the rights to his novel.

ADAM. The rights to *Tender Currency*?

(TEDDY *nods. Beat.*)

Why would he think that?

TEDDY. I don't know.

ADAM. Who knows about this?

TEDDY. Me. D.W. The lawyers.

ADAM. Do you think Cole's found some proof? That the novel was his?

TEDDY. No. It was Saul's.

ADAM. Right.

TEDDY. It's a stunt. For attention. You know what Cole's like.

ADAM. Maybe he's changed.

TEDDY. People don't change, you just get to know them better. We know him: he's a manipulator and a liar. Mama died of a broken heart practically.

ADAM. She died of cancer, Ted. Cigarettes.

TEDDY. There are studies that prove that grief breeds cancer.

ADAM. Studies don't prove, they fail to falsify.

TEDDY. I'm just saying, I understand why Sophie said no. The guy has some nerve coming back tail held high.

ADAM. Yeah, the nerve of the guy, being a success. It's not like that's a real value in this family.

(*The sound of a car honking, pulling up the driveway.*)

TEDDY. What are you trying to say?

ADAM. Your wife's here Ted.

TEDDY. Please finish this conversation.

ADAM. By the way, congratulations on your promotion.

TEDDY. Thanks, I earned it.

ADAM. I know you did.

TEDDY. What's that supposed to mean?

ADAM. I think you've got a pretty good idea. SOPH, POP'S HERE.

TEDDY. I don't appreciate it when you use your anger to undermine my feelings.

ADAM. I don't appreciate it when you use your therapy to undermine my anger.

TEDDY. You know, that kind of negative energy is going to catch up with you someday.

ADAM. That what your shrink tells you?

TEDDY. It wouldn't kill you to be nice once in a while.

JULIA. (*From off right.*) Honey, we're home!!

(JULIA, *28, carries in* SAUL's *suitcase.* SAUL, *70, follows with his briefcase.*)

ADAM. (*To* JULIA.) I thought you were ten minutes away. What'd you do, race here?

TEDDY. (*Taking the suitcase from her.*) She does it all the time, even with the baby in the car.

SAUL. Would a baby stop Chuck Yeager? Throw that bag down, you son of a bitch, and bring me a drink.

TEDDY. It isn't even two o'clock.

SAUL. Consider it daylight savings and grant an old man a few festive hours. (*To* ADAM.) What, you don't greet your father?

ADAM. Happy birthday Pop.

SAUL. This place! Coming down the drive, I could smell it, the musk and wood…. And I thought, what's the damage this time? But then: everything's so beautiful. You've made it perfect, Son, damn near it. Wish your mother could have seen it.

ADAM. She always wanted it like this, didn't she?

(SAUL *sees* COLE's *vase on the side table.*)

SAUL. Ah! Presents! This looks nice. Who sent this?

ADAM. Cole.

SAUL. Throw it away. (*Switching tacks.*) Julia, I know there's a grandchild for me around here, but I don't hear one. Is it a mute?

TEDDY. She's asleep.

SAUL. Wake her.

JULIA. If I do, you'll have to quiet her down.

SAUL. A female baby is just a very small woman. She'll do what I say.

TEDDY. She's barely two months old—

JULIA. What are you gonna do, Solomon, cut her in half?

SAUL. Someone's a clever little cunt...

TEDDY. DAD!

ADAM. (*To* JULIA.) Sophie said to tell you she's started the cake.

JULIA. I told her I'd do it.

TEDDY. (*Re: the vase.*) Take that with you, okay?

>   (*She goes inside with the vase.*)

Saul, I'm going to set your suit out, and then we should talk about tonight?

>   (TEDDY *waits for his response.* SAUL *tosses him his hat.* TEDDY *goes inside.* SAUL *stares out at the lake. Moment of silence.*)

ADAM. Long trip?

SAUL. Should make it more often. Good for me.

ADAM. You need to sit down?

SAUL. Do I look like I do? So. You still like it out here?

ADAM. Keeps me busy. Taking care of the house, keeping the trees alive.

SAUL. If it's keeping you from writing—

ADAM. No.

SAUL. So you're writing then? Another novel? What's it about?

ADAM. ...It's new.

>   (SAUL *looks at his son long and hard. He reaches into his breast pocket and pulls out a long, thin box wrapped in fancy paper.*)

SAUL. Go ahead, open it.

ADAM. It's your birthday, you shouldn't be giving me presents.

SAUL. Tell me something I don't know.

>   (ADAM *opens it. Inside is a typewriter ribbon.*)

ADAM. What is this?

SAUL. Typewriter ribbon.

ADAM. I know what it *is*.

SAUL. Look, kid, you've spent some time out here, it's been two years. It's time to move on.

ADAM. Pop, this isn't something you just get over.

SAUL. Sure you can. Think of it as a dybbuk. It's taken hold of you, but you can beat it.

ADAM. I'm not possessed, Dad.

SAUL. Look, we all miss the hell out of him. But you've got to move on. Make a fresh start. Put that ribbon in the typewriter in the cottage, and write something. Write anything. You'll feel better. Probably write better too. Now get your sister, I've got something for her.

(ADAM *is completely still for one long moment, then abruptly goes inside.* SAUL *is alone. Some unnameable emotion crosses his face like a cloud over the sun. The moment passes;* SAUL *crosses to his briefcase. There is a sudden hitch in his step—he teeters and then rights himself. He opens his briefcase and begins removing copies of his book and placing them on the table.* SOPHIA *throws open the door.*)

SOPHIA. Poppa!

SAUL. My joy!

(*They embrace.*)

SOPHIA. Happy birthday Poppa. Are you excited about tonight?

SAUL. I'll be happy to have this over and you home again. Here, close your eyes.

(*She does. He looks for the correct copy in his stack of books.*)

This is a little early for your birthday…

SOPHIA. (*Her eyes still closed.*) You remembered!

SAUL. (*Locking the briefcase.*) Three days after mine, how could I forget?

SOPHIA. Two days after yours.

SAUL. What?

SOPHIA. June 25th, two days after yours.

SAUL. You want your present or not?

(*She nods. He hands her a copy of his book,* Self Made Man: A Life in Print. *A large picture of his face on the cover.*)

Open.

SOPHIA. (*She opens her eyes.*) Oh Poppa. It came out perfectly.

SAUL. Look inside.

(*He turns the book open to the title page. She reads.*)

SOPHIA. "For my Sophia, my wisdom, my joy. So you remember your old man. Solomon Weber. P.S. Look at page…"

SAUL. 310. (*He takes the book from her, thumbs through, and stabs his finger at a page.*) Read.

SOPHIA. "I sit in my library most days now—"

SAUL. No, no, next—

SOPHIA. "All men have the potential to be great men"?

(*He nods.*)

"Not because of what they do, but because of what they make. Having spent my life helping others make great things, I ask myself, what have I created? Then I think of my children—Adam, Sophia and Theodore—and realize that every man can be great if he is willing to see his children as his great work. People ask me, 'How did you, having come from nothing, an immigrant, uneducated, become this, a literary hero?' I say—" (*Her voice breaks.*) Oh, Poppa.

SAUL. "My children taught me all that I am. Without them, I would have been nothing." Something to show your grandchildren, eh?

(SOPHIE *looks away.*)

Sophela. You'll have children, I'm never wrong.

SOPHIA. And with whom will I be having these children?

SAUL. You in some sort of rush to replace your old man?

SOPHIA. I'm thirty-eight on Sunday.

SAUL. Don't say that, you make me feel old.

SOPHIA. You're Solomon Weber, you'll never be old.

SAUL. I'm practically dead already! They're keeping me alive on drugs. Vitamin this, vitamin that. I should tell you now, I'm not going to make it another summer.

(*Over the following, we see, but* SOPHIA *and* SAUL *do not:* ADAM *comes halfway through the door, carrying a basket of linens. At the sight of them, he hesitates. He decides to wait, and tucks himself in the doorway to watch them.*)

SOPHIA. You always say that, every time you finish a book, "I'm not going to make it…"

SAUL. Book doesn't hit stores until Tuesday. Watch me closely 'til then, no sudden moves. I thought it was all over with Julia on the way here!

SOPHIA. What do you think of her? I know at the wedding you were a little…

SAUL. The wedding, ph, who knows weddings. I couldn't like her more. Pretty, funny as hell.

SOPHIA. Yeah…

SAUL. Sophela.

SOPHIA. No, I like her.

(SAUL *laughs.*)

I mean, she's fine. Pretty.

SAUL. Jealous?

SOPHIA. Shouldn't I be?

SAUL. Well, God knows you aren't going to win any pageants, Sophie. Listen to your old man. When I first started at Knopf, it was all these fine young men. Upstanding, aristocrats. And here I was, with my nose, my manners, my foods…. To them, I was a Polack, a peasant, everything my parents died trying to escape. But I was hungry, so I played their game. Took the books with the immigrant themes, wrote poems to the Statue of Liberty—I was proud to be an American. Soon, I am making such progress, they want to show me off. So? They invite me into their homes.

SOPHIA. Daddy, you've told me this a thousand—

SAUL. I'm getting to my point. You want to hear it?

SOPHIA. (*She can't help herself.*) Yes.

SAUL. They take me into their homes. White foods, white floors, and white, blond goddesses. Their sisters!

(*Behind them, we see* TEDDY *come to the door carrying a bundle.* ADAM *holds up a hand to stop him. The two of them silently watch the scene unfold below them.*)

Now I was, contrary to belief, not a handsome man. But this was America. America: A Spick plays a Towelhead, the matinee ladies swoon. And I was the Sheik! You see, these handsome men, these pretty boys, they didn't know what it was to struggle. And so it is with our friend Julia. That's the problem with beauty: it only knows how to be desired, it doesn't know its own nature. But I worked. I yearned. I looked deep into the eyes of these sisters, these mothers, these fiancées, and my eyes said, "I want you." There is no greater seduction. It's in your blood. When your mother met me, she called me a troll, but she slept with me five days later. And she was playing hard to get.

TEDDY. You still wanted her after she called you that?

(*His voice startles* SOPHIA. SAUL *laughs.*)

SAUL. When a woman looks like June, you forgive a lot.

ADAM. My memory is, she did most of the forgiving.

SAUL. What are you boys scheming back there? You gonna off your old man?

TEDDY. Just bringing you the baby.

(SAUL *rises.*)

Olivia June Weber. Don't tell Julia she's up.

(TED *places the child in her grandfather's arms.* SAUL *uncovers her face. She is sleeping, stirring, not quite two months old.* ADAM *and* SOPHIA *stand to the side, forgotten.*)

SAUL. What a face…an angel. Her mother's looks, thank God.

SOPHIA. I should help Julia. The stove is temperamental.

(*She goes inside with her copy of the book.* SAUL *strokes the baby's face.* TEDDY *watches him.*)

SAUL. Olivia…. The most beautiful of Shakespeare's women.

TEDDY. We're going to call her Liv for short.

SAUL. "O, when mine eyes did see Olivia first, Methought she purg'd the air of pestilence."

(*Liv begins to cry.*)

Okay, okay. Okay. Calm down. I think it's time to go back to Mama. Julia! Julia!

(SAUL *goes inside, carrying the baby a little away from his body.* TEDDY *follows. We hear from inside…*)

Sophie, what the hell did you do with the furniture? It's all backwards. *(They are gone.* ADAM *touches the locked briefcase. He picks up the portable phone and walks over to the box that held* COLE's *present. He dials a number off* COLE's *card. Waits until someone picks up.)*

ADAM. Yeah can I speak with him? Will you tell him Adam Weber called? Yes, my father. We're having a party out here tonight, did Cole receive his invitation? Yeah, there's been some confusion, we think some of the invitations went missing. He's on our list. Of course I'm sure, I'm looking at it right now. Will you tell him my father asked for him specifically? Eight o'clock, the Great Barrington house. He knows how to find it.

(Lights out.)

Scene 2

It is late afternoon—magic hour. Christmas lights have been strung, but are not turned on. A lone figure stands on the porch, his back to us, peeking through the doorway. He emerges, and we see: COLE MADDOX, *a wolf in a tuxedo. He walks to the other side of the porch, surveys the property.* JULIA *appears behind him in the doorway, presenting her back as she puts on an earring. Her black dress is half-unzipped.*

JULIA. Baby, can you get this for me?

COLE. Wrong baby.

JULIA. *(She turns, blushes.)* Oh! I…I thought my husband…

COLE. It's fine, I get that all the time. *(Gesturing at her zipper.)* Do you need a hand?

JULIA. I don't think we've met.

COLE. Cole Maddox.

JULIA. Oh!

COLE. Prodigal something.

JULIA. I should have…. From your photos. Your book jackets. I loved your stories when I was in high school.

COLE. That's depressing. What's your name?

JULIA. Julia. Grimes. Weber.

(She extends her hand. He takes it. Holds onto it. Inspects her.)

COLE. Saul's new wife?

JULIA. Teddy's.

COLE. Poor Teddy.

(She withdraws her hand.)

JULIA. Look, we're not really prepared for guests yet…

COLE. I thought I'd pop up early, catch the worm. As it were.

JULIA. Well, the worm as it were is taking a nap. Do you mind waiting?

COLE. Will you keep me company?

JULIA. No, I'm going inside to alert the authorities to your presence. Do you want a drink while you wait?

COLE. Anything. Scotch, neat, preferably.

JULIA. There's punch.

COLE. Old times.

> (JULIA *goes to the punch bowl. Pauses.*)

JULIA. I'm sorry, do you mind?

> (*She gestures at her zipper.* COLE *comes behind her, zips it.*)

The hook?

> (*He hooks it.*)

Thanks.

> (*Beat. She looks at the cup in her hand, then gives it to him, empty.*)

Here, I'm sure you know your way around a punch bowl.

> (*She heads to the door.*)

COLE. Pleasure to meet you…

JULIA. Julia.

COLE. I hadn't forgotten.

> (JULIA *goes into the house.* COLE *watches her go. Begins to whistle a low, sad tune—a nervous habit. He goes to the tree and inspects his initials carved there. Behind him, the door opens, revealing* SOPHIA, *in old clothes—sneakers, tee, shorts—and her hair wet from the shower. She watches him.*)

SOPHIA. Cole.

COLE. (*Turning at her voice.*) Good Lord. Sophie.

SOPHIA. You can't be here.

COLE. Look at you.

SOPHIA. I'm serious.

COLE. You haven't changed a bit.

SOPHIA. (*Picking up the portable phone.*) I'll call you a car.

> (COLE *starts to approach her. She won't look at him, dials the cab company.*)

COLE. Put down the phone.

SOPHIA. You have to leave.

COLE. Aren't you happy to see me?

SOPHIA. Poppa's right inside.

COLE. You want to bring me to him?

SOPHIA. No.

COLE. He invited me.

SOPHIA. No, he didn't. You have to go.

COLE. Sophela.

SOPHIA. Seriously.

COLE. Serious Sophie.

SOPHIA. Stop it.

COLE. My little Sophism.

SOPHIA. Cole—

(*He embraces her. She is stiff, then a sudden shudder as she relaxes.*)

Oh.

COLE. What?

SOPHIA. …You smell like you.

COLE. Hah. You smell like home.

(*The phone makes a noise—someone from the cab company picked up.* SOPHIE *responds.*)

SOPHIA. (*Into the phone.*) I'm sorry. Wrong number.

(*She hangs up.* COLE *keeps his eyes on her. She blushes.*)

COLE. You don't look a day older.

SOPHIA. Yes I do. You do.

COLE. God Sophie, way to cushion the blow.

SOPHIA. No! It looks good. Distinguished.

COLE. I was going for distinguished; I think it's just coming out grey. You look well. Are you well?

SOPHIA. Sure, I'm great.

COLE. The old man?

SOPHIA. Great.

COLE. I heard you're living with him?

SOPHIA. It's temporary. He won't hire help, so…. You know: aging parents.

COLE. No, I don't know. One advantage of being an orphan, I guess.

SOPHIA. Oh, God, I'm sorry. I wasn't thinking.

COLE. Don't worry, that was a pity ploy to butter you up. I've actually been in contact with my mom.

SOPHIA. That's amazing! How did you find her?

COLE. Money. Are you still writing?

SOPHIA. (*Like a series of questions.*) I'm doing a piece, um, for the *Times*? On experimental oncology? But mostly I teach.

COLE. High school? College?

SOPHIA. Um, Columbia J-School? Journalism? Grad?

COLE. Yeah, I think I've heard of it. Sophie. That's huge.

SOPHIA. Yeah, big surprise, I'm not a failure after all.

COLE. No, no, I just hadn't heard. Adam must be living easy. *Red Grass.* Amazing the legs on that book. (*Beat.*) How is he? I wanted to call, but then I didn't know what to say, and then it felt too late…. Did they ever figure out what happened?

SOPHIA. Theo's blood alcohol content was…above what it should have been. But there's never any wind on the lake and he was a good swimmer. He knew not to take the boat out alone.

COLE. A little young to be drinking.

SOPHIA. Fifteen. You and Adam were up to much worse.

COLE. Fifteen. Jesus. Time flies.

SOPHIA. I've wondered, how you were.

COLE. You don't watch my show?

>   (*The door slams open.* ADAM *carries a bottle of single malt whiskey.*)

ADAM. Cole Maddox. You son of a bitch.

COLE. Adam Weber. You brought me a drink.

ADAM. Old times.

COLE. Old times. (COLE *drinks.*) Jesus. Adam Weber.

ADAM. So, the TV business: do they blow you before or after the meeting?

COLE. Oh, usually during.

ADAM. Efficient.

COLE. I do my best.

ADAM. And how's the little woman?

COLE. Woman singular?

ADAM. Cold Heart Maddox. It won't last forever, you know, you're not in your twenties anymore…

COLE. Funny, the girls still are. You're looking good. Thinned out. Suits you. Writing much?

ADAM. A bit.

SOPHIA. Really?

ADAM. Just 'cause you don't see it, doesn't mean I'm not—

SOPHIA. I didn't say that, I just thought—

COLE. So what's your book about?

ADAM. Always after my ideas. Can't get me that easily.

COLE. Please. Remember that time in Nice?

ADAM. With the car?

SOPHIA. What car?

COLE. You cracked before we'd gone a mile.

SOPHIA. What car?

COLE. That was no car, that was an Alfa.

ADAM. Cole threatened to leave me on the side of the road if I didn't tell him the plot of my next novel.

COLE. His fault, for getting out to piss.

ADAM. Made me run after him for miles.

COLE. Less than one mile. Before you cracked.

ADAM. You always stooped to conquer.

COLE. Stooped? What about when you had Teddy send me that letter?

SOPHIA. What letter?

COLE. Your big brother had your baby brother—who couldn't have been more than twelve—write, pretending to be my agent, to ask my intentions for my next book.

ADAM. A plan that, as I recall, worked.

COLE. Ted did his signature perfectly. Lucrative skill, he should have kept it up.

SOPHIA. Yeah, forgers get really far in life.

(TED *enters, stage right, carrying a poster board with the cover of* SAUL's *autobiography printed on it, his face ten times larger than life.*)

ADAM. Speak of the devil. Ted, look who's here!

TEDDY. Oh. Hi.

COLE. Hi.

TEDDY. What are you doing here?

COLE. It was a last-minute decision.

(*Beat.*)

TEDDY. Well, you're welcome. Do you need a...?

COLE. No, Adam got me... (*Gestures with his drink.*)

TEDDY. Of course. Well. Got to get this in to Sophie—

SOPHIA. I'm right here, Ted.

TEDDY. Right. So I'll put it inside then. (*He starts in, stops.*) Saul know you're here?

COLE. I don't think so.

TEDDY. The party isn't until eight.

COLE. I was hoping to speak with him before the—

TEDDY. He'll be out in a minute, I've got to shave him.

COLE. Out here?

TEDDY. He likes the view.

(TEDDY *goes inside. Pause.*)

SOPHIA. He's touchy about Daddy sometimes.

COLE. I'm sure it's just the occasion. He's normally very civil to me.

SOPHIA. *Normally?*

COLE. At trade shows and so forth. We collect the same books—early Modern—so we see each other, have a drink. He…never told you?

(ADAM *pours a drink for himself, drains it.*)

SOPHIA. Adam?

(*He pours another.*)

I can't watch this.

(*She goes into the house without a word.* ADAM *drains his glass, slams it down.*)

ADAM. So. You see him a lot?

COLE. Occasionally.

ADAM. Did he tell you?

(COLE *doesn't reply.*)

Did he tell you?

COLE. Adam.

ADAM. Jesus.

COLE. I know. But look at it from my perspective—

ADAM. I told myself that you hadn't heard. That somehow, in the smallest community of a very small city in this very small world you had somehow not heard. Because, clearly, if you had—

COLE. Adam—

ADAM. Had heard that my child—my only child—had died—you might have sent a card.

COLE. I know, and if I could go back—

ADAM. You think you can do whatever the fuck you want and we'll all just forgive you.

COLE. Forgive me? I don't need your fucking forgiveness. You should be asking for mine.

ADAM. For what?

COLE. "I've got your back kid!" "No worries!" "I know it's yours!"

ADAM. I never said it was yours.

COLE. You know it was! More mine than his.

ADAM. That's not how it seemed.

COLE. No? Then why did you promise you'd back me up?

ADAM. I'm not doing this with you.

COLE. You promised you'd be there for me, and when my ass was on the line you disappeared.

ADAM. You're the one who left.

COLE. You bailed on me! You left me hanging! And then, years later, your kid dies, which is terrible, yes, but—

ADAM. "Terrible"?!

COLE. What am I supposed to imagine? That you're waiting to hear from me? That you want me around? And then you call up after a decade, call my fucking secretary, and you expect me to show up and apologize?

ADAM. You're right. Only an idiot would think you might have the decency to care about anything other than your fucking reputation.

(COLE *shoves him.*)

COLE. Take that back.

ADAM. Don't touch me.

(COLE *shoves him again.*)

COLE. I said take it back.

ADAM. Make me.

(COLE *goes for him. They fight, angry and desperate, clutching at each other.* SOPHIA *comes through the door, brought out by the noise. She runs down to separate them.*)

SOPHIA. Stop it!! Stop it!

(Her *attempts do little. The fight gets more vicious, and is suddenly over,* ADAM *hurt.*)

ADAM. Fuck!!!!!!!!!!!

SOPHIA. Are you okay?

ADAM. No, I'm not okay! Fuck!

SOPHIA. Let me see.

ADAM. Fuck.

COLE. What, is it your shoulder?

ADAM. Where the fuck did you learn that?

COLE. I've been taking martial arts. Here.

(He *starts to rotate* ADAM's *shoulder.* ADAM *lets him. Quiet for a moment.*)

ADAM. Martial *arts*?

COLE. Tae Kwon Do.

ADAM. Jesus.

COLE. You're in good shape, you should come some time. There are great classes in the city.

ADAM. Where? Chinatown?

COLE. I go to a guy on 27th and Broadway. It's a huge stress reliever.

SOPHIA. So, what, that's it? Fight over?

> (*They look at each other.* ADAM *extends a hand. They shake.*)

I can't believe you guys. You could have really hurt yourselves.

COLE. She sounds like your mom, right?

ADAM. Completely.

SOPHIA. You guys are children, you're fucking infants. You're two steps away from frying ants and torturing snakes.

COLE. We never tortured them—

ADAM. We just played with them a little.

COLE. Those traps we made were pretty amazing though.

SOPHIA. Yeah, for never having caught anything.

ADAM. You shut up.

SOPHIA. Or what, you'll fight me?

COLE. We would never hit a girl.

SOPHIA. The "No Girls Allowed Club"? I think hitting girls was pretty much your chartered mission.

COLE. Well, then let's take her down to the fort and enforce some club rules. (*Sudden silence.*) What?

SOPHIA. That's where we spread Mama's ashes. She didn't want anything fancy. We planted some willows.

> (*Beat.*)

COLE. You think I could see that? I mean, not now, obviously, but—

SOPHIA. Why not? I'll show you. Knowing Daddy, he won't be out for ages.

COLE. No, I shouldn't presume—

ADAM. Go. It'll give me a chance to warm him up. Pour him a drink, tell him a few lies. By the time you get back he'll be cracking out the altar for the sacrificial lamb.

SOPHIA. Okay, okay, enough.

> (COLE *and* SOPHIA *get up and start to exit, down the steps to offstage left.*)

COLE. Magic hour. I used to be afraid of these woods at night.

SOPHIA. Don't worry, I'll protect you.

COLE. Okay, wiseass.

(They exit, SOPHIE leading. ADAM notices the dark. Flips on the Christmas lights. JULIA enters from the house, dolled up. She carries a copy of SAUL's book. ADAM whistles.)

ADAM. I'll give you this, kid: you sure know how to make an entrance.

JULIA. I'm still carrying all this baby weight.

ADAM. Not a day older than the day I met you.

JULIA. I look nineteen? *(She throws herself down on the chair.)* What happened to Cole? Did you chase him away?

ADAM. Not at all. Sophie's keeping him occupied.

JULIA. Ted thinks he has an agenda.

ADAM. I don't think that's in question. Liv asleep?

JULIA. Babysitter's got her 'til eleven p.m. Everything looks rosier when someone else is watching your kid. *(She looks out at the lake.)* God, it's like time doesn't pass here.

ADAM. Time passes.

JULIA. We had some good times, those first few years, didn't we? Sitting here with some beers, waiting out the summer storms.

ADAM. *(A private joke.)* Sally Ann Thunder Ann Whirlwind *Crockett.*

  (They laugh, affectionate.)

JULIA. And then you passed me on to Ted.

ADAM. I didn't pass you on.

JULIA. Yeah you did.

ADAM. You were the best writer in my class, Ted was a young editor. I thought it would be good for you to know each other, at least professionally.

JULIA. Okay.

ADAM. You were closer to my son's age than to mine.

JULIA. You're right.

ADAM. And you fell for him. Am I wrong?

JULIA. You're not wrong.

ADAM. So?

JULIA. I don't know.

  (She puts her hands over her face. ADAM doesn't move.)

ADAM. Are you okay?

JULIA. I don't know.

ADAM. Is there anything I can do?

JULIA. I don't know. Don't touch me.

ADAM. I wasn't going to. The move to L.A. must have been tough.

JULIA. (*She takes her hands from her face.*) No, it's great. I love L.A., I can go days without seeing anyone. In New York it was like I couldn't move without committing myself to something. I've never written so well in my life.

ADAM. You're writing?

JULIA. Don't sound so surprised.

ADAM. No, it's just: you just had a baby.

JULIA. Yeah, so I'm home all day. What's your point?

ADAM. Nothing, I think it's great that you're home with her. I stayed home too. I just didn't get much writing done.

JULIA. I'm averaging twenty pages a day.

ADAM. That's…wonderful.

JULIA. It is, isn't it?

(*She turns away from him. He sits next to her.*)

Everything's wonderful: the baby's quiet and the house is huge and Ted is great. The other morning, he left tulips on my pillow so they'd be the first thing I saw when I woke up. I'm so fucked up.

ADAM. No.

JULIA. I feel like the Talking Heads or something, you know: "Is this my beautiful wife?" Because it doesn't feel like mine. Any of it. (*A beat.*) But, you know, Ted's great.

ADAM. Yes, we've established that. Look, I don't know what to tell you. I was a disaster at marriage, and my parents, God knows, weren't any better. Family solution: sleep with someone else. That's my great advice.

(*Beat.*)

JULIA. I think I'm writing to avoid her. The baby. I'm a terrible mother.

ADAM. No, it's normal. A little postpartum.

JULIA. I am way too productive to be postpartum.

(*Silence.*)

ADAM. How are things with your mom?

JULIA. Phenomenal. (*Stands up, shaking off her mood. Picks up SAUL's book.*) So, did he make this stuff up?

ADAM. I wouldn't know, I haven't read it.

JULIA. You mean…

ADAM. What.

JULIA. Nothing.

ADAM. Julia, what?

JULIA. They didn't…. Teddy said they had told you.

ADAM. No.

JULIA. Ah.

ADAM. What? What does it say?

JULIA. Just…stuff.

ADAM. Julia.

JULIA. About his affairs. Your dad's. He says you'd cover for him. When he brought women to the house. That you'd lie to your mom, lie to everyone, and say that the girls were yours instead. Not that that's necessarily true. Um. Is it? True?

(*Long beat.*)

ADAM. So…. Every person here tonight…. No. Every person…. (*Beat.*) It's really going to sell, isn't it? What else does he say?

JULIA. Nothing. Adam, it'll blow over.

ADAM. (*Quiet.*) What does it say?

(*Beat.*)

JULIA. He says your novels weren't good until he edited them. He says the only reason *Red Grass* was a bestseller was because he rewrote parts. He says your relationship with your mom was unnaturally close. He says you slept with your students. He says that's why your marriage ended. (*Beat.*) He's not very nice to anyone in it. It's not just you.

ADAM. Is he nice to Teddy?

JULIA. …He doesn't really mention Teddy.

(*Silence.*)

ADAM. How long until people get here?

JULIA. Adam, anyone can see that he's lying. They're outrageous lies.

ADAM. (*He picks up the book.*) Is this your copy?

(*The door flies open: SAUL, in his tuxedo and a pair of desperately old sneakers.*)

SAUL. All right! Where are we performing this operation?

(*SAUL walks down the steps, swatting JULIA with his towel. TED is just behind him, carrying an old-fashioned shaving kit and a glass of water. ADAM looks at his father and his brother like they are apparitions.*)

TEDDY. (*To ADAM.*) Where is he?

SAUL. Where is whom?

TEDDY. Some guests arrived.

SAUL. What kind of idiot shows up three hours early for a party? Jeff Kominsky? Adam, stop standing there like a mute and get me a drink.

(*ADAM takes SAUL's book off right and disappears into the woods.*)

SAUL. Where's he going?

JULIA. I think to read your book.

TEDDY. Fuck.

> (SAUL *sits on the chaise lounge. He is perfectly calm.*)

SAUL. Don't be vulgar Theodore. It doesn't suit you.

TEDDY. He's gonna kill us.

SAUL. He's gonna kill me, you have nothing to do with it. Read the fucking Greeks. (*To* JULIA.) Honey, get me a drink and make it a double.

TEDDY. You should talk to him.

SAUL. He's going to read it either way. (*To* JULIA.) Honey?

JULIA. An Old Fashioned?

> (SAUL *makes the OK sign with his hand, and* JULIA *goes inside.* TEDDY *wavers.*)

SAUL. Teddy: if he wants to speak with me, he knows where I live. Now, are you going to shave me or not?

> (TEDDY *begins to set out the shaving accoutrement: cake of soap, brush, glass of water, and a straight-edged razor.*)

Good. I'm glad we're all in agreement. (*He tucks the towel around his neck.*) What a view. Look at the view, Theodore.

> (TEDDY *looks for a second.*)

We've had this place longer than we've had you. Bought it in escrow for a little more than the price of a Cadillac, and I can't tell you how much I'd get for it now. But I'll never collect on it. Leave it for you to enjoy.

TEDDY. That's very generous Pop.

SAUL. But you: you'll pay off, won't you? Take care of your old man?

TEDDY. I doubt you'll need much taking care of.

SAUL. But if I do.

TEDDY. We'll get you the best care, you know that.

SAUL. What do you mean, get me the best? You'll take care of me.

TEDDY. Sophie takes care of you.

SAUL. But if something happens, I can't earn? You're my son, you'll take care of me.

TEDDY. Pop.

SAUL. Pop what?

TEDDY. We live in L.A. now. You wouldn't want to live out there.

SAUL. Why not?

TEDDY. You can't drive.

SAUL. I'll walk.

TEDDY. The house is in the hills, you wouldn't be able to get around.

SAUL. So you'll drive me.

TEDDY. I work eighty hours a week.

SAUL. So Julia'll drive me.

TEDDY. I couldn't ask her to do that.

SAUL. Why not?

TEDDY. It'd be a burden.

SAUL. She's your wife.

TEDDY. Yeah.

SAUL. She got you by the balls? She got you wrapped up in her pussy?

TEDDY. I just don't like to think of my wife as a slave, okay?

SAUL. Oh.

TEDDY. Strange concept I know.

SAUL. You were always such a romantic. Don't be stupid about women, Son. They're never worth it.

(*Beat.* SAUL *begins to sing, a drinking song. Lustily.*)

"Show me the way to go home. I'm tired and I want to go to bed. I had a little drink about an hour ago, and it went right to my head."

TEDDY. Hold still.

SAUL. "Wherever I may wander, over land or sea or foam, you can always hear me singing this song, show me the way to go home…" Come on, kid, you remember the second part. Your favorite—with all the big words. Come on. "Indicate the direction…" Sing it to me.

TEDDY. Pop.

SAUL. "Indicate the direction"…

TEDDY. …"Of my habitual abode, I'm fatigued and I desire to retire."

(*We begin to hear voices coming up from the direction of the lake.*)

SAUL & TEDDY. "I had an alcoholic beverage sixty minutes ago, and it went right to my cerebellum. Wherever I may perambulate, on terrafirma or H2O, you can always hear me crooning this tune…"

(*From downstage left,* SOPHIE *and* COLE *emerge from the woods.* SAUL *sees them, stops singing.* TEDDY *does not see them.*)

TEDDY. "Indicate the direction of my habitual abode!"

(*Silence.* TEDDY *turns around, sees* COLE. *Half of* SAUL's *face is white with shaving cream and the other not.*)

SAUL. Teddy, is something detaining your arm or have you abandoned the project altogether?

TEDDY. Dad.

SAUL. Fine, give it to me.

SOPHIA. Say hello.

SAUL. Give me the razor.

> (JULIA *emerges from the house, carrying his drink.*)

JULIA. I couldn't find any maraschinos—

> (*Sees what is happening, goes right back inside.* SAUL *takes the razor from his son.*)

SAUL. What is this, a man can't get a shave or a drink around here. Julia?

> (*She comes out again and hands him the drink.* SAUL *begins to shave himself.*)

COLE. Saul.

SOPHIA. Daddy. Talk to him.

SAUL. Hold up the mirror for me Sweetness.

COLE. Saul.

SOPHIA. Daddy.

SAUL. What do you want? You want talk? You want *speech*? You want *text*? Fine. (*To* COLE.) You're trespassing.

COLE. I was invited.

SAUL. Trespassing. Sophie, call the cops.

COLE. You asked me to come.

SAUL. I asked you? A person doesn't ask vermin to infest his home. Forget the cops, Sophie, call an exterminator.

COLE. Someone called me, today, and asked me to come. If you didn't, who did?

> (*Silence.* SAUL *looks around at his children. No one speaks.*)

SAUL. Sharper than a serpent's tooth…. (*To* COLE.) Okay, my little guest. You've seen the old man, now leave.

COLE. Not until we've talked.

SAUL. You hear this? This is talk, we're talking.

> (COLE *walks up the steps of the house.*)

Sorry, no charlatans in the house.

COLE. I'm not in the house.

SAUL. Get off my fucking porch.

COLE. You don't want me here, next time take my calls.

SAUL. I've never received any calls from you.

COLE. I've had my lawyers on your office every day for the past month.

SAUL. They must have an old number.

COLE. Fuck you, the number works fine.

SAUL. You're so cute when you're angry.

COLE. You can insult me. I'm not here for your approval.

SAUL. Are you positive? Because it sure looks like—

COLE. (*Reaching into his breast pocket.*) I got my lawyers to draw up some papers.

SAUL. Is that supposed to scare me?

COLE. I'll leave as soon as you sign them.

SAUL. If you want to scare me, you're going to have to work a lot harder than that.

COLE. I just want my due.

(SAUL *stands.*)

SAUL. You want what you've always wanted: to suck at some tit, grub out all you can, and run away. You want to suck tit? This one's all dry. Go cry to your mother. I think she'll stick around now that you're paying her bills.

(SAUL *goes inside. The door slams behind him. A moment of unbelievable silence, then: the baby begins to scream.*)

TEDDY. Oh God Damn it all to Hell.

(TEDDY *goes in.*)

COLE. Call me a car.

SOPHIA. You can't leave.

COLE. I don't need his fucking permission. It was my novel.

(COLE *gets up.* SOPHIA *stops him.*)

SOPHIA. I will talk to him. He will talk to you. Please don't leave. Promise me you won't leave until I come back.

(*A long beat.* COLE *nods.*)

Thank you.

(*She goes inside.* COLE *covers his face with his hands and screams into them. Beat. He opens his eyes.* JULIA *has been standing there, quietly cleaning up the shaving kit.*)

COLE. Don't feel obliged to stay out here. With the charlatan.

JULIA. Is that what you are?

COLE. Ask your husband. Ask your father-in-law.

(*He reaches into his pocket for a cigarette.*)

JULIA. Ted doesn't like to talk about it. And I was raised not to ask impolite questions. But I'll make an exception for you.

COLE. Do you have a light?

JULIA. Do you have one of those for me?

COLE. I thought you were a nursing mother.

JULIA. I thought you were an asshole.

COLE. Thanks for reminding me.

(*She hands him the matches. He lights both cigarettes and hands one to her.*)

So, what do you know?

JULIA. You lived here, with them. Saul published *A Tender Currency*. You left.

COLE. Ted must really not want to talk about it.

JULIA. He doesn't like to talk about a lot of things.

COLE. That bothers you?

JULIA. It makes my job harder.

COLE. Your job as his wife?

JULIA. Are you going to tell me or not?

> (*He takes a moment to smoke.* JULIA *keeps her eyes on him.*)

COLE. Huge advance press on this book. This autobiography. Huge orders in stores.

JULIA. So they say.

COLE. You know why? Because Saul is so *famous*.

JULIA. He does fine.

COLE. No, he is a *famous* writer. Do you know what he was *famous* for when I met him? Finding new talent. That's all. In certain circles he was known as a good editor with a good eye, who judged a short story contest at the *Atlantic Monthly*, which I entered and won. Of course, the contest was for college students, and since I was at the time trying to pass eighth grade at Allegheny Middle School, I had to forfeit the prize. But when Saul found out my age, and what I'd done, and that I, like him, had been orphaned…. He offered me a better prize. I could leave my shitty school and my foster home and Pittsburgh, and I could live with him in his beautiful house with his beautiful family, and he would help me become a writer. So I came. I lived with them. I wrote, we worked. My first book of short stories was a hit, the second one bigger. They adopted me. Member of the family. All I ever wanted.

JULIA. And then…

COLE. And then, when I was, I expect, a little older than you…. How old are you?

JULIA. That's a rude question.

COLE. You must be older than you look. I was twenty-eight and I couldn't follow up. Overdue on my first novel, well bone dry. Saul approaches me with a proposal. He wants to try his hand at this "writing" thing. He has an idea for a novel about an orphan boy who makes good. He even has a title: *A Tender Currency*. But he's nervous; he wants a partner. And he chooses…me. Not Adam. Me. It would be our secret collaboration. Our surprise.

JULIA. And then…

> (*He thinks. She waits.*)

COLE. Have you ever been with someone where the sex was really bad?

JULIA. Is that like a come-on?

COLE. If you like them enough, you keep thinking, "It'll get better." And then it doesn't and the love starts to wear off, and you start to think "I could do better"? That's what reading Saul's first draft was like. I wanted so badly for it to be good. But it being...so bad: it got me going. I put it all in there: my mother, my father. Things I hadn't thought about since I left Pittsburgh. It was painful: write what you know. After a couple polishes I sent Saul my draft. And that was it. Never saw it again. I thought maybe I'd hurt his feelings, straying so far from what he wrote. But he was kind, convivial. Fatherly. (*A beat.* COLE *seems very far away.*) And the next thing I know Knopf is going to publish our novel. Except now it's his novel. He claims I gave it a read. He has my draft, I have no proof. End of story.

JULIA. You didn't make copies?

COLE. I trusted him.

JULIA. So your draft just disappeared?

COLE. I ransacked the house, went through the safe.

JULIA. The book isn't Saul's at all?

COLE. I didn't say that. But if there was going to be one name on that manuscript, it should have been mine.

JULIA. Someone must have been able to testify—

COLE. The only other person who read my draft was Adam.

JULIA. Adam didn't say anything?

COLE. He said it was his father's work.

    (*A pause.*)

JULIA. Adam isn't a liar.

COLE. No, but he isn't exactly the bravest person I've ever met.

JULIA. Why didn't you sue?

COLE. I had no proof. My word against theirs. So I left the family, I left the business, I got a job writing for TV. The network liked me, I got my own show, cop show, drawing on my hoodlum youth. I've done fine.

JULIA. Do you miss writing?

COLE. I am a writer. You know how hard we have to work in TV? *Proud Days* is a good show.

JULIA. Do you feel guilty?

COLE. About what?

JULIA. Getting out.

COLE. Do you know much about foster homes?

JULIA. I'm from Greenwich.

COLE. You learn pretty quickly that the guilt of the survivor is a waste of energy. I gave up on guilt a long time ago. (*Beat.*) You should be pleased with yourself, I never talk about this.

JULIA. Why not? You come off so well in this story.

COLE. All right. It's my turn to ask you some questions.

JULIA. I don't have any secrets.

COLE. Why are you with Teddy?

>   (*A sudden chill.*)

JULIA. I love him.

COLE. Really?

JULIA. He's my husband.

COLE. He's a safe choice.

JULIA. He's a good man.

COLE. He's scared and he's safe. What happened to you that makes you think you have to pick someone like that?

JULIA. Are you kidding me? Teddy's *scared*? Adam isn't *brave*? Do you know what it took to survive this family?

COLE. Yeah. I'm the only one who did.

JULIA. You didn't survive it, you climbed on top of it.

COLE. You don't know shit about me sweetheart.

JULIA. It takes you ten years to show up here? If someone stole my book, I'd hit them so hard they'd never stand up again.

COLE. You and what army?

JULIA. I don't need an army, I have a spine. You have one shitty thing happen to you, and you never write again.

COLE. You want to talk shitty things happening?

JULIA. Bla bla bla your childhood. You're an adult, act like one.

COLE. Why do you think I'm here?

JULIA. So prove me wrong. Stay and clean up your fucking mess.

>   (SOPHIA *comes to the doorway, interrupting.*)

SOPHIA. Cole? Saul won't…. Do you want me to call you a car? We could try again in the city.

>   (*Beat.*)

COLE. I'm not going anywhere.

>   (*Lights out. Intermission.*)

Scene 3

Around eleven p.m. Remnants of food on the table, the candles flickering or out. JULIA sits on the steps of the porch, nursing Liv. From behind the audience, where dinner and dancing are in full swing on a pavilion by the lake: laughter and TEDDY's voice.

TEDDY. (*Offstage.*) Well, some of us may be trying to determine if we're sober enough to drive—and if you're not, I can recommend a lovely bed and breakfast down the road—but for everyone who's willing, please stay and drink and dance until the champagne's gone!

(Applause, music. SOPHIA enters from the house, wearing a dress she is not comfortable in and carrying a bottle of champagne, a slim book, and her shoes. She watches JULIA for a moment, then pops the champagne. JULIA jumps.)

SOPHIA. Sorry.

JULIA. …Didn't see you come up.

SOPHIA. Came in the back. Have you seen Adam?

JULIA. He's still in the cottage, I think.

(SOPHIA starts back inside.)

It's a beautiful party. In spite of Cole and Adam and everything. You did perfectly.

SOPHIA. …I just tried to remember what my mom did.

JULIA. You wanna take a break? Keep me company?

(JULIA pats the steps next to her.)

SOPHIA. Um. Okay.

JULIA. Great.

(SOPHIA sits. Silence.)

JULIA. I like the lights you put in the trees.

SOPHIA. Adam's idea.

JULIA. They're pretty. (*Silence.*) Those are nice shoes. Where did you get them?

SOPHIA. I don't know. I bought them for my mom's funeral; that was like ten years ago. (SOPHIE *holds up the bottle she's holding.*) Is this going to bother you?

JULIA. Why would it?

SOPHIA. (*Gesturing at Liv at her breast.*) Aren't you not supposed to drink?

JULIA. That's a pretty long list. "Not supposed to."

(Liv stirs, and JULIA adjusts her, moving her to the other breast. The awkwardness of her naked breasts; JULIA attempts to shift SOPHIA's attention to the book in her hand.)

JULIA. What's that?

SOPHIA. *Heart's Needle.* W. D. Snodgrass. It's a book of poems.

JULIA. Actually, it's just one long poem. In that edition.

SOPHIA. Okay.

JULIA. Sorry, I thought since you were carrying it around…

SOPHIA. I just picked it up. Adam mentioned it; I wanted to look at it.

JULIA. What did he say?

SOPHIA. You can take it if you're so interested.

> (SOPHIA *tosses the book down. It makes a little resounding sound. In the pause that ensues,* JULIA *reaches out with her free hand and folds back the pages one by one, like someone soothing the brow of a child or lover. When she speaks, it is very softly.*)

JULIA. Snodgrass wrote it for his daughter, after he lost her in his divorce. The title comes from a story, this ancient Job-like story, about a man who has gone mad. He won't come down from this tree, not for anything. They tell him his parents have died. Nothing. His siblings, nothing. They tell him his daughter is dead, and he breaks a little—"A daughter is the needle of the heart"—but he won't budge. Finally, they tell him his son has died. He comes down from the tree.

SOPHIA. You gave this to him.

JULIA. Adam turned me onto Snodgrass in college. I couldn't think of anything else to give him. After.

> (*A little silence.* JULIA *closes the book.* SOPHIA *peels the label off the champagne.*)

SOPHIA. She's beautiful. Liv.

JULIA. Really? It's hard to get perspective. I'm an only child, so I never.… It must have been great, having brothers.

SOPHIA. It was a lot of testosterone for one house.

JULIA. How old were you when Cole came?

SOPHIA. I don't know. He was fourteen, so I guess I was about ten.

JULIA. He was an orphan?

SOPHIA. No. His dad was gone and his mom was on drugs. So, foster care. But his foster parent beat him, so Dad brought him home.

JULIA. God. Like a stray dog.

SOPHIA. He wasn't a bad kid.

> (JULIA *watches* SOPHIA's *face change.*)

Just…weird.

JULIA. Weird?

SOPHIA. He had this thick accent, and all this terrible slang. He had to have plastic sheets, because he'd get night terrors and wet the bed. He didn't know how to dress, he ate like an animal. I thought Mother was going to faint the first time she saw him at the table.

JULIA. How'd she get him to behave?

SOPHIA. He wanted to belong.

(*JULIA watches SOPHIA's face as she remembers.*)

JULIA. You ever think about having kids?

SOPHIA. It's never been an option. I bet you always wanted kids.

(*JULIA laughs.*)

So what happened?

JULIA. I met Ted.

SOPHIA. I guess love will do that to you.

JULIA. Or writer's block. I'm joking. Love.

(*Beat.*)

SOPHIA. (*Genuinely trying.*) I'm sorry if we haven't been enthusiastic enough. About the baby. It's hard to process, so soon after Theo. It's good to have another kid in the family though.

JULIA. We weren't trying to replace him.

SOPHIA. No, no, of course not. But for us it's a little difficult right now, that's all.

JULIA. You think it's easy for me? You think I don't—

(*JULIA is suddenly silent. SOPHIA doesn't know what to say. Then, fighting back unexpected tears…*)

Being with Theo was the only reason I thought I could be a mother in the first place. Seeing him and Adam, it made me want to…. I helped teach him to swim.

(*She gets up abruptly, taking Heart's Needle.*)

You shouldn't talk about things you don't understand.

SOPHIA. I'm sorry.

JULIA. I'm going to put her down.

SOPHIA. Julia, I'm sorry.

JULIA. Yes, Sophie, I know.

(*JULIA goes inside. After a breath, SOPHIA throws her shoe, hard, down the path stage left. It almost hits COLE, walking up carrying his jacket.*)

COLE. Hey!

SOPHIA. Oh, God! I didn't see you! I'm so sorry.

COLE. I'm never going to forgive you. Have you seen Saul?

SOPHIA. He isn't down there?

COLE. He seems to have vanished.

SOPHIA. The men in my family have a way of doing that.

COLE. Ted's down there.

SOPHIA. Ted's always there.

COLE. I'm going to check the house.

SOPHIA. Saul's not up here. You should go back to the party. Enjoy your admirers.

COLE. People are just surprised to see me. It's annoying actually, every time I turn around someone's asking about my show.

SOPHIA. Yeah, that sounds annoying.

COLE. What about you? Aren't you supposed to be hostessing?

SOPHIA. I had to get drunk.

COLE. You can't do that down there?

SOPHIA. Not alone.

COLE. (*He laughs.*) Poor Sophie.
  (*He sits behind her and begins to massage her shoulders. She startles away.*)

SOPHIA. What are you doing?

COLE. Rubbing your back.

SOPHIA. No.

COLE. Why not?

SOPHIA. I hardly know you.

COLE. We grew up together.

SOPHIA. A long time ago.

COLE. But we know each other. I know you.

SOPHIA. Don't say that.

COLE. I do, I know you. You wore braces as a kid, you listen to an ungodly amount of Creedence Clearwater Revival. You like to have your back scratched.

SOPHIA. I'm not—I don't like to be touched.

COLE. When did that happen? (*Beat.*) Same old Cole. Who still listens to Creedence…

SOPHIA. You don't.
  (*He bursts into song: "I Heard it Through the Grapevine," loud and earnest.*)
Stop.
  (*He sings louder.*)
Seriously.
  (*He sings right to her.*)
Okay, okay, you can rub my *back.* Jesus.
  (*He begins to massage her shoulders.*)

COLE. So I'm taking a poll: is your Dad going to hide from me all night?

SOPHIA. He's not hiding.

COLE. He's either surrounded by twenty people or off in a corner with his most loyal cronies. I haven't been able to get close to him, let alone talk to him.

SOPHIA. Just be grateful he hasn't tried to kick you out again. That must mean something.

COLE. It means he doesn't want a scene.

SOPHIA. It *is* hard for him, Cole. I know it is.

COLE. I bet.

SOPHIA. For years he wouldn't let us mention your name. If your show is on, he goes into his study and doesn't come out.

COLE. Guilt can make a man do strange things.

SOPHIA. Not guilt.

COLE. What then?

(*A pause.* SOPHIA *looks out at the lake.*)

SOPHIA. A person can live a long time with a feeling. Just because he doesn't express it.... He has a heart. Even if no one sees it.

COLE. Say something then.

SOPHIA. Say…what?

COLE. Talk to him for me.

SOPHIA. Why? (*She pulls away from him.*) Why are you even here Cole? I told you not to come.

COLE. I never miss a good party.

(*She stands as if to go.*)

I'm lonely Soph. I wanted to not feel that way for one night. Can't you understand that?

SOPHIA. I'm sure you have plenty of friends to keep you company.

COLE. It's not the same. You get older, you start to want something more. So you stop fucking 22-year-olds, you get a therapist, you eat right. And when that doesn't work, when you're still…so fucking alone…there's nothing to do but go home. So I found my mother, but it wasn't the family I missed. I missed you. Is that so terrible of me? Am I not allowed?

(*She looks at him. He seems earnest. She sighs, sits.*)

SOPHIA. Of course you're allowed.

(*They are side by side.*)

Marriage… you never…?

COLE. I kept saying I'd stop when I met the right one. But I never did. Or I was a coward. Something. You?

SOPHIA. …There was someone.

COLE. Who?

SOPHIA. It didn't really pan out.

COLE. Why not?

(*She doesn't answer.*)

Well, at least he's out there. There's hope for you.

SOPHIA. What about you? Any hope?

(JULIA *comes through the door, carrying the baby.*)

JULIA. Oh, sorry, I didn't mean to interrupt anything.

COLE. Don't leave. We were talking about love. You're the expert around here.

JULIA. No, really, I just wanted some air.

COLE. We insist. Don't we Soph?

SOPHIA. I thought you were putting the baby to bed.

JULIA. She cries every time I put her down.

(SOPHIA *stands.*)

SOPHIA. Well, we should head back before they send a search party.

JULIA. You guys go. The babysitter's gone and Ted doesn't want Liv around the cigar smoke.

COLE. (*To* JULIA.) I'll stay with you.

SOPHIA. (*To* COLE.) Don't you want to find Saul?

COLE. From here I can catch him coming or going. (*To* JULIA.) I'd like to keep you company.

JULIA. You can do as you please.

(*Beat.* SOPHIE *looks from* COLE *to* JULIA *and back.*)

SOPHIA. Great. Glad we got that cleared up.

(*She stalks off.*)

COLE. If you find him, come get me!

(SOPHIE's *gone. Awkward silence.*)

JULIA. Don't worry, it's personal. She's always hated me.

COLE. Look, what I said earlier—

JULIA. It doesn't matter.

COLE. I was angry, and I shouldn't have taken it out on you—

JULIA. No, it was my fault. Saying that you weren't—that your childhood wasn't—

COLE. It's fine.

JULIA. I didn't know what I was talking about. Can we start over?

COLE. Cole Maddox, prodigal asshole.

(*She laughs. The laughter fades. Pause.*)

JULIA. What were you and Sophie talking about?

COLE. Love, I guess. Marriage. Why do people get married? (*A beat.*) I'm asking you: why do they get married?

JULIA. You're kidding.

COLE. Not personally, in general. Is it always out of fear?

(*Silence.*)

JULIA. I met Ted.

COLE. Love at first sight.

JULIA. Sort of. I fell in love with his bed. The rest came after.

COLE. You wouldn't be the first person to mistake sex for love.

JULIA. I meant the actual bed. It was super nice.

COLE. Never underestimate a good sleep. Where do you live in New York?

JULIA. Los Angeles.

COLE. Love that neighborhood.

(*She laughs.*)

I come to L.A. sometimes.

JULIA. On business?

COLE. Sometimes.

(*Beat.* COLE *reaches over and strokes Liv's head. He holds his hand there, very close to* JULIA's *breast. Charged. His fingers may graze her skin.*)

JULIA. It's the loneliest place in the world.

COLE. Los Angeles?

(COLE *takes his hand away.*)

JULIA. You think I'm stupid.

COLE. Just young.

JULIA. I don't feel young.

COLE. That's one of the young things about you.

JULIA. Does that bother you?

COLE. Not yet. What's your book about?

JULIA. What?

COLE. Ted says you're writing your first novel. What's it about?

JULIA. I can't tell you.

COLE. You aren't superstitious…

JULIA. I'm not stupid, either.

COLE. So don't be stupid.

(*Beat.*)

JULIA. Can you keep a secret?

COLE. No, but I can make an exception.

JULIA. You have to. It's…delicate.

COLE. Cross my heart.

(*Pause.*)

JULIA. It's about the family. This family, the Webers. I mean, it's fictionalized, but they're my inspiration. The family dynamics. Fathers and sons, competition, survival. How sometimes the things we do for love make us unworthy of love. I mean, there's some of my family in it too. My mother.

COLE. Am I in it?

(*She shrugs.*)

I'm flattered.

JULIA. You should read it before you say that.

COLE. Anytime you want me to. I could probably help you get it optioned early, get you more money when you find a publisher. Or has Ted offered it to Knopf already?

JULIA. Ted doesn't know. What it's about. He's so protective about the family. If he finds out…

COLE. *When* he finds out.

JULIA. *If* I try to get it published.

COLE. Is the book good?

JULIA. I mean, it's not Faulkner…

COLE. Is it good?

JULIA. It's the best thing I've written.

COLE. If you want to be part of this family, you should burn what you have and write something else.

JULIA. Are you joking?

COLE. Someone said that once a family produces a writer, that's the end of the family. You have a great husband and a beautiful baby.

JULIA. What if I have to?

(*Little silence as they look at each other. He reaches out and touches her hair.*)

COLE. All those questions before? About Saul and me? Was that just research?

JULIA. Research?

COLE. For your book?

(*She leans in and kisses him. Unseen to them,* TEDDY *emerges from the woods. He sees them kiss. They do not see him tucked in the shadows.* JULIA *breaks the kiss.*)

JULIA. Does that feel like research?

COLE. Kind of.

(*She kisses him again. The kiss gets a little intense.*)

COLE. I think you better put the baby down.

JULIA. Go to the boathouse. I'll meet you there.

(JULIA *gets up, goes for the front door.* TEDDY *steps out from the shadows and strides toward the porch.*)

TEDDY. You missed my toast!

(JULIA *whirls around.* COLE *stands.*)

COLE. Teddy! We were just wondering where you were.

TEDDY. At the party, where else would I be? Are you still looking for Saul?

COLE. Have you seen him?

TEDDY. Down by the water.

COLE. Thanks.

(COLE *doesn't move.*)

TEDDY. If you run you might catch him.

COLE. Right. Right. Be right back.

(COLE *goes off. Beat.*)

JULIA. He was helping me with Liv. She cries every time I put her down. He was just helping me.

TEDDY. I'm glad you had company.

JULIA. Sophie was here too. We had a good talk.

TEDDY. I could have used some company. Down there.

JULIA. I'm sorry.

TEDDY. I missed you.

JULIA. I'm sorry.

(*Beat.*)

TEDDY. Dad keeps disappearing.

JULIA. I'm sure everyone's too drunk to notice.

TEDDY. People keep congratulating me on his book.

JULIA. You did a great job.

TEDDY. On my father's autobiography.

JULIA. Anyone can see you're not riding on his coattails. I mean, it's not like you work for him.

TEDDY. Actually, when I edit his autobiography, it is like I work for him.

JULIA. Then you should have said no.

TEDDY. Sometimes it isn't that easy.

JULIA. What's the worst he could have done, disowned you?

TEDDY. Never mind.

JULIA. We don't need his money.

TEDDY. I said, never mind. I felt a little uncomfortable down there, and I wanted you with me. That's all.

JULIA. The baby—

TEDDY. I said, I understand. So, you and Cole are getting along?

JULIA. We had a good talk.

TEDDY. That's great. I'm glad.

> (TEDDY *undoes his tie and begins to retie it.* JULIA *watches him.*)

JULIA. He says you were like brothers.

TEDDY. No we weren't. Maybe with Adam.

> (*Beat.*)

JULIA. You don't have to tell me.

TEDDY. There's nothing to tell. Cole belonged to Dad and Adam belonged to Mom, and so the two of them were kind of a team.

JULIA. Who did you belong to?

> (*Silence.* TEDDY *finishes with his tie.*)

TEDDY. Is this straight?

JULIA. It's fine. It was fine before.

TEDDY. Let's go back down.

JULIA. If Adam and Cole were like brothers, why didn't Adam back him up about *Tender Currency*?

TEDDY. Is that what Cole told you? That Adam bailed on him?

JULIA. Isn't that what happened?

TEDDY. Cole tried to get Adam to gang up on Dad, to agree that it was Cole's book. Adam came to his senses.

JULIA. The book wasn't Cole's at all?

TEDDY. It's Dad's. You've read it; everything he's written since sounds just like it.

JULIA. Everything he's written since hasn't been as good.

TEDDY. Famous first novels. Let's go down.

JULIA. So his autobiography, that sounded like the novel too, even before your edit?

TEDDY. Julia. I'm going to count to three, and then we're going back down to this party.

JULIA. Why won't you ever talk about this?

TEDDY. It doesn't matter.

JULIA. It matters to me.

TEDDY. It happened. It's over. There's nothing I can do about it. Can we just drop the subject?

JULIA. Fine. Of course. How stupid of me to try to talk about something.

TEDDY. Why, is there something you'd like to talk about?

(*Pause.*)

JULIA. I won't mention it again.

TEDDY. I'm taking care of this, you don't have to.

JULIA. Fine. I don't actually care.

(*Beat.*)

TEDDY. Do you remember when I proposed to you? Do you remember what you said?

JULIA. I said I'd marry you.

TEDDY. Before that. Do you remember?

JULIA. Let's go down to the party.

TEDDY. You said I must not really know you, because if I did, I wouldn't love you. I wouldn't want to be married to you. Julia. You were wrong. I know you…so much better than you could ever know. And I love you. I love every part of you. Even the parts—

JULIA. Let's stop okay?

TEDDY. Even that part. (*Beat.*) Join the party. I know you want to.

JULIA. The baby.

TEDDY. I'll take her. Go on. You should have a good time while we're here.

JULIA. Why do you always have to be so nice to me?

TEDDY. I'm your husband. I'd do anything for you.

(*Suddenly, she kisses him. He kisses her back. She breaks the kiss and looks at him hard, holding his face in her hands.*)

JULIA. You know I love you, don't you?

TEDDY. Of course. I love you too. We're going to be very happy.

JULIA. (*Letting go of him.*) One dance and I'll come to bed.

TEDDY. Jules?

JULIA. What?

(*Very gently, he pulls up the front of her dress from where it was pulled down to nurse. He tucks the hair that has fallen behind her ear. With his thumbs, he cleans mascara smudges from under her eyes.*)

TEDDY. Beautiful.

(*She leaves; TED is alone on the porch, watching her go. He looks down at the baby in his arms. Waltz music starts up. TEDDY dances with the baby.*)

Who's my girl? Who's my little girl? What a beautiful baby girl.

(*ADAM enters: disheveled, unsteady, holding SAUL's autobiography. TEDDY sees him.*)

TEDDY. I can explain.

ADAM. Don't.

TEDDY. I wasn't in charge here.

ADAM. I don't want to hear it.

TEDDY. You have to believe me.

ADAM. God, I'm hungry.

>   (*He eats food off the plates on the table.*)

TEDDY. Adam, there was nothing I could do. It was practically finished when I got to it. I begged Dad to cut it, or at least change the tone. He wouldn't hear me.

ADAM. Just drop it. Whatever you have to say: I don't care. I know why you did it, and I'm done with it. I'm done.

>   (ADAM *sits heavily in* SAUL's *chair.*)

Well this is one beautiful goddamn night for a party. What is that?

>   (*He points.* TED *holds up the baby.*)

Oh yeah. That's good.

TEDDY. Want to hold her?

ADAM. No.

TEDDY. My arms are killing me. I've been like this for hours. Give me a break?

>   (*Beat.* ADAM *doesn't move, but he doesn't say no.* TEDDY *passes him the baby, very carefully.*)

Watch her head.

ADAM. I know.

>   (ADAM *is now holding the baby. Something changes in him; a sudden flood of emotion.* TED *watches him take her in. He sits on the stool next to* ADAM.)

TEDDY. Nice huh?

ADAM. The smell.

TEDDY. Need me to take her?

ADAM. No, I'm good.

TEDDY. Sometimes I can't believe how much love I have. Before Liv…I couldn't understand. I had no idea what it must have been like—

ADAM. You have to be careful at this age. Their immune systems are so new. A cold can kill them. We live in modern times, and kids still die in their sleep. Then they get older, and you've really got to be vigilant. Doorknobs, electric sockets, the corners of tables: it's like the world's designed to hurt them, and you're the only thing that's stopping it. You can't look away for a moment.

TEDDY. We all have to protect the things we love.

ADAM. She's a good baby. I don't think you were ever this good. As soon as you started walking, you were into everything, running around, trying to keep up with us. If you fell, no matter what, you'd pick yourself up and keep going. You drove Momma crazy. She'd make me hold you. You'd put your head right here.

(ADAM *gestures to the crook of his neck.*)

TEDDY. I don't remember that.

ADAM. You don't remember much.

TEDDY. No. I do. The important stuff. Coney Island with Dad. Mom's turkey meatloaf. When you bashed my nose in. How you told me I was worthless. Stuff like that.

ADAM. Tough love.

TEDDY. Didn't feel like that.

ADAM. You want what I got? Treated like God's gift?

TEDDY. Couldn't have hurt.

ADAM. Going out in the world like that, no clue how to protect yourself? I spared you that pleasure. Greatest gift you ever got: the freedom not to be Poppa's boy. You should thank me.

TEDDY. Give me my child.

ADAM. What else do you remember, Ted? The fights? How he lied? You remember her crying? No, because I took care of you.

TEDDY. I never asked for your protection.

ADAM. You think it's an accident you're a success? You think you could have gotten here with Mom and Pop raising you? (*Gestures with Liv.*) I saw you when you were this helpless, and I said, his life will be better. And I didn't do it to be thanked. I did it because I loved you. (*Beat.*) I loved you, I hated you, but I knew you deserved better. Our golden boy.

TEDDY. Don't call me that.

ADAM. That's what you're going for. Right? The rightful heir? Drop it, kid. It's a losing battle, take it from me.

TEDDY. Adam, I'm not…

(*A silence. The two brothers stare at each other.*)

Please let me take her inside now. There really is a chill.

(*Beat.* ADAM *loosens his grip.* TED *takes the baby from him, starts into the house.*)

TEDDY. It would mean a lot to Pop if you made it down to the party.

ADAM. Whatever you say chief.

TEDDY. Then get changed.

(*He goes inside.* ADAM *leans against the house. From off left, we hear the sound of* SAUL *singing his drinking song.* ADAM *picks up the autobiography.* SAUL *enters, leaning on a stick he found in the woods. He sees* ADAM*, and stops singing.* SAUL *climbs the steps and goes to his box of cigars.*)

SAUL. Not that it matters, but you might have made an appearance. Tipped your hat. Gave the impression that you're still a member of this family.

ADAM. Am I? Still a member of this family?

SAUL. Don't be pathetic.

ADAM. What did you always say? "Family first." (ADAM *holds up the book.*) Family *first*?

SAUL. So you didn't like it, so what, another book. Burn it, sell it, use it for a doorstop.

ADAM. All those years of keeping my mouth shut, and you publish this?

SAUL. There are people down there that I've fucked or fucked over, and they're sitting there enjoying my food, and my wine, and my view. If those people can do that, you certainly can. Get dressed.

ADAM. You could have picked one. One thing. Ma, or the women, or my book, or my.… But all of them? All of them?

SAUL. What do you want from me? It's supposed to be an honest book. All I did was tell the truth.

ADAM. It isn't the truth, it's an evisceration! Our guts are hanging out!

SAUL. When I read your first draft of *Red Grass*, I thought my son is going to make something of himself because he understands the number one principle in publishing: Sex sells.

(*Beat.*)

ADAM. Whatever Cole's here for, he's after you, and this time I'll deliver. I'll say I lied. I'll say the book was his.

SAUL. Don't be stupid. The book was mine.

ADAM. The facts didn't matter then; why should they matter now?

SAUL. The facts were, it was mine. My idea, my story, my words. You read it, you remember.

ADAM. I don't, though. I don't remember his draft anymore. What if I was wrong?

SAUL. Look, Cole shows up, you feel guilty because that's how he wants you to feel. He's a pro. But you have no reason to feel guilty. You hear me? You were a smart kid. You knew his writing better than anyone. And you knew he did not write that book. That's not a crime.

ADAM. But who was I to judge? I'm your son. I would have done anything for you.

SAUL. You did what was right.

ADAM. I didn't know what was right. I only knew what was good for you. And I would do anything for you, Pop. Anything. I *did* anything for you, at any cost.

SAUL. That's what it means to be a family.

ADAM. This isn't a family, it's a pack of wolves. We're all killing ourselves for some tiny scrap of the *carcass* that passes for your love. I gave you everything, and this is how you repay me. You had no right. No right.

SAUL. It's my life, I can write what I want.

ADAM. Our life, Pop. My life. My secrets. Things I didn't want anyone knowing! Things I worked my whole life to keep from Sophie and Theo!

SAUL. Teddy.

ADAM. What?

SAUL. Things you didn't want Teddy knowing. You said Theo.

(ADAM *realizes what he's said. He sits, buries his head in his hands.*)

It'll make good money. You know who's going to see that money? I'm not going to live much longer, but you'll be a rich man.

ADAM. (*Into his hands.*) Never.

SAUL. What?

ADAM. I'm done living off you.

SAUL. My whole life I've worked for you. I made a place for you in America.

ADAM. I don't care.

SAUL. You don't care? I gave you a name that means power and money, even a little bit of class. Those are commodities you could work your whole life for, your whole life, and never achieve, and I gave it to you! Free of charge! You don't throw that away for pride.

ADAM. I'm done living off your money.

SAUL. You don't have a choice.

(*Beat.*)

ADAM. No. I do, Pop. I have a choice. (*Change of tone.*) What do you say we go down and join our friends?

SAUL. What do you mean, you have a choice?

ADAM. Pop, we have so much to celebrate tonight. Why don't I just pop inside, get dressed, and we'll pop down to this party.

SAUL. Adam, if you're implying…. Look. This has been a hard year, couple of years, but that's no reason. Suicide is for the weak.

(ADAM *laughs.*)

You think that's funny? You remember my cousin Karl. I had to take the gun out of his—

ADAM. I know. I'm laughing because there's no need for a gun. I'm sick, Pop. Real sick. (*Relishing the word.*) Cancer.

      (*Silence.* ADAM *has the look of a man who has just turned over a winning card.*)

SAUL. Where?

ADAM. My lungs.

SAUL. Your *lungs?*

ADAM. Mind if I have a cigar now, Pop?

      (SAUL *grabs the box from out of his reach.*)

Come on, it's been fifteen years.

SAUL. Has it metastasized?

ADAM. What does it matter?

SAUL. Has it metastasized?

ADAM. I'm dying anyway.

SAUL. Has it metastasized?

ADAM. No.

SAUL. You see a doctor?

ADAM. Last month.

SAUL. What stage?

ADAM. What do you care?

SAUL. Adam.

ADAM. They think if they go in and remove the tumors and give me chemo right away, they think they might get it.

      (SAUL *breaks away from his son.*)

SAUL. Then that's what we'll do. Now get dressed.

ADAM. No. That's not what we'll do.

      (*Pause.*)

SAUL. It doesn't take a genius, Adam: the doctors say jump, you jump.

ADAM. It's one expensive jump.

SAUL. Forget the cost. Make the appointment, send me the bills.

ADAM. I don't want your money.

SAUL. You trying to kill yourself? Take the money.

ADAM. No.

SAUL. Take the fucking money. Sick my ass, it hasn't even metastasized.

ADAM. Yet.

SAUL. It's not like your mother, how it ate her up. It's a new field now. Dying! You can get that out of your head. You're my son, if anyone can beat this you can.

ADAM. Pop. Do you hear me? I don't want your money and I don't want treatment. Then you'll know what it is to lose a son.

(*Beat.*)

SAUL. Is that a threat?

ADAM. It's a fact.

(COLE *walks up the lawn.* ADAM *sees him.*)

COLE. Saul.

ADAM. You should remember this night, Pop. Tonight, you have all your sons.

COLE. (*To* SAUL.) Don't move.

(SAUL *starts at his voice, starts to leave.* ADAM *grabs his arm, pushes him down in the chair.*)

ADAM. (*To* COLE.) We've been waiting for you.

SAUL. Let go of me.

ADAM. Scared, Saul? You should be.

SAUL. I said, let go.

ADAM. Not 'til you hear what he has to say.

COLE. Let him go.

ADAM. I'm happy to hold him.

COLE. Let him go. He couldn't run even if he wanted to. Could you?

(SAUL *elegantly shakes off his son's hands.*)

SAUL. Thank you, Cole. Forgive my son, he's unused to company. Adam, you can leave now.

COLE. He can stay.

SAUL. No, it's time for him to go.

ADAM. I'm not leaving him alone this time, Pop. You want one of us, you have to deal with us both.

SAUL. Adam. I will not rule out the possibility that something may be slowly eating away at your brain, so I will put this very simply. You have been exceedingly clear with me that you wish to quit my company. By the same token, I will tell you as plainly as I can: you are unwelcome, your presence is unwanted, I no longer wish to look at you or speak with you or even breathe the same air. If Cole desires your company instead of mine, he may leave with you. If he wishes to speak with me, he will stay.

(*There is a moment of stillness on stage.* ADAM *looks at* COLE. COLE *looks at him, and then at the ground. He is going to stay with* SAUL. ADAM *looks back at his father.*)

SAUL. Have I made myself clear?

ADAM. Yes. You have. I understand perfectly. Thank you.

(He steps off the porch, walks with a slight halter down toward the party by the lake. As he passes COLE, *he pauses for a moment.* COLE *does not look at him.* ADAM *exits.* COLE *removes the papers from his pocket.* SAUL *stands.)*

COLE. Stay where you are.

SAUL. I'm getting you a cigar.

COLE. I don't want one.

SAUL. Don't be uncouth, they're Cubans. *(He reaches into a box and takes out a cigar, lays it on the table beside him.)* You remember your first cigar? You sucked on it like a reefer. Once upon a time, my sewer rat. You were a good kid when I met you.

COLE. I was an idealist when I met you.

SAUL. You were fourteen, of course you were an idealist. That was the thing we all liked most about you. Purity of heart. Then you smelled money.

COLE. You shoved it under my nose.

SAUL. Money, money, money. Well, you know where the safe is. The combination's still your birthday. If you're going to steal from me, you might as well do it the old-fashioned way.

(COLE throws down the papers in front of SAUL.)

COLE. Sign here.

SAUL. What is it?

COLE. The rights to *A Tender Currency*. You're going to give them to me.

SAUL. The rights to my novel?

COLE. You're going to give them to me like you should've ten years ago, or I'll tell everyone how you stole from me.

SAUL. I took you into my house. I gave you food and shelter and clothes and a family and an education and an agent and a publisher and a career. Who stole from whom?

COLE. That didn't give you the right to take my story. I'm not leaving until you sign this.

SAUL. This is private property. I'll call the cops.

COLE. I'll talk to Adam. It looks like he'll back me up.

SAUL. No. You sided with me just now, and he likes to nurse a grudge.

COLE. We're not children anymore. He'll do what's right.

SAUL. And be robbed of his inheritance? Coley, look at yourself. You don't need the money. Why would you take food out of the mouths of your sister and brothers?

COLE. They're not my family.

SAUL. They depend on that money. You want to turn them out in the streets?

COLE. I just want the rights.

SAUL. You want the money, which is why you've come now. My biography's going to make the rights far the more valuable. Monetarily.

COLE. I'll give them the money, I don't care. I just want the rights.

SAUL. Why?

COLE. It doesn't matter.

SAUL. I'm curious. Why would you want the rights if you don't want the money?

COLE. Just sign the fucking papers.

SAUL. Coley. If you don't tell me why, I'm never going to sign, and the fact is, you won't be able to make me. So, take a gamble, and tell me: why?

(Beat.)

COLE. Talk around town is, you want to turn it into a movie.

(SAUL *laughs.*)

SAUL. Is that all? The book's been kicking around for years.

COLE. Yes, but rumor is Universal wants to make it next year, and you don't have a script.

SAUL. And now that I have finished my biography, I'll have plenty of time to write it.

COLE. It's my movie to write, Saul.

SAUL. Sweet offer, but I think I'll do fine on my own.

COLE. You can have the producing credit, you'll get your fee. What do you care who writes it?

SAUL. It was my first novel. Of course I care.

COLE. It was my life, and I'm done letting you put your dirty hands all over it. Sign the papers and let me leave.

SAUL. Or what?

COLE. Or I'll walk down to that party, and I'll tell everyone here it was my book—

SAUL. Don't make me laugh.

COLE. And then I'll go on *Larry King* and tell everyone else.

SAUL. I doubt Larry King would be interested—

COLE. He is.

(A beat. SAUL lets that sit.)

SAUL. Explain something to me.

COLE. Sign—

SAUL. I'll sign your papers, I want you to explain something to me.

(COLE *shifts on his feet.*)

Your mother was sick, your brother—

COLE. June wasn't my mother.

SAUL. Your brother was getting divorced. We needed you here. We'd given you everything you ever wanted. Why did you leave like that, Coley?

COLE. You stole my manuscript.

SAUL. I stole nothing from you. We were doing what we had always done: trading ideas, working as a team, helping each other out. "Spring Bride"? You couldn't have written that without me. Not that I begrudged it, it is a parent's privilege to watch his son grow. Even now, my greatest pleasure is to see your name on your show every week.

(*A pause.* COLE *doesn't say anything.*)

Of course I'll sign your papers. How could I refuse? You're my son. I'd do anything you asked.

(*Another beat.* COLE *still doesn't speak.* SAUL *reaches in his breast pocket for a pen.* COLE *watches as he begins to sign the papers. Then, suddenly—*)

COLE. You know I write the whole show myself.

(SAUL *looks up. His eyes are bright.*)

SAUL. I know.

COLE. That's very rare in television.

SAUL. I know.

COLE. You watch it?

SAUL. Every week.

(SAUL *goes back to signing. After a second…*)

COLE. Well?

SAUL. Well, what?

COLE. Do you like it? Do you think it's any good?

SAUL. Some weeks.

COLE. Not always?

SAUL. Everyone has an off week.

(SAUL *goes back to signing papers.*)

COLE. Which episodes did you like?

SAUL. I can't recall.

COLE. Did you like the one with the rapist and the priest?

SAUL. It was fine. You need these initialed too?

COLE. What was wrong with it?

SAUL. Cole. What do you want from me? You come here, you storm my house—

COLE. I know.

SAUL. I've signed your papers. What more can I possibly give you?

COLE. (*Very soft.*) I just—miss you sometimes.

SAUL. Sorry, my hearing isn't what it used to be.

COLE. I said I miss it sometimes. Having someone like you around to work with. Now… I look at the blank page, and I don't even know what I'm looking at anymore. I know what works, and I do it. But I don't know what I'm doing it for. That's all.

SAUL. Oh. I missed you too.

(COLE *reaches out and clasps* SAUL's *shoulder with his hand.* SAUL *clasps his hand. They are very still.* COLE *releases his hand and covers his face.* SAUL *hands him a handkerchief.* COLE *wipes his face with it.*)

COLE. God, I don't know what's wrong with me. I'm just so tired. They've signed us for three more seasons, and I have no clue how I'm going to do it. I can't even tell what my life's like anymore. I never leave the writer's room.

SAUL. Take a break. Turn the show over to someone for a season. Come here and rest.

COLE. I can't. There isn't anyone I trust.

SAUL. Just take the summer here. Write something for yourself. It'll do you good.

COLE. I can't. I don't have anything left.

(*Beat.*)

SAUL. Coley, do you remember when you first came to live with us? Do you remember the day I brought you home? You were so scared you could not make yourself get out of the car. You remember what you told me?

COLE. …I said, "I can't. I think my legs are broken."

SAUL. So I walked away and left you in the car. After a while, you came inside. Nothing's broken, Coley. You're just scared to use what you've got.

COLE. That's why I want to write the screenplay for *Tender Currency.* Write what I know again.

SAUL. Turn a new page. Write something new. A novel maybe.

COLE. I can't. I don't have any other stories to tell.

SAUL. You have other stories.

COLE. Like what?

SAUL. Isn't that how we got in trouble in the first place?

COLE. That's not funny.

SAUL. Go home. Go to therapy. Call me when you're ready to work.

(SAUL *moves toward the house. Suddenly…*)

COLE. There is one idea. I don't know. All I have is notes. Memories. A little dialogue.

SAUL. I'm listening.

COLE. It's…it's about the family. This family. The Webers. And me. It'll be fictionalized, of course, but that's my inspiration. The family dynamics: fathers and sons, competition, survival. And how…sometimes the things we do for love make us unworthy of love. There'll be my history too—my mother. (*Beat.*) What do you think? Is there a book there? If you hate it, I won't write it.

SAUL. Cole. I've never been prouder.

> (*He reaches out.* COLE *steps into his embrace. They hold each other for a long quiet moment, before* SAUL *breaks from* COLE's *grip and walks toward the house.*)

COLE. Where are we going?

SAUL. I'm going to bed. It's been a long night, and I've already said my farewells.

COLE. But—

SAUL. Call me in the city. We'll discuss your career.

COLE. My career?

SAUL. I've got my book tour, but you can see me when I'm back. Call Sophia to coordinate.

COLE. That'll be months.

SAUL. Yes.

COLE. Why would we wait that long?

> (SAUL *stops, smiles. He fishes into his pocket, pulls out a key, and tosses it to* COLE. ADAM *enters from the woods, unseen by the two men. He is carrying a bottle of whiskey, half empty.*)

SAUL. There's a new ribbon on the typewriter in the cottage. Stay there tonight. In the morning, we'll discuss. I'll be back here at the end of the week, and I'll expect to see twenty pages.

> (SAUL *goes inside.* COLE *looks at the key in his hand, then up to see* ADAM. *Silence.*)

ADAM. He sign your papers?

COLE. What?

ADAM. What you came here for.

COLE. …He gave me the key to the cottage. He asked me to stay.

ADAM. You accepted?

COLE. He offered to help me write again.

ADAM. You accepted?

COLE. ...I want to come home.

(*Beat.* ADAM *takes a long swig from the bottle, then wrenches it from his mouth with sound of release. He climbs the stairs and prepares a cigar for himself.*)

ADAM. Then we should celebrate.

COLE. Are you okay?

ADAM. Never better. (*He lights the cigar, puffs. He raises the bottle to* COLE.) To your triumphant return. May we all rest in peace.

(ADAM *drinks. Lights out.*)

Scene 4

Morning. About nine a.m.—too early, and yet late enough that it is already too hot. SOPHIA, *in her pajamas and an apron, is cleaning up. From offstage, the sound of tinny music, as if coming from someone's Walkman—which it is.* COLE *emerges from the woods, in jogging gear, out of breath, in an old tee shirt and running shorts. The music is from 1986, the shorts are from the early seventies. This may be the first real sense we get of the outside world.* SOPHIA *looks up at his footsteps.*

SOPHIA. What...what...

(*She can't muster words.* COLE *climbs the steps, throws the Walkman on the table, picks up a glass of water and dumps it over his head. Shakes his head like a dog.*)

COLE. June in the Berkshires, might as well be Calcutta. Fuck. (*Gestures toward the tee and shorts.*) Found these in the cottage, hope that's okay.

SOPHIA. I...I thought you'd gone.

COLE. Your dad asked me to stay.

SOPHIA. No.

COLE. I'm going to take some time off, work here for a while. I'm calling my people Monday.

SOPHIA. What happened? Yesterday...

COLE. I don't know. I just think it's time. (*He pulls the wet tee shirt away from his body and looks at the lettering on it.*) Who in God's name went to Great Barrington High?

SOPHIA. Theo.

COLE. Oh shit. (*He peels the wet shirt off, hangs it in the tree.*) Hopefully that won't take too long to dry.

(*When he looks back around, he sees that* SOPHIA *has her head buried in her lap. She seems to be crying.*)

I'm sorry. I didn't know it was his. It's not stained or anything.

(SOPHIA *raises her head. She is halfway between laughter and tears.*)

SOPHIA. I can't believe you're back!

COLE. Oh, Sophela, don't cry!

SOPHIA. You're really staying?

COLE. Right down in that cottage.

SOPHIA. For the summer?

COLE. For as long as you'll have me.

> (TEDDY *enters from the house. He looks haggard, as if he hasn't slept.* SOPHIA *sees him.*)

SOPHIA. Teddy! Cole is staying!

TEDDY. Yeah, Adam told me. Have you put the coffee on yet?

COLE. Up early?

TEDDY. Never got to bed.

SOPHIA. Liv kept you up?

TEDDY. All night.

SOPHIA. Poor baby. I'll go brew a fresh pot. (SOPHIA *darts up the steps, turns at the door.*) Cole, I'll bring you some fresh sheets and things. It's such a mess down there.

COLE. Don't bother. I love the smell of mildew.

> (*She laughs, goes inside.* TEDDY *reaches over and turns off the Walkman.*)

She's like a kid. So excited.

TEDDY. Cole.

COLE. Yeah?

TEDDY. We need to talk.

COLE. (*Suddenly guarded.*) Okay.

TEDDY. Why don't you sit down?

COLE. I'm fine.

TEDDY. If it's all right with you, I'd prefer your discretion in this matter.

COLE. If this is about last night I can explain.

TEDDY. Explain what?

COLE. Nothing. What?

TEDDY. Around five this morning, I was in the living room with the baby, when Saul came in. He asked me to give this to you.

> (TEDDY *holds up a letter, which he has taken from his breast pocket.*)

COLE. What is it?

TEDDY. I think the letter should explain everything.

COLE. Explain what?

TEDDY. Cole, over the past few years, I've come to consider you a friend, so I'd really prefer not to be the one to do this. But Dad didn't want Adam and Sophie to know. Please, just read it.

(*Beat. COLE rips the letter open and reads it.*)

COLE. What…what does he mean he doesn't want to see me?

TEDDY. I don't know, I haven't read it.

(COLE *holds the letter out to him.* TEDDY *reads.*)

COLE. He makes it sound like I manipulated him. Right? Like I seduced him.

TEDDY. It seems he's had a change of heart.

COLE. He gave me the keys to the cottage. He practically begged me to stay. Why would he kick me out now?

TEDDY. Who knows? He's always done exactly what he's wanted, and fuck the cost.

COLE. Maybe this is a test. Like: if I were a loyal son, I would stay even though he tells me to go. Do you think it's a test? (*Starting inside.*) Why am I asking you?

TEDDY. I wouldn't go in there. You know how he is when he's angry.

COLE. He's angry?

TEDDY. Remember when Adam crashed his Bentley? And Saul ran around the house with a baseball bat breaking Adam's stuff?

(*He pulls from under the table: the shards of COLE's vase, broken in sharp pieces.*)

COLE. Jesus.

TEDDY. I got him to rest a little now, but…

(*Beat.*)

COLE. I wish your mom were still around. She could always talk him down.

(*Beat.*)

TEDDY. Well… Never mind.

COLE. What?

TEDDY. Nothing, I was just going to say I could try talking to him, but I don't want to get between you two. Unless you think it would help…

COLE. It couldn't hurt. Would you feel comfortable doing that for me?

TEDDY. Look, I promised Dad that you'd be gone by the time he got up, so we're both dead if he catches you here. Let me drive you to the station, and when I get back, I'll have a long talk with him. For all we know, you could be back here by Monday.

COLE. You'd do that for me?

TEDDY. You're my brother.

(COLE *embraces him.*)

Okay. Get your stuff.

(TEDDY *puts the broken vase back under the table.*)

COLE. What'll we tell Sophie? And Adam?

TEDDY. Don't worry, I'll handle it after you're gone. I'll grab my keys, you get changed and meet me back here in ten.

(*They shake.* SOPHIA *enters from the house. She has changed into a pretty sundress and has something tied around her neck like a cape.*)

SOPHIA. What are you shaking on?

TEDDY. (*Locking eyes with* COLE.) It's a guy thing, you wouldn't understand. (*As he heads into the house.*) I'm going to run to town, let me know if you need anything.

(TED *goes inside.*)

SOPHIA. Hey, look. (*She strikes a pose for* COLE.) "Stronger than a locomotive, faster than a speeding bullet. Is it a bird, is it a plane?"

(*He isn't laughing. She drops the pose, holds out the cape so he can see it.*)

I found your old Superman sheets.

COLE. I can see that.

SOPHIA. Okay, the storm windows are still up on the cottage; we should probably take them down. You up for some manual labor?

COLE. Sure.

SOPHIA. 'Cause you might need a shirt or something. The sun's so crazy, it's not even ten a.m. and you could definitely burn.

(*Long beat.*)

COLE. Sophie.

SOPHIA. You're leaving, aren't you?

COLE. Kind of.

SOPHIA. Kind of.

COLE. Ted will explain everything.

SOPHIA. Ted's making you leave?

COLE. No, no, no. No. This is—this is between me and your dad.

SOPHIA. Is Daddy up? What did he say to you?

COLE. Nothing. This is temporary. I'll be back soon. I promise.

SOPHIA. Did I do something?

COLE. Of course not.

SOPHIA. Then what?

COLE. Sophie. Believe me when I tell you: I am coming back. Okay?

SOPHIA. When?

COLE. Sophie.

SOPHIA. Okay.

> (*He goes.* SOPHIA *stands for a moment, then unties the sheets from around her neck. She attempts to fold them alone.* ADAM *walks in stage right, groggy.*)

Hey.

> (*He nods, barely awake.*)

Cole's here, but he's leaving soon.

ADAM. Cole's leaving?

SOPHIA. He says he's coming right back. Are you okay?

ADAM. Trouble breathing last night.

> (*He sees the tee shirt in the tree.*)

SOPHIA. You should have woken me.

ADAM. (*Re: the shirt.*) What's that doing there?

SOPHIA. Don't worry, I'll take it down as soon as it's dry. Here, sit.

> (*She helps him into a chair. After a moment.*)

ADAM. I told Pop.

SOPHIA. You told him…? How did he take it?

ADAM. He wants me to start chemo. He offered to pay.

SOPHIA. Did you tell him you've been trying alternative treatment?

ADAM. I don't want to do that anymore.

SOPHIA. So, chemo?

ADAM. No.

SOPHIA. Radiation, then. (*A beat.*) Adam. You can't give up. This is treatable.

ADAM. I'd rather just live out here, plant some seeds…

SOPHIA. This isn't Walden Pond. This is your life.

ADAM. Exactly. It's my life, I'll do as I please.

> (*A pause.*)

SOPHIA. What did Daddy say to you?

ADAM. Nothing.

SOPHIA. You can't die just to piss him off.

> (ADAM *looks away.*)

Die because you can't take it anymore, die because you've tried everything the doctors say and you still can't beat it, die after you're so sick of chemo that you'd rather hang yourself, but for God's sake, don't die to spite him. He's not worth your life.

ADAM. Practice what you fucking preach.

SOPHIA. What?

ADAM. You heard me. "He's not worth your life."

SOPHIA. I'm not.… Someone has to take care of him.

ADAM. How convenient for you that that's true.

SOPHIA. Don't you think I'd rather have.… I didn't choose this. He's old, he needs help.

ADAM. Leave me alone Sophie, and I'll leave you alone. We're both free to waste our lives.

SOPHIA. Well, if that's your attitude, I'm not keeping this secret for you anymore. Tell Ted or I will.

(JULIA *comes out of the house.*)

JULIA. Tell Ted what?

ADAM. That I'm madly in love with you, clearly.

JULIA. Oh, clearly.

(*She goes and sits on* ADAM's *lap.*)

ADAM. You look beautiful this morning.

JULIA. Ha ha.

ADAM. Seriously, you look like you got laid.

JULIA. Ted took care of Liv last night. I just got some sleep for once. You smell like a cigar, have you been smoking?

SOPHIA. You were smoking?

(COLE *enters from the cottage, dressed in his suit again.*)

COLE. Morning.

ADAM. Sophie said you're leaving.

COLE. I'll be back as soon as I can.

JULIA. You're going?

COLE. Gotta get back to the city. (*He pulls out a card, hands it to her.*) My card. For when you're ready. I'd love to read the manuscript.

JULIA. I'll think it over.

(*Unnoticed,* SOPHIE *goes into the house.*)

ADAM. You're leaving right now? Don't you want to say goodbye to Pop?

COLE. Better not, I think. Ted'll explain.

(TED *comes out of the house with a scrap of paper.* JULIA *gets up.*)

TEDDY. Ad, I've started a grocery list, take a look. Julia, do we need diapers?

JULIA. Always. I'll come, keep you company.

TEDDY. I'm sure my sister could use your help in the kitchen. Addy?

ADAM. Looks fine.

TEDDY. We should get going.

(COLE *pulls* ADAM *into a hug, holds him close.*)

COLE. Call me if Saul changes his mind.

TEDDY. All right, let's not miss this train.

COLE. I'll see you soon.

(TEDDY *and* COLE *exit,* ADAM *and* JULIA *stand to see them off.*)

ADAM. You're going to show him your book?

JULIA. I haven't decided yet.

(SOPHIA *sticks her head out the door.*)

SOPHIA. Julia, the kitchen's not going to clean itself.

(*We hear* TEDDY's *voice from offstage.*)

TEDDY. Sorry, I'll be back in a sec! (TEDDY *reenters. Sees the girls.*) I forgot the grocery list, have you seen it anywhere?

SOPHIA. It's right there on the table.

TEDDY. Anything else you need?

SOPHIA. Nothing. Julia?

(*She gestures inside.* JULIA *looks at* TEDDY.)

JULIA. Are you sure you don't want my company?

TEDDY. Positive. Go help my sister.

JULIA. I should check on the baby anyway.

(JULIA *follows* SOPHIA *inside.* TEDDY *waits until he's heard them retreat, and then leans over* ADAM.)

TEDDY. Do me a favor? Give this to Dad for me?

(*He removes, from his pocket, a second letter, which looks identical to the first.*)

It's from Cole. He gave it to me to give to Saul. Didn't want Sophie to know. Can you pass it on for me?

(ADAM *takes the letter from him and opens it.*)

It's for Dad, you're not supposed to read it. Stop. Stop.

(*Silence.* ADAM *coolly finishes reading, then looks up at* TEDDY.)

ADAM. Got it.

(TEDDY *looks at him, wordless. After a moment, he picks up the grocery list he has left on the table, and runs back off stage right.*)

TEDDY. Found it!

(*Silence. The sound of a motor starting.* SOPHIA *reenters, starts stacking up dishes. After a moment…*)

SOPHIA. I'm his only daughter, Adam. I have to care for him. It's not a choice, it's my duty.

ADAM. You always have a choice.

(SAUL *comes out the door. He looks like shit.*)

SAUL. Fuck. Jesus God.

SOPHIA. Could we start the day a little less profanely?

SAUL. Ungodly early…

SOPHIA. The rest of us have been up for hours.

(SOPHIA *goes into the house.*)

SAUL. Can't handle my liquor now. God damn. Tell Sophia to bring my coffee to the cottage. And another for Cole.

(SAUL *starts to head off toward the cottage.*)

ADAM. He isn't down there.

SAUL. Asked him to stay. Don't bother us 'til lunch.

ADAM. Pop, he's gone. Ted's driving him to the station right now. Look for yourself.

(SAUL *looks, sees the car is gone. Beat. Laughs.*)

SAUL. You can't pull that shit on me. What do you want to do, kill me? Cole, get out here! Game's up!

(ADAM *holds out the letter.*)

What's that?

ADAM. Just read it.

SAUL. No. What does it say?

ADAM. Just read it.

SAUL. I don't have my glasses.

(ADAM *opens the letter, reads.*)

ADAM. "Saul. I thought when I came here that there was something you could give me. But I realized that whatever was between us died a long time ago. Forgive me for leaving so abruptly, but I couldn't bear to face you this morning. Do not attempt to contact me in the city. Let the past rest in peace." And then his signature.

(*After a beat,* SAUL *takes the letter from him and peruses it. Then…*)

SAUL. Get the car.

ADAM. Sit down Pop.

SAUL. We can still catch him.

ADAM. He can leave if he wants to. He's a grown man.

SAUL. No one leaves me unless I tell them to go!

ADAM. He's gone Pop.

SAUL. Get the goddamn car.

ADAM. You can run after him all you want, you can't make him come back.

SAUL. Watch me.

ADAM. You can't make him stay.

SAUL. I can make him do whatever the fuck I want!

ADAM. Not anymore.

SAUL. Adam. Get the goddamn car!

    (SAUL's *knee gives out. He stumbles, falls,* ADAM *tries to catch him.*)

ADAM. Pop!

SAUL. I'm fine, I'm…it's just this damn heat.

ADAM. You're bleeding.

SAUL. I'm bleeding?

    (ADAM *lifts up* SAUL's *pajama pant leg to reveal a badly scuffed knee.* ADAM *starts to administer water to it with a napkin from the table.*)

Is it bad? Do I need stitches?

ADAM. It's just a scrape. You're fine.

SAUL. I'm fine?

ADAM. You're fine.

    (SAUL *watches his son.*)

SAUL. He's not coming back?

    (*Beat.* SAUL *puts his head between his knees. After a moment, we see that he is weeping.*)

ADAM. Pop?

SAUL. He's gone.

ADAM. Pop.

SAUL. What am I going to do?

ADAM. It's okay Pop!

SAUL. I can't lose him again!

ADAM. You have us. We're here.

SAUL. What am I gonna do without him?

ADAM. You're fine. It isn't any different than before. You lived without him for years.

SAUL. But he was my boy! To have him and to lose him…for no reason! You can't understand what that means.

    (ADAM *stands, stricken.* SAUL *realizes what he has said.*)

I didn't mean that.

    (ADAM *walks away from his father.*)

I didn't mean it. Come here.

    (ADAM *pulls Theo's shirt down from the tree.*)

Addy? Get over here.

(ADAM *does not turn around. He stares at the shirt in his hands.*)

ADAM. You know, when they called me—to say they found his body—I was sure it wasn't him. He was asleep, safe in Danny Triello's top bunk, the same as every Saturday night since he started having sleepovers. *I would know if my son was gone*, I kept saying. The whole way over to the morgue, I felt so sorry for the poor parents of whoever was lying there waiting to be identified. Even when I saw him, I thought, that's not my boy. That body lying there—that's the body of a man. When I realized it was…*him*… The first thing I felt was some petty shame. Like I had let him down by not recognizing how grown-up he'd become. My child: not a child anymore. And you know what my very next thought was? While I held his hands and stroked his hair, as I signed the papers and collected his things and drove back to this—empty home. You know what I kept thinking? (ADAM *looks down, straight into* SAUL's *eyes.*) "Why were we stupid enough to have only one kid?"

(*A silence between the two men.*)

SAUL. Adam.

(ADAM *moves toward the door.* SAUL *tries to hold him.*)

Where are you going?

ADAM. At least one of us deserves a second chance.

(ADAM *picks up the phone just inside and dials a number.*)

SAUL. Who are you calling?

ADAM. (*Into the phone.*) Dr. Derounian, this is Adam Weber, you diagnosed me last month? Yeah, I have some questions about chemotherapy that I'd like to run past you. (ADAM *starts into the house.*) Would it be possible for you to see me this week?

(ADAM *is gone.* SAUL *is alone. He tries to get up, but he can't make himself.*)

SAUL. Adam! Adam, come back here! (SAUL *tries to get up.*) Sophie? (*He waits. No one comes.*) Julia? (*Still no one.*) Come on, I need… (*He tries to pull himself up, but he can't get any further.*) Adam, get out here! I can't…

(*He looks up:* SOPHIE *is in the doorway.*)

Sophela.

SOPHIA. Papa.

SAUL. I can't…

(*He reaches for her. She doesn't move. Lights out.*)

End of Play.

ROANOKE
by Michael Lew
music and lyrics by Matt Schatz

Playscripts, Inc.
website: www.playscripts.com
email: info@playscripts.com
phone: 1-866-NEW-PLAY (639-7529)

BIOGRAPHIES

Michael Lew is a three-time Heideman Award finalist three years in a row. His plays include *Stockton* (EST workshop production); *A Better Babylon* (Victory Gardens workshop); *Yit, Ngay* (published in *Plays and Playwrights 2006*); *Neanderthal Love* (Sloan Commission); *microcrisis*; *Bury the Iron Horse;* and *Paper Gods*. His shorts include *Roanoke* (Humana Festival); *In Paris You Will Find Many Baguettes but Only One True Love* (Humana Festival/Heideman Award winner/InspiraTO Festival winner); *Tenure* (24 Hour Plays on Broadway); *Moustache Guys* (Second Generation; published by Playscripts, Inc.); *The Roosevelt Cousins, Thoroughly Sauced* (Sam French Festival winner); *Magician Ben Vs. The Wizard Merlin* (published by Smith & Kraus); and *Hawaiian Shirt* (Heideman Finalist). Residencies include Youngblood (EST), Ma-Yi Writers' Lab, Second Generation, Old Vic New Voices, and TCG Young Leaders of Color. He is a 2003 graduate of Yale College.

Matt Schatz is a New York City-based playwright and songwriter, who was a finalist for the 2009 Fred Ebb Award for Musical Theatre Songwriting (with composer/collaborator Dina Pruzhansky). Matt's plays and musicals have been presented, commissioned and/or developed by Actors Theatre of Louisville, Ensemble Studio Theatre, Manhattan Theatre Club, Luna Stage, Midtown International Theatre Festival, Page 73, Interborough Repertory Theater and others. Matt is a three-time recipient of an EST/ Sloan Commission, a two-time Shubert Fellow and has been a finalist/semi-finalist for the Page 73 Playwriting Fellowship, the Princess Grace Playwriting Fellowship and the Public Theater's Emerging Writers Group. Member: The BMI Advanced Musical Theatre Workshop and the Dramatists Guild. Alumnus: P73's "Interstate 73," Youngblood Playwrights Residency at EST. M.F.A.: Carnegie Mellon University. Official website: mattschatz.com.

ACKNOWLEDGMENTS

Roanoke premiered at the Humana Festival of New American Plays in March 2009. It was directed by Steven Rahe with the following cast:

FLORENCIA .... Anna Kull
STEVE .... Steven Rausch
MELANIE .... Katie Kreisler
SIR WALTER RALEIGH .... Andy Nogasky

and the following production staff:

Scenic Designer.. Paul Owen
Costume Designer .... Lindsay Chamberlin
Lighting Designer .... Nick Dent
Sound Designer... Benjamin Marcum
Properties Designer.. Mark Walston
Wig Designer.. Heather Fleming
Stage Manager .... Paul Mills Holmes
Assistant Stage Manager .... Debra Anne Gasper
Dramaturg... Julie Felise Dubiner
Assistant Dramaturg... Brendan Pelsue

Originally developed with Youngblood (Graeme Gillis and RJ Tolan, Artistic Directors) at Ensemble Studio Theatre, New York City.

CHARACTERS

FLORENCIA—a rookie reenactor
STEVE—a rookie reenactor
MELANIE—the head of reenactor recruitment
SIR WALTER RALEIGH—a sixteenth-century tobacconist

TIME

The Present.

PLACE

Roanoke Colony Living Museum.

MUSIC NOTE

Sheet music is available. Please contact Matt Schatz at his website, mattschatz.com.

For Matt Conlon, Florencia Lozano, Melanie Nicholls-King, and Steve Sanpietro

Steven Rausch, Andy Nogasky, Katie Kreisler, and Anna Kull
in *Roanoke*

33rd Annual Humana Festival of New American Plays
Actors Theatre of Louisville, 2009
Photo by Harlan Taylor

ROANOKE

STEVE *and* FLORENCIA *are in rehearsal clothes.* STEVE *sips Cheerwine.*

STEVE. Blast! A pox on this Roanoke Island.

FLORENCIA. A pox on it.

STEVE. A pox on this blasted pox pox blast pox Roanoke.

FLORENCIA. Look ye good fellow. For I have found (*With careful emphasis.*) cornnnnn.

STEVE. Corn? Corn say ye? How did ye find ye corn on this blasted Roanoke Island? She's a witch! A witch I tell ye! I saw Goodie Good with the devil!

FLORENCIA. (*Full scream.*) NOOOOOOOOO! NOOOOOOOOOOOOOOOO! NOOOOOOOOOOOOOOO!

MELANIE. Ok stop. What the fuck are you doing?

STEVE. What?!

MELANIE. This is Roanoke, not Salem. There were no witch hunts at Roanoke.

STEVE. It's just this line I remembered from when I was in *The Crucible.* At Juilliard.

MELANIE. You two are the worst reenactors I've ever had the misfortune of training. Florencia, you did better that time.

FLORENCIA. (*Sincerely flattered.*) Thank you.

MELANIE. Shut up. Don't get cocky. This is the Roanoke Living Museum, people. The Lost Colony. And if you think you can traipse around being cocky…

FLORENCIA. All I said was "thank you."

MELANIE. SHUT. UP. If you're here to be cocky, go apply to some rinky-dink shitshow living museum like Williamsburg.

STEVE. Aw—tell me about it! With those trust-fund babies in their million-dollar lofts and refusing to shower.

MELANIE. I was talking about *Colonial* Williamsburg, you shit. Not Williamsburg, Brooklyn. Look. Steve—is it? You may have "New York theatre chops" but in Roanoke there's no intermission. You're going to have social studies teachers pestering you with minutiae. Punk kids trying to derail you with their iPods and their automatic weapons. Unless you're on top of your shit, staying *in* character *while* you shit—which will be in a chamber pot and not on a toilet—you are not going to make it as a reenactor.

FLORENCIA. Melanie, all I want is to combine my love of reenacting with my passing interest in cooperage.

MELANIE. So you wanna be a barrel maker, is that it Florencia? Good. Good. How 'bout you, Broadway?

STEVE. Well after I graduated *the Juilliard…*

MELANIE. Shut it Broadway. Nobody cares about my failed acting career. I mean your failed acting career. And what the hell are you drinking?

STEVE. It's Cheerwine. It's great! Kind of like cherry-flavored Dr. Pepper but…

MELANIE. I know what Cheerwine is, Broadway, I'm from here. What are YOU doing drinking it?

STEVE. Um…drinking it.

MELANIE. Not anymore you're not. Cheerwine stains your tongue and makes you burp cherries. Cheerwine is for the gift shop—not for reenactors. We have to maintain absolute historical accuracy.

STEVE. We're not even in costume yet. Couldn't I pour it into a flask and… HEY!

(*She grabs the bottle, chugs it, burps, crumples the bottle and tosses it.*)

MELANIE. If you spill Cheerwine on your doublets and jerkins it'll make us look amateur and I can't afford that right now. I need to keep raking in field trip money so I can dredge up the Dare County swampland, put in a roller coaster, and give Colonial Williamsburg a run for its money.

STEVE. But what does a roller coaster have to do with living museums?

MELANIE. You just eat, breathe and shit in Elizabethan and leave that to me.

FLORENCIA. You're really going to dredge up the Dare County swampland?

MELANIE. Well it won't dredge itself.

FLORENCIA. But that's where I live.

MELANIE. Yeah, so? My parents are buried there. But if razing your childhood home gets me one step ahead of those Williamsburg fuckwads then sister you'd better pick up some packing tape. All right enough chitchat. The candlemaker needs fresh tallow so I've gotta go slaughter some pigs. While I'm gone I want you to reenact being colonial scarecrows. *Arms up!* Higher! Good.

(*She exits. Their arms are up.*)

STEVE. Wow. You really think she'll slaughter those pigs?

(*Horrible offstage bleating. MATT enters in full Walter Raleigh regalia.*)

MATT. Ah. The new recruits. (*Cracks his neck each way, then his knuckles.*) Perfect.

FLORENCIA. Who are you, good fellow?

MATT. I. Am Sir Walter Raleigh. Raleigh! He who was jailed in the Tower of London. Raleigh! He whose surname serves as the moniker for this state's capital city. Raleigh! He the tobacconist whose likeness is emblazoned on these. (*He shows a pack of Raleigh Cigarettes with MATT's face plastered on it. Poses like the picture. Throws the cigs at STEVE.*)

STEVE. Whoa.

MATT. But I don't know any of that because— Don't! Smoke those in here, Boy, what's wrong with you? —But I don't know any of that because it's 1587 and I'm colonizing this barren island not for the first but the *second time!* Because that's how Sir Walter Raleigh *rolls.* Sir Walter Raleigh don't *quit.* It's not that Sir Walter Raleigh can't stop—it's that Sir Walter Raleigh WON'T stop. Now. Who do you think you'll be playing?

STEVE. Well, Melanie says I'll be playing Raleigh.

MATT. No, idiot. *I'm* Raleigh. (*He slaps STEVE across the face with his glove.*)

STEVE. Maybe I'll play Raleigh if you need a sick day.

MATT. Raleigh don't *take* sick days. YOU will play a Croaton Indian. Yes, the Croatons. That mysterious Indian tribe whose mysterious tribal name was mysteriously carved on a tree once the Roanoke settlers mysteriously disappeared from this colony. *Mysteriously.*

STEVE. Um I don't think I can pass for an Indian. I look pretty Hispanic.

MATT. That's what war paint is for, Enrique. However, history has long forgotten these savages' native tongue so I hope you're good at emotive grunting.

FLORENCIA. Look ye good fellow. What character shall I play?

MATT. Why it sounds like you're in character already.

FLORENCIA. (*Sincerely flattered.*) Thank you.

MATT. Shut up—don't get cocky.

FLORENCIA. How's that cocky? All I said was…

MATT. SHUT. UP. You'll be playing Virginia Dare, the first non-heathen born in the New World.

FLORENCIA. You mean Virginia Dare like Dare County? Omigod. I *live* in Dare County! Fuckin' A! I mean…fuckin' A, good fellow.

MATT. Fucking A, Virginia Dare. Let us drink to the new world. (*He drinks Cheerwine.*)

STEVE. Are you drinking Cheerwine? I thought we weren't supposed to…

MATT. Walter Raleigh is *thirsty!* Now. Raleigh will play a gawking Yankee tourist. You stay in character. Ready? Go. (STEVE *grunts emotively.*) Why hello there ladies and injuns. I'm a big moneybags Yankee tourist. Can I take your *photograph* with my *camera?*

FLORENCIA. What is that devil box? I'm just Virginia Dare, a simple cooper born into this craft of barrel-making. Merry, nuncle, behold ye this cask I have crafted from hoops and wooden staves.

MATT. What staves? You're not holding anything.

FLORENCIA. (*Breaks character.*) Oh I'm sorry I was miming it. Won't we have wooden barrels?

MATT. HA! Lookit you rookie reenactors. Lookit how easily Raleigh dupes you into dropping character.

FLORENCIA. Aw man!

MATT. What if I burned my hands off at the blacksmith's? You'd probably be running around screaming "Where's the *first aid kit*? Where's the *antibiotics*? Where's my *cell phone* so I can use *electricity* to call *911!*

FLORENCIA. If you burned your hands off of course I'd call 911!

MATT. In 1587 we didn't HAVE the number "nine." It wasn't invented yet.

FLORENCIA. But!

MATT. I once saw a three-year-old jump into the bay. I was standing next to a life vest but do you think I touched it? No, Raleigh fashioned a raft by felling six trees and weaving together some lashings. By the time Raleigh was done with the lashings, the boy had drowned naturally as God intended.

FLORENCIA. Holy shit. You watched a three-year-old drown?

MATT. God is a harsh master. (*Whispers, leg up.*) And so is the sea. (*Awkward pause.*)

STEVE. Does anyone have a light for these cigarettes?

MATT. Raleigh does not have a "light" here in Roanoke, for fire has not been invented in this year of our Lord 1-5-8-7.

FLORENCIA. Hey I'm not sure that's right. You're saying that Roanoke had no *fire*?

MATT. Take it from Raleigh. Raleigh takes naught but cold showers and eats naught but a slurry of cold hardtack and raw bacon.

FLORENCIA. How can there be a blacksmith if you have no fire?

MATT. The blacksmith…melds his alchemy through cold fusion. Which he achieves by striking together two rocks.

FLORENCIA. Did you say "cold fusion"?

MELANIE. (*Enters.*) I swear to God nothing burns brighter than fresh pig tallow. (*Sees MATT.*) You again! Matt, I thought I fired you!

MATT. Fired me? Or couldn't stand seeing me after I dumped you?

MELANIE. *Please* don't do this here Matt.

STEVE. YO! You dated Walter Raleigh?

MELANIE. He's not Walter Raleigh. He's Matt the ex-parking attendant.

MATT. Ex-*lover* parking attendant.

MELANIE. How did you even get in here? Did you steal that getup from wardrobe?

MATT. Raleigh takes what Raleigh wants! Raleigh founded this colony!

MELANIE. Get out of here or I'm calling security.

MATT. You'll rue this day. There's a reason they call it the Lost Colony!

MELANIE. Is that a threat?

MATT. No. Shit I mean yes. Yes that's a threat. Look, just please don't fire me!

MELANIE. What are you talking about "don't fire you"? I fired you three weeks ago.

MATT. Raleigh's been hiding inside of the pig troughs. Raleigh's been subsisting on cold hardtack and discarded Cheerwine.

FLORENCIA. I don't see what the problem is, Melanie. Walter Raleigh was just teaching us character work.

MELANIE. He's NOT Walter Raleigh!

FLORENCIA. (*Rises dramatically.*) Yes he is! And I'm Virginia Dare and I dare to love him!

MELANIE. You're fired.

FLORENCIA. Aw man. I knew I should've gone to college!

MELANIE. (*To* STEVE.) And you're fired too!

STEVE. Me? But what did I do?!

MELANIE. Everyone is fired!

STEVE. I can't go back to New York. I can't go back to playing bit parts in ten-minute plays!

MATT. And Raleigh can't go back to the Old World lest he be jailed in the Tower of London.

MELANIE. What's wrong with you people? Reenacting is about capturing history. This is serious work—it's not an excuse to dress up and goof off and be cocky…Florencia.

FLORENCIA. All I'm doing is standing here!

MELANIE. Why are you all so obsessed with Walter Raleigh? The truth is Raleigh was four feet tall and a crook.

    (STEVE *and* FLORENCIA *gasp.*)

MATT. That may be, Melanie. But reenacting is about more than historical accuracy. It's about capturing the *spirit* of our bygone heroes. Raleigh is much more than Raleigh! Raleigh is *twenty* feet tall. Raleigh's hair shines like silk and he smells like a newborn baby. I am Sir Walter Raleigh!

STEVE. I am Sir Walter Raleigh!

FLORENCIA. I am Sir Walter Raleigh! (*Quickly blurted.*) And also Virginia Dare. (MELANIE *throws up her hands and turns away but Raleigh pulls out a pitch pipe, sounds it, and sings to her.*)

MATT.

RALEIGH
WAS ONE AMAZING BLOKE
RALEIGH
DISCOVERED ROANOKE
RALEIGH
THE REASON THAT WE SMOKE
IS RALEIGH
SIR RALEIGH

STEVE AND FLORENCIA.

RALEIGH
HE DIED AT TWENTY-FOUR
RALEIGH
GAVE MONEY TO THE POOR
RALEIGH
HE WON THE CIVIL WAR
DID RALEIGH
SIR RALEIGH

MATT, STEVE, AND FLORENCIA.

RALEIGH WAS SWEET
AND LIGHT ON HIS FEET
RALEIGH WAS JEWISH

MATT.

WHEN YOU REENACT
IT DON'T HAVE TO BE FACT
IT JUST NEEDS TO SOUND TRUE-ISH

MELANIE. Really?

FLORENCIA. Just give it a try.

MELANIE.

RALEIGH
MAY NOT HAVE BEEN A MAN
RALEIGH
WAS AN ENORMOUS FAN
OF DALI,
AND ELIA KAZAN
WAS WALLY
WALLY RALEIGH

KIDS AND RALEIGH. Yeah!

ALL. (*Back and forth.*)
> HE'D GRANT A MAN THREE WISHES
> HIS BRISKET WAS DELICIOUS
> HE MAY HAVE BEEN FICTITIOUS…TOO
> RALEIGH WAS A COMMIE
> RALEIGH WAS YOUR MOMMY
> RALEIGH IS ME
> RALEIGH IS YOU

ALL. (*Together.*)
> RALEIGH
> WAS OFTEN MELANCHOLY
> RALEIGH
> WAS RALEIGH RALEIGH RALEIGH
> AND NOW HERE IS THE GRAND FINALE
> FOR RALEIGH
> FOR RALEIGH!
> RALEIGH.

> (*They pose in a tableau.*)

ALL. (*Whispered.*) Raleigh.

> (*Lights out.*)

End of Play.

WILD BLESSINGS:
A CELEBRATION OF WENDELL BERRY

adapted for the stage by
Marc Masterson & Adrien-Alice Hansel

from the writing of Wendell Berry

original music & musical direction by
Malcolm Dalglish

BIOGRAPHIES

Wendell Berry was born in Henry County, Kentucky, in 1934. He holds a B.A. and M.A. from the University of Kentucky. Mr. Berry has taught at Georgetown College, Stanford University, New York University and his alma mater. The author of over 40 books of poetry, essays and fiction, Mr. Berry has been the recipient of numerous awards, including the Guggenheim Foundation Fellowship, Rockefeller Foundation Fellowship, National Institute of Arts and Letters Award, American Academy of Arts and Letters Jean Stein Award, Membership in the Fellowship of Southern Writers, John Hay Award and the Cynthia Pratt Laughlin Medal from The Garden Club of America. He lives and works with his wife, Tanya Berry, on their farm in Kentucky.

Marc Masterson is the Artistic Director of Actors Theatre of Louisville. In ten seasons of leadership at Actors Theatre, Mr. Masterson has produced more than 200 plays in Louisville, expanded and deepened arts education programs, and spearheaded community-based projects, including commissions and site-specific productions of regional stories and artists. He is an award-winning director, with more than 100 professional productions to his credit, who enjoys working on new plays as well as innovative productions of classics. As a producer, he has brought new artists to Louisville audiences, including playwrights August Wilson, Craig Wright, Theresa Rebeck and dozens of Humana Festival playwrights. He led the creation of Actors Theatre's first Education Department and numerous community outreach efforts. Mr. Masterson earned an M.F.A. from the University of Pittsburgh and a B.F.A. from Carnegie Mellon University, and subsequently taught at both universities. He currently serves on the Executive Committee of Theatre Communications Group.

Adrien-Alice Hansel is the Director of New Play Development at Actors Theatre, where she heads the Literary Department. She has served as production dramaturg on roughly 45 plays at Actors, including *A Midsummer Night's Dream, Hedwig and the Angry Inch, A Raisin in the Sun, Spunk, 9 Parts of Desire, The Crucible* and *Underneath the Lintel* and the Humana Festival premieres of plays by Craig Wright, Naomi Wallace, Gina Gionfriddo, The Civilians, Charles Mee, Jordan Harrison, Adam Bock, Anne Bogart and SITI Company. She holds an M.F.A. from the Yale School of Drama, where she served as the Associate Literary Manager of Yale Repertory Theatre, was an Assistant Editor of *Theater* magazine and dramaturged both classic and new plays. Ms. Hansel is the co-editor of six anthologies of plays from Actors Theatre and serves on the board of the Kentucky Foundation of Women, which promotes social justice by funding feminist art.

Malcolm Dalglish is a hammer dulcimer player and composer whose work draws on his background in choir, theatre and folk music. He has over fourteen recordings on Windham Hill, Rounder and other labels. *Into the Sky*, *Hymnody of Earth* and *Pleasure* feature the poetry of Wendell Berry. He has composed over eighty commissioned works for choirs worldwide and runs an outdoor singing camp in the summer. He attended Cincinnati Conservatory of Music and acted in a resident theatre company at Oberlin College with Herbert Blau, Bill Irwin and Julie Taymor. His solo show *Wild, Wild, Word Show*, ran at Cincinnati Playhouse and other theatres nationwide. His operetta, *Free Range, A Baseball Dream*, toured China in 2008. Performances include Carnegie Hall, Avery Fisher Hall, the Smithsonian, the Kennedy Center and NPR's *Prairie Home Companion*.

ACKNOWLEDGMENTS

Wild Blessings: A Celebration of Wendell Berry premiered at the Humana Festival of New American Plays in March 2009. It was directed by Marc Masterson with the following cast (in alphabetical order):

Helen-Jean Arthur
Malcolm Dalglish
Tracy Conyer Lee
Larry John Meyers
Phil Pickens

and the following production staff:

Scenic Designer	Michael B. Raiford
Costume Designer	Lorraine Venberg
Lighting Designer	Brian J. Lilienthal
Sound Designer	Matt Callahan
Properties Designer	Doc Manning
Video Designer	Donna L. Lawrence
Stage Manager	Paul Mills Holmes
Production Assistant	Sara Kmack
Stage Management Intern	Cadi Thomas
Dramaturg	Adrien-Alice Hansel
Assistant Dramaturg	Rachel Lerner-Ley
Assistant Director	Jacob Stoebel

This play was developed at the Perry-Mansfield Performing Arts New Works Festival, June 2008.

POEM LIST

1. The Mad Farmer Manifesto: The first amendment
2. Sabbath, 1982: X
3. Manifesto: The Mad Farmer Liberation Front
4. May Song
5. The Guest
6. The Mad Farmer in the City
7. A Letter
8. The Mad Farmer, Flying the Flag of Rough Branch, Secedes from the Union
9. Sabbath, 1991: The Farm
10. A Letter, part two
11. The Fear of Love
12. The Mad Farmer Revolution
13. The Country of Marriage
14. Walking at Night
15. The Wheel
16. The Dance
17. Rising
18. The Clearing
19. Song (2)
20. How to be a poet *(to remind myself)*
21. The Sycamore
22. The Wild Geese
23. The Satisfactions of the Mad Farmer
24. Some Further Words
25. Window Poems
26. Sabbath, 1982: V
27. My Great Grandfather's Slaves
28. The Morning's News
29. Questionnaire
30. Sabbath, 2007: I
31. Sabbath, 1986
32. The Blue Robe
33. Boone
34. At a Country Funeral
35. The Contrariness of the Mad Farmer
36. Rising, part two

These poems were originally published in:

The Collected Poems of Wendell Berry, 1957-1982, North Point Press, 1987
A Timbered Choir: The Sabbath Poems 1979-1997, Counterpoint, 1999
Given: Poems, Counterpoint, 2006
The Progressive Magazine, December 2007
The American Poetry Review, January/February 2009

CHARACTERS

ACTOR 1, an older man
ACTOR 2, a younger man
ACTRESS 1, an older woman
ACTRESS 2, a younger woman
MUSICIAN

NOTE ON PRODUCTION

In the original production, the set included a screen to project poem titles and images as indicated in the stage directions. Other productions may find this useful; we believe the piece could work without projections as well.

Tracy Conyer Lee, Phil Pickens, and Larry John Meyers
in *Wild Blessings: A Celebration of Wendell Berry*

33rd Annual Humana Festival of New American Plays
Actors Theatre of Louisville, 2009
Photo by Harlan Taylor

WILD BLESSINGS:
A CELEBRATION OF WENDELL BERRY

The Mad Farmer Manifesto: The first amendment

MUSICIAN.

To be sane in a mad time
is bad for the brain, worse
for the heart. The world
is a holy vision, had we clarity
to see it—a clarity that men
depend on men to make.

Sabbath, 1982

Sung.

ALL.

The dark around us, come,
Let us meet here together,
Members one of another,
Here in our holy room,

Here on our little floor,
Here in the daylit sky,
Rejoicing mind and eye,
Rejoining known and knower,

Light, leaf, foot, hand, and wing,
Such order as we know,
One household, high and low,
And all the earth shall sing.

Manifesto: The Mad Farmer Liberation Front

ACTOR 2.

Love the quick profit, the annual raise,
vacation with pay. Want more
of everything ready-made. Be afraid
to know your neighbors and to die.
And you will have a window in your head.

ACTRESS 2.

When they want you to buy something

they will call you. When they want you
to die for profit they will let you know.

ACTOR 1.

So, friends, every day do something
that won't compute.

ACTRESS 1.

Love the Lord.

ALL.

Love the Lord.

ACTOR 1.

Love the world.

ALL.

Love the world.

ACTOR 2.

Love someone who does not deserve it.

ACTRESS 2.

Denounce the government and embrace
the flag. Hope to live in that free
republic for which it stands.

ACTOR 1.

Give your approval to all you cannot
understand. Praise ignorance, for what man
has not encountered he has not destroyed.

ACTRESS 1.

Put your faith in the two inches of humus
that will build under the trees
every thousand years.

ACTRESS 2.

Expect the end of the world. Laugh.
Laughter is immeasurable. Be joyful
though you have considered all the facts.

ACTOR 2.

Go with your love to the fields.
Lie down in the shade. Rest your head
in her lap. Swear allegiance
to what is nighest your thoughts.

ACTOR 1.

As soon as the generals and the politicos
can predict the motions of your mind,
lose it. Leave it as a sign

to mark the false trail, the way
you didn't go. Be like the fox
who makes more tracks than necessary,
some in the wrong direction.

ACTRESS 1.

Practice resurrection.

ALL.

Practice resurrection.

May Song

Sounds of a city and images of urban decay. A young man walks with his suitcase.
The squeal of a subway. Light passing and moving.

ACTRESS 1.

The window flies from the dark
of the subway mouth

into the sunlight
stained with the green
of the spring weeds

that crowd the improbable
black earth
of the embankment,

their stout leaves
like the tongues and bodies
of a herd, feeding

on the new heat,
drinking at the seepage
of the stones:

the freehold of life,
triumphant
even in the waste

of those who possess it.

The Guest

More traffic sounds; a busy street at lunchtime—a crush of people, some lone
figures, from many walks of life.

ACTRESS 2.

Washed into the doorway

by the wake of the traffic,
he wears humanity
like a third-hand shirt
—blackened with enough
of Manhattan's dirt to sprout
a tree, or poison one.
His empty hand has led him
where he has come to.
Our differences claim us.
He holds out his hand,
in need of all that's mine.

And so we're joined, as deep
as son and father. His life
is offered me to choose.

My stranger waits, his hand
held out like something to read,
as though its emptiness
is an accomplishment.
I give him a smoke and the price
of a meal, no more

—not sufficient kindness
or believable sham.
I paid him to remain strange
to my threshold and table,
to permit me to forget him
—knowing I won't. He's the guest
of my knowing, though not asked.

The Mad Farmer in the City

Sounds of traffic. The younger man walks through the urban space.

ACTOR 2.
I heard the earth singing beneath the street.
Singing quietly myself, I followed the song
among the traffic. Everywhere I went, singing,
following the song, the stones cracked,
and I heard it stronger. I heard it strongest
in the presence of women.

(ACTOR 2 *sees and moves around* ACTRESS 1 *as he speaks.*)
There was one I met
who had the music of the ground in her, and she

was its dancer. "O Exile," I sang, "for want of you
there is a tree that has borne no leaves
and a planting season that will not turn warm."
Looking at her, I felt a tightening of roots
under the pavement, and I turned and went
with her a little way, dancing beside her.

(ACTRESS 2 *waits for a bus.*)

And I saw a black woman still inhabiting
as in a dream the space of the open fields
where she had bent to plant and gather. She stood
rooted in the music I heard, pliant and proud
as a stalk of wheat with the grain heavy. No man
with the city thrusting angles in his brain
is equal to her. To reach her he must tear it down.
Wherever lovely women are the city is undone,
its geometry broken in pieces and lifted,
its street and corners fading like mist at sunrise
above groves and meadows and planted fields.

A Letter

Noise again—engines and traffic. Images of tall buildings, blocking the sunlight.

ACTOR 1.

The cities have forgot the earth,
and they will rot at heart
till they remember it again.
In the streets, abstraction
contends with outcry,
hungering for men's flesh.

In the city I measure time
by the life of no living thing,
but by the running down
of engines. I grew a skin
that did not know the sun.

The streets of the broken city
bring in the vogue of the revolutionary
—another kind of politician, another
slogan sayer, ready to level the world
with a little truth. Those who wait
to change until a crowd agrees
with their opinions will never change.

The Mad Farmer, Flying the Flag of Rough Branch, Secedes from the Union

Image of a small-town square. First a drum underscores, then the dulcimer, possibly other instruments, as the Mad Farmer describes his vision of the world.

ACTRESS 1.

From the union of power and money,

ACTOR 2.

from the union of power and secrecy,

ACTOR 1.

from the union of government and science,

ACTRESS 2.

from the union of government and art,

ACTOR 2.

from the union of science and money,

ACTRESS 1.

from the union of ambition and ignorance,

ACTOR 1.

from the union of genius and war,

ACTRESS 2.

from the union of outer space and inner vacuity,

ACTOR 2.

the Mad Farmer walks quietly away.

ACTRESS 1.

There is only one of him, but he goes.
He returns to the small country he calls home,
his own nation small enough to walk across.

ACTOR 1.

He goes shadowy into the local woods,
and brightly into the local meadows and croplands.

ACTRESS 2.

He goes to the care of neighbors,
he goes into the care of neighbors.

ACTRESS 1.

He goes to the potluck supper, a dish from each house
for the hunger of every house.

ACTOR 2.

He goes into the quiet of early mornings
of days when he is not going anywhere.

ACTRESS 2.

Calling his neighbors together into the sanctity of their lives separate and together

ACTOR 1.

in the one life of their commonwealth and home,
in their own nation small enough for a story
or song to travel across in an hour, he cries:

ACTOR 2.

"Come all ye conservatives and liberals
who want to conserve the good things and be free,
come away from the merchants of big answers,
whose hands are metalled with power;
from the union of anywhere and everywhere
by the purchase of everything from everybody at the lowest price
and the sale of anything to anybody at the highest price;
from the union of work and debt, work and despair;
from the wage-slavery of the helplessly well-employed.

ACTRESS 1.

From the union of self-gratification and self-annihilation,
secede into care for one another and for the good gifts of Heaven
and Earth.

ACTRESS 2.

Come into the life of the body, the one body
granted to you in all the history of time.

ACTOR 1.

Come into the body's economy, its daily work,
and its replenishment at mealtimes and at night.

ACTRESS 1.

Come into the body's thanksgiving, when it knows and acknowledges
itself a living soul.

ACTOR 2.

Come into the dance of the community, joined
in a circle, hand in hand, the dance of the eternal
love of women and men for one another
and of neighbors and friends for one another."

ACTRESS 2.

Always disappearing, always returning,
calling his neighbors to return, to think again
of the care of flocks and herds, of gardens
and fields, of woodlots and forests and the uncut groves,
calling them separately and together, calling and calling,
he goes forever toward the long restful evening
and the croak of the night heron over the river at dark.

ACTOR 2.

 Amen.

<h3 align="center">Sabbath, 1991: The Farm</h3>

The country—a different feel. Image of a run-down farm: a field pockmarked with dry runoff beds, overrun with weeds and thistles; a farmhouse neglected and unsturdy. Our first view of the land that will become a farm.

ACTRESS 1.

 Go by the narrow road
 Along the creek,

ACTOR 1.

 a burrow
 Under shadowy trees
 Such as a mouse makes through
 Tall grass,

ACTRESS 1.

  so that you may
 Forget the wide road you
 Have left behind, and all
 That it has led to.

 You'll see it suddenly
 Lie open to the light
 Amid the woods:

ACTOR 1.

  a farm
 Little enough to see
 Or call across.

ACTRESS 1.

 That is the vision, seen
 As on a Sabbath walk:
 The possibility
 Of human life whose terms
 Are Heaven's and this earth's.

ACTOR 1.

 You make the farm
 That must be daily made
 And yearly made, or it
 Will not exist.

ACTRESS 1.

    By this expenditure
    You make yourself a place;
    You make yourself a way
    for love to reach the ground.

A Letter, part two

Dusk on the farm. Sounds of nature.

ACTOR 2.

    That was a lovely time we had out there,
    Those months of talk and laughter, correcting us.
    Now back in Kentucky, far from you again,
    I often think of those days and nights, and long
    For their music and their mirth. And then
    I remind myself: the past is gone. Remember it.

    Returning, I always put on a new body,
    Waking in wet dawn and going to work.

    I come into the community of the creatures:
    lily and fern, thrush and sycamore,
    they turn to the light, and to the earth again.
    Light and leaf, man and wife,
    bird and tree—each one
    a blind dancer, whose partner sees.

ACTRESS 2.

    And friend and friend,
    together though only in thought,
    our bond is speech
    grown out of native ground
    and laughter grown out of speech
    surpassing all ends.

The Fear of Love

Sung.

ACTOR 2.

    I come to the fear of love
    As I have often come
    To what may be desired
    And to what must be done.

BOTH.

>Only love can quiet the fear
>Of love and only love can save
>From diminishment the love
>That we must lose to have.

ACTRESS 2.

>We stand as in an open field,
>Blossom, leaf, and stem,
>Rooted and shaken in our day,
>Heads nodding in the wind.

BOTH.

>Only love can quiet the fear
>Of love and only love can save
>From diminishment the love
>That we must lose to have.

>Only love can quiet the fear
>Of love and only love can save
>From diminishment the love
>That we must lose to have.

The Mad Farmer Revolution

Guitar vamp underneath.

ACTOR 1.

>The mad farmer, the thirsty one
>went dry. When he had time
>he threw a visionary high
>lonesome on the holy communion wine.

ACTRESS 2.

>"It is an awesome event
>when an earthen man has drunk
>his fill of the blood of a god,"
>people said, and got out of his way.

ACTOR 2.

>He plowed the churchyard, the
>minister's wife, three graveyards
>and a golf course. In a parking lot
>he planted a forest of little pines.

ACTRESS 1.

>He sanctified the groves,
>dancing at night in the oak shades

with goddesses. He led
a field of corn to creep up
and tassel like an Indian tribe
on the courthouse lawn. Pumpkins
ran out to the ends of their vines
to follow him.

ACTOR 1.

Ripe plums
and peaches reached into his pockets.
Flowers sprang up in his tracks
everywhere he stepped. And then
his planter's eye fell on
that parson's fair fine lady
again.

ACTRESS 2.

"O holy plowman," cried she,
"I am all grown up in weeds.
Pray, bring me back into good tilth."

ACTOR 2.

He tilled her carefully
and laid her by, and she
did bring forth others of her kind,
and others, and some more.

ACTRESS 1.

They sowed and reaped till all
the countryside was filled
with farmers and their brides sowing
and reaping. When they died
they became two spirits of the woods.

ACTOR 2.

On their graves were written
these words without sound:

ACTOR 1.

(*Sings.*) "Here lies Saint Plowman.

ACTRESS 2.

(*Sings.*) Here lies Saint Fertile Ground."

MEN.

(*Sing.*) "Here lies Saint Plowman

WOMEN.

(*Sing.*) Here lies Saint Fertile Ground."

ALL.

> (*Sing.*) "Here lies Saint Plowman
> Here lies Saint Fertile Ground."
>
> "Here lies Saint Plowman
> Here lies Saint Fertile Ground."

The Country of Marriage

Images of a country church; light music plays under. The two couples speak to each other.

ACTOR 1.

> I dream of you walking at night along the streams
> Of the country of my birth, warm blooms and the nightsongs
> Of birds opening around you as you walk.
> You are holding in your body the dark seed of my sleep.

ACTRESS 1.

> This comes after silence.
> Was it something I said
> That bound me to you, some mere promise
> Or, worse, the fear of loneliness and death?

ACTOR 2.

> A man lost in the woods in the dark, I stood
> Still and said nothing. And then there rose in me,
> Like the earth's empowering brew rising
> In root and branch, the words of a dream of you
> I did not know I had dreamed. I was a wanderer
> Who feels the solace of his native land
> Under his feet again and moving in his blood.
> I went on blind and faithful. Where I stepped
> My track was there to steady me. It was no abyss
> That lay before me, but only the level ground.

ACTRESS 2.

> Sometimes our life reminds me
> Of a forest in which there is a graceful clearing
> And in that opening a house,
> An orchard and garden,
> Comfortable shades, and flowers
> Red and yellow in the sun, a pattern
> Made in the light for the light to return to.
> The forest is mostly dark, its ways
> To be made anew day after day, the dark

Richer than the light and more blessed,
Provided we stay brave enough to keep going in.

ACTOR 1.

How many times have I come to you out of my head
With joy, if ever a man was,
For to approach you I have given up the light
And all directions. I come to you
Lost, wholly trusting as a man who goes
Into the forest unarmed. It is as though I descend
slowly earthward out of the air. I rest in peace
in you, when I arrive at last.

ACTRESS 1.

What I am learning to give you is my death
to set you free of me, and me from myself
into the dark and the new light. Like the water
of a deep stream, love is always too much. We
did not make it. Though we drink till we burst
we cannot have it all, or want it all.
In its abundance it survives our thirst.

ACTRESS 2.

In the evening we come down to the shore
to drink our fill, and sleep, while it
flows through the regions of the dark.
It does not hold us, except we are returning
to its rich waters thirsty. We enter,
willing to die, into the commonwealth of its joy.

ACTOR 1.

I give you what is unbounded, passing from dark to dark,
containing darkness: a night of rain, an early morning.
I give you the life I have let live for love of you:
a clump of orange blooming weeds beside the road,
the young orchard waiting in the snow, our own life
that we have planted in the ground, as I
have planted mine in you.

ACTRESS 2.

I give you my love for all
beautiful and honest women that you gather to yourself
again and again, and satisfy—and this poem,
no more mine than any man's who has loved a woman.

Walking at Night

Sung.

MUSICIAN.

> How many times have I come to you,
> Out of my head with joy?
>
> How many times have I come to you,
> Out of my head with joy?
>
> I give you the life I have let live for love of you
> Dreaming, I see you there,
>
> Along the streams of the country of my birth,
> Warm blooms and the night songs of birds
> Opening around you.
>
> Walking at night, the water flowing,
> Walking at night, through the regions of the dark,
> Walking at night, it does not hold us,
> Walking at night, we keep returning,
> Returning thirsty, returning thirsty.
>
> You are the known way leading always to the unknown,
> And you are the known place
> To which the unknown is always leading me back.
>
> You are the known way leading always to the unknown,
> And you are the known place
> To which the unknown is always leading me back.

The Wheel

At a country dance. The MUSICIAN *speaks as the caller; actors watch the dance as he describes it.*

MUSICIAN.

> At the first stroke of the fiddle bow
> the dancers rise from their seats.
> The dance begins to shape itself
> in the crowd, as couples join,
> and couples join couples, their movement
> together lightening their feet.
> They move in the ancient circle
> of the dance. The dance and the song
> call each other into being.

ACTOR 1.

Soon they are all one—rapt in a single
rapture, so that even the night
has its clarity, and time
is the wheel that brings it round.

The Dance

The dance and music continues and builds.

ACTOR 1.

I would have each couple turn,
join and unjoin, be lost
in the greater turning
of other couples, woven
in the circle of a dance,
the song of long time flowing
over them, so they may return,

turn again unto themselves
out of desire greater than their own,
belonging to all, to each,
to the dance, and to the song
that moves them through the night.

(The music shifts and slows down.)

ACTRESS 2.

What is fidelity? To what
does it hold? The point
of departure, or the turning road
that is departure and absence
and the way home? What we are
and what we were once
are far estranged.

ACTOR 2.

For those
who would not change, time
is infidelity. But we are married
until death, and are betrothed
to change. By silence, so,
I learn my song. I earn
my sunny fields by absence, once
and to come.

ACTRESS 1.
> And I love you
> as I love the dance that brings you
> out of the multitude
> in which you come and go.
> Love changes, and in change is true.

Rising

Early morning light—dawn the day after. Young man follows older man through the fields.

ACTOR 2.
> Having danced until nearly
> time to get up, I went on
> in the harvest, half lame
> with weariness. And he
> took no notice and made
> no mention of my distress.
> He went ahead, assuming
> that I would follow. I followed,
> dizzy, half blind, bitter
> with sweat in the hot light.
> He never turned his head,
> a man well known by his back
> in those fields in those days.
> He led me through the long rows
> of misery, moving like a dancer
> ahead of me, so elated
> he was, and able, filled
> with desire for the ground's growth.
> We came finally to the high
> still heat of four o'clock,
> a long time before sleep.
> And then he stood by me
> and looked at me as I worked,
> just looked, so that my own head
> uttered his judgment, even
> his laughter. He only said:

ACTOR 1.
> "That social life don't get
> down the row, does it boy?"

ACTOR 2.

> I worked by will then, he
> by desire. What was ordeal
> for me, for him was order
> and grace, ideal and real.
> That was my awkward boyhood,
> the time of his mastery.
> He troubled me to become
> what I had not yet thought to be.

The Clearing

Images of manual farm labor unfold through the poem.

ACTRESS 2.

> As the vision of labor grows
> grows the vision of rest.
> Work clarifies
> the vision of rest. In rest
> the vision of rest is lost.

ACTRESS 1.

> But no matter, life
> must be served. Wake up,
> leave the bed, dress
> in the cold room, go under
> the stars to the barn, come
> to the greeting of hunger,
> the breath a pale awning
> in the dark. Feed
> the lives that feed
> lives.

ACTOR 1.

> Make clear what was overgrown.
> Cut the brush, drag it
> through the sumac and briars, pile it,
> clear the old fence rows,
> the trash dump, stop
> the washes, mend the galls,
> fence and sow the fields,
> bring cattle back to graze
> the slopes, bring crops back
> to the bottomland. Here
> is where the time of rain is kept

take what is half ruined
and make it clear, put it
back in mind.

ACTOR 2.

An evening comes
when we finish work and go,
stumblers under the folding sky,
the field clear behind us.

Song (2)

ACTRESS 2 *greets* ACTOR 2 *from the fields. A moment, looking at their work. The satisfaction of well-earned weariness. Images of a farmhouse—kitchen, sitting room, bedroom. Sung.*

ACTOR 2.

My gentle hill, I rest beside you
I rest beside you in the dark.
Rest in a place warmed by my body—
Rest in a place where I belong.

ACTRESS 2.

My gentle hill, I rest beside you
I rest beside you in the dark.
Rest in a place warmed by my body—
Rest in a place where I belong.

BOTH.

Where by ardor, graces, work,
and loss, I belong.

How to Be a Poet (*to remind myself*)

ACTOR 2 *sits at his desk by a window.*

ACTRESS 1.

Make a place to sit down.
Sit down. Be quiet.
You must depend upon
affection, reading, knowledge,
skill—more of each
than you have—inspiration,
work, growing older, patience,
for patience joins time
to eternity.

ACTOR 1.

> Any readers
> who like your work,
> doubt their judgment.
>
> Breathe with unconditional breath
> the unconditioned air.
> Shun electric wire.
> Communicate slowly. Live
> a three-dimensioned life;
> stay away from screens.
> Stay away from anything
> that obscures the place it is in.
> There are no unsacred places;
> there are only sacred places
> and desecrated places.

ACTRESS 2.

> Accept what comes from silence.
> Make the best you can of it.
> Of the little words that come
> out of the silence, like prayers
> prayed back to the one who prays,
> make a poem that does not disturb
> the silence from which it came.

The Sycamore

An image of a huge tree, silhouetted against the sky. ACTOR 2 *visualizes and writes as* ACTOR 1 *speaks.*

ACTOR 1.

> In the place that is my own place, whose earth
> I am shaped in and must bear, there is an old tree growing,
> a great sycamore that is a wondrous healer of itself.
> Fences have been tied to it, nails driven into it,
> hacks and whittles cut in it, the lightning has burned it.
> There is no year it has flourished in
> that has not harmed it. There is a hollow in it
> that is its death, though its living brims whitely
> at the lip of the darkness and flows outward.
> Over all its scars has come the seamless white
> of the bark. It bears the gnarls of its history
> healed over. It has risen to a strange perfection
> in the warp and bending of its long growth.

It has gathered all accidents into its purpose.
It has become the intention and radiance of its dark face.
It is a fact, sublime, mystical and unassailable.
In all the country there is no other like it.
I recognize in it a principle, an indwelling
the same as itself, and greater, that I would be ruled by.
I see that it stands in its place, and feeds upon it,
and is fed upon, and is native, and maker.

The Wild Geese

Music plays under.

ACTRESS 2.

Horseback on Sunday morning,
harvest over, we taste persimmon
and wild grape, sharp sweet
of summer's end. In time's maze
over the fall fields, we name names
that went west from here, names
that rest on graves. We open
a persimmon seed to find the tree that stands in promise,
pale, in the seed's marrow.

(Musical bridge.)

Geese appear high over us,
pass, and the sky closes.
Abandon, as in love or sleep,
holds them to their way, clear
in the ancient faith: what we need
is here. And we pray, not
for new earth or heaven, but to be
quiet in heart, and in eye
clear. What we need is here.

ALL.

(Chanted, four times.)

And we pray, not
for new earth or heaven, but to be
quiet in heart, and in eye
clear.

MUSICIAN.

(Sung simultaneously, twice.)

What we need is here.

The Satisfactions of the Mad Farmer

Images of community life unfold—the sowing and reaping of fields; a church social; children running; a garden in late summer; cows and sheep in their fields; a barn, with its hay up and tools in place; winter in the woods; a meal at a full table.

ACTRESS 2.

Growing weather; enough rain;
the cow's udder tight with milk;
the peach tree bent with its yield;
honey golden in the white comb;

ACTOR 2.

the pasture deep in clover and grass,
enough, and more than enough;

the ground, new worked, moist
and yielding underfoot, the feet
comfortable in it as roots;

ACTOR 1.

the early garden: potatoes, onions,
peas, lettuce, spinach, cabbage, carrots,
radishes, marking their straight rows
with green, before the trees are leafed;

ACTRESS 1.

raspberries ripe and heavy amid their foliage,
currants shining red in clusters amid their foliage,
strawberries red ripe with the white
flowers still on the vines—picked
with the dew on them, before breakfast;

ACTOR 2.

grape clusters heavy under broad leaves,
powdery bloom on fruit black with sweetness
—an ancient delight, delighting;

ACTRESS 2.

the bodies of children, joyful
without dread of their spending,
surprised at nightfall to be weary;

ACTOR 1.

the bodies of women in loose cotton,
cool and closed in the evenings
of summer, like contented houses;

ACTRESS 1.

the bodies of men,

able in the heat and sweat and weight and length
of the day's work, eager in their spending,
attending to nightfall, the bodies of women;

ACTOR 2.

sleep after love, dreaming
white lilies blooming
coolly out of the flesh;
after sleep, enablement
to go on with work, morning a clear gift;

ACTRESS 2.

the maidenhood of the day,
cobwebs unbroken in the dewy grass;

ACTRESS 1.

the work of feeding and clothing and housing,
done with more than enough knowledge
and with more than enough love,
by those who do not have to be told;

ACTOR 1.

any building well built, the rafters
firm to the walls, the walls firm,
the joists without give,
the proportions clear,
the fitting exact, even unseen,
bolts and hinges that turn home
without a jiggle;

any work worthy
of the day's maidenhood;

ACTOR 2.

any man whose words
lead precisely to what exists,
who never stoops to persuasion;

ACTRESS 1.

the talk of friends, lightened and cleared
by all that can be assumed;

ACTRESS 2.

deer tracks in the wet path,
the deer sprung from them, gone on;

ACTOR 2.

live streams, live shiftings
of the sun in the summer woods;

ACTOR 1.

> the great hollow-trunked beech,
> a landmark I loved to return to,
> its leaves gold-lit on the silver
> branches in the fall: blown down
> after a hundred years of standing,
> a footbridge over the stream;

ACTRESS 1.

> the quiet in the woods of a summer morning,
> the voice of a pewee passing through it
> like a tight silver wire;

ACTOR 2.

> a little clearing among cedars,
> white clover and wild strawberries
> beneath an opening to the sky
> —heavenly, I thought it,
> so perfect; had I foreseen it
> I would have desired it
> no less than it deserves;

ACTOR 1.

> fox tracks in snow, the impact
> of lightness upon lightness,
> unendingly silent.

ACTRESS 2.

> What I know of spirit is astir
> in the world. The god I have always expected
> to appear at the woods' edge, beckoning,
> I have always expected to be
> a great relisher of the world, its good
> grown immortal in his mind.

Some Further Words

ACTOR 1.

> Let me be plain with you,
> I am an old-fashioned man. I like
> the world of nature despite its mortal
> dangers. I like the domestic world
> of humans, so long as it pays its debts
> to the natural world, and keeps its bounds.
> I like the promise of Heaven. My purpose
> is a language that can pay just thanks

and honor for those gifts, a tongue
set free from fashionable lies.

Neither this world nor any of its places
is an "environment." And a house
for sale is not a "home." Economics
is not "science," nor "information" knowledge.
A knave with a degree is a knave. A fool
in a public office is not a "leader."
A rich thief is a thief.

The world is babbled to pieces after
the divorce of things from their names.
Ceaseless preparation for war
is not peace. Health is not procured
by sale of medication, or purity
by the addition of poison.

I don't like machines,
I mean the dire machines that run
by burning the world's body and
its breath. When I see an airplane
fuming through the once-pure sky
or a vehicle of the outer space
imitating a star at night, I say,
"Get *out* of there!" as I would speak
to a fox or a thief in the henhouse.

When I hear the stock market has fallen,
I say, "Long live gravity! Long live
stupidity, error, and greed in the palaces
of fantasy capitalism!" I think
an economy should be based on thrift,
on taking care of things, not on theft,
usury, seduction, waste, and ruin.

My purpose is a language that can make us whole,
Though mortal, ignorant, and small.
The world is whole beyond human knowing,

                 We live as councils
of ghosts. It is not "human genius"
that makes us human, but an old love,
an old intelligence of the heart
we gather to us from the world,

from the creatures, from the angels
of inspiration, from the dead—

Think of the genius of the animals,
every one truly what it is:
gnat, fox, minnow, swallow, each made
of light and luminous within itself.
They know (better than we do) how
to live in the places where they live.
And so I would like to be a true
human being, dear reader—a choice
not altogether possible now.

Window Poems

Images of winter on the farm beside a river. Light through the window as ACTOR 2
sits at the desk. The sound of a clock ticking.

ACTOR 2.
>Window. Window.
>The wind's eye
>to see into the wind.
>The eye in its hollow
>looking out
>through the black frame
>at the waves the wind
>drives up the river,
>whitecaps, a wild day,
>the white sky
>travelled by snow squalls,
>the trees thrashing,
>the corn blades driven,
>quivering, straight out.

ACTOR 1.
>This is the wind's eye,
>Wendell's window
>dedicated to purposes
>dark to him, a seeing into
>days to come, the winds
>of the days as they approach
>and go by. He has come
>mornings of four years
>to be thoughtful here
>while day and night

cold and heat
beat upon the world.

ACTOR 2.

In the low room
within the weathers,
sitting at the window,
he has shed himself
at times and been renewed.

ACTRESS 1.

The country where he lives
is haunted
by the ghost of an old forest.
In the cleared fields
where he gardens
and pastures his horses
it stood once,
and will return. There will be
a resurrection of the wild.
Already it stands in wait
at the pasture fences.
It is rising up
in the waste places of the cities.
When the fools of the capitals
have devoured each other
in righteousness,
and the machines have eaten
the rest of us, then
there will be the second coming
of the trees. They will come
straggling over the fences
slowly, but soon enough.
The highways will sound
with the feet of wild herds,
returning. Beaver will ascend
the streams as the trees
close over them.
The wolf and the panther
will find their old ways
through the nights. Water
and air will flow clear.
Certain calamities
will have passed,

and certain pleasures.
The wind will do without
corners. How difficult
to think of it: miles and miles
and no window.

ACTRESS 2.

Sometimes he thinks the earth
might be better without humans.
He's ashamed of that.
It worries him,
him being a human, and needing
to think well of the others
in order to think well of himself.
And there are
a few he thinks well of,
a few he loves
as well as himself almost,
and he would like to say
better. But history
is so largely unforgivable.
And now his mighty government
wants to help everybody
even if it has to kill them
to do it—like the fellow in the story
who helped his neighbor to heaven:

ACTOR 1.

"I heard the Lord calling him,
Judge, and I sent him on."

ACTRESS 2.

According to the government
everybody is just waiting
to be given a chance
to be like us. He can't
go along with that.
Here is a thing, flesh of his flesh,
that he hates. He would like
a little assurance
that no one will destroy the world
for some good cause.

ACTRESS 1.

Until he dies, he would like his life
to pertain to the earth.

But there is something in him
that will wait, even
while he protests,
for things to turn out as they will.

ACTOR 2.

Out his window this morning
he saw nine ducks in flight,
and a hawk dive at his mate
in delight.

ACTOR 1.

The day stands apart
from the calendar. There is a will
that receives it as enough.
He is given a fragment of time
in this fragment of the world.

ACTOR 2.

He likes it pretty well.

Sabbath, 1982

A young couple together at home. She is pregnant.

ACTRESS 2.

A child unborn, the coming year
Grows big within us, dangerous,

ACTOR 2.

And yet we hunger as we fear
For its increase: the blunted bud
To free the leaf to have its day,
The unborn to be born.

ACTRESS 2.

                    The ones
Who are to come are on their way,
And though we stand in mortal good
Among our dead,

ACTOR 2.

                    we turn in doom
In joy to welcome them, stirred by
That Ghost who sits in seed and tomb,

ACTRESS 2.

Who brings the stones to parenthood.

My Great Grandfather's Slaves

Images of slaves working the tobacco fields.

ACTOR 1.

Deep in the back ways of my mind I see them
going in the long days
over the same fields I have gone
long days over.

ACTRESS 1.

I see the sun passing and burning high
over that land from their day
until mine, their shadows
having risen and consumed them.

ACTOR 2.

I see them obeying and watching
the bearded tall man whose voice
and blood are mine, whose countenance
in stone at his grave my own resembles,
whose blindness is my brand.

ACTOR 1.

I see them kneel and pray to the white God
who buys their souls with Heaven.

ACTOR 2.

I see them approach, quiet
in the merchandise of their flesh,
to put down their burdens
of firewood and hemp and tobacco
into the minds of my kinsmen.

ACTRESS 1.

I see them moving in the rooms of my history,
the days of my birth entering
the horizon emptied of their days,
their purchased lives taken back
into the dust of birthright.

ACTOR 1.

I see them borne, shadow within shadow,
shroud within shroud, through all nights
from their lives to mine, long beyond
reparation or given liberty
or any straightness.

ACTRESS 1.

> I see them go into the bonds of my blood
> through all the time of their bodies.

ACTOR 2.

> I have seen that freedom cannot be taken
> from one man and given to another,
> and cannot be taken and kept.

ACTRESS 1.

> I know that freedom can only be given,
> and is the gift to the giver
> from the one who receives.

ACTOR 1.

> I am owned by the blood of all of them
> who ever were owned by my blood.

ALL.

> We cannot be free of each other.

The Morning's News

Images of dawn on a farm.

ACTRESS 2.

> To moralize the state, they drag out a man,
> and bind his hands, and darken his eyes
> with a black rag to be free of the light in them,
> and tie him to a post, and kill him.
> And I am sickened by the complicity in my race.
>
> To kill in hot savagery like a beast
> is understandable. It is forgivable and curable.
> But to kill by design, deliberately, without wrath,
> that is the sullen labor that perfects Hell.
>
> The morning's news drives sleep out of the head
> at night. Uselessness and horror hold the eyes
> open to the dark. Weary, we lie awake
> in the agony of the old giving birth to the new
> without assurance that the new will be better.
>
> I look at my son, whose eyes are like a young god's,
> they are so open to the world.
> I look at my sloping fields now turning
> green with the young grass of April. What must I do
> to go free? I think I must put on

a deathlier knowledge, and prepare to die
rather than enter into the design of man's hate.

Questionnaire

Doorbell.

ACTOR 2.

    1. How much poison are you willing
    to eat for the success of the free
    market and global trade? Please
    name your preferred poisons.

ACTRESS 1.

    2. For the sake of goodness, how much
    evil are you willing to do?
    Fill in the following blanks
    with the names of your favorite
    evils and acts of hatred.

ACTRESS 2.

    3. What sacrifices are you prepared
    to make for culture and civilization?
    Please list the monuments, shrines,
    and works of art you would
    most willingly destroy.

ACTOR 1.

    4. In the name of patriotism and
    the flag, how much of our beloved
    land are you willing to desecrate?
    List in the following spaces
    the mountains, rivers, towns, farms
    you could most readily do without.

ACTRESS 2.

    5. State briefly the ideas, ideals, or hopes,
    the energy sources, the kinds of security,
    for which you would kill a child.
    Name, please, the children whom
    you would be willing to kill.

Sabbath, 2007

ACTOR 2.

    I dream by night the horror
    that I oppose by day.

The nation in its error
and by its work and play

destroys its land, pollutes
its streams, and desecrates
air and light. From the roots
it dies upward, our rights,

divinely given, plundered
and sold by purchased power
that dies from the head downward,
marketed hour by hour.

That market is a grave
where goods lie dead that ought
to live and grow and thrive,
the dear world sold and bought

to be destroyed by fire,
forest and soil and stone.
The conscience put to hire
rules over flesh and bone.

To take the coal to burn
they overturn the world
and all the world has worn
of grace, of health. The gnarled,

clenched, and forever shut
fist of their greed makes small
the great Life. Hollowed out,
the soul like the green hill

yields to the force of dearth.
The crack in the despot's skull
descends into the earth,
and what was bright turns dull.

Sabbath, 1982

Sung a cappella.

MUSICIAN.

Slowly, slowly, they return
To the small woodland let alone:
Great trees, outspreading and upright,
Apostles of the living light.

Patient as stars, they build in air
Tier after tier a timbered choir,
Stout beams upholding weightless grace
Of song, a blessing on this place.

They stand in waiting all around,
Uprisings of their native ground,
Downcomings of the distant light;
They are the advent they await.

Receiving sun and giving shade,
Their life's a benefaction made,
And is a benediction said
Over the living and the dead.

In fall their brightened leaves, released,
Fly down the wind, and we are pleased
To walk on radiance, amazed.
O light come down to earth, be praised!

The Blue Robe

Image of a farmhouse, lights inside blazing against the night.

ACTRESS 1.
How joyful to be together, alone
as when we first were joined
ACTOR 1.
in our little house by the river
long ago,
ACTRESS 1.
except that now we know
each other, as we did not then;
ACTOR 1.
and now instead of two stories fumbling
to meet, we belong to one story
that the two, joining, made.
ACTRESS 1.
And now
we touch each other with the tenderness
of mortals, who know themselves:
ACTOR 1.
how joyful to feel the heart quake
at the sight of a grandmother,

old friend in the morning light,
beautiful in her blue robe!

Boone

Image of a sycamore in winter.

ACTRESS 1.

In winter the river hides its flowing under the
ice—even then it flows,
bearing interminably down; the black crow flies
into the black night;
the bones of the old dead ache for the house fires.

Death is a conjecture of the seed
and the seasons bear it out;
the wild plum achieves its bloom,
perfects the yellow center of each flower,
submits to violence—
extravagance too grievous for praise;
there are no culminations, no
requitals.

Freed of distances
and dreams, about to die,
the mind turns back to its approaches:
what else have I known?
The search
withholds the joy from what is found,
that has been my sorrow;
love is no more than what remains of itself.
There are no arrivals.

At the coming of winter
the birds obey the leviathan flock
that moves them south,
a rhythm of the blood that survives the cold
in pursuit of summer;
and the sun, innocent of time
as the blossom is innocent of ripeness,
faithful to solstice, returns—
and the flocks return;
the season recognizes them.

If it were possible now,

I'd make myself submissive
to the weather
as an old tree, without retrospect
of winter, blossoming,
grateful for summers hatched from thrushes' eggs
in the speckled thickets
                                    —obedient
to darkness,
be innocent of my dying.

At a Country Funeral

Image of a country church and cemetery. "Abide With Me" hummed under.

ACTOR 2.

Now the old dead wait in the open coffin
for the blood kin to gather, come home
for one last time, to hear old men
whose tongues bear an essential topography
speak memories doomed to die.

ACTRESS 2.

But our memory of ourselves, hard earned,
is one of the land's seeds, as a seed
is the memory of the life of its kind in its place,
to pass on into life the knowledge
of what has died.

ACTOR 1.

                    What we owe the future
is not a new start, for we can only begin
with what has happened.

ACTRESS 1.

                        We owe the future
the past, the long knowledge
that is the potency of time to come.

That makes of a man's grave a rich furrow.

ACTRESS 2.

The community of knowing in common is the seed
of our life in this place. There is not only
no better possibility, there is no
other, except for chaos and darkness,
the terrible ground of the only possible
new start.

ACTOR 2.

> And so as the old die and the young
> depart, where shall a man go who keeps
> the memories of the dead, except home
> again, as one would go back after a burial,
> faithful to the fields, lest the dead die
> a second and more final death.

The Contrariness of the Mad Farmer

ACTOR 1.

> I am done with apologies. If contrariness is my
> inheritance and destiny, so be it. If it is my mission
> to go in at exits and come out at entrances, so be it.
> I have planted by the stars in defiance of the experts,
> and tilled somewhat by incantation and by singing,
> and reaped, as I knew, by luck and Heaven's favor,
> in spite of the best advice. If I have been caught
> so often laughing at funerals, that was because
> I knew the dead were already slipping away,
> preparing for a comeback, and can I help it?
> And if at weddings I have gritted and gnashed
> my teeth, it was because I knew where the bridegroom
> had sunk his manhood, and knew it would not
> be resurrected by a piece of cake.
> When they said, "I know that my Redeemer liveth,"
> I told them, "He's dead." And when they told me
> "God is dead," I answered, "He goes fishing every day
> in the Kentucky River. I see Him often."
> When they asked me would I like to contribute
> I said no, and when they had collected
> more than they needed, I gave them as much as I had.
> When they asked me to join them I wouldn't,
> and then went off by myself and did more
> than they would have asked. "Well, then," they said
> "go and organize the International Brotherhood
> of Contraries," and I said, "Did you finish killing
> everybody who was against peace?" So be it.
> Going against men, I have heard at times a deep harmony
> thrumming in the mixture, and when they ask me what
> I say I don't know. It is not the only or the easiest
> way to come to the truth. It is one way.

Rising, part two

Music plays under.

MUSICIAN.
>And that is our story,
>not of time, but the forever
>returning events of light,
>ancient knowledge seeking
>its new minds.

ACTRESS 2.
>The man at dawn
>in spring of the year,
>going to the fields,
>visionary of seed and desire,
>is timeless as a star.

ACTOR 1.
>Any man's death could end the story:
>his mourners, having accompanied him
>to the grave through all he knew,
>turn back, leaving him complete.

ACTRESS 1.
>But this is not the story of a life.
>It is the story of lives, knit together,
>overlapping in succession, rising
>again from grave after grave.

ACTOR 2.
>Ended, a story is history;
>it is in time with time
>lost. But if a man's life
>continue in another man,
>then the flesh will rhyme
>its part in immortal song.
>
>By absence, he comes again.

ACTRESS 1.
>There is a kinship of the fields
>that gives to the living the breath
>of the dead.

ACTRESS 2.
>   The earth
>opened in the spring, opens
>in all springs.

ACTOR 1.
>Nameless,
>ancient, many-lived, we reach
>through the ages with the seed.

End of Play.

UNDER CONSTRUCTION
by Charles L. Mee

BIOGRAPHY

Charles L. Mee has written *Big Love* (2000 Humana Festival), *True Love*, *First Love*, *bobrauschenbergamerica* (2001 Humana Festival), *Vienna: Lusthaus*, *Orestes 2.0*, *Trojan Women: A Love Story*, *Summertime* and *Wintertime*, among other plays, all of them available online (www.Charlesmee.com). Among other awards, he is the recipient of the lifetime achievement award from the American Academy of Arts and Letters. His work is made possible by the support of Richard B. Fisher and Jeanne Donovan Fisher.

ACKNOWLEDGMENTS

Under Construction premiered at the Humana Festival of New American Plays in March 2009. It was directed by Anne Bogart with the following cast (in alphabetical order.):

Akiko Aizawa
J. Ed Araiza
Leon Ingulsrud
Ellen Lauren
Tom Nelis
Barney O'Hanlon
Makela Spielman
Samuel Stricklen
Stephen Duff Webber

and the following production staff:

Scenic Designer	Neil Patel
Costume Designer	James Schuette
Lighting/Video Designer	Brian H. Scott
Sound Designer	Darron L West
Properties Designer	Mark Walston
Music Arranger	Rachel Grimes
Stage Manager	Elizabeth Moreau
Production Assistant	Dave Sleswick
Dramaturg	Sarah Lunnie
Assistant Dramaturg	Rachel Lerner-Ley
Assistant Director	Alicia Dhyana House
SITI Executive Director	Megan Wanlass Szalla

Under Construction was created and performed by SITI Company.

Presented in association with SITI Company with support from the Andrew W. Mellon Foundation, New York Theater Program, administered by the New York Foundation for the Arts and the National Endowment for the Arts. The Guthrie Theater provided early development support for this project. The script was posted on the internet and people were invited to contribute to scenes from the play, although none have been incorporated into the final script.

SETTING

America in the Fifties and the present, the red states and the blue states, where we grew up and where we live today.

A NOTE ON THE TEXT

This piece was composed with the dramaturgical collaboration of Tom Damrauer. It was, in part, inspired by, and samples some texts from, John O'Hara, Allen Ginsberg, William Burroughs, Jason Rhoades, John Cage, Sloan Wilson, instructional films of the Fifties, Mary Roberts Rinehart, Lydia Lunch, Barney Rosset, Garson Kanin, Sinclair Lewis, Charles Bukowski, Lester Bangs, David Woynarowicz, Annie Sprinkle, Jennie Holzer, Carla Nowlin, Lydia Gaston, and Richard Rorty.

The Ensemble
in *Under Construction*

33rd Annual Humana Festival of New American Plays
Actors Theatre of Louisville, 2009
Photo by Harlan Taylor

UNDER CONSTRUCTION

At the doorway entering the theatre
an artist's easel will have a blackboard on it
announcing:
Tonight we will be performing scenes
6
79
29
22
67
107
18
57
122
5
41
This version of the script is the way it's been done
with the SITI Company,
and it seemed to us that these scenes,
in this order, are wonderful.
But, in the future, when others do it,
it may be that they will want to throw out some of these scenes,
write some new ones,
change the order of things.
And so, in this way, the piece will remain,
like America,   .
permanently
under construction.

PROLOGUE

Bing Crosby sings "Dear Hearts and Gentle People."
I love those dear hearts and gentle people
Who live in my home town
Because those dear hearts and gentle people
Will never ever let you down

They read the good book
From Fri 'til Monday
That's how the weekend goes
I've got a dream house

I'll build there one day
With picket fence and ramblin' rose

I feel so welcome each time I return
That my happy heart keeps laughin' like a clown
I love the dear hearts and gentle people
Who live and love in my home town

There's a place I'd like to go
And it's back in Idaho
Where your friendly neighbors smile and say hello
It's a pleasure and a treat
To meander down the street
That's why I want the whole wide world to know
(I love those dear hearts)
I love the gentle people
(Who live in my home town)
Because those dear hearts and gentle people
Will never ever let you down

> (*It may be that a few members of the cast enter,*
> *take their position as backup singers,*
> *and sing the chorus parts along with him.*)

They read the good book
From Fri 'til Monday
That's how the weekend goes
I've got a dream house
I'll build there one day
With picket fence and ramblin' rose

I feel so welcome each time that I return
That my happy heart keeps laughin' like a clown
I love the dear hearts and gentle people
Who live and love in my home town

(Home, home, sweet home
Home, home, sweet home
Home, home, sweet home
Home, home, sweet home)

Scene 6. Thanksgiving

> *A table*
> *people enter all talking in a hubbub*
> *several conversations at once*

as they bring in bowls of mashed potatoes, cranberry sauce,
string beans…

SOMEONE SAYS. The point is,
of course they are both games
and they both are played in a rectangular area
and the players go back and forth from one end to the other
but, in football,
all the players gather in a huddle
and the quarterback decides on the play
and then the players all go out and execute the play
and it is over
and so it goes starting and stopping and starting and stopping
with plans and more plans
whereas in basketball the whole thing is
you take out the ball
and you make it up as you go along
like life
it's an open thing
so this is why I say
the game people should really talk about
is not football
but basketball.

ANOTHER PERSON. Or hockey.

FIRST PERSON. Right. Or hockey.

ANOTHER PERSON. Hockey. I don't know about hockey.

> (*And the following conversation about getting organized*
> *occurs at the same time as the sports conversation—*
> *two conversations going on at once around the dinner table.*)

SOMEONE ELSE. I think it's time we got organized.
No more rushing for the train in the morning.
We need to have a leisurely breakfast before work.
No more instant coffee.
No more grabbing a piece of toast on the way to the station.
We need to start living life sanely.
No more hotdogs and hamburgers for dinner.
We're going to start making stews and casseroles.
No more television.

ANOTHER PERSON SAYS. What?

THE FIRST VOICE AGAIN. No more television. I'm going to give the
  damn set away
and we're going to sit in a family group and read aloud.

ANOTHER PERSON SAYS. And you ought to get your mandolin fixed,
Billy, we could have friends in and sing.
THE FIRST VOICE AGAIN. No more passive entertainment.
No more homogenized milk.
We're going to save two cents a quart and shake it ourselves.
We need to start doing the things we believe in.

> *(and then* MOM *enters with turkey*
> *saying turkey turkey turkey turkey turkey*
> *and the others exclaim:*
>
> *oh, wonderful!*
> *turkey! turkey!*
> *and cranberry sauce!*
> *I love Thanksgiving…*
>
> *and dinner table conversation resumes*
> *as people serve themselves turkey and mashed potatoes.)*

SOMEONE. Of course it could be
you didn't see last weekend's games.
SOMEONE ELSE. I did.
FIRST PERSON. Not everyone did.
The fact is,
if you didn't go to the games,
you can just shake hands with half the student body,
because they didn't go either.

> *(random overlapping talk*
> *would you pass the cranberry sauce, please,*
> *thank you*
> *would you like a drumstick?*
> *have you had gravy?….)*

And some of the kids
when they were asked whether they went to the last game
what did they say?
they said, oh I had a date, or
I didn't have any way to get there.
And what I say is:
Sure, sure, you had a date,

and what's wrong with going to a basketball game on a date?
And, as for not having a ride,
you can always ask around and find one.
Because
if the team thinks that the game is important enough to play,

then the student body should think it important enough
to attend and to show the school spirit.
To have top teams
we have to have a winning student body
that wants its teams to come out ahead!

> (*The* FATHER *stands to make a toast about Thanksgiving.*)

THE FATHER. Now, then
one thing I think we can all agree about
I think we can all agree
this is a moment to remember how grateful we are for all we have
for being able to gather with one another
for the warmth of home and family
and a time of safety—
because
when you look back
not so long ago, in the past, people lived in places
with thick stone walls and thick iron bars over the windows
and they had towers on top of the big houses
where the family could all retreat in case they were attacked
and pour boiling oil down on top of the people
who were trying to get into their house
but these days we don't think about that any more
these days there is nothing between us and a hurled rock
but a big picture window made of glass
this is how safe we are
and so we count our blessings
we look back over the past year and take pleasure
in what we have done
and say to ourselves, even though Bill may not have done so well with his
    geometry but
it's not a tragedy

> (*he goes on and on and on*
> *so that people begin getting up one by one from the table*
> *excusing themselves*
> *first the* MOM *to go to kitchen to check the pie:*
> *"I'm just going to check on the pie."*)

and after all it seems he couldn't help himself
although, frankly, I don't think
he should have blamed his mother
mothers are not always to blame

> (*then the* GRANDMOTHER *slips away from the table:*
> *"I'm just going to help Sally in the kitchen."*)

sometimes the kids have to take the blame themselves
because when a girl gets pregnant in high school
she ought to leave, that's all

> (*then the* SON *has a phone call:*
> *"Sorry, Dad, I have a phone call."*)

her boyfriend should stay and finish high school
so that he can get a good job when he gets out
that's my opinion

> (*then* ANOTHER SON *forgot something—left his skates outside:*
> *"Oh, god, I think I left my skates outside!"*)

but she should go home and have the baby
and then, when the baby is a little older
maybe the mother can get a job at the checkout counter
at the A & P...

> (*So, at the end,*
> *the* DAD *is alone*
> *with two* GIRLS
> *and he leaves, defeated, saying*
> *"I'll just help clear the table."*
>
> *The two* GIRLS *are left behind.*
>
> *One of the* GIRLS *begins to say what she wants.*
> *Perhaps the other joins in.*
> *Maybe some of the* OTHER WOMEN *straggle back in*
> *and they join in voicing the list of desires, too.*
> *They shouldn't repeat one another's lines—*
> *each should have their own lines.*)

What I want.
I want to be respected.
I want my family to be proud of me.
I want to be creative.
I want whiter teeth.
I want more money.
I want better knees.
I want better skin.
I want a better body.
I want an end to war.
I want a tighter ass.
I want a better job.
I want to eat what I want and not gain weight.
I want people to care.

I want a better life for the poor.
I want to feel.
I want to be strong.
I want to skydive.
I want to do a back handspring.
I want to be protected.
I want to be safe.
I want to have nightmares
and wake up and share them with my lover.
I want to fuck like a teenager but with the knowledge of an adult.
I want what I don't have.
I want there to be justice.

> (*And now all together as a chorus*
> *the same lines at the same time.*)

THE WOMEN. I want what everyone else has.
I want more than you have.
I want what people don't know about.
I want good friends who are there for you and tell you what you need to hear
and make you laugh so hard you pee in your pants.

> (*Deafening hard rock music from the present moment—*
> *not the Fifties—*
> *so that we have moved from then to now in an instant—*
> *and the* WOMEN *break into a wild, ecstatic, enraged, abandoned,*
> *insane messy hair dance*
> *at the end of which*
> *they simply stop*
> *and walk off without ceremony.*
>
> *It could be that there should be a large television set*
> *to one side, for the entire performance,*
> *and it should have continuous programming on it,*
> *so that there could be news, the history channel,*
> *home movies,*
> *other random stuff—*
> *the context for everything we see,*
> *or else just some more random home movies.*)

Scene 41. The Backyard

The DAD *and his* SON *with golf clubs.*

NARRATOR. In class it's not so bad but when school's out and the others
go off to enjoy themselves, well, if you're what they call a shy guy, that's when
you really feel it. The awful loneliness of being new in town. You don't know

how to make people like you and you find yourself holding a grudge against them. You're standing on the outside looking in. You might have something to contribute to their conversation, but nobody cares whether you do or not. There's a barrier and you don't know how to begin breaking it down. You imagine they keep watching the way you look, the way you act. They think you're different. So you head for home. What else?

DAD. Hello, Phil. How's everything?

PHIL. Okay, I guess Dad, but school here isn't like it was back in Morristown. I don't think I ever will fit in, not here. I'm different from the guys in this town.

DAD. What about the other fellas, what do they do? What do they like?

PHIL. Gosh Dad, I don't know. I never noticed.

DAD. Why not try to find out?

NARRATOR. Now there's an idea. Maybe a good idea. Worth a try anyway, and tomorrow's not too soon to start. Pick out the most popular boys and girls in school and keep an eye on them. Who are they, now? Some of them are right here in this class. Andy McIntire for instance. People like him all right. Chick Gallagher rates high in popularity too. There's Jane Davenport. She is popular with the boys and girls. And Jack Gilbert, what's he got that makes people like him so much? Andy's got something to say and Jack's listening. He really seems interested. Come to think of it, Jack's always interested in what people are talking about. Maybe that's why he hits it off so well with everybody. Look at Jack and Beezy over there. Girls seem to like them. Why? What's the angle? They do act kind of polite. At least they seat the girls and give their orders to the waiter. They aren't loud like some of the guys.

CHICK. Cherry coke, chocolate coke, milkshake and malt, double chocolate malt, okay, I got it.

BOB. Oh!

Excuse me. I've got the orders for this table.

CHICK. I'm sorry, Bob. I was just helping out during rush hour.

BOB. Gee, thanks a lot Chick, that's swell.

PHIL. You know Dad, there's a mixer Friday night, I, uh, I wasn't going to go but in the drugstore the other day, Chick said I ought to come.

DAD. Good idea, Phil.

PHIL. Well, Dad, there is a girl I'd like to take, Mary Lou Wright. But, I'm not sure she'd go with me. I've never even talked to her. I'd probably fall all over myself. Besides, she's popular. She's probably got a date by now.

DAD. Well, it is pretty late to ask a girl. Why don't you just go stag.

PHIL. I think I will. You know, I think it will be easier after I've had a chance to talk to her at the mixer. You know what? I kind of think I'm going to fit in after all.

Scene 76. Blog

In the '80's movie Beehive *by Frank Moore and Jim Self
and filmed by Barry Shils
two people in giant bee costumes fly through the air.*

*Meanwhile a guy comes out on stage,
puts his feet into moonboots that are secured to the floor
and rocks back and forth*

while a young woman speaks into a microphone.

So, this is her blog, or podcast:

BLOG. So I haven't updated this blog in forever.
So Yeah.
I live in New York now.
My apartment is pretty sweet.
We're right behind Lincoln Center,
and it sounds dumb but I feel rejuvenated
everytime I walk through it.
I get the feeling like "this is why I'm here."
I wish I knew more people here.
I kinda feel like this nobody in a sea of nobodies,
which has never really happened to me before.
It'll change soon. I hope.
SO life is okay.
It's a bit scary, but life is okay.
Stuff is a-happenin'.
Which is a good thing. I hope!
I had this WEIRD ASS nightmare last night.
I was in a parking lot
coming out of an event or a concert of some sort
and these evil cat people came in a black van
and got out and wreaked havoc on the place
blowing things up and killing people with their claws
and I got away in a backseat of someone's car,
and for some reason I was taken to my friend Kim's house,
but it wasn't where Kim really lives,
it was my house,
but Kim lived there in my dream,
and I was telling her about the killer cat people
and she thought I was crazy,
and then I was in the backyard
and I saw the black van pull up front

and these 20-somethings got out,
but I realized that they were actually
the cat people disguised to not look cat-ish
and be completely human,
and I tried to make myself not seen
and walked to the neighbors' backyard
and somehow I wound up hiding in their bathroom
only for the door to be busted in by the cat people
and my friend Kim,
who I was alerted was a cat person as well.
And then I woke up
and I thought:
What does this all mean?

Scene 74. Travelling Salesman

> A SALESMAN *comes into a hotel room*
> *puts his sample case on the bed*
> *turns down the covers,*
> *gets in bed*
>
> *he takes one book after another out of his sample case*
> *and we hear a* VOICEOVER—*the voice of a woman—*
> *reading the jacket copy*
> *as he turns the book over in his hand*
> *and skims the pages*

VOICEOVER.
Beebo Brinker
by Anne Bannon
Lost, lonely, boyishly appealing—
this is BEEBO BRINKER.
She landed in New York,
fresh off the farm…
her only certainty was
that she was different.
So innocent
she did not notice
that women watched her
when she entered the room.

Odd Girl Out
by Anne Bannon
She was the brain, the sparkle,
the gay rebel of the sorority,

and wonder of wonders,
she chose Laura as her roommate.
That was how it began.
Suddenly they were
alone on an island
of forbidden bliss.

Women in the Shadows
by Anne Bannon
A guarded look across the room.
That was all she dared to do,
and this was Greenwich Village
where almost anything goes….
She had learned long ago
that she could never love a man—
that only another woman could excite her.
And Laura found the strange,
sloe-eyed girl exciting.

I Am a Woman
by Anne Bannon
          (THE SALESMAN *speaks with the voiceover.*)
VOICEOVER & THE SALESMAN. She looked around the cellar
with Laura following her gaze.
"I know most of the girls in here…
I've probably slept with half of them."
          (*The* VOICEOVER *fades out, leaving* THE SALESMAN *to speak alone.*)
THE SALESMAN. "I've lived with half of the half
I've slept with.
I've loved half of the half
I've lived with.
L for love," Beebo said,
looking into space.
"L for Laura."
She turned and smiled at her.
"L for Lust
and L for the L of it,"
          (*The* VOICEOVER *fades back in with* THE SALESMAN.)
VOICEOVER & THE SALESMAN. "L for Lesbian
L for let's—"
VOICEOVER. "Let's,"
she said,

and blew smoke softly
into Laura's ear.

> (*and then* THE SALESMAN *sits, looking disconsolately out front,
> while on the back wall behind him we see this scene from*
> On the Waterfront.)
>
> TERRY. (*Struggling with an unfamiliar problem of conscience and loyalties.*)
> Yeah—yeah—I guess I do—but there's a lot more to this whole
> thing than I thought, Charley.
>
> CHARLEY. You don't mean you're thinking of testifying against—
> (*Turns a thumb in toward himself.*)
>
> TERRY. I don't know—I don't know! I tell you I ain't made up my
> mind yet. That's what I wanted to talk to you about.
>
> CHARLEY. (*Patiently, as to a stubborn child.*) Listen, Terry, these piers
> we handle through the locals—you know what they're worth to us?
>
> TERRY. I know. I know.
>
> CHARLEY. Well, then, you know Cousin Johnny isn't going to
> jeopardize a set up like that for one rubber-lipped—
>
> TERRY. (*Simultaneous.*) Don't say that!
>
> CHARLEY. (*Continuing.*) —ex-tanker who's walking on his heels—?
>
> TERRY. Don't say that!
>
> CHARLEY. What the hell!!!
>
> TERRY. I could have been better!
>
> CHARLEY. The point is—there isn't much time, kid.
>
>> (*There is a painful pause, as they appraise each other.*)
>
> TERRY. (*Desperately.*) I tell you, Charley, I haven't made up my mind!
>
> CHARLEY. Make up your mind, kid, I beg you, before we get to
> four thirty-seven River….
>
> TERRY. (*Stunned.*) Four thirty-seven—that isn't where Gerry G…?
>
>> (CHARLEY *nods solemnly.* TERRY *grows more agitated.*)
>
> Charley…you wouldn't take me to Gerry G…?
>
>> (CHARLEY *continues looking at him. He does not deny it. They
>> stare at each other for a moment. Then suddenly* TERRY *starts out
>> of the cab.* CHARLEY *pulls a pistol.* TERRY *is motionless, now,
>> looking at* CHARLEY.)
>
> CHARLEY. Take the boss loading, kid. For God's sake. I don't want
> to hurt you.
>
> TERRY. (*Hushed, gently guiding the gun down toward* CHARLEY's *lap.*)
> Charley…. Charley…. Wow….
>
> CHARLEY. (*Genuinely.*) I wish I didn't have to do this, Terry.

(TERRY *eyes him, beaten.* CHARLEY *leans back and looks at* TERRY *strangely.* TERRY *raises his hands above his head, somewhat in the manner of a prizefighter mitting the crowd. The image nicks* CHARLEY'*s memory.*)

TERRY. (*An accusing sigh.*) Wow....

CHARLEY. (*Gently.*) What do you weigh these days, slugger?

TERRY. (*Shrugs.*) ...eighty-seven, eighty-eight. What's it to you?

CHARLEY. (*Nostalgically.*) Gee, when you tipped one seventy-five you were beautiful. You should've been another Billy Conn. That skunk I got to manage you brought you along too fast.

TERRY. It wasn't him! (*Years of abuse crying out in him.*) It was you, Charley. You and Johnny. Like the night the two of youse come in the dressing room and says, "Kid, this ain't your night—we're going for the price on Wilson." It ain't my night. I'd of taken Wilson apart that night! I was ready—remember the early rounds throwing them combinations. So what happens— This bum Wilson he gets the title shot—outdoors in the ballpark!—and what do I get—a couple of bucks and a one-way ticket to Palookaville. (*More and more aroused as he relives it.*) It was you, Charley. You was my brother. You should of looked out for me. Instead of making me take them dives for the short-end money.

CHARLEY. (*Defensively.*) I always had a bet down for you. You saw some money.

TERRY. (*Agonized.*) See! You don't understand!

CHARLEY. I tried to keep you in good with Johnny.

TERRY. You don't understand! I could've been a contender. I could've had class and been somebody. Real class. Instead of a bum, let's face it, which is what I am. It was you, Charley.

(CHARLEY *takes a long, fond look at* TERRY. *Then he glances quickly out the window.*

and when THE SALESMAN *leaves his hotel room— which maybe he does in the middle of the movie?— his sample case is left behind.*)

Scene 114. Reality TV auditions

a live video cameraman comes on to videotape whatever happens on stage

and then others straggle back in and now everyone wants to be on camera and gets in front of it

and does bits to get noticed
everyone does audition pieces as though for a reality TV show
someone walks on a beam
while a couple keeps falling down a set of steps like rag dolls.
Whatever special gifts the actors have.

And, during this, another piece of text is spoken—
For example, JOHN CAGE:

JOHN. I think the real changes that will take place
in society will take place primarily
through our renunciation of government
and our concern with the earth as a problem
in relation to the living of human beings.
I think that modern art and modern music
have served to draw the attention of the individuals
to the enjoyment of the world around them.
And when you see that work in art
then you can have more courage that it will work
in the world outside of art.

I think it was Steve Reich who said
it was clear I was involved in process,
but it was a process the audience didn't participate in
because they couldn't understand it.
I'm on the side of keeping things mysterious,
and I have never enjoyed understanding things.
If I understand something
I can put it on a shelf and leave it there.
If I understand something,
I have no further use for it.
So I try to make a music which I don't understand
and which will be difficult for other people to understand, too.

Scene 22. The barber shop

THE BARBER SAYS. The question naturally comes up:
what is an acceptable haircut, and what isn't
and the truth is
you need to ask if you don't want to get into trouble
does a boy have his mother's permission?
this boy went home one day with a crew cut
the first time he had ever been to the barbershop on his own
and when he got home his mother made him wear a hat
even though it was the middle of summer

and when his father came home
his father was upset
and you wouldn't think a haircut
could cause such trouble in a marriage
but a haircut is a very big deal
the mother would never let her son
come back on his own to the barbershop for a haircut
and so, just at the age when the boy should have been discovering
how to be an independent person
he was crushed
his spirit was crushed
and so, in the end,
he never grew up to be a confident self-assured person

> (*a guy is getting a haircut*
> *while other guys stand around*
> *listening to this chatter*
> *and the dairy queen maids are hanging around, too*
>
> *And the* NARRATOR *steps up to a microphone and says:*)

NARRATOR. Nonetheless,
things can still work out
if a boy and girl know how things ought to go.
Take, for example, The First Date.
John calls for Mary at her home at the appointed time.
Mary is ready for John
and answers the door herself when he rings
(because he has come to see her, not some member of her family.)
She greets him pleasantly
and leads him into the living room
where her parents are waiting to meet him.
Mary introduces John to her parents by saying something like,

MARY. "Mother, this is John.
Dad, you remember John plays center on the team."

NARRATOR. This little lead as a part of the introduction
gives Dad and John something to talk about the first thing.
Dad may ask a simple question
on how the team is doing this season.
John is put at his ease and answers,
while Mother and Dad relax and enjoy getting acquainted with him. In a few
    moments Mary picks up her coat and,
smiling at John,
indicates that they had probably better be on their way.

If John holds the coat for Mary,
she accepts his assistance graciously;
if he does not,
she slips into her coat without comment and prepares for departure. As the
    couple is about to leave,
Mary turns to her parents and says,

MARY. "We are going to the Bijou for the double feature"

NARRATOR. (or whatever),

MARY. "you know. We should be home before midnight."

NARRATOR. This declaration of plans
and specifying of time for homecoming
has a double purpose.
It lets her folks know that she is taking responsibility
for getting in before it is too late,
and prevents them from putting down the parental foot too hard. Further,
    such initiative on Mary's part
lets John know what is expected of him in getting Mary home.
If Mary has already talked over their plans with her parents
before John has arrived,
her last minute announcement is simply
a confirmation for all four of them.
The couple leave,
with John opening the door for Mary,
while she accepts the courtesy with a smile.
When they reach the box office,
Mary steps back and looks at the display cards
while John buys the tickets.
Inside, if there is an usher,
Mary follows him while John follows her down the aisle.
If there is no usher on duty,
John goes ahead and finds seats while Mary follows.
Once seated, John helps Mary slip out of her coat and get settled. They enjoy
    the show
without annoying their neighbors with talking, giggling,
or other disturbing behavior.
Out of the theater,
John may suggest something to eat
or he may conduct Mary to the place of his choice.
At this point, Mary is careful to let John take the lead.
When he asks her what she would like to have,
she thoughtfully hesitates
until she sees what price range he has in mind.

She says something along the following line,

MARY. "What is good here, John?"

NARRATOR. or

MARY. "What do you suggest?"

NARRATOR. If John recommends the steak sandwich with French fries, or the double-gooey sundae with nuts, this gives Mary the general idea of what he is prepared to spend. If she is friendly and shrewd she may note that John, in his desire to do the right thing, is suggesting something extravagant. If so, she will ask for something that she knows costs a little less. But if John says,

JOHN. "Which do you like better, coke or root beer?"

NARRATOR. Mary graciously keeps within these bounds. Over their food, John and Mary talk about the movie they have just seen or friends they have in common or anything that is of mutual interest. As they leave the restaurant, John pays the check and Mary thanks him by saying simply,

MARY. "That was good; thank you, John."

NARRATOR. Once back to Mary's house, Mary gets out her key, unlocks the door, and then turns to John with a smile. She says,

MARY. "It's been a lovely evening. Thank you, John,"

NARRATOR. or something similar that lets John know she has enjoyed the date. John replies,

JOHN. "I have enjoyed it too. I'll be seeing you."

NARRATOR. Then she opens the door and goes in without further hesitation. Since this is the first date, neither John nor Mary expect a good-night kiss.

(*and the barber chair is left behind on stage when the scene ends.*)

Scene 29. The Homecoming GI

greeted by everyone
and he tells what he hopes for now

GI. What I hope now
is to be in the living room after dinner
with my sister
with her silver locket around her neck
my mother, with large pearl earrings and a beige cardigan
my father, in his casual holiday dress,
gray flannel trousers, hand-knit argyle socks
a red and green plaid Pendleton shirt
standing with easy confidence
holding a china cup and saucer in his hand
my Irish Setter Pat
stretched out on the carpet
elegant and soulful
I myself, stretched out on the leather couch
wearing a navy blue pullover
the game on television
the backyard barbecue talking about the Cubs
big Chuck Buckley wearing an apron and a chef's hat
standing at the grill holding in one hand a spatula
in the other a Scotch and water
the robust good cheer
football and the economy
the rise and fall of the Dow Jones
the best route to drive to the golf club in Park Ridge
the tweed jacket
the football-letter sweater
the goodness of intentions
the deep pleasure in things as they are
the gratitude for the given order of things.

> (and then a YOUNG WOMAN *speaks to the returning* GI
> *and says:*)

THE YOUNG WOMAN SAYS. What I want:
I want to graduate
and go to college
Northwestern, I hope it will be Northwestern
and my husband earns a lot of money
and we have thirteen kids
twelve boys and one girl
a football team, one sub, and a cheerleader.
What I always tell the freshmen is:
Study now,
because you can't learn it all in your senior year.

AND THE GI SAYS. Right.

OTHER GUYS SAY. That's right.

> (*That's for sure.*
>
> *and the* GI *is followed out, a hero, by the guys*
>
> *and his suitcase is left behind*
> *Other things that might be left behind in the course of the evening:*
> *a cheerleader's megaphone*
> *a soldier's hat*
> *a prayer book*
> *a pair of shined shoes*
> *a football helmet*
> *a baseball glove*
> *a pair of Chuck Taylor Converse red high-top sneakers*
> *a barber's shaving mug.*)

Scene 103. Women

THE WOMAN SAYS. The blue-collar worker is the backbone of our society,
Society needs the services and products they provide, whether the workers them-
selves dream of something better or not. Many of them love their jobs, too—
that doesn't change that quite a few of them
aren't qualified to do much else.
There's no shame in that.
Not that this is why I did it.
Not that I am saying that.

Luckily, that was never my reason.
I was not forced into it in that way.
It was my choice.

Not everyone can be a prostitute.
You do need a special talent.
It's definitely a hell of a hard fucking job.
You need enormous amounts of patience,
enormous amounts of compassion.
You have to put up with a lot of shit.
It's like being in a war—
you're in a war zone.
You're in a society which is misogynistic and full of sexual guilt,
and you take that shit on.
It can get to you.
I compare it a lot to being a nurse.

I had a transsexual, hermaphroditic lover for a while—
a female to male transsexual,
surgically made hermaphrodite.
A new option for people.
That's one of the great things about living these days.
My new lover is totally androgynous.
I think it's beautiful.

These days, you see men dressing as women wearing monkey boots,
and women dressing as men but with false eyelashes.
Now, everything's getting mixed together
which I really like.
And strap-on dildos, of course,
are really being used a lot to play with gender.
Women are getting these big dicks—
it's great.
And they really know how to use them.
It's so real.
And of course it never gets soft.

My friend Trish is really good at thrusting.
Women aren't generally as good at thrusting,
but she has really got it down.
Her dick is totally real to her
and I suck it like it's real
and I feel like she feels everything that I do.
It's just beautiful.
The technology has vastly improved.
When I first got into porno movies
they were tied on with pieces of elastic
and were really flimsy.
These were invented by men,
but now women are designing these fabulously beautiful
leather strap-on things.

Scene 18. The Barbershop Quartet

a BARBERSHOP QUARTET *forms out of the group*
and steps forward to sing
a classic barbershop quartet song
such as:

BARBERSHOP QUARTET SINGS.
lit-tle lil-ly was oh so sil-ly and shy,
and all the fel-lows knew,

she would-'nt bill and coo,
ev-'ry sin-gle night some smart fel-low would try,
to cud-dle up to her,
but she would cry;

"ma," he's mak-ing eyes at me, "ma," he's aw-ful nice to me,
"ma," he's al-most break-ing my heart,
I'm be-side him, mer-cy let his consc-ience guide him;
"ma," he wants to mar-ry me, be my hon-ey bee,
ev-'ry min-ute he gets bold-er,
now he's lean-ing on my should-er, "ma," he's kiss-ing me.

lil-ly was so good, ev-ery bo-dy could tell,
you'd nev-er see her roam,
she'd al-ways stay at home,
all the neigh-bors knew lit-tle lil-ly too well,
for when the boys would call,
they'd hear her yell;

"ma," he's mak-ing eyes at me, "ma," he's aw-ful nice to me,
"ma," he's al-most break-ing my heart,
if you peek in, can't you see I'm goin' to weak-in'
"ma," he wants to mar-ry me,
be my hon-ey bee,
ma I'm meet-ing with re-sist-ance,
I shall holl-er for as-sist-ance,
"ma," he's kiss-ing me.

Scene 49. Bad Stuff

A guy comes out with bloody hands,
blood up to his elbows
and he stands and shows them to the audience
as three young women wearing Victoria's Secret lingerie
are brought in on leashes by a guy with a whip
and a black cripple, badly burned from head to foot,
stumbles in, falls, and writhes on the ground
and another guy brings in a guy on a leash who hops up and down
and an old Mafia don comes in wearing sunglasses and stands there
and a guy comes in on his knees,
walks on his knees along the front of the stage
and goes out again
all the while some great popular music is playing.

And it may be that
on the rear wall
is projected a still, or moving scroll
with as much of this Jenny Holzer text on it
as seems enough:

> *a little knowledge can go a long way.*
> *a lot of professionals are crackpots.*
> *a man can't know what it is to be a mother.*
> *a positive attitude means all the difference in the world.*
> *a sense of timing is the mark of genius.*
> *a sincere effort is all you can ask.*
> *all things are delicately interconnected.*
> *ambivalence can ruin your life.*
> *any surplus is immoral.*
> *anything is a legitimate area of investigation.*
> *at times your unconsciousness is truer than your conscious mind.*
> *bad intentions can yield good results.*
> *being alone with yourself is increasingly unpopular.*
> *being happy is more important than anything else.*
> *children are the hope of the future.*
> *decency is a relative thing.*
> *don't place too much trust in experts.*
> *eating too much is criminal.*
> *enjoy yourself because you can't change anything anyway.*
> *every achievement requires a sacrifice.*
> *everyone's work is equally important.*
> *exceptional people deserve special concessions.*
> *good deeds eventually are rewarded.*
> *grassroots agitation is the only hope.*
> *if you live simply there is nothing to worry about.*
> *ignoring enemies is the best way to fight.*
> *illness is a state of mind.*
> *it's better to be a good person than a famous person.*
> *it's not good to operate on credit.*
> *it's vital to live in harmony with nature.*
> *just believing something can make it happen.*
> *keep something in reserve for emergencies.*
> *killing is unavoidable but nothing to be proud of.*
> *listen when your body talks.*
> *men are not monogamous by nature.*
> *murder has its sexual side.*
> *pain can be a very positive thing.*

people are responsible for what they do unless they are insane.
people won't behave if they have nothing to lose.
raise boys and girls the same way.
redistributing wealth is imperative.
religion causes as many problems as it solves.
remember you always have freedom of choice.
romantic love was invented to manipulate women.
sometimes science advances faster than it should.
sometimes things seem to happen of their own accord.
starvation is nature's way.
sterilization is a weapon of the rulers.
the desire to reproduce is a death wish.
the family is living on borrowed time.
the idea of revolution is an adolescent fantasy.
the new is nothing but a restatement of the old.
the only way to be pure is to stay by yourself.
true freedom is frightful.
you are a victim of the rules you live by.
you can't expect people to be something they're not.

Scene 472. L.A.

This could be spoken by a man or a woman:
My head is a lot better in L.A.
There's always a feeling when I am sitting here
driving around in the car,
coming back into the studio,
in and out in my head,
and in and out of reality…
If you know my work,
you know that things are never finished…
so
then you have a lot of narrative threads
that interweave self-portraiture
fictional characters
cultural commentary
and much more
drama
humor
slapstick
critique
theatricality

entrepreneurship
attitude
quests
discoveries
self-sampling
internal recycling
auto-cannibalism
revelations
cosmologies.
Coming together and coming apart
and becoming something else
free-form
random
nonhierarchical
everywhere and nowhere.
And then you need an overview
because
or at least a point of view
because
all trees and no forest
means there isn't any difference between here and there
even though you still want to be
everywhere and nowhere.
It's all a blur
and the blur could be permanent
that would be OK
a blur, that's a cool thing, too.
I understand art as the pursuit of something.
As it is pulling me in this direction
I don't quite understand why I am going in this direction.
It is important that each piece creates
a territory for me to go in
like a direction that is opening up.
In this piece, which is called "Perfect World,"
the thing is you can fall off of it
and it can kill you.
You can walk on this surface
but it has these holes
these cracks
and then these soft spots,
these traps,
where it's just papered over.

I wanted to build this thing
which somehow mimics real life.
I am not interested in artists who close things down,
I am interested in situations which open things up.
That is just an optimistic perspective.
I want to build a work which includes the public
but does not exclude the artist.
If you imagine you have children
one is a drug addict with crack
one is a drug addict with ecstasy
one is thirteen and has four kids
and one is kind of a genius.
It is important to see each one
in relationship to the other one
in relationship to yourself.
It is about seeing where all the positive parts are
in the things that you have created.
You have to deal with them.
You have to like them all the same.
Because what we have come to learn
is that the future is made
not by arguing well
but by speaking differently.
And speaking differently:
that's the job of poets.
Because truth is not something we discover;
truth is something we create.
How it is to be a human being
is something we decide
not because of how it has always been
but because
whether or not it has ever been that way before,
this is who we want to be
and how we want to behave
now.
Just because, in the past, there have been slaveholders
and patriarchs
we are not destined to live the same way forever.
The reason people study history
is so that they can see
the way things are

is not the only way they have been
or the only way that they can be.
It is up to us to see what human nature can become.

Scene 5. Hair Brushing

Four WOMEN *all brush one* GIRL's *hair and then each other's.*

SOMEONE SAYS. What they say is there are rules.
And everyone knows what they are.
Number One.
Have dinner ready:
Plan ahead, even the night before,
to have a delicious meal—on time.
This is a way of letting him know
that you have been thinking about him
and are concerned about his needs.
SOMEONE ELSE SAYS. Number Two.
Prepare yourself.
Take fifteen minutes to rest so you will be refreshed when he arrives.
Touch up your makeup
put a ribbon in your hair
and be fresh looking.
Be a little zestful and a little more interesting.
SOMEONE ELSE SAYS. Number Three.
Minimize the noise.
At the time of his arrival
eliminate all noise of washer, dryer, dishwasher or vacuum.
Be happy to see him.
Greet him with a warm smile
and be glad to see him.

(*And then there is a* RADIO VOICEOVER *and the* GIRLS *answer variously yes, no, etc. etc. all in a jumbled unison.*)

RADIO VOICE. Are you fit for marriage? To help you decide for yourself, the author presents in this article several tests that are being used throughout the country to determine individual fitness for marriage. By taking the three tests that follow and studying the results, you can measure your own marital aptitudes. Give serious thought to the result and you will find it's likely taking out a personal love-insurance policy that pays dividends throughout your married life.
Are you 21 or over?

VARIOUS VOICES. Yes Yes No Yes No

RADIO VOICE. Are or were your parents happily married?

VARIOUS VOICES. Very happy Average Above average I'd say average Unhappy

RADIO VOICE. Were you happy as a child?

VARIOUS VOICES. Very happy Unhappy Average Average

RADIO VOICE. To what degree were you punished as a child?

VARIOUS VOICES. Often and severely Rarely but severely Never Often but mildly Mildly

RADIO VOICE. Where did you first learn about sex?

VARIOUS VOICES. Don't remember From other children From strange adults Books

RADIO VOICE. What is your present attitude toward sex?

VARIOUS VOICES. Disgust Necessary evil Indifferent Pleasant anticipation Intense interest

RADIO VOICE. Have you ever wanted to be of the opposite sex?

VARIOUS VOICES. Never As a child, yes As an adolescent As an adult As an adult? Yes!

RADIO VOICE. How do you rate with your partner in mental ability?

VARIOUS VOICES. Slightly inferior Definitely inferior Very similar Slightly superior Very superior

RADIO VOICE. How do you rate with your partner in willingness to cooperate?

VARIOUS VOICES. Definitely inferior Very similar Slightly superior Very superior

RADIO VOICE. Is your religion the same as your partner's?

VARIOUS VOICES. Yes No Yes Yes No

RADIO VOICE. Have you a tendency to be careless or disorderly?

VARIOUS VOICES. Yes No Yes No

RADIO VOICE. Are you uncommonly bossy?

VARIOUS VOICES. Yes No Yes No Yes

RADIO VOICE. For the Man: Does he insist on having his own way?

VARIOUS VOICES. Always Frequently Occasionally Seldom Never

RADIO VOICE. For the Woman: Has she a mean disposition?

VARIOUS VOICES. Frequently Seldom Never Never

RADIO VOICE. When his luck goes bad does he brood over it and look for your sympathy?

VARIOUS VOICES. Yes No Sometimes Yes No

RADIO VOICE. Does she try to please you?

VARIOUS VOICES. Always Frequently Occasionally Seldom Never

RADIO VOICE. Is he usually stubborn and insistent in his demands?

VARIOUS VOICES. Yes No Sometimes Yes No

RADIO VOICE. Can you get him to change his mind?

VARIOUS VOICES. Always Frequently Occasionally Seldom Never

RADIO VOICE. Does she try to make you miserable if you so much as look at another woman?

VARIOUS VOICES. Yes No Yes, no Yes

RADIO VOICE. Does he expect you to shower him with attention and affection in public?

VARIOUS VOICES. Yes No Yes No Yes

RADIO VOICE. Does she create scenes in public places?

VARIOUS VOICES. Yes No Yes Yes Yes

RADIO VOICE. Do you believe implicitly in your partner's:
Good Judgment?

VARIOUS VOICES. Yes No Yes No

RADIO VOICE. Honesty?

VARIOUS VOICES. Yes Yes Yes No

RADIO VOICE. Fidelity?

> (*Silence.*)

Scene 79. Film Noir

NARRATOR. When they reached the dark hallway,
she slowed their walk.

WESLEY. Tired?

VANESSA. No.
It's just that I want to be kissed.

NARRATOR. She looked at him gravely.
He walked away, and she followed him.
It was a long time before he spoke.

WESLEY. When you get to be my age,
you won't take things so lightly.

VANESSA. I don't take them lightly now.

WESLEY. You may be a minx, for all I know.

VANESSA. I'm not sure what that means.

WESLEY. Look it up.

VANESSA. Where?

WESLEY. Well, I have a fine dictionary in my cabin.
Let's both look it up.

NARRATOR. He wished that he could have cut that last speech.

VANESSA. Let's go to mine
where there are no dictionaries at all.

NARRATOR. With a surge of dizzying feeling
he wanted her more than he had ever wanted anything.
Vanessa led him toward her cabin.
The night steward sitting in the corridor said,
Good evening,
and vanished.
She whispered:

VANESSA. Won't you come in?
I'll make you some scrambled eggs.

NARRATOR. She laughed, stepped into the cabin,
held open the door,
and he was drawn magnetically in.
She closed the door.
They stood in the blackness and she waited a full minute
before turning on a light.
She moved to the table and fixed two drinks.

WESLEY. Not until I know who you are.

NARRATOR. She handed him his glass and took a thoughtful sip from her own.

VANESSA. Vanessa Foley

NARRATOR. she said

VANESSA. and I'm sort of mad about you.

WESLEY. Sort of.

VANESSA. Really.
Another story:

NARRATOR. They passed from the road into a meadow.
The long grasses whispered to their slow tread.
He ignored the heavy dew
which soaked his shoes
until he realized that he was not caring for her…

WILBUR. Sakes alive! You'll catch your death of cold.
Let's sit on this gate.

NARRATOR. He had spoken so softly that the charm was not shattered,
and, swathed in glory,
they perched on the three-barred wooden gate
of a barbed wire fence.
She sat on a lower bar and leaned her head against his knee.
He instinctively stroked her cheek.

WILBUR. I've never felt so happy before.
I don't want ever to lose you.
Can't we be married?

I'm not worthy…

MYRTLE. Wilbur, you don't love me!
It's just the moonlight and walking with a woman.
You don't know what you want yet.
You wouldn't propose to me if it were a hot afternoon,
a muggy, wilty afternoon, and we were walking down Main Street.

WILBUR. But you do like me. And when we're both lonely…

MYRTLE. Probably no one will ever love me as I want.
Why should they?
I'm just a little hat trimmer with a love for tea and cats!

WILBUR. You aren't. You are the one person I could love
if you could only understand how much I mean it.

NARRATOR. And as he said it
he knew he didn't quite mean it;
he knew he was merely living up to the magic moment,
and he listened to his own high-pitched voice
going on in poetic periods unnatural to him…

WILBUR. When I look into your eyes
I see all the fairy stories my mother used to read to me…

MYRTLE. But you don't want a lady storyteller.
You want a nice home
and somebody to send out the laundry for you.
I understand. I often want a home myself.
But I'm funny. I distrust sentimentality.
You ought to think what you're saying…

NARRATOR. Suddenly she was crying
in sobs accumulated through years of loneliness.
She crouched on the lower bar of the gate
and hid her eyes against his knee.
Her hat fell off and her hair was a little disordered.
Yet this touch of prosaicness did not shock him.
It brought her near to him,
made her not a moon wraith, but a person like himself.
He patted her shoulder till she sat up and laughed a little,
and they strolled back toward the town.

And he: the overwrought self
that had sung of love and fairy tales was gone.
But he felt toward her
a sincere and eager affection.

Scene 42. *http://actiongirls.com/*

a movie of sex and violence together
naked or nearly naked women with bows and arrows
and submachine guns and rocket launchers
bomb and shoot bad guys
and blow up buildings
at an incredibly rapid rate;
previews from this movie are available from the website URL above

Scene 55. The Family Car

and everyone gets out at the Drive-In
holding cokes and popcorn
and sets up folding chairs
and watches the movie of The Perversion,
a documentary made for classrooms in the Fifties,
in which a man stands behind a desk in front of a map
of the United States and says:

GEORGE. Hello there.
I'm George Putnam.
I'd like to begin with a fact
a simple yet shocking fact
and it is this:
a flood tide of filth is engulfing our country
in the form of newsstand obscenity
and is threatening to pervert
an entire generation of our American children.
We know that once a person is perverted
it is practically impossible for that person
to adjust to normal attitudes in regard to sex.
Yet much of this material has been described
as an illustrated, detailed course in perversion.
Abnormal sex, crime, and violence—
it is also a fact that no matter who buys this material
seventy-five to ninety percent of it ends up in the hands of our children.
Now you might ask yourself
why this sudden concern?
Pornography and sex deviation
have always been with mankind.
This is true.
But, now, consider another fact:
never in the history of the world have the merchants of obscenity

the teachers of unnatural sex acts
had available to them
the modern facilities for disseminating this filth:
high-speed presses, rapid transportation,
mass distribution.
All have combined to put the vilest obscenity
within reach of every man, woman, and child in the country.
In the past few years this obscenity traffic
and salacious newsstand literature
have become increasingly worse
not only in content but in volume
this traffic continues to increase and flourish
for one reason
it is big business
profitable business
for the mercenary persons who produce it
and for its more than eight hundred distributors.
The United States Supreme Court has described it as
dirt for dirt's sake.
We describe it as
dirt for money's sake.
Obscene literature is a two billion dollar a year business
that's two billion dollars.
Through this material, youth can be stimulated
to sexual activity for which he has no legitimate outlet
he is even enticed to enter the world of homosexuals
lesbians, sadists, masochists and other sex deviants.
The psychiatric terms for these unnatural sex acts
are unknown to most decent adults in our country
but through these salacious materials
these abnormalities are corrupting the minds and the hearts
of our children.

> (*As the movie goes on and on,*
> *one by one*
> *the members of the family leave*
> *to get a coke, a popcorn—*
> *"gonna get a coke, be right back…"*
> *and they never return.*)

Perversion for profit.
Here is the most vicious
the most insidious feature of these publications—
they constantly portray abnormal sexual behavior as

being normal.
They glorify unnatural sex acts
they tell youngsters that it's smart, it's thrilling,
it provides kicks to be a homosexual, a sadist
and every other kind of deviant.

> *(So finally the stage is empty,*
> *as the movie sound fades*
> *and then:)*

Scene 57. The Dugout

> *all the guys come out*
> *with gloves and baseball bats and sing a song*

> *Maybe they sing this Frank Sinatra song*
> *or some other:*

Out of the tree of life I just picked me a plum
You came along and everything's startin' to hum
Still, it's a real good bet, the best is yet to come.

Best is yet to come and babe, won't that be fine?
You think you've seen the sun, but you ain't seen it shine.

a-Wait till the warm-up's underway
Wait till our lips have met
And wait till you see that sunshine day
You ain't seen nothin' yet.

The best is yet to come and babe, won't it be fine?
Best is yet to come, come the day you're mine.

Come the day you're mine
I'm gonna teach you to fly
We've only tasted the wine
We're gonna drain the cup dry.

Wait till your charms are right for these arms to surround
You think you've flown before, but baby, you ain't left the ground.

a-Wait till you're locked in my embrace
Wait till I draw you near
a-Wait till you see that sunshine place
Ain't nothin' like it here.

The best is yet to come and babe, won't it be fine?
The best is yet to come, come the day you're mine.

Come the day you're mine
And you're gonna be mine.

> *(When they leave,*
> *they leave their baseball bats behind.)*

Scene 83. Union Station

> *everyone arriving at Christmas*
> *with briefcases and hats and newspapers?*
> *some or all holding a Christmas stocking?*
> *Christmas carols are playing*
> *or are they all singing a Christmas carol?*
> *and then everyone rushing off in different directions?*
>
> *Or do they all rush through*
> *while we hear a* VOICEOVER *giving this recipe:*

VOICEOVER.

2	cups cooked rice
1/2	cup finely chopped red onion
2	large eggs, lightly beaten
1/4	cup finely chopped cilantro
2	tablespoons butter or margarine, melted
1	tablespoon diced jalapeños
2	teaspoons cornstarch
1/3	cup packed dark brown sugar
2	tablespoons ketchup
2	tablespoons dark rum
1	lime, juiced
2	cups coffee, sweetened
10	tablespoons vanilla-flavored syrup, divided
4	egg yolks
3	tablespoons superfine sugar
1	pound mascarpone cheese
4	packages lady fingers, 1 dozen per package
3	cans (14 1/2 fl. oz. each) reduced-sodium chicken broth
2	packages (16 oz. each) frozen cut broccoli
1	small onion, coarsely chopped
1	teaspoon bottled minced garlic
1/2	cup water
1/4	cup all-purpose flour
1	cup shredded cheddar cheese
1	tablespoon butter
2	teaspoons finely chopped ginger

1/8	teaspoon ground allspice
2	large cloves garlic, crushed
1	teaspoon olive oil
1/2	teaspoon salt
1/8	teaspoon ground black pepper
1	package (9 ounces) Fettuccine
1	tablespoon olive oil
1	tablespoon red wine vinegar
1/4	cup (1 ounce) grated Parmesan cheese
1	pound fresh tomatoes, chopped
1/4	cup chopped fresh basil or 1 tablespoon dried basil, crushed

Scene 85. Howl

*We hear a saxophone
and we are in a coffee house in North Beach, San Francisco.*

Some people sit at tables, smoking.

BUKOWSKI *sits up center at a small table with a microphone
and a glass of something.*

BUKOWSKI. My Father
was a truly amazing man
he pretended to be
rich
even though we lived on beans and mush and weenies
when we sat down to eat, he said,
"Not everybody can eat like this."

And because he wanted to be rich or because he actually
thought he was rich
he always voted Republican
and he voted for Hoover against Roosevelt
and he lost
and then he voted for Alf Landon against Roosevelt
and he lost again
saying, "I don't know what this world is coming to,
now we've got that goddamned Red in there again
and the Russians will be in our backyard next!"

I think it was my father who made me decide to
become a bum.
I decided that if a man like that wants to be rich
then I want to be poor.

and I became a bum.
I lived on nickels and dimes and in cheap rooms and
on park benches.
I thought maybe the bums knew something.

but I found out that most of the bums wanted to be
rich too.
they had just failed at that.

so caught between my father and the bums
I had no place to go
and I went there fast and slow.
never voted Republican
never voted.

buried him
like an oddity of the earth
like a hundred thousand oddities
like millions of other oddities,
wasted.

> (BUKOWSKI *gets up from the table,*
> *gathers up his papers*
> *and walks away*
>
> ANOTHER POET, *a woman, comes up,*
> *sits down at the same table*
>
> *someone plays guitar*
> *or other happenings/performance events occur*
> *without reference to the reading*
> *while she reads:)*

THE WOMAN POET. He's got me down on my knees
and I can't even focus on anything I have no time to understand
the position of my body or the direction of my face I see
a pair of legs in rough corduroy and the color of
the pants are brown and
surrounded by darkness
and there's a sense of other people there
and yet I can't hear them breathe or hear their feet or
anything
and his hand suddenly comes up against the back of my head
and he's got his fingers locked in my
hair and he's shoving my face forward and twisting my head
almost gently
but very violent in that gentleness and I

got only half a breath in my lungs the smell of
piss on the floorboards and this fleshy bulge in his
pants getting harder and harder as my face
is forced against the front of his pants
the zipper tears my lips I feel them getting bruised
and all the while he's stroking my face and tightening his fingers
around the locks of my hair and
I can't focus my eyes my head being pushed and pulled and
twisted and caressed and it's as if I have no hands
I know I got hands I had hands a half hour ago
I remember lighting a cigarette with them
lighting a match
and I remember how warm the flame was when I lifted it
toward my face and my knees are hurting from the floor
it's a stone floor and my knees are
hurting 'cause they banged on the floor
when he dragged me down the cellar stairs
I remember a door in the darkness
and the breath of a dog his dog
as it licked my hands when I reached out to stop
my headlong descent its tongue licking out at my
fingers and my face slams down
and there's this electric blam inside my head
and it's as if my eyes suddenly opened on the large sun
and then went black with the switch thrown down
and I'm shocked and embarrassed
and his arms swing down he's lifting me up saying
lookin' for me?, and he buries his face
in my neck and I feel the saliva
running down into the curve of my neck
and my arms are hanging loose
and I can see a ceiling and a dim bulb tossing back and forth.

        (*so this is like a spoken word performance at City Lights bookshop*
        in San Francisco in the Fifties

        We hear a recording of Burroughs reading The Exterminator *or* Junky *from*
        The Outlaw Bible *p 89*
        while a woman does a happening dance
        and/or a guy is on the side doing amplified finger-sound performance
        or
        a guy on roller skates with kite wings
        while Karen Finley smears herself
        or Charlotte Moorman, naked, plays the cello

and/or a naked woman runs after a spotlight,
throwing spinach greens into the pool of light

[there are recordings of Burroughs in his distinctive voice
that could be played over a piece of choreography or performance.]

and/or there could be a GUY *at the table,*
who lip-syncs Burroughs' text
though he shouldn't try to lip-sync it exactly,
but be a whole sentence behind or ahead of the voiceover
looking puzzled about why the sound doesn't sync with his lips
while we know it is because he's high on something.)

BURROUGHS. During the war I worked for A. J. Cohen Exterminators ground floor office dead-end street by the river.

I used my own car a black Ford V8 and worked alone carrying my bedbug spray, pyrethrum powder, bellows and bulbs of fluoride up and down stairs.

"Exterminator! You need the service?"

A fat smiling Chinese rationed out the pyrethrum powder—it was hard to get during the war—and cautioned us to use fluoride whenever possible. Personally I prefer a pyrethrum job to a fluoride. With the pyrethrum you kill the roaches right there in front of God and the client whereas this starch and fluoride you leave it around and back a few days later a southern defense worker told me "They eat it and run around here fat as hawgs."

When it comes to bedbugs there is a board of health regulation against spraying beds and that of course is just where the bugs are in most cases. Now an old wood house with bedbugs back in the wood for generations only thing is to fumigate…. So here is Mamma with a glass of sweet wine her beds back and ready…

I look at her over the syrupy red wine…. "Lady we don't spray no beds. Board of health regulations you know."

"Ach so the wine is not enough?"

She comes back with a crumpled dollar. So I go to work…bedbugs great red clusters of them in the ticking of the mattresses. I mix a little formaldehyde with my kerosene in the spray it's more sanitary that way and if you tangle with some pimp in one of the Negro whorehouses we service a face full of formaldehyde keeps the boy in line. Now you'll often find these old Jewish grandmas in a back room like their bugs and we have to force the door with the younger generation smooth college-trained Jew there could turn into a narcotics agent while you wait.

"All right Grandma, open up! The exterminator is here."

She is screaming in Yiddish no bugs are there we force our way in I turn the
bed back…my God thousands of them fat and red with Grandma and when
I put the spray to them she moans like the Gestapo is murdering her nubile
daughter engaged to a dentist.

(*project Robert Frank film* Pull My Daisy? [*without the soundtrack.*]
while a YOUNG BLACK WOMAN *erupts with* "*Howl.*")

A YOUNG BLACK WOMAN. I saw the best minds of my generation
destroyed by madness, starving hysterical naked,

dragging themselves through the negro streets at dawn looking for an angry fix,
angelheaded hipsters burning for the ancient heavenly connection to the
starry dynamo in the machinery of night,
who poverty and tatters and hollow-eyed and high sat up smoking in the
supernatural darkness of cold-water flats floating across the tops of
cities contemplating jazz,

What sphinx of cement and aluminum bashed open their skulls and ate up
their brains and imagination?
Moloch! Solitude! Filth! Ugliness! Ashcans and unobtainable dollars! Children
screaming under the stairways! Boys sobbing in armies! Old men
weeping in the parks!
Moloch! Moloch! Nightmare of Moloch! Moloch the loveless! Mental Moloch!
Moloch the heavy judger of men!
Moloch the incomprehensible prison! Moloch the crossbone soulless jailhouse
and Congress of sorrows! Moloch whose buildings are judgment!
Moloch the vast stone of war! Moloch the stunned governments!
Moloch whose mind is pure machinery! Moloch whose blood is running
money! Moloch whose fingers are ten armies!
Moloch whose breast is a cannibal dynamo! Moloch whose ear is a smoking
tomb!
Moloch whose eyes are a thousand blind windows! Moloch whose skyscrapers
stand in the long streets like endless Jehovahs! Moloch whose
factories dream and croak in the fog! Moloch whose smokestacks
and antennae crown the cities!
Moloch whose love is endless oil and stone! Moloch whose soul is electricity
and banks! Moloch whose poverty is the specter of genius! Moloch
whose fate is a cloud of sexless hydrogen! Moloch whose name is
the Mind!

America I'm putting my queer shoulder to the wheel.

Scene 68. No Pig

A GUY *comes out to speak.*
After a few moments, while he speaks,
ANOTHER GUY *comes out*
and begins to dance—
without any musical accompaniment—
dancing not even to the spoken text,
rather just dancing in his own quiet world.

GUY. We ended up living in a tiny apartment
in a house owned by an Indian couple in Flushing, Queens.
My stepmother cried the whole first night.
We've come to America, and look at this apartment!
It was one of those Archie Bunker neighborhoods.
You know when you watch *All in the Family,*
that first aerial shot with all those tiny homes
right next to each other?
That's exactly where we lived.
I got left back a year at the local public school
because I didn't know English.
I didn't know how to say
"May I go to the bathroom?"
or
"I don't know what you're saying."
My desk was right in front of the teacher's desk
and I would sit there all day and not go to the bathroom
until I went home.
Then I got a little picture book
and I would point to a picture of a toilet
and the teacher would know, OK,
it's time to go to the bathroom.
My teacher told my stepmother at a parent-teacher conference
that I wasn't learning English fast enough.
When I came home
my father was extremely upset with me.
He told me, in Farsi, that I must be stupid.
I had the hardest time trying to tell the cafeteria lady
that I couldn't eat pork.
My father taught me how to say, NO PIG! NO PIG!
It took about a month for the cafeteria lady
to realize I couldn't eat pork.
Whenever they were having pork products,
she would make me a peanut butter and jelly sandwich,

which was horrible, because I hated peanut butter and jelly!
So I didn't eat anything.
Then my father told me to say chicken,
but I would say "kitchen" instead of chicken.
It took me so long to differentiate between the two.
Imagine me:
"KITCHEN! NO PIG! NO PIG!"

Scene 92. The Woman in the Red Dress

music overwhelms the scene
and the woman in the red dress enters dancing

then a guy enters
another guy enters
a bunch of people are entering from every direction
wild music
unsynchronized frenzy
until finally all ten or twelve are making the same gesture together, scattered over
the stage, but dancing the same gestures and moves

and maybe this could happen, too:

at a certain point,
a woman is lying on the floor
a guy leans down and locks lips with her
and raises her from the floor into a flamenco-like dance
with lips permanently locked in a kiss
they go on and on and on and on and on
until he passes out and falls to the ground in a heap
she turns to another guy and locks lips with him immediately
and they dance
but she stops them, interrupts the dance
to tell him he is dancing the wrong way
they lock lips and dance again
she stops to correct him again
ditto
ditto
until she spins around, grabs the sleeve of his shirt
and rips it
then he is pissed
they argue
they argue and argue and argue and argue and argue
till the guy turns front and takes a dance posture

and flexes his bicep
he flexes his bicep to the music
five guys join him in bicep flexing dance
all in unison
then they all do a hip thrust
very macho
then turn upstage and wiggle their butts
(not SO macho.)
they move through other male display dance moves
finger snapping, etc.
then three women step up and do the same male display moves.

Scene 88. The Wedding Cake

We see the video by Laleh Khorramian
from the P.S. 1 show Greater NY 2005
in which paper cutouts of pen and ink drawings
brightly colored
fall and fall and fall and fall from the sky
everything is falling
while tragically moving music plays underneath it
and the immense absurdly baroque wedding cake "Sweet Nothing"
by Kirsten Hassenfeld (from the same P.S. 1 show)
rises from a trap door.
(The work of both these artists can also be seen on the internet.)

Scene 36. Mrs. Bridge

woman in red dress
entering, dancing solo
with floor lamp
looking for a place to put it
no dialogue here, just music?
Benny Goodman or Guy Lombardo or Bing Crosby
trying the lamp here, not liking it,
trying it there, not liking it,
trying it somewhere else,
finally placing the lamp and exiting

Scene 67. The Commuter Platform

just a guy with gray flannel suit, fedora, briefcase
met at the station by his wife

JAY. Camila, I don't want to hurt you,
but I'd better say this and get it over.

CAMILA. Say what, Jay?

JAY. I want a divorce.

NARRATOR. Just like that.
No preamble. No explanation.
A clean surgical cut and then it was all over.
Or was it?
For she was merely looking bewildered.

CAMILA. Are you joking?

JAY. Do I look as though I'm joking?

CAMILA. I see. You want a divorce.
But what for? I don't...

JAY. What does any man want a divorce for?

CAMILA. You're not telling me you want to marry again?
At your age! I don't believe it!

JAY. I'm not Methuselah!

NARRATOR. Her chief feeling was one of intense amazement.
Perhaps she would suffer later.
She supposed women did suffer over things like this.

CAMILA. Then there is another woman?

JAY. What do you think I'm telling you?

CAMILA. And you're in love with her?
Well, if you want a divorce, you'll get it.
You always get what you want.

JAY. I had hoped you'd be reasonable about this thing, Camila.
After all, you're a sensible woman.
As to getting what I want,
you've always had what you wanted, haven't you?

CAMILA. I've always had what you wanted me to have.
There's a difference.

NARRATOR. He stared at her.
This was not the Camila he knew at all.
She was letting him go lightly, easily,
without a struggle. It hurt his pride,
and it demanded assuagement.

JAY. It isn't as though I really meant anything to you.
I haven't meant anything to you for years.

NARRATOR. And, to her eternal credit,

she used what amounted to her last breath
to turn away from the railroad platform
toward the car, and, pausing for a moment,
to turn back and throw a barb instead of a sop.

CAMILA. I wouldn't say that, Jay.
You've supported me.

NARRATOR. Then she left,
leaving him staring after her
as though he had never seen her before.

(*and his fedora and briefcase are left behind.*)

Scene 96. Cell Phones

Hello? Hello? Trish!
etc. etc.

the talker continues as all the other actors
look straight out at audience
finally another of them takes a cell phone call
is her lover breaking up with her? or is it difficult?
and then all twelve people are on cell phones at the same time
having the same conversation
about a love affair
a breakup
each taking different lines of the same conversation
or of archetypal conversations around this event
archetypal lines

Scene 99. I Remember

While television news footage of war—
and, or, if there is more than one screen,
of war and race riots and other violence—
is projected,
this text is spoken by one man.
or else one man begins
and then one or two or three others join him.

I remember many Sunday afternoon dinners
of fried chicken or pot roast.

I remember my father's collection of arrow heads.

I remember loafers with pennies in them.

I remember game rooms in basements.

I remember "come as you are" parties.
Everybody cheated.

I remember drugstore counter stools with no backs,
and swirling around and around on them.

I remember two-dollar bills. And silver dollars.

I remember "Double Bubble" gum comics
and licking off the sweet "powder."

I remember catching myself with an expression on my face
that doesn't relate to what's going on anymore.

I remember the little "thuds" of bugs
bumping up against the screens at night.

I remember when polio was the worst thing in the world.

I remember my first cigarette. It was a Kent.

I remember my first erections.
I thought I had some terrible disease or something.

I remember the only time I ever saw my mother cry.
I was eating apricot pie.

I remember when, in high school,
if you wore green and yellow on Thursday
it meant you were queer.

I remember an American history teacher
who was always threatening to jump out the window
if we didn't quiet down. (Second floor.)

I remember Liberace.

I remember pony tails.

I remember driftwood lamps.

I remember potato salad.

I remember salt on watermelon.

I remember lightning.

I remember my father in a tutu.
As a ballerina dancer in a variety show at church.

I remember getting erections in school
and the bell rings

and how handy zipper notebooks were.

I remember not looking at crippled people.

I remember chalk.

I remember daydreams of dying
and how unhappy everybody would be.

I remember the sound of the ice cream man coming.

I remember once losing my nickel in the grass
before he made it to my house.

I remember that life was just as serious then
as it is now.

> *(And then, at the end,*
> *hard rock music comes on,*
> *they all dance*
> *in the same way the women did at the beginning of the piece—*
> *a wild, ecstatic, enraged, abandoned,*
> *insane messy hair dance*
> *at the end of which*
> *they simply stop*
> *and walk off without ceremony.)*

Scene 128. Antony

> *An empty stage, while we hear*
> *Antony and the Johnsons sing one of their songs—*
> *"Twilight"*
> *or "River of Sorrow"*
> *or "Rapture"*
> *or "Hope There's Someone"*
>
> *And it may be that a solo dancer enters quietly—*
> *a young girl dancing contemplatively,*
> *sweetly, gently, vulnerably—*
> *or a solo male dancer doing the same,*
> *or a dancer with Downs Syndrome.*

Scene 123. The Gathering

> *The community gathers again*
> *like the gathering around the Thanksgiving table at the beginning*
> *but look how everyone has changed!*

musical intro

Each person brings in something
and puts it down somewhere
so that items on the stage accumulate

VERY old guy in print house dress and clogs

a guy in a dress with a red crown of flowers
comes downstage and smokes cigarette smiling
just that, no more, and is happy

a guy enters and sits on box
he has on a straitjacket
watches TV on packing crates
he frees his hands and eats bread and sings along with TV
making drumming motions with his hands

narrator wanders with sheaf of papers in hand
inadequate

a guy in a monkey suit

a woman in a beautiful black dress enters
and paces while she smokes
she is angry, hostile
as though challenging anyone's right to challenge her smoking
or her being there
and, in the end, she just turns upstage and rushes out

a guy wearing a roller blade on only one foot
going in circles
while another guy rolls around with yellow high heeled shoes on his hands

a clown wearing a clown hat, carrying a briefcase

Asian woman appears in chinky/junky outfit
looking like one of the dancers in the Strange Mushroom company
she leaves,
returns in red shirt, white undies
with a pillow in her arms
looking for someone
and turns abruptly and leaves at once
she returns wearing a white shirt and tie and glasses
like an office worker
—as though she has been trying out identities that will be acceptable

guy puts on fifteen shirts

and eight pairs of pants
then has a fit getting out of them
throwing them around
making pile of laundry and diving into it

a little guy wearing a wedding dress

others?

what they bring:
like workmen assembling a Rhoades piece
http://www.davidzwirner.com/artists/5/
chandelier of neon words such as Taco,
Oval Office
sign on a piece of cardboard: Quality Control
pickle jars
four immense white boxes with red ribbons
as though Christmas gifts from Harry and David
a huge installation of Styrofoam balls
plywood
FedEx boxes
and handcarts
desk chairs with wheels
boxes of foam
boxes of plastic wrap
huge vertical column plastic bags full of foam
piles of CDs
aluminum tubes
buckets
construction workers' plastic helmets
boards
a film projector
a shovel
a scanner
upside-down yellow rain boots
poster for Marilyn Chambers, Behind the Green Door, *adults only*
computer components
construction site striped yellow and black tape
caution signs
road blocks—wooden horses
heavy-duty orange electrical extension cords
if there are tables with things on them
the tables might be turned over onto their sides
so that foam balls and rubber balls roll out across the stage

fans blowing shit

so it looks at the end like this:
http://www.theatredelaville-paris.com/voeux2005/voeux.htm
(or has this page been removed from the internet?)

Scene 138. Beach Boys

and then everyone suddenly breaks out into
a dance
to what might as well be Italian Beach Boys music
it goes on and on and on
or they might do a version of one of the "Life Goes On" songs
by Johnny Cash or the Beatles or LeAnn Rimes or Tu Pac
or one of the dozens of other versions
happily ecstatically

maybe the version by Gary Chapman:
Cecil was a hard-workin' simple man
He raised six sons and a daughter
One of them became my father
His opinion was he was here to live
Till he was too weak to work any longer
Then he became much stronger
And like a leaf on a tree he would bud in the spring
And then fall to the ground in the autumn
And in death he would leave to this earth reasons for life.

And life goes on
Until it stops.
And a man walks on
Until he drops.
And when life ends
Well it's better still
'Cause another life goes on.
Life goes on, another life goes on
It always will
Life goes on.

Daddy married Mom when he was seventeen
They had me and my sister and brother
We all still love each other
Some day Dad will go to where his dad is
And I bet Cecil laughs when he sees him
'Cause they always were the best friends

Just as sure as there's dirt here beneath my feet
There is surely a heaven above me
And I live in a hope that is far beyond my days

That life goes on
Until it stops.
And a man walks on
Until he drops.
And when life ends
Well it's better still
'Cause another life goes on.
Life goes on
Another life goes on.

Life goes on
Until it stops.
And I believe a man walks on
Until he drops.
And when life ends
Well it's better still
'Cause another life goes on.
Life goes on, another life goes on
It always will.

Life goes on
Life goes on
Oh, yeah, ooo
Life goes on.

> (*do they all settle down on beach blankets
> amidst the chaos?*
>
> *or are they seated again at the Thanksgiving dinner table?*)

Scene 147. The Future

> *woman with computer (and headphones) dancing
> she comes out alone,
> stands there, opens computer,
> puts on headphones—we can't hear what she hears
> then she dances solo to this unheard music—
> and, after a couple minutes* JOHN CAGE *comes in
> and speaks his text at a microphone while she continues to dance to the unheard
> music.*

CAGE. My attitude toward old age

is one of gratitude for each day.
It strikes me
that since there's obviously a shorter length of time left
than I've already had
I'd better hurry up
and be interested in whatever I can.

I remember that it seemed to be essential
when I was in my twenties
to focus my attention on one thing
and I made a choice between music and painting.
I chose music.
But now it seems perfectly natural to open out
to every single thing I possibly can do
because I'm not going to be here much longer.
The best thing is to enjoy to do
as much as possible while I am here.

The business of the great things from the past
is a question of preservation and the use of things
that have been preserved.
I don't quarrel with that activity,
and I know that it will continue.
But there is another activity,
one to which I am devoted,
and it is the bringing of new things into being.
The difference between these two things
is the difference between spring and summer.

And so it is out of this chaos,
this accumulation of history and novelty,
that we begin building.
We are in the constant process of construction
making and remaking
from where we are and what we have.
This is what human beings do.
This is the human project
as long as we are alive.

    (*and then the celebratory music:*

    Aaron Copland's "Fanfare for the Common Man"

and the lights go to black
and when they come up
does Copland play for the curtain call, too?)

End of Play.

ADDITIONAL SCENES FOR ANYONE WHO WANTS THEM

Scene 51. The Brooklyn Girl

The actors all come out
put chairs in a row across the stage
and sit with their backs to the audience
watching for several minutes the video by Laurel Nakadate
from the P.S. 1 show Greater NY 2005
in which a young Asian girl wearing a Girl Scout sash stands
with fireworks going off behind her
and then we see squirrels close up
and then we see her dragged across a beach by a guy
and then we see her lying on a highway overpass with a dead bird
and then we see her dancing in her bra and underpants on her bed
as we see her figure out how to grow up
and make her own world to live in.
(Laurel Nakadate's work can also be seen on the internet.)

Scene 54. The Epileptic Dances

while twelve others just stand there watching,
to music by Mozart.
Or it could be someone with some extreme motor skill difficulty
dances
while the others watch
and then,
toward the end,
the others join in the dance, too,
not mocking the dancer
but appreciating and emulating his aesthetic.

Scene 68. The Arts

A country store.

A string quartet comes on,
finds chairs,
adjust their instruments, tune up,
and we just listen to some beautiful Bach
while how-to drawings from the Great Artists school
or paint-by-numbers paintings
are projected

And after a while, over the music,
Bill Dow steps up and reads his poem:

BILL DOW. Many people from many lands
Are living here as one.
They work together, learn together
For them living is fun.

This nation of ours is a powerful one,
It's known from shore to shore.
But as it grows, as everyone knows,
Cooperation is needed even more.

Rivers, valleys, mountains, plains,
Make up our beautiful land.
America is a wonderful place,
Made by God's own hand.

Scene 61. Rain Delay

We hear the song
"It's Raining Men"
by Paul Jabara and Paul Shaffer

Humidity's rising
Barometer's getting low
According to all sources
The street's the place to go.
'Cos tonight for the first time
At just about half-past ten
For the first time in history
It's gonna start raining men.

It's raining men Hallelujah!
It's raining men, Amen!
It's raining men Hallelujah!

It's raining men, Amen!

Humidity's rising
Barometer's getting low
According to all sources
The street's the place to go.
'Cos tonight for the first time
At just about half-past ten
For the first time in history
It's gonna start raining men.

It's raining men Hallelujah!
It's raining men, Amen!
I'm gonna go out
I'm gonna let myself get
Absolutely soaking wet.

It's raining men, Hallelujah!
It's raining men!
Every specimen
Tall blond dark and mean
Rough and tough and strong and lean.

God bless Mother Nature
She's a single woman too
She took on a heaven
And she did what she had to do
She taught every angel
To rearrange the sky
So that each and every woman
Could find her perfect guy.

It's raining men.
Go get yourself wet, Girl
I know you want to.

I feel stormy weather moving in
About to begin
Hear the thunder
Don't you lose your head
Rip off the roof and stay in bed.

It's raining men Hallelujah!
It's raining men, Amen!
It's raining men Hallelujah!
It's raining men, Amen!

It's raining men Hallelujah!
It's raining men, Amen!
It's raining men Hallelujah!
It's raining men, Amen!

> (*And, while we hear the song*
> *the Shea Stadium ground crew*
> *starts to cover the stage with a huge blue tarp.*
>
> *They have to pause frequently in their work*
> *to do unison dances to the song.*
> *This is humiliating to different degrees for each of them.*
>
> *And then,*
> *while the ground crew finishes the job*
> *the umpires come on and do a dance with umbrellas*
> *they are totally straight-faced but there is a lot of hip shaking.*
>
> *At the end of the dance*
> *the ground crew joins the umpires for a full cast rain delay dance.*)

Scene 48. Sex

> *There is a constant simulcast projection on a big screen*
> *of live action as it is happening in the moment on stage,*
> *and also pre-recorded stuff*
> *of the same* ACTOR *we are seeing on stage,*
> *but of her in the dressing room*
> *then leaving the dressing room*
> *then standing just off-stage preparing to come on*
> *then leaving the stage*
> *and returning to her dressing room*
> *and also two small TV sets on a bar with irrelevant movies playing, and projected*
> *over the set and back wall as a whole,*
> *another continuous Hollywood movie*
> *while she speaks:*

ACTOR. "Two weeks is a long time without sex,"
I heard someone say yesterday.
When you've been married twelve years
and you've got children,
sex every two weeks, hell, every two months,
is cause for celebration.
Forget about exchanging loving glances across any part of the house.
I am either fixing my kids' lunches
or figuring out where someone's homework folder is.

Let's face it.
Romantic sentiments including sex
have no place in a marriage with children.
When they all turn eighteen
perhaps there'll be time for such pursuits,
but will we still know each other then?
I am looking at a picture of my husband's grandparents
standing in front of their pharmacy
on 89th and Lexington Avenue in Manhattan.
I am told this picture was taken in the Fifties
during the pharmacy's heyday.
Riva and Sol worked here morning till night,
only taking quick lunch breaks
upstairs in their one bedroom apartment.
It was also here that they raised their daughter,
my mother-in-law.
I have often wondered what sort of marriage they had.
In the picture Riva stands proud,
determined and independent.
Sol's demeanor is resigned,
almost defeated.
I doubt if they ever had a chance to
exchange loving glances at each other during the day,
much less at night when they tumbled into bed.
Theirs was the American dream.
Two Jewish immigrants who had done well
and sacrificed much.

SLASHER
A HORRIFYING COMEDY

by Allison Moore

BIOGRAPHY

Allison Moore is a displaced Texan living in Minneapolis, where she was a 2007-2009 Bush Artist Fellow and a 2008-2009 McKnight Advancement Grantee. Her plays include *End Times* (Kitchen Dog Theater; Dallas Critics Forum Award), *American Klepto* (Fresh Ink/Illusion Theater), *Hazard County* (2005 Humana Festival), *Split* (Guthrie Theater commission), *Urgent Fury* (2003 Cherry Lane Mentor Project; Mentor: Marsha Norman) and *Eighteen* (2001 O'Neill Playwrights Conference). Ms. Moore is a two-time Jerome Fellow and two-time McKnight Fellow through The Playwrights' Center. Her new adaptation of Willa Cather's novel, *My Ántonia*, for Illusion Theater will be produced in their 2009-2010 Season. Ms. Moore holds a B.F.A. from Southern Methodist University and an M.F.A. from the University of Iowa's Playwrights Workshop.

ACKNOWLEDGMENTS

Slasher premiered at the Humana Festival of New American Plays in March 2009. It was directed by Josh Hecht with the following cast:

FRANCES McKINNEY ....Lusia Strus
CHRISTI GARCIA and others.......................Christy McIntosh
MARC HUNTER .... Mark Setlock
SHEENA McKINNEY ....Nicole Rodenburg
HILDY McKINNEY .... Katharine Moeller
JODY JOSHI .... Lucas Papaelias

and the following production staff:

Scenic Designer.. Paul Owen
Costume Designer ....Jennifer Caprio
Lighting Designer .... Russell Champa
Sound Designer..Matt Callahan
Properties Designer..Doc Manning
Wig and Make-up Design.................................Heather Fleming
Dialect Coach .... Rinda Frye
Fight Director..k. Jenny Jones
Stage Manager ....Robin Grady
Production Assistant.. Melissa Blair
Dramaturg..Amy Wegener
Assistant Dramaturg... Brendan Pelsue
Casting... Alaine Alldaffer Casting
Directing Assistant ....Nathan Green

Slasher was developed with the generous support of The Playwrights' Center's New Plays on Campus Program and 2008 PlayLabs Festival (Minneapolis, Minnesota); the Lark Play Development Center (New York City); and Playwrights Horizons (New York City). The play was written with the support of a Bush Artist Fellowship as well as a McKnight Advancement Grant from The Playwrights' Center.

CAST OF CHARACTERS

SHEENA McKINNEY, 21, girl-next-door kind of pretty. Not book-smart, but a survivor.

HILDY McKINNEY, 15, Sheena's little sister. Smarter than Sheena, but less capable in a crisis.

FRANCES McKINNEY, 40-50, their mother. Angry, thwarted feminist with a questionable disability. Gets around her house with the aid of a Li'l Rascal scooter. Loud.

MARC HUNTER, 35-40, a D-list director and recovering alcoholic and sex addict. Tells everyone he's younger than he is.

JODY JOSHI, 23, an undergrad film school dude. Capable, knows his stuff, but kind of a kiss-ass.

CHRISTI GARCIA, 23-30, Assistant Director of the Holy Shepherd Justice League. Very put together, as if she's always ready to make a statement on camera. Not to be underestimated.

BRIDGET/MARCY/BETH/MADISON, attractive young women who are killed in various ways, all to be played by the actor playing Christi Garcia.

WOMAN/ CAR HOP/ RADIO ANNOUNCER/ NEWS ANCHOR, also to be played/voiced by the actor playing Christi Garcia.

SETTING

In and around Austin, Texas, 2007. Frances' run-down house; a Hooters-style bar; a Sonic drive-in; another house where they film.

STYLE NOTE

As the play progresses, Sheena's life begins to resemble a horror movie; acting and production choices should reflect this.

Lusia Strus and Nicole Rodenburg
in *Slasher*

33rd Annual Humana Festival of New American Plays
Actors Theatre of Louisville, 2009
Photo by Harlan Taylor

SLASHER

Prologue

Flashback, 1992. The construction site. Darkness. Night. Sound of rain.

WOMAN'S VOICE. No…no, please….

> (*A crack of thunder, and a flash of lightning reveals FRANCES, searching for the source of the voice.*)
>
> (*Another flash of lightning, and we see two shadowy figures—a WOMAN and MARC. They are outside on the deserted construction site. MARC crouches over the WOMAN, who lies in a compromised position.*)

WOMAN. No!

> (*A loud crack of thunder. The WOMAN lets out a piercing scream.*)
>
> (*FRANCES, her face twisted in rage, gives a primal yell in response.*)
>
> (*Blackout.*)
>
> (*In the darkness, the sound of FRANCES falling violently.*)

Scene 1

Present day. Sound of rain continues.

Sound of a car door slamming.

HILDY. (*Offstage.*) Wait!

SHEENA. (*Offstage.*) Run!

> (*Sound of the two girls squealing as they run through the rain. Sound of keys in the door. Lights up as the front door opens into the living room of an old house. SHEENA and HILDY step into the house, shaking off the storm. They carry a bag of groceries and a box from a chicken joint. FRANCES lies awkwardly on the floor. She wears an old bathrobe and slippers. A motorized scooter sits empty on the other side of the room.*)

FRANCES. I've been waiting for you.

SHEENA. (*Annoyed.*) Jesus Christ.

HILDY. Mom! Are you all right?

SHEENA. What happened.

FRANCES. What do you think happened? Get my scooter.

> (HILDY *gets the scooter.*)

SHEENA. Let her get it herself.

FRANCES. Thank you for your concern, Sheena.

SHEENA. The physical therapist showed you how to get up.

FRANCES. According to her I should be training for a damn marathon.

SHEENA. Walking ten minutes three times a day is not—

FRANCES. I FELL.

    (*As* HILDY *helps* FRANCES *into the scooter,* SHEENA *reaches into* FRANCES' *pocket, grabs a bottle of pills.*)

SHEENA. How many did you take?

FRANCES. Give me those!

    (SHEENA *dodges* FRANCES, *counts the pills.*)

I've been lying on the floor for three hours, all you care about is—

SHEENA. Is today the eleventh?

HILDY. Tenth. (*To* FRANCES.) We got chicken?

FRANCES. It's not enough that I'm disabled, you have to humiliate me, too. Why don't you call Marshall Davis, huh? He would loooove to see me lying on the floor, not able to get up. He'd pay to see that. Get me flat on my back so everybody at City Hall can take their turn—

SHEENA. Mother!

FRANCES. STEPPING ON ME.

You can stop counting. I've been a good little cripple.

SHEENA. Today is the tenth, your prescription was refilled on the first—

FRANCES. So I took an extra—

SHEENA. FOUR extra—

FRANCES. Whatever—

SHEENA. Which is why you were passed out for three hours and forgot to tell me Hildy's practice was cancelled.

FRANCES. It was a choice between taking a couple of extra pills and screaming in agony for half the day! Now give them back.

    (SHEENA *hands* FRANCES *the pill bottle.*)

SHEENA. Did you hear from that attorney?

FRANCES. Coward. Ball sucker.

HILDY. You want ice tea?

FRANCES. No thank you, Dear.

SHEENA. So he's not taking the case.

FRANCES. Didn't even have the guts to call me himself. Made his secretary do it for him.

SHEENA. Hildy?

HILDY. (*To* FRANCES.) There's mashed potatoes?

    (SHEENA *gathers her things to leave.*)

FRANCES. She's probably not even his secretary. He just employs her so he can claim the blowjobs as a business write-off.

SHEENA. Please eat something tonight.

FRANCES. Where are you going?

SHEENA. I picked up a bunch of shifts.

FRANCES. Well, there goes the dean's list.

SHEENA. How else are we going to fix the A.C.?

FRANCES. You wouldn't have to pick up shifts if they weren't paying you third-world wages—

SHEENA. They're not.

FRANCES. Two dollars and fourteen cents an hour is what women in Mexico make for pulling used limes out of Corona bottles.

SHEENA. I'm late.

FRANCES. You know why they get away with paying you that? Because most tipped workers are WOMEN. If you got the other servers together to protest, stage a walkout—

SHEENA. We'd be replaced in a day and a half, and then *no one* in this house would have a job. (*To* HILDY.) I'm closing tonight, do you have a ride in the morning?

HILDY. Yep.

FRANCES. They underpay you on purpose to force you to giggle and flirt and generally debase yourself so all the dickless little men will leave you a big tip!

SHEENA. I do NOT debase myself!

> (*Immediate shift to:*)

Scene 2

The Bar. SHEENA *takes off her jacket, revealing a tight V-neck T-shirt that reads "BUSTERS" in big letters across the chest. It's her uniform. She picks up a tray and quickly puts on a big smile for* JODY *and* MARC, *who sit at a table in the bar.*

SHEENA. Hey Jody!

JODY. 'Sup, Sheena.

SHEENA. Be right with you.

> (SHEENA *exits.* MARC *watches her go uncomfortably, like he's in a dentist's office.*)

JODY. So you were saying?

MARC. I was saying, what I was saying is, that it's an allegory.

JODY. Absolutely—

MARC. Which is the case with most horror movies, the good ones, anyway. They tell us about our deepest fears, not just personally but as a society.

JODY. Definitely.

MARC. Take *Hostel*, right? The whole movie trades on this fear that super rich Europeans *get off* on torturing Americans.

JODY. Well, yeah, but, I mean. They do, right?

(*Beat.* MARC *does not laugh.*)

Just, illustrating your point—

MARC. That's good.

JODY. That we really think rich dudes are total sadists—

MARC. When you let that underlying fear inform every shot, *that's* when you transcend the genre. That's what separates the breakout hit from just another slasher flick—*Texas Chainsaw Massacre* being the original example.

JODY. Oh man, from the word go that film is unbelievable—

MARC. Because of the threat. That's what was so revolutionary.

JODY. Well, that and Tobe Hooper's insane editing—I mean, forty edits per minute—

MARC. Blah blah blah, fine. His editing is great, but it would have meant nothing if he hadn't— At a time when the media's favorite whipping boy was the so-called "Me Generation," he makes a film that says: yes, young people do smoke pot and drink beer and have sex, *but they are innocent.* The threat comes from the adults.

JODY. I see what you mean.

MARC. And not adults like "The Man" or "The Suit," no no no no no. It's the *family*. The movie hits on this deep fear that the family structure itself is ultimately responsible for the most unspeakable violence and terror.

JODY. Absolutely.

MARC. This project I'm working on now, it's really about what happens to a man when he's forced to, to repress and even hate his own, natural, sexual desires.

JODY. Right.

MARC. He should be loving these women—they're beautiful young women —he *wants* to love them, but he's been told that sex is evil. And so he has to kill them.

JODY. Yeah.

(SHEENA *reenters and waits on them.*)

SHEENA. I'm back.

MARC. You are.

SHEENA. What can I get for you?

MARC. Club soda and lime, please.

SHEENA. You got it. (*To* JODY.) And I already know what you want—
(*She starts to exit.*)

JODY. Actually, can I, uh, just get an ice tea?

SHEENA. Um. Sure?

JODY. Thanks.

(SHEENA *exits.*)

MARC. You're a regular, huh?

JODY. Well, half the filmmakers in town hang out here, so if you want to know what's going on—

MARC. It's the hub.

JODY. Exactly.

MARC. When I was here there was a place off Magnolia, I hope to God it's been condemned. Can't remember how many times I found McConaughey or Zellweger passed out on the bathroom floor there—

JODY. Right.

MARC. Oh wait, that was me!

JODY. Right.

MARC. Had a little tendency to, uh, overindulge—

JODY. I've been there, brother.

MARC. But you don't drink anymore?

JODY. Oh. I'll have a beer now and again, just—

MARC. Just not now.

JODY. Well, this is a meeting, right?

MARC. Is it? I mean, you called me, buddy.

JODY. All right, okay, so. So I heard through the grapevine that you need a first assistant.

MARC. Interesting. What else did you hear?

JODY. Nothing, really.

MARC. Uh-huh.

JODY. Well, just that you've got a 21-day shooting permit up in Round Rock that started today, but Jenna Long pulled out of her contract yesterday and took most of your investors with her. But since you're on the hook with the Texas Film Commission and you've already paid up your insurance and deposit on cameras, you're planning to shoot anyway.

MARC. Wow.

JODY. It's a pretty small town.

MARC. Let's assume what you've said is, more or less true. Why should I give you the job.

JODY. I'm ready, dude. In the past two years I've shot and cut five short films, three of them horror.

MARC. But you've never worked on a feature.

JODY. Well—

MARC. Because, see, here's the thing: if we miss a shot, Jody, if we have to do extra set-ups because someone's not paying attention, I'm literally throwing money away.

JODY. I hear you, brother—

MARC. Not *my* money. But money that I worked very hard to raise. This film gets made in the next twenty days, or it does not get made—and it not getting made is not an option.

JODY. I'm Johnny on the spot—

MARC. You graduate already?

JODY. Um, technically, no, but—

MARC. You're still a student.

JODY. I'm just missing, like, a math class—

MARC. *You can still access the editing room at the University?*

JODY. Oh. Oh! Yeah. Definitely.

MARC. Well.

JODY. Access is easy, brother.

MARC. The first assistant is gonna have a lot of responsibility.

JODY. I can handle it.

MARC. And it's gonna be old-school. I'm talking twenty-three hours a day and being grateful for that one hour off. So I need to know: how bad do you want this.

JODY. I'd sell my mom for it.

MARC. Is your mom hot?

JODY. Not really.

MARC. It's a joke.

JODY. Right.

MARC. Sort of.

JODY. Um—

MARC. I'm joking about your mother, specifically—I mean unless you're lying to me and she's one of those really hot moms—

JODY. No.

MARC. Because I have a rule now about not dating anyone under 30, so.

JODY. Oh.

MARC. It's a recent thing.

JODY. I mean, that's cool, man—

MARC. It is. It is cool. You should try it.

JODY. Sure.

MARC. I'm telling you, once you date a woman who is 32 or 33, 35 even? How old are you?

JODY. Twenty-three.

MARC. Talk to me when you've lived in L.A. for fifteen years.

JODY. So does this mean—

(SHEENA *brings their drinks.*)

SHEENA. One soda with lime and one ice tea. Can I get y'all anything else right now?

JODY. I'm good.

MARC. I'm so sorry I didn't mention this before, but—is it Sheena? I like kind of *a lot* of lime.

SHEENA. Oh—

MARC. I should have said something when I ordered, but this one's a little small and—

SHEENA. Let me get you another one.

MARC. You don't mind?

SHEENA. Not at all! You just want one or two or—

MARC. One will be fine. Thank you.

(SHEENA *exits, he watches her go.*)

God, I miss Texas. You have no idea.

JODY. So, the location is in Round Rock?

MARC. It's dynamite. It's suburban and rural all at the same time. I swear to God, find the right location, and you're halfway there.

JODY. I just saw your film, um, *Initiation Rites?* And the locations in that are—

MARC. You what.

JODY. Your movie, from last year?

MARC. How did you, where did you get it.

JODY. I downloaded it.

MARC. Great. That's really great—

JODY. Did I do something wrong—

MARC. I was told they were never going to release it—

JODY. I was just online, and—I mean, you directed that, right, it's yours?

MARC. Did I direct it? Yes, if you can call it "directing" when you're forced to cast five of the six principals with relatives of the investor—

(SHEENA *brings the lime.*)

SHEENA. Here you—

MARC. (*Barreling through, holds up his finger to* SHEENA.) And then deal with his demands that entire scenes be reshot to show his girlfriend at a more flattering angle—

JODY. Yo, I didn't mean to—

MARC. Which I would have done in the first place, if she'd HAD a flattering angle. (*To* SHEENA.) The way you walked across the bar just now to deliver a slice of lime to an agitated but I assure you a very grateful customer—you displayed more intention in that simple action than the lead so-called actress in *Initiation Rites* did for a single moment in the entire movie.

SHEENA. She must've really sucked.

MARC. That, Sheena, is the understatement of the year. When they didn't get a distributor, I thought: thank God, at least no one else will have to suffer through her performance. The entire film was a waste, except for maybe one shot.

JODY. *The scene in the woods!* With the low-angle shot looking up at her. I mean, right?

(*Beat.* MARC *sees that* SHEENA's *interested.*)

MARC. Go on.

JODY. It was right after, what was her name—

MARC. *"Gabriella."*

JODY. Right. She's just chopped up the guy and buried him. She takes a step, and the camera is right there. Her bare foot sinks into the mud and you slowly pan up her body. There's blood and dirt caked on her arms and legs, and the trees are towering up behind her. And it's like: she's as powerful and as silent as those trees.

MARC. That's the one.

JODY. It's a great shot.

SHEENA. It sounds cool.

MARC. (*To* SHEENA, *this is all for her.*) We got on location and it just came to me, you know?

JODY. Totally—

MARC. (*To* SHEENA.) That's the thing about directing, you gotta be open all the time, filming in your head constantly, "What if we shoot it this way, what if we put the camera there—"

SHEENA. Right.

JODY. That is so true—

MARC. (*Still to* SHEENA.) People think it's about mapping everything out ahead of time, but to make a great film, you prepare, you prepare, and then you throw it all out the window and fly.

JODY. Right on, brother.

MARC. Don't say "brother." It makes you sound like an asshole.

JODY. Um—

MARC. Scream for me.

SHEENA. Excuse me?

MARC. I'm sorry, I'm being rude. Marc Hunter, I'm a film director.

SHEENA. I figured that out.

MARC. I'm going to be shooting a movie here in town and it just so happens that I need to recast a couple of roles.

SHEENA. Um, I'm not an actress.

MARC. Why don't you let me be the judge of that.

SHEENA. You want me to just scream? Right here in the bar.

MARC. I don't want you to "just scream." I want you to scream like…like you're all alone in a house. You're housesitting, friends of your parents. You thought it would be fun. Make your boyfriend a fancy dinner, make love to him in front of the fireplace. But your boyfriend won't be there 'til late and you're upstairs in that king-sized bed, all alone when you hear a noise: drip, drip, drip. It's coming from the attic. You call your boyfriend, he says it's probably just a leak. Get a bucket, he says, and he'll deal with it in the morning. So you find a bucket and a flashlight and ascend the creaking stairs into the deep darkness of the attic. You reach the top of the steps, pull on the light string, and click: the bulb is burned out. You don't want to go, but you have to now. You take a step, flash the light in front of you, and you see a pool of blood, it stretches back to an old wheelchair that's been tipped over, blood gathering beneath it, and there it is, drip, drip, dripping right in front of you and you look up to the rafters and you see it:

SHEENA. (*Screams. It's a knockout.*)

MARC. Yes!

JODY. Wow.

MARC. You were right there, you really saw it—

SHEENA. Holy crap—

JODY. That was amazing—

MARC. You're brilliant! Pretty but not too pretty, with that believably innocent quality—but at the same time I totally buy that you'd put up a hell of a fight—

JODY. Oh yeah!

MARC. You are the perfect Last Girl.

SHEENA. The last what?

MARC. The Last Girl. The last one to be killed. You're not SAG, or AFTRA are you?

SHEENA. What?

JODY. No.

MARC. (*He hands her his card.*) Email me your address, I'll get you a contract tomorrow. Shooting starts Thursday morning.

SHEENA. But, I have class. And I work and—

JODY. So ditch!

SHEENA. I can't just quit my job.

MARC. Well, Sheena, I hate to tear you away from all this, but, um: I'm offering you a role in a feature film.

SHEENA. How much do I get paid?

MARC. The non-union rate is five hundred a week. Principal shooting starts Thursday, and it goes without saying that you need to be 100 percent available, because as it turns out, time actually is money, and we're already behind schedule.

SHEENA. I want ten grand.

JODY. What?

MARC. Um—

SHEENA. Ten grand, plus a percentage of gross.

MARC. I'm sorry, the non-union rate is—

SHEENA. I make $500 a week here.

MARC. Okay, fair enough. I'll tell you what: we can do $800 a week.

SHEENA. No.

MARC. We don't normally negotiate this kind of thing—

SHEENA. If I'm the last girl to get killed, that means I'm in most of the movie.

JODY. That's true.

MARC. (*To* JODY.) Shut up. (*To* SHEENA.) I'll give you fifteen hundred dollars a week, okay? But that's it—

SHEENA. Ten grand, plus one percent gross.

MARC. Only investors get gross—

SHEENA. Then I want twenty grand.

MARC. Okay, did no one ever explain that when you negotiate, the high bidder generally comes down toward the low bidder until you reach a compromise somewhere in the middle?

SHEENA. You just hired a girl in a bar with no experience to play the Last Girl in your movie? Shooting starts the day after tomorrow, you're already behind schedule and I'm guessing every day you spend looking for a new Last Girl is gonna cost you a hell of a lot more than twenty grand.

MARC. I'll give you ten grand.

SHEENA. Twenty.

MARC. Ten, plus one percent net.

SHEENA. No.

MARC. Two percent net—

SHEENA. I don't believe in net.

MARC. Fifteen grand, and that's my final offer.

SHEENA. Done.

MARC. Thank God.

JODY. Holy shit.

SHEENA. I'm in the movie?

MARC. Welcome to *Bloodbath*.

SHEENA. Oh my God! I can't believe it! I'm so excited! I have to, I have to go quit my job!

(SHEENA *exits.* MARC *slams his club soda, gets up.*)

MARC. I have to get out of here, I have to explain to my one remaining investor what the hell just happened.

JODY. But, wait! You never actually said—

MARC. You're in. You'll get gas money, cold tacos on the set and two points net—and don't even think about negotiating.

JODY. You are not gonna regret this, broth—Marc.

MARC. Stop by my hotel in the morning and pick up the script. And start tracking down a meat hook, the biggest claw-foot bathtub you can find, and a wheelchair.

(*Sound of whirring.*)
(*Immediate shift to:*)

Scene 3

FRANCES' *house.* FRANCES *whirs by on her scooter. A knock is heard. She opens the front door to reveal* CHRISTI, *who stands holding a clipboard.*

CHRISTI. Hi, how are you doing today?

FRANCES. That depends, are you Mormon?

CHRISTI. Um, *no*—

FRANCES. I like the Mormons. You can say anything, they just smile.

CHRISTI. I'm Christi Garcia, I'm Assistant Director of the Holy Shepherd Justice League? We're in the area to let people know about an important issue that—

>(FRANCES *slams the door in* CHRISTI's *face, cutting her off.* CHRISTI *knocks again.* FRANCES *opens the door.*)

CHRISTI. Are you aware that there's an abortion clinic being built across the street from the mall? It's going to be six blocks from LBJ High School.

FRANCES. Sounds convenient.

>(CHRISTI *hands her a flier.*)

CHRISTI. Holy Shepherd is staging a protest tomorrow, all the information is right here—

FRANCES. What's to protest? Get an abortion, stop for an Orange Julius, still make it to cheerleading practice.

CHRISTI. Cynicism comes from a lack of hope, Mrs…?

FRANCES. *MS.*

CHRISTI. It comes from deep despair. I am living proof of what young people can accomplish when they reject our anything-goes culture and embrace the values of self-respect and chastity.

FRANCES. I bet you're a big hit at parties.

CHRISTI. I refuse to stand by and let the cancer of immorality spread unchecked. When you decide you want to take action, when you're ready to help create a better society—

>(FRANCES *slams the door in her face once more. There is another knock.*)

FRANCES. Look, I already—

>(*She opens the door.* JODY *is standing there with a script.*)

You're definitely not a Mormon.

JODY. Um, I'm looking for Sheena? I need to drop this off for her. Is she here—

FRANCES. What is this.

>(FRANCES *grabs the script from him.*)

JODY. The script, for the movie? Are you her mom? Marc asked me to drop it off and—

FRANCES. *Bloodbath.*

JODY. Yeah.

FRANCES. A Film by Marc Hunter.

JODY. It's actually not bad—

FRANCES. Marc Hunter—

JODY. A couple of clever twists, and—

FRANCES. Marc with a "C"—

JODY. He's the—

FRANCES. Smarmy, beady-eyed hustler who went to school here?

JODY. Hey, you know him.

(FRANCES *zips into the house, taking the script.*)

(*She pops a handful of pills.*)

JODY. So, okay, I mean, you are Sheena's mom, right? Sheena lives here?

FRANCES. Get out.

(FRANCES *starts to charge him.*)

JODY. I'm going, I'm going!

FRANCES. Wait!

(*He stops.*)

What exactly is Sheena doing with this movie.

JODY. She's in it? She's, like, the main girl.

FRANCES. I see.

JODY. She's gonna be amazing. You should hear her scream.

FRANCES. Oh, I will.

(*Immediate shift to:*)

Scene 4

Sonic. The car. SHEENA *in the driver's seat. She leans out to order into the drive up box.* HILDY *sits next to her.*

DRIVE UP VOICE. (*Garbled mess.*)

SHEENA. Hi, two chicken strip dinners, an order of chili cheese fries, and two Diet Cokes please.

DRIVE UP VOICE. (*More garbled mess.*)

HILDY. Get something for Mom.

SHEENA. I did. I'm going out, genius.

HILDY. With who?

SHEENA. None of your business. I do have a life.

HILDY. Okay?

(SHEENA *puts on a pair of very hip sunglasses.*)

When did you get those?

SHEENA. Today. I needed a new pair.

HILDY. That why you were so late?

SHEENA. Actually, I was late because I was getting the muffler replaced. The muffler on this car that takes you everywhere—not that you even noticed that you couldn't hear me coming four blocks away.

HILDY. Oh. Yeah, it is a lot quieter!

SHEENA. Look, you need to start taking more responsibility.

HILDY. I already clean the whole house.

SHEENA. For rides, for getting yourself to and from places. I mean, what do you think is gonna happen when I'm done with school?

HILDY. I'll get my license in June.

SHEENA. And you're gonna drive what car?

HILDY. I don't know.

SHEENA. Well, I'm not gonna be around forever, so you need to get used to it.

HILDY. What's going on.

SHEENA. What's going on is that I'm twenty-one years old, I'm supposed to have my own life, not be taking care of you all the time. I'm not your mother.

HILDY. I know that.

SHEENA. Plus I've been cast in a movie.

HILDY. What?!

> (CAR HOP *arrives with bags of food and drinks.* SHEENA *passes them off to* HILDY, *gives the* CAR HOP *a bill.*)

CAR HOP. Two chicken strip dinners, one chili cheese fry, two Diets, nine forty-seven please.

HILDY. You're lying.

SHEENA. Here's ten, keep the change.

CAR HOP. Thanks.

> (CAR HOP *exits.*)

HILDY. You're a marketing major!

SHEENA. So?

HILDY. Seriously?

SHEENA. *Yeah.* The director is in from L.A. He came in to Buster's last night with this film guy I kind of know and the next thing, he's offering me a part.

HILDY. It's not porn, is it?

SHEENA. NO!

HILDY. I'm just asking.

SHEENA. It's a horror movie, all right, and I'm the lead, I'm the Last Girl.

HILDY. The last what?

SHEENA. The Last Girl, the last to be—I'm basically the main character, so I have to be on the set all the time. You're gonna have to get rides and figure out dinner and stuff.

HILDY. Have you told Mom?

SHEENA. No, and you're not going to either.

HILDY. She's gonna freak.

SHEENA. She is a freak.

HILDY. You know how she gets about horror movies—

SHEENA. Which is why no one is telling her.

HILDY. You don't think she's gonna notice you're gone all the time.

SHEENA. Not as long as her prescription doesn't run out.

HILDY. When she finds out, I want to be there to see it.

SHEENA. Do you know how many girls would kill for a chance like this?

HILDY. Oh, sorry, I assumed you were going to *be* killed—

SHEENA. I'm serious!

HILDY. Or forced to saw off your own arms, or get gutted by a maniac or whatever—

SHEENA. *They're paying me fifteen thousand dollars, okay?* Fifteen grand that's gonna fix the A.C. and pay for your SAT prep course, and get me the hell out of here when I graduate so I don't end up working at Buster's for the rest of my life. So I don't really care right now about Mom's "feminist critique of the horror genre." Because let me tell you something: *It cannot be exploitation when they are paying me this much money.*

HILDY. This is gonna be so rad.

SHEENA. You know what? Tell her. I don't care. She can't stop me. I mean, seriously, she hasn't left the house for almost a year. What's she gonna do?

(*Immediate shift to:*)

Scene 5

FRANCES' *house.* HILDY *and* SHEENA *step into the house holding their Cokes and the Sonic bag.* FRANCES *sits on her Rascal, ready for battle. She holds the copy of the script.*

FRANCES. You.

HILDY. Uh-oh.

SHEENA. What is that?

FRANCES. This?

(*She rips a single page from the script.*)

SHEENA. Don't!

FRANCES. Oh, I thought you didn't know what it was.

SHEENA. Where did you get it.

FRANCES. I was actually hoping that you DIDN'T know—

SHEENA. Give it to me—

FRANCES. Because this, *this* is a chronicle of female degradation, one hundred and five pages in which a virginal young woman named "Sloan" is terrorized—

(FRANCES *rips another page.*)

SHEENA. Mother!

FRANCES. (*And another.*) —sexually objectified—

SHEENA. Stop!

FRANCES. (*And another.*) TORTURED AND RAPED AFTER BEING BATHED IN ANOTHER WOMAN'S BLOOD.

HILDY. Gross.

FRANCES. No, Hildy. "Gross" is a booger. "Gross" is vomit, or feces. *This* is a contagion in which the most reprehensible acts are packaged as entertainment— not just entertainment, but as TITILLATION, so that men like Marc Hunter will continue to think that it's HOT to see women RAPED AND KILLED! I am going to track him down and cram every single page down his throat, page after page until his dangly little uvula is castrated by a thousand paper cuts and he chokes on his own blood! Or maybe I'll just burn it.

(SHEENA *makes a quick grab for the script, but* FRANCES *zips away on her scooter. A chase.*)

SHEENA. I won't let you!

FRANCES. Where are the matches!

SHEENA. I am doing this movie!

FRANCES. OVER MY DEAD BODY!

SHEENA. I can arrange that!

FRANCES. I will lock you in the closet before I let that happen! I will force-feed you the collected works of Betty Friedan! I will not allow you to be tortured and humiliated—

SHEENA. I WANT TO BE TORTURED, OKAY?

FRANCES. What did you just say.

SHEENA. I want to be tied up, and look scared and scream my head off, and you know why? BECAUSE IT'S A MOVIE.

FRANCES. I am not hearing this.

SHEENA. I AM IN A MOVIE! I'm the STAR! And I didn't just get the part! I NEGOTIATED! I demanded more money and I GOT IT! YOU'RE SUPPOSED TO BE PROUD OF ME!

FRANCES. I'm supposed to be proud you want to be degraded?

SHEENA. IT'S NOT REAL, MOTHER! I'M IN CONTROL!

FRANCES. You're actually retarded, aren't you?

SHEENA. You know what? I'm outta here.

> (SHEENA *bounds up the stairs. Sound of drawers opening and closing.* FRANCES *comes to the foot of the stairs, talking up at* SHEENA.)

FRANCES. I always knew you weren't smart, but I didn't think you were actually STUPID. Have you learned NOTHING? Watching me bang my head on the glass ceiling, day after day—

> (SHEENA *reappears at the top of the stairs.*)

SHEENA. You haven't worked in years.

FRANCES. I HAVE CHRONIC FATIGUE!

SHEENA. You want to stop me from making this movie?
Here's your chance: Come up here and stop me.

> (*An expectation.*)

FRANCES. Don't mock me.

SHEENA. I dare you. Walk up these stairs and admit that there's nothing wrong with you, and MAYBE I won't do the movie.

HILDY. Sheena, what are you doing?

SHEENA. The choice is yours, Mom.

HILDY. You know she can't go up stairs.

SHEENA. Oh yes she can. She just doesn't want to.

FRANCES. That's not true.

SHEENA. I want you to admit that you're a lazy, bitter drug addict—

HILDY. Sheena, stop it.

SHEENA. Who would rather rail about injustice than GET A JOB—

FRANCES. You're beyond cruel.

SHEENA. What's cruel is pretending you're too tired to even walk across a room, and forcing your daughter to support you so you can spend all your time screaming that you've been discriminated against.

FRANCES. I HAVE been discriminated against—

SHEENA. The city gave Marshall Davis that cleaning contract because you couldn't do the job.

FRANCES. I DID the job.

SHEENA. You took a whole day to clean one floor!

FRANCES. Hello! I'm DISABLED, of course it's going to take me longer.

SHEENA. You are such a victim! God! You talk about how people are so afraid of strong, powerful women "like you." But no one is afraid of you, and you know why? Because you don't DO ANYTHING! Ever since Dad left you've done nothing! Well I'm actually DOING something now, and you can't stop me.

(SHEENA *disappears onto the second floor.*)

FRANCES. Oh, so this is your big statement? Well, I've got a question for you: Who controls the film? Who controls the money, huh? I'll give you a hint: it's not you! You and the rest of your generation, you're all too busy getting boob jobs and counting carbs to notice that WOMEN ARE STILL ROYALLY SCREWED. They pat you on the head, tell you discrimination is over. Who needs equal rights when you've got the WNBA? They trot out Condoleezza Rice once a month like she's the EQUALITY BONG, fire up the Katie Couric Hooka on the nightly news so you're all too stoned to notice that WE STILL ONLY MAKE 76 CENTS ON THE DOLLAR!

(SHEENA *barrels down the stairs with a bag of clothes and climbs over* FRANCES *like she's a piece of furniture.*)

SHEENA. Get out of my way.

FRANCES. I am not going to let you—OW!

HILDY. Stop it!

FRANCES. You are NOT taking my car.

SHEENA. It's MY car, Mom. I bought it after you totaled the last one ramming into Marshall Davis' Expedition.

HILDY. Where are you going.

FRANCES. If you do this movie, I am disowning you, Sheena. I'll never speak to you again.

HILDY. Mom!

SHEENA. Fine.

HILDY. Sheena!

SHEENA. She's all yours.

HILDY. You can't leave. What am I supposed to do?!

SHEENA. You're the genius. Figure it out.

FRANCES. They've turned my own daughter against me.

SHEENA. No, you did that all on your own.

(*Immediate shift to:*)

Scene 6

Lobby Bar. SHEENA *approaches* MARC, *who sits at a table with a club soda and an open bottle of beer.*

SHEENA. Marc, I'm so sorry to keep you waiting—

MARC. It's okay.

SHEENA. I know it sounds lame, "the dog ate my script," but seriously, if you met my dog—

MARC. It's not a big deal. I've got another copy up in my room. (*Catching himself.*) Which I will bring down to you.

SHEENA. (*Off the beer.*) Is this for me?

MARC. Well, it's not for me.

SHEENA. You are so nice, and I feel like such a loser. You asked me to meet you here to talk about the movie, and acting, and I haven't even read the script—

MARC. No, no, it's better this way, actually. Because here's the thing: I don't want you thinking about things too much.

SHEENA. Okay?

MARC. I'm serious. That's the biggest mistake actors make. Over-preparation. You've got such a great, open quality, Sheena, and to *be* your character, to really *be* Sloan? That's all you need.

SHEENA. Really?

MARC. Absolutely. Acting is all about being in the moment. They shouldn't even call it "acting." They should call it *reacting.* Because that's what you're doing.

SHEENA. I never thought of that.

MARC. It's very instinctual. And that's what you've got. Losing Jenna Long and, honestly, a good chunk of the budget with her, that was, hard to take. But now? I really think you're gonna be better.

SHEENA. Me?

MARC. You're gonna be the new Jenna Long.

SHEENA. Holy crap.

MARC. It's a big deal.

(*Beat.*)

SHEENA. (*Searching.*) She's the, girl from, from that show, right?

MARC. On FX, yeah. And she's good. But I don't want to work with people who've been through the L.A. meat grinder. That's why I wanted to shoot in Texas.

SHEENA. Right.

MARC. I mean, who needs the attitude when I can find such an unspoiled, untainted, unbelievably attractive, young actress right here.

SHEENA. Um, wow.

MARC. I mean it's also cheaper—it's a lot cheaper. But to this day some of the best work I ever saw and ever did happened right here. Matt McConaughey didn't know what he was doing any more than the rest of us. We just did it, you know? Filming out of the back of some shitty van, trespassing on construction sites. That's what I'm after with this one.

SHEENA. You know Matthew McConaughey?

MARC. I know a lot of people.

SHEENA. Oh my God.

MARC. In L.A., that's all anybody cares about: who do you know, who's attached to your project. It has nothing to do with vision. You should move there. As soon as you can.

SHEENA. What?

MARC. I mean, if you're at all interested in having a career as an actress, which I think you could.

SHEENA. Really?

MARC. Absolutely. But if you're gonna do it, don't wait.

SHEENA. Well, I have to finish school.

MARC. No you don't. I mean, do whatever you want, but L.A. is obsessed with youth. And I hate to say it, but it's especially true for women. The women who wait, or God help them, the ones who go to grad school and THEN move to L.A. when they're 25? They either end up teaching Pilates or doing porn.

SHEENA. 25 isn't old.

MARC. How old do you think I am.

SHEENA. I don't know, like, 30?

MARC. I am. I am thirty. Which is old for a man in L.A., but it's still not as old as a 25-year-old actress.

SHEENA. That's crazy.

MARC. The only unknown 25-year-olds who work get cast as the fat friend. And you, Sheena, are not a fat friend.

SHEENA. There's actually a "fat friend" category?

MARC. Um, *Yeah.* It's pretty competitive, actually. There aren't that many fat roles, and, well, nobody wants a fat Pilates instructor, if you know what I'm saying.

SHEENA. *They cast the fat friend in porn?*

MARC. *Niche porn.*

SHEENA. You're making this up.

MARC. I've got pay-per-view. We can go up to my room and settle this right now.
    (*Beat. Did he say what I think he just said?*)

SHEENA. What?

MARC. *That's reacting.*

SHEENA. Wait, what?

MARC. God, you're perfect, so in the moment—

SHEENA. I was?

MARC. You're gonna be amazing on camera. I want you to remember this, Sheena, this exact moment. How you were open and listening and just ready to react. If you do that on set? I promise you: I will capture it, and you will blow everyone away. Will you trust me enough to do that?

SHEENA. Yes, I will.

> (*They look at each other. A moment of connection.* MARC *begins to caress her, almost unconsciously.* SHEENA *is unsure how to react.*)

MARC. How's your beer, is it good?

SHEENA. Yeah, I like Shiner.

MARC. Me too.

SHEENA. Oh, I thought you didn't drink.

MARC. I don't. You want another?

SHEENA. That's okay—

MARC. Let me get you another—

SHEENA. Marc, are you trying to get me drunk?

MARC. No! God, no—

SHEENA. I'm just teasing—

MARC. No, I need to attack this head on. I can feel, that there's a little attraction happening—

SHEENA. Um—

MARC. But you should know that I have absolutely sworn off all, romantic entanglements with women under thirty.

SHEENA. Okay.

MARC. So I've come clean about that. If I hadn't, you know, my sponsor would've crucified me.

SHEENA. Totally.

MARC. And it's nothing personal, Sheena. You're a, beautiful young woman. But now that I'm, thirty, I've found I'm just much more in tune with women who are, a little older.

SHEENA. I really wasn't trying to—

MARC. It's understandable.

SHEENA. I'm so sorry if I was doing something that made you think—I'm just a little scattered, I had this big blowout with my mom, so it's been—

MARC. It's okay—

SHEENA. Kind of a crazy day. I mean almost everything I own is in this bag right now? I have no idea where I'm even staying tonight, so I'm just a little, whatever—

MARC. You don't know where you're staying?

SHEENA. But starting now, I am one hundred percent focused. I am gonna work so hard, Marc. I'm gonna be open, and in the moment, and I will do absolutely everything you tell me to do.

MARC. Well, that's, music to a director's ears.

SHEENA. Good. So should we go up to your room now?

MARC. Um—

SHEENA. I mean, I have to get the script, right?

(*Immediate shift to:*)

Scene 7

FRANCES' *house. Night. She sits in her scooter at the table. She's lined up all her pills across the table. A mallet is nearby.*

FRANCES. Marc Hunter. You like to watch. You like to hear women scream, don't you. I should have taken you down when I had the chance. Come on, Frances.

(*She counts the pills.*)

Onetwothreefourfivesixseveneightnine… Seventeen. Seventeen little lovelies, lovely blues. This was all part of their plan, wasn't it? Keep her doped up, keep her quiet! You have to get rid of them, Frances. Think about him. Sadistic little prick, it all happened because of him and his movie. Just do it. Do it. DO IT!

(FRANCES *swings the mallet, screaming and smashing the pills to bits.* HILDY *runs down the stairs.*)

HILDY. Mom!

FRANCES. AAAAAAARRRRRGGGGHHHHHAAA!

(HILDY *watches as* FRANCES *smashes all the pills in a flurry of banging.*)

(*An expectation.*)

HILDY. Why did you just hammer all of your pills?

FRANCES. Because I'm not taking them anymore.

HILDY. What.

FRANCES. I'm done. Finished. Cold turkey.

(FRANCES *suddenly puts her face to the table and takes a full snort of the pill powder.*)

Get me the dust buster!

HILDY. What are you—

FRANCES. Now, before I change my mind!

    (*Immediate shift to:*)

Scene 8

    The Set. A suburban kitchen. MARC *is agitated, pacing.* JODY *is on his cell phone. Walkie-talkies dangle from both* MARC's *and* JODY's *necks.*

MARC. Where is he?

JODY. (*To* MARC.) He says the directions he got were—

MARC. How far away is he?

JODY. (*Into the phone.*) How far are you from the set—? (*To* MARC.) He doesn't know, he's looking for a place to ask directions but—

MARC. Why didn't he call when he realized he was lost—

JODY. (*Overlapping.*) He kept thinking it was gonna be—

MARC. Instead of WAITING until he was already late to call—

JODY. (*Into the phone.*) I know, man, it's cool, it's just—

MARC. IT IS NOT COOL.

JODY. (*Into the phone.*) Okay, okay, yeah, Pedernales is like—

MARC. Hang up the phone.

JODY. (*Into the phone.*) I think you're too far south, man, you're—

MARC. (*Shouting into his walkie-talkie.*) I SAID HANG UP THE PHONE.

JODY. (*Into the phone.*) I'll call you back.

    (JODY *hangs up.* SHEENA *has entered, wearing her film costume—a form-fitting tank top with a bright cropped hoodie, and short shorts.*)

SHEENA. It all fits.

MARC. Great, yes. You look great.

SHEENA. Thanks.

MARC. You look really— All right, Jody, you're going to stand in for Brian, we're gonna mark through the scene. I'll get all the shots I can of Sheena, while you get back on the phone and see if you can get that idiot here before we get further behind.

JODY. Got it.

MARC. So. You open the door, the first shot is the two of you crossing the threshold, your magical weekend getaway. BRIAN, you find the light switch—

JODY. Over here—

MARC. Yes, and the lights come on and you both look around slowly, slowly. SLOAN, you're nervous, but you're not scared—

SHEENA. Not yet—

MARC. Definitely not. You're excited, you're apprehensive, you want him to like you.

SHEENA. Right.

MARC. BRIAN, you're mostly thinking about how smart you are for getting the keys from your uncle's buddy so you can fuck Sloan's brains out.

JODY. Got it.

MARC. But in a sweet way. Hit this mark, we'll do a nice 360 around the two of you, thinking all of these things, so we see how harmless and normal the place looks.

JODY. Right.

MARC. Then BRIAN, hit your mark here for the line, "See? What did I tell you?"

JODY. Right.

MARC. SLOAN you stay right here, still a little apprehensive.

(MARC *demonstrates for* SHEENA.)

"Are you sure he said it was okay? You hardly know this guy."

(*To* JODY.)

Brian:

JODY. (*In a leading man voice.*) "He gave me the key, didn't he?"

MARC. Yes. Grab hands.

JODY. "Don't worry, he's out of town until Monday. We've got the place all to ourselves."

SHEENA. (*Imitating* MARC's *vocal quality and body language.*) "Until everybody else gets here."

MARC. Good.

JODY. "It'll be fun."

SHEENA. "I know. I just wanted this weekend to be…special."

JODY. "It will be. I promise."

MARC. And the shot goes back to Sloan as Brian moves to the next room.

JODY. "Come on, check it out."

MARC. (*To* SHEENA.) The camera's still on you, scanning your face, you decide to follow your man, and walk out of the shot.

(JODY's *phone rings.*)

JODY. It's him.

MARC. Go.

(JODY *steps away to answer the phone.*)

Once he's gone—

SHEENA. Look, before Jody comes back—I just wanted to say thanks, again, for letting me crash in your room last night.

MARC. Don't mention it.

SHEENA. You totally saved me, and I really didn't intend to impose, or—

MARC. No, no—

SHEENA. Or make you uncomfortable, you know—

MARC. I was, totally comfortable. I mean it's not like we were sleeping together!

SHEENA. No! I know!

MARC. I mean, they give you two beds, someone may as well use the, the other one.

SHEENA. I just I wanted to say thanks. I got ahold of my friend Heather, I'm gonna stay with her now—

MARC. Great. That's great—

SHEENA. So it won't happen again.

MARC. Well, you know, any time you want to—or if things at Heather's are, whatever, you know you can always, always—

(MARC's *phone rings—an inappropriately sexy song. He silences it immediately.*) I'll get that later, let's skip ahead. Madison calls, she's having car trouble, they're gonna be late. You and Brian have been playing hide and seek, it's sexy, it's playful, at some point you lose the jacket?

SHEENA. (*She takes off the jacket.*) Right.

MARC. So you're exploring the house. Something seems strange, and now you can't find Brian. Is this part of the game? Maybe. You step in here to look, hit this mark.

SHEENA. (*In her movie voice.*) "Brian? Come on, where are you?"

MARC. The room is empty. You notice the family photos: a stern minister with a very young Victor and the beautiful Elise, *who you realize looks almost exactly like you.* You see the framed newspaper clipping about Elise's death. A cold wind blows through the room. You shudder, and turn and see: the door to the porch is mysteriously open. You hit this mark here. Now you're getting worried.

SHEENA. "Brian?"

MARC. You hear a noise. You go to the porch, but it's not coming from there. What is it? Your senses are on high alert, your nipples should be like rocks.

SHEENA. What?

MARC. Skip it. You shut the door, shivering. You listen, trying to figure out where the noise is coming from. You hear it, coming from in here. But that can't be, that's impossible. Hit this mark—

SHEENA. "Come on, this isn't funny."

MARC. Open the door and—

(SHEENA *opens the freezer door.* BRIDGET, *a brunette, spills out. She's virtually naked, her neck and wrists have been slit.*)

SHEENA. (*Screams.*)

MARC. *YES!*

SHEENA. Oh my God.

BRIDGET. Hey. I'm Bridget.

MARC. Oh, I'm sorry, did you guys not meet yet?

SHEENA. No.

MARC. Bridget's dead girl number one.

BRIDGET. The unsuspecting realtor who gets it in the first ten minutes.

SHEENA. Right. Nice to meet you.

MARC. (*To* SHEENA.) That reminds me: You're not claustrophobic, are you?

SHEENA. Um—

> (*Immediate shift to:*)

Scene 9

> FRANCES' *house.* FRANCES *is on the phone. She digs through an old toolbox as she waits to leave a message. Some tools she considers and then discards back into the toolbox. When she finds a tool she likes, she sets it out on the table, like a surgeon assembling her instruments.*
>
> *Just as* FRANCES *begins to leave the message,* HILDY *enters with a sad-looking pair of soccer shoes. When she hears* FRANCES *speak, she stops short, unseen by* FRANCES. *As* HILDY *listens, she slowly backs away, becoming more and more anxious.*

FRANCES. Mr. Hunter, this is Belinda Chapman from Channel Five News. I'm a, real *fan* of your work, all the way back to your earliest days here in Austin.

> (*She finds a hatchet, hefts it in her hand, sets it on the table.*)

Oh yes. And I would LOVE to interview you about your new project. *Bloodbath?* I have to say, it sounds like a real crowd pleaser.

> (*She snaps a large needle-nose pliers in the air, adds them to her selected tools.*)

So, I thought we'd meet at the set. I think that'd be best. I really want to get an up-close look at your—

> (*She revs a cordless drill.*)

—artistic process. I am really looking forward to this. You name the time, Mr. Hunter. And I will be there.

> (HILDY *pulls out her phone.*)
>
> (*Immediate shift to:*)

Scene 10

Break Room—The Set. SHEENA *and* MARCY. SHEENA *is still in her costume, and now has mud streaks up her legs.* MARCY *is a redhead who appears to have had half her face burned off. The other half of her face is perfect. They drink Diet Cokes and eat chips. An occasional scream is heard—filming continues nearby.*

MARCY. God I can't wait to get home and wash this stuff off.

SHEENA. I bet.

(A scream is heard. They continue their conversation.)

MARCY. Amanda's good, though. I mean this stuff she did on my face, with the burns—

SHEENA. It's, amazing.

MARCY. It totally looks like someone held me down on a hot griddle. Which is good, because, you know, I was held down on a hot griddle!

SHEENA. Right.

(SHEENA's phone rings, she silences it.)

MARCY. So when do you get killed?

SHEENA. Um, later. At the end, actually.

MARCY. You're the Last Girl?

SHEENA. Yeah.

MARCY. Wow, that's gotta be cool. How do they do it?

SHEENA. I get impaled, I think.

MARCY. Awesome. Save the best for last, right?

SHEENA. Marc said it might change, but I think I get to take Victor down with me.

(Her phone rings again, she silences it.)

He's been keeping me chained up while he kills everyone else, because I look like his dead sister?

MARCY. Uh-huh.

(More screaming, SHEENA talks over it.)

SHEENA. After he washes me in all the blood he's collected, he wants to put me in one of Elise's old dresses. That's when I make a break for it. He comes after me and we end up crashing through the railing, and I fall and get impaled on the same spike as Brian. Victor freaks, 'cause he wasn't gonna kill me, he was gonna keep me? So it's like I'm Elise dying all over again. And while he's trying to keep me from bleeding out, I grab his knife and gut him!

MARCY. Cool!

SHEENA. *(Her phone rings again.)* Ugh.

MARCY. Someone really wants to talk to you.

SHEENA. It's my sister. She's been calling all day because my mom is, my mom is crazy.

MARCY. I totally know what you mean.

SHEENA. No, I mean, she's literally crazy. And I feel bad my sister has to deal with her, but, I just, I need a break from it all.

> (*Sound of a chainsaw. A* WOMAN *screams, "No, no, please!"*)

I need to have some normalcy for once, you know?

MARCY. Totally.

SHEENA. My sister's probably freaking out about some stupid thing my mom is saying she's gonna do. But she never actually DOES anything. She's all talk. And if I answer, I'm just gonna get sucked back in.

MARCY. Then I say don't do it.

SHEENA. I deserve to have some fun, right?

MARCY. Hell yeah! Oh, crap.

SHEENA. What?

MARCY. (MARCY *pulls something out of her mouth.*) Part of my burn flaked off.

SHEENA. Let me see.

MARCY. Amanda's gonna kill me.

SHEENA. Oh, I'm sure she can fix it.

MARCY. I better go. I'll see you.

SHEENA. Yeah.

> (SHEENA's *phone rings again, she silences it.*)
> (*Immediate shift to:*)

Scene 11

> HILDY, *on the phone in a tight light—she is hiding somewhere in the house.*

HILDY. Sheena? Look, I know you're busy being mutilated and all, but seriously, Mom has flipped her can. She stopped taking her pills, Sheena. Mom is SOBER. She got Dad's old tools and set up target practice with the staple gun, and now she's making me help her build explosives! She wants to blow up the guy who's directing the movie. She keeps talking about how she's not gonna be a joke on the ten o'clock news this time? I seriously think she's gonna do something so please pick up your freakin' phone!

FRANCES. (*Offstage.*) Hildy!

HILDY. I'm freaking out, I don't know what to do and I need new soccer shoes by Friday! Call me.

FRANCES. (*Offstage.*) Hildy come here!

(HILDY *sneaks out of her spot and enters the living room where* FRANCES *sits, in her scooter.*)

HILDY. I'm right here, Mom.

FRANCES. Where?

(*There is a board with wires sticking out of it on the table now, along with an assortment of tools and plastic bottles—a ridiculous attempt to make a bomb.* FRANCES *is a wreck, she's twitching and shaking. The rumpled remains of the script, and the Holy Shepherd flier, are strewn about.* HILDY *stands out of* FRANCES' *line of vision, packing her backpack, putting on her bike helmet.*)

HILDY. I was looking for more plastic.

FRANCES. Get it and let's finish.

HILDY. Um, I have to go to school, Mom.

FRANCES. Screw school!

HILDY. You're shaking.

FRANCES. Just ignore it.

HILDY. And sweating a lot—

FRANCES. It'll stop in a minute.

HILDY. I really think I should call Dr. Mosier—

FRANCES. NO! That pill-pushing prick. He's practically been force-feeding me narcotics for the last fifteen years! Trying to keep me from DOING SOMETHING. Well, NOT ANYMORE.

HILDY. Okay, Mom: I know this is not really about fixing the toaster.

FRANCES. Keep working.

HILDY. You could go to jail for building a bomb.

FRANCES. Bomb? Who said anything about a bomb.

HILDY. The instructions you printed off the Internet say it.

Look, I know you're upset about Sheena and the movie, but I mean you've already got a deferred sentence for trying to run over Marshall Davis after he got the cleaning contract—

FRANCES. I THOUGHT I WAS PRESSING THE BRAKE.

HILDY. If you try to blow up this director they are gonna put you away.

FRANCES. Do you know how many crimes go unsolved each year? How many criminals are never brought to justice? Murderers and rapists—

HILDY. Mom—

FRANCES. HUNDREDS. THOUSANDS. Half the time the police don't even LOOK.

HILDY. I think they're gonna look for a bomber.

FRANCES. If they'd been looking, they would have caught him before it happened again! Then that self-righteous dyke getting on the news saying I should have done something. Well NOW, I am going to DO SOMETHING. And this time, NO ONE is going to be LAUGHING!

(HILDY *has quietly taken the key to* FRANCES' *scooter.*)

What are you doing. Hey! HEY!

(HILDY *stands out of reach, holding the key.*)

HILDY. I'm taking your key, I swear this is for your own good.

(FRANCES *reflexively presses the button on her chair; nothing happens. A moment of horror.*)

FRANCES. *Give it back.*

HILDY. I'm going to school.

FRANCES. Give me my key!

HILDY. Promise you'll just stay here until I get back, okay?

FRANCES. Hildegard McKinney—

HILDY. *I don't think you're faking.* Okay? I know Sheena does, and a lot of other people. My friends, and most of my teachers. Coach Conner—

FRANCES. That health Nazi always hated me—

HILDY. But if you were only pretending to be disabled, that would mean that all this time—my whole life basically—you've never been there. That you've never come to any of my soccer games or the awards assembly or anything, not because you couldn't but because you didn't want to.

FRANCES. Hildy, you know that's not true—

HILDY. (*Overlapping.*) And I know that's not true! You want to be a good mom, it's just. You're in a lot of pain. Right?

(*An expectation.*)

FRANCES. I hurt *so much.*

HILDY. I know.

FRANCES. I never wanted to be like this. They did this to me. You see that, don't you? Things were supposed to get better—

HILDY. They will—

FRANCES. No, no, they won't, not unless we do something—

HILDY. I'm taking your key, okay?

FRANCES. We have to stop them, Hildy—

HILDY. Because then you'll be safe here. Because you can't go anywhere without your chair, right?

FRANCES. You're so smart, I know we can do it—

HILDY. So I'm putting a bottle of water, and, and a Hot Pocket on the table for you—

FRANCES. We can finish it!

HILDY. I'll just be at school—

FRANCES. Don't leave me!

(HILDY *turns on the radio.*)

HILDY. You can listen to the news, and when I get home—

FRANCES. We have to take a stand—

HILDY. I'll be back, I swear.

FRANCES. Hildy, don't go, don't—

(HILDY *exits.*)

FRANCES. HILDY! Stupid Internet instructions! Think. Think, Frances.

RADIO. ...In breaking news, a bomb went off this morning at the site of the proposed Emma Goldman clinic on Payne Avenue. Anti-abortion protesters organized by Holy Shepherd Church gathered at the site last night in an effort to prevent the clinic from opening. In a statement released earlier today, church leaders denied any involvement in the bombing. Fortunately, no one was injured. In other news...

(FRANCES *springs into action. She grabs the phone cord, pulls it to her. She finds the Holy Shepherd flier, dials the number, waits for someone to pick up.*)

FRANCES. Yes, may I speak to— (*She refers to the sheet of paper.*) Christi Garcia? Thank you, I'll hold.

(*Immediate shift to:*)

Scene 12

The Set. BETH, *a blonde in soccer mom clothes strides onto the set where* MARC *is getting* JODY *into costume and instructing him.*

MARC. (*To* JODY.) Keep your face front, so we get a good shot of the mask, that's the most important thing.

JODY. Right—

BETH. Where the hell is Tyler?

MARC. He's been replaced, all right?

BETH. Jesus Christ.

MARC. Why is this so baggy?

JODY. Dude, Tyler was a lot bigger than me, but maybe I can—

MARC. Lose it. Just go with the mask.

JODY. Yeah.

(SHEENA *enters, watches.*)

MARC. When you start pushing her through the saw, make sure you really sell it, I want to see how much effort it takes to cut through her skull.

JODY. Got it.

SHEENA. Where's Tyler? Why is Jody dressed like Victor now?

BETH. Didn't you hear? It's amateur night.

MARC. (*To* BETH.) It's gonna be fine!

BETH. Sorry, Mr. Scorsese. (*To* SHEENA.) I'm so moving to L.A., just as soon as I finish grad school.

MARC. Let's get set up for the take. Get your mask on, SLOAN'S MOM, get into position.

> (JODY *puts on a creepy mask, while* BETH/SLOAN'S MOM *slips her arms through two ropes attached to a table so that she appears to be tied down.*)

JODY. Do you want me to say the lines?

MARC. Yeah—just keep the scene going. We'll dub it later if we have to.

> (MARC's *phone rings. He hands it to* SHEENA.)

Damnit—this is that reporter again. Find out when she's coming for the interview.

SHEENA. Sure—

> (SHEENA *stuffs the phone in her armpit and runs for an exit.*)

MARC. (*Into his walkie.*) Standing by.

JODY. (*Grabbing his walkie from his back pocket.*) Standing by.

> (*He stuffs it back in his pocket.*)

MARC. And action!

BETH/SLOAN'S MOM. I know you have my daughter, and you won't get away with it!

> (*Sound of the circular saw starts as* SHEENA *steps off the set into a tight spotlight. Lights go out on the set, but we continue to hear the sound of the saw and screaming as filming continues.*)

SHEENA. (*Into the phone.*) Hello? Hello? (*She's missed the call.*) Crap. (*She looks at the number to redial and sees:*) Oh my God…Mom?!?

> (*Immediate shift to:*)

Scene 13

> FRANCES' *house. Sound of knocking.* FRANCES *crawls or rolls across the floor to the door. She opens it, revealing* CHRISTI, *who carries her clipboard and some brochures.*

FRANCES. What took you so long?

CHRISTI. I was a little tied up.

FRANCES. Well don't just stand there, come in.

(CHRISTI *awkwardly steps over* FRANCES.)

CHRISTI. I must say, I was surprised you called me, Ms. McKinney.

FRANCES. You're not the only one.

CHRISTI. The Lord works in mysterious ways.

(*She watches* FRANCES *struggle for a moment.*)

Can I help you up, or—

FRANCES. I'm FINE.

CHRISTI. All right then. I brought some information about Holy Shepherd, and of course, the information about the Justice League that you requested. I also wanted to let you know about our pick-up service, Riders to Joy? We have two transport vans that are fully handicap accessible and—

FRANCES. Are you driving one now?

CHRISTI. Um, no Ma'am. I'm driving my personal vehicle?

FRANCES. That's all right, that'll work.

CHRISTI. Excuse me?

FRANCES. Look, let's cut to the chase. I called you because I want to stop this.

(*She hands* CHRISTI *the script.*)

It's despicable.

CHRISTI. *Bloodbath.* These movies are just awful.

FRANCES. We have to stop them. Every other minute there's a *Law and Order* with a prostitute dead in an alley, a *CSI* with a stripper face-down in a vat of Jell-O—

CHRISTI. You're shaking a little, are you okay?

FRANCES. Sometimes I think if I see one more "artistic" shot of a beautiful young woman who's been beaten or tortured or raped, I will go completely crazy.

CHRISTI. Don't you worry. The Justice League has a plan.

FRANCES. What are we gonna do.

CHRISTI. We have a letter you can send to your local TV stations and movie theatres—

FRANCES. No no no—

CHRISTI. When advertisers hear from consumers—

FRANCES. Nobody pays attention to that stuff—

CHRISTI. When they see an effect on the bottom line—

FRANCES. I'm talking about fire bombs!

CHRISTI. What.

FRANCES. Why the hell do you think I called you? I heard about the bombing this morning—

CHRISTI. Ms. McKinney—

FRANCES. You people know how to get shit done, and you get away with it, too!

CHRISTI. Pastor Dan issued a statement, Holy Shepherd had NOTHING to do with that—

FRANCES. I want to kill him. The director, the producer, everyone who's involved—

CHRISTI. We do not advocate the use of violence as a means to—

FRANCES. You don't have to pretend with me—

CHRISTI. The Justice League is not—

FRANCES. By any means necessary!

We may not agree on everything, but you and I both know that letters won't change anything. We have to *do something* to get their attention. My daughter has been brainwashed by this, this trash, and I'm gonna lose her.

We have to stop them. We have to save them.

CHRISTI. What did you have in mind?

FRANCES. I know where they're filming. I got the director's number off the script, and said I was from Channel Five. Then he sang like a canary. The house is half a mile from your church. All I need is a ride.

(*An expectation.*)

CHRISTI. Is that mess of wires supposed to be a bomb?

FRANCES. You tell me.

(*Split scene: The Set.* SHEENA *runs into an isolated place, she has twigs sticking out of her hair, like she's been running through the woods.*)

JODY. (*Offstage.*) Sheena?

SHEENA. (*Calling off to* JODY.) Just a second! (*To herself.*) I have to check my messages.

(CHRISTI *and* SHEENA *dial their phones.*)

FRANCES. Who are you calling?

CHRISTI. My friend Piper. Her dad's an explosives expert at the ATF?

(*She waits for Piper to pick up.*)

Since Pastor Dan hired me, I've implemented a three-hundred-and-sixty-degree strategy that includes outreach, publicity, utilization of the courts, and covert ops.

SHEENA. (*As she listens to* HILDY's *message.*) Oh my God.

FRANCES. *Covert ops.*

CHRISTI. (*To the phone.*) Hey Piper, it's Christi, call me back, 'k?

SHEENA. *Oh my God!*

(CHRISTI *hangs up.*)

FRANCES. You're like a perky little general.

CHRISTI. That's what it takes to battle evil. And we're gonna strike at the source.

SHEENA. *Oh my freakin' God!*

(*Immediate shift to:*)

Scene 14

The Set. SHEENA *runs to* JODY.

SHEENA. Jody! Look, I need your help—

JODY. As soon as Marc is done with Madison, you need to be in position for the chase—

SHEENA. Listen to me. Marc thinks someone from Channel Five is coming.

JODY. Yeah, I talked to her earlier.

SHEENA. Did you tell her where we are, she *knows* where the location is?

JODY. Yeah.

SHEENA. Crap. I have to go.

JODY. What?!

SHEENA. I'm sorry but this is—

JODY. They're gonna be done any minute!

SHEENA. I think my mom wants to kill Marc!

JODY. What?

MARC. (*Offstage, coming through the walkie around* JODY's *neck.*) *Quiet on the set!*

SHEENA. I should have answered my phone—

JODY. What are you talking about?

SHEENA. He's the guy! He's—seriously, she thinks he ruined her life!

JODY. Marc?

SHEENA. Yes! He was making this movie—he must have been in college. He snuck onto my dad's construction site because he was filming there at night—

JODY. Right.

SHEENA. There'd been a whole series of rapes that summer. It was all over the news. My mom was obsessed, she was part of this women's action group? So one night my dad doesn't come home—probably because he's off with his secretary. My mom goes to the construction site to try to find him. When she gets there she hears this woman screaming. She sees all these people standing around, so she calls the cops—

JODY. Because she thinks—

SHEENA. Yes! And then she calls the TV station and says: the Austin serial rapist is here, right now! The cops are about to nab him, here's the address!

JODY. Nooo—

SHEENA. The TV crews get there first, and all they find is Marc and a bunch of kids filming this scene. It becomes a big joke on the ten o'clock news. And that night another woman is raped! The cops say if my mom hadn't called in a false report they would've caught the guy.

JODY. Whoa.

SHEENA. And this bitch from the women's group gets on the news and says if my mom really thought a woman was being raped, she should have done more to stop them. My mom completely loses it, my dad runs off with his secretary and now I'm making a movie with the SAME GUY.

JODY. Holy coincidence, Batman.

SHEENA. She's making my little sister try to build a—she's gonna try to kill him.

JODY. Okay, isn't your mom, like, in a wheelchair?

SHEENA. Look, I will be back as soon as I can—

(SHEENA *turns and runs smack into* CHRISTI.)

(*Screams.*)

CHRISTI. There's gonna be a lot less of that going on now.

(*She gives a card to* JODY.)

Christi Garcia, Assistant Director of the Holy Shepherd Justice League.

(MARC *comes running in behind her.*)

MARC. I told you, this is a closed set.

CHRISTI. I just wanted to let the rest of your crew know that filming is about to shut down.

JODY. What?

CHRISTI. Holy Shepherd has filed an injunction barring you from using this property on behalf of the owner.

(*She produces a document.*)

JODY. We have all the permits!

CHRISTI. Mr. Parrish didn't understand the nature of the movie you all would be making here.

MARC. He understood the money I paid him to use this dump!

CHRISTI. We'll have you shut down by Monday, so it really would be best for you to just leave now. (*To* SHEENA.) You know, you don't have to take your clothes off to make people like you.

SHEENA. Excuse me?!

CHRISTI. But first you have to like yourself.

MARC. Look, unless you flash a badge in the next three seconds—

CHRISTI. Mr. Parrish is a member of Holy Shepherd—

MARC. (*To* JODY.) Call the cops, dial 911, RIGHT NOW.

(JODY *dials*.)

CHRISTI. There's no need, I'm leaving. But I'll be back. Judge Monson is scheduled to hear the case first thing Monday morning. He's a very fair man. I should know. He's my uncle.

(*Hands* SHEENA *a card*.)

When you're ready to treat yourself with respect, close your legs and call me.

(CHRISTI *exits as* SHEENA *shouts after her*.)

SHEENA. Hey!

MARC. Sheena, find Amanda, tell her we're skipping ahead—

SHEENA. Marc—

MARC. Tell her she has to do all of Madison's make-up and wounds for the meat hook scene *now*.

JODY. The meat hook scene?

SHEENA. Marc, I have to go home.

MARC. What?

JODY. That's almost at the end of the movie!

SHEENA. I know it's bad timing, but—

MARC. No one's going anywhere.

SHEENA. But it's an emergency!

MARC. You leave, I will come after you for delay of production and take every cent you've got. (*To* JODY.) Jody, anything that can be shot someplace else, take it off the schedule. Make sure we've got all the exteriors—

JODY. Look, I'm all about working fast, but—

MARC. Good—

JODY. We've only been shooting for two days!

MARC. We have to work faster—

JODY. We barely have enough footage to cover 20 minutes of film—

MARC. So get moving!

JODY. Just call your investor and ask him to—

MARC. *There is no investor!* All right? I am financing this entire movie with a three-hundred-thousand dollar second mortgage on my six-hundred square foot condo, most of which is already spent! And I will be damned if I am going to be homeless at thirty-seven years old!

SHEENA. You're thirty-seven?

MARC. NO! Now we are going to shoot enough film in the next forty-eight hours to edit together SOMETHING that I can sell to a video distributor, even if it kills me. So until the cops show up to shut us down, *nobody leaves the set.* Now move!

>(*Immediate shift to:*)

Scene 15

Split Scene. SHEENA *steps downstage into a spotlight, pulls out her phone and dials as:*

HILDY *enters the house, wearing her backpack and bike helmet.*

HILDY. Mom? Mom?

>(*She sees the empty scooter.*)

Crap!

>(*Her phone rings. She answers it.*)

HILDY. Oh my God, Sheena—

SHEENA. I just got your messages and—

HILDY. I swear to God, I didn't think she could leave—

SHEENA. What?

HILDY. You said it yourself, she hasn't left in a year, and I had to go to school—

SHEENA. What's happening?

HILDY. She's gone! She's not here—

SHEENA. What?!

HILDY. I really didn't think she could do it, I even took her key! Her scooter's still here, but she's gone—

SHEENA. She was building a bomb and you left her alone?!

HILDY. I had a chemistry quiz!

SHEENA. Okay, all right. She couldn't have gotten very far, right? She doesn't have money for a cab, I have the car. Even if she's planning to blow up Marc, she'd have no way of getting here, right?

>(HILDY *finds the flier from Holy Shepherd.*)

MARC. (*Offstage.*) Sheena! Get in here!

HILDY. This is weird.

SHEENA. What?

HILDY. It's just, this flier. It's from some church group, she circled the phone number over and over.

SHEENA. Oh my God, what's the name of the church?

HILDY. Holy Shepherd? It's for something called the Justice League.

SHEENA. Crap.

MARC. (*Offstage.*) SHEENA!

(*Immediate shift to:*)

Scene 16

Break Room—The Set. MADISON, *a perky blonde, sits alone in a prop wheelchair, listening to her headphones. She sings to herself, an upbeat pop song like "Love Shack" by The B-52s. She has what appears to be a gigantic meat hook going through her back and out her chest.*

MADISON. (*Singing.*) …the Love Shack is…we can get to-ge-ther-er…

(FRANCES *appears behind* MADISON, *doing a commando-style crawl, advancing on* MADISON.)

MADISON. (*In a low voice.*) Love Shack Baby.

(FRANCES *has outfitted herself with an old tool belt containing various tools that could be used as weapons.* FRANCES *crawls up behind* MADISON, *waiting for her opportunity.*)

MADISON. (*Still singing.*)

Bang bang bang on the door baby…

I can't hear you.

BANG BAN-GGGAAAAAHHH!!!

(*As* MADISON's *mouth opens wide,* FRANCES *stuffs a bandana in it, stifling her scream.*)

(*Immediate shift to:*)

Scene 17

The Set. A tight light follows SHEENA, *as though she is being tracked by a camera. They are filming. She runs a few steps, trips and falls.*

SHEENA/SLOAN. (*In her movie voice.*) "No!"

(*She turns back towards her pursuer, pushing herself away from him.* JODY, *dressed as* VICTOR, *advances menacingly towards her, wearing his signature mask.* SHEENA *remains on the floor, backing herself into a corner.*)

SHEENA/SLOAN. "No, no please—"

JODY/VICTOR. "Oh yes."

(VICTOR *reaches* SHEENA, *grabs her*—)

SHEENA/SLOAN. (*Screams.*)

(*She struggles to get away, but* VICTOR *handcuffs* SHEENA *to an old radiator. She whimpers and cries.*)

SHEENA/SLOAN. "No no no no…"

JODY/VICTOR. "You shouldn't have worn this. You knew Daddy wouldn't like it."

> (*In a swift movement,* VICTOR *rips* SHEENA's *shirt down the center, leaving her stomach and chest exposed except for her bra.*)

"Now it's time for your bath."

> (*The light follows* VICTOR *as he turns to a bathtub of blood. Above it is an empty harness where* MADISON *is supposed to be.*)

MARC. CUT. Where the hell is Madison? She's supposed to be in the shot!

JODY. I told her to get in position ten minutes ago—

MARC. (*Calling.*) MADISON!

SHEENA. You want us to reset—

MARC. NO. Stay where you are, we can take it from the reveal— (*Calling.*) MADISON IF YOU DON'T GET ON THIS MEAT HOOK IN THE NEXT 60 SECONDS—

> (*All the lights go out.*)

JODY. What the—

SHEENA. Oh my God.

MARC. Great. This is just great.

SHEENA. Marc, there's something I should tell you.

MARC. Did you see the fuse box in the laundry room?

JODY. I'm already on my way—

SHEENA. No! Wait, please—

MARC. GO.

> (JODY *exits.*)

SHEENA. Marc, you have to unlock me.

MARC. Just STAY WHERE YOU ARE.

SHEENA. Seriously, I have a really bad feeling about this.

> (MARC *laughs.*)

I didn't tell you before because I didn't want you to think I was crazy, but—

MARC. (*He laughs more.*) You have a *bad feeling* about this?

SHEENA. Listen to me—

MARC. I lost my star, all my investors, quite possibly the only piece of property I've ever owned, and you have a BAD FEELING?

SHEENA. I THINK MY MOTHER IS HERE!

> (*The lights flick on.* FRANCES *is there, in the wheelchair. She wears a hockey mask, a la Jason from* Friday the 13th, *her hand on her holstered cordless drill.*)

SHEENA. (*Screams.*)

FRANCES. Hello, Marc.

MARC. Who are you?

SHEENA. Mom, please!

MARC. Wait, this is your mother?

(FRANCES *takes the mask off.*)

FRANCES. We'll see who's laughing in five minutes.

MARC. I'm sorry, you can stay for a couple of takes, but you've got to keep quiet and stay out of the way.

FRANCES. You'd like that wouldn't you?

SHEENA. Nobody wants you here, so just leave!

FRANCES. Keep us all tied up and whimpering, like Sheena. (*To* SHEENA.) You're really in control now.

SHEENA. I am in control!

MARC. Do I know you?

FRANCES. If it weren't for me, you wouldn't even have your pathetic little career—

SHEENA. We'll call the police.

FRANCES. You'd still be working construction, but thanks to all the free publicity—

MARC. Wait a minute—

FRANCES. I should have done this fifteen years ago.

MARC. (*It dawns on him.*) You!

FRANCES. That's right. The middle of the night, a woman is dragged to a construction site, beaten and raped—

MARC. It was a movie!

FRANCES. I forgot, it's all okay because it isn't REAL. It's in SERVICE of the STORY. Isn't that what you said to Channel Five? "It's not about depicting violence against women, it's about telling the story!"

MARC. Well, yeah!

FRANCES. DID YOU EVER STOP TO THINK THAT MAYBE WE NEED SOME DIFFERENT STORIES?!?!

(MARC *attempts to leave the room,* FRANCES *maneuvers to stop him, revving the drill.*)

FRANCES. Oh no you don't. I want justice, and this time I'm gonna get it.

SHEENA. You can't stop us!

FRANCES. I've already taken down everyone else in the place.

MARC. What.

FRANCES. Your bloody little bimbos, that punk who came to the house—

SHEENA. What did you do?

FRANCES. The make-up girl? She was spunky.

MARC. (*Calling.*) Jody!

SHEENA. Mother, they will put you away for this!

MARC. I'm calling the cops.

> (MARC *starts to dial,* FRANCES *trips him, his phone goes flying. She points the drill at him like a gun.*)

FRANCES. DON'T MOVE!

> (MARC *holds his hands up in spite of himself.* JODY *creeps into the room unseen by* FRANCES. *He has several bleeding cuts on his arms, and duct tape wrapped around his head.* SHEENA *sees* JODY, *they silently make a quick plan.*)

I can't let you do this, Sheena. You were supposed to finish what we started. But you just take whatever they force on you and then pretend it's what you wanted in the first place!

SHEENA. It IS what I want!

FRANCES. You're dragging us all back down!

SHEENA. I am pulling myself up! You know why there are so many horror movies? BECAUSE PEOPLE LIKE THEM! That's it!

> (MARC *sees* JODY.)

It's not some huge conspiracy to degrade women, or keep women down. Because the last time I checked, women have all the same rights as men! If a woman doesn't get a job, it's because she's not as qualified! If she gets paid less, it's because she didn't negotiate as well. And let me tell you something else:

> (SHEENA *gives a sign to* JODY *and* MARC.)

The WNBA is on the verge of bankruptcy, not because people are afraid to see women as strong and powerful, but because CHICK BASKETBALL IS BORING!

> (JODY *and* MARC *spring on* FRANCES. MARC *grabs the drill as* JODY *tapes her mouth shut.*)

FRANCES. HEY! HEY— (*As they get the tape over her mouth.*) MRWRUGH! HOMRWMIGITIZ!

MARC. Tie her hands up.

JODY. Hold her down!

> (JODY *ties her hands.*)

MARC. Hurry. Just hold still! You're not going anywhere.

FRANCES. MURMIGURMITO!

JODY. There. That should hold for a little while.

> (*They have finished the job.* FRANCES *sits in the wheelchair, hands bound, gagged with tape. She is seething, but for once, she is silent.* MARC *moves her out of the way.*)

MARC. We'll deal with her later.

SHEENA. I'm not stupid, Mother, I know what I'm doing.

JODY. All right. I'm gonna untie Madison and call the cops.

MARC. No.

JODY. What.

MARC. We're gonna keep going.

JODY. Dude—

MARC. We'll just let her calm down.

JODY. She wrestled me down on a bed of carpet tacks!

MARC. WE ARE FINISHING THE MOVIE.
Get Madison, and get reset for the shot.

    (*JODY exits.*)

SHEENA. Marc, I am so sorry.

    (*MARC goes to her, crouches down next to her, tenderly.*)

MARC. Are you okay?

SHEENA. I'm fine. I'm just embarrassed, all of this is happening because of me.

MARC. You don't have anything to be embarrassed about.

SHEENA. You really think we can leave her tied up there while we shoot?

    (*They look at FRANCES. She tries to scream.*)

MARC. Yep.

SHEENA. When we get a break, I'll call her doctor.

MARC. All right. Now get ready to be impaled.

    (*JODY enters with MADISON. Her meat hook is ridiculously crushed, her costume comically askew.*)

JODY. Um, we've got a little bit of a problem.

MARC. Okay, okay, Amanda can fix this.

JODY. Dude—

MARC. AMANDA!

JODY. She left! She was a little traumatized, you know?

MARC. All right. All right, Madison, honey, you doing okay?

MADISON. Yeah, I guess—

MARC. Good.

    (*MARC rips her hook off.*)

MADISON. Ow!

MARC. Here.

(MARC *takes the knife off his belt, swiftly cuts the straps off her tank top so she looks like she's wearing a tube top.*)

MADISON. (*As he cuts her straps.*) Oh! Oh!

(*He gets a bottle of blood, squirts it on her.*)

MARC. Okay, what else?

(*He grabs a short, spiky wig.*)

Put this on!

(*She puts the wig on.* MARC *and* JODY *futz with her costume and hair for a second. They stand back and look at her.*)

MARC. What do you think?

JODY. You don't think anyone's going to recognize her from earlier?

MARC. She's gonna be a corpse in 15 seconds.

JODY. She looks great.

MARC. PLACES.

(JODY *pulls on* VICTOR's *mask as they scramble to get into position.*)

MADISON. What are we doing?

JODY. I have no idea.

MADISON. Okay.

MARC. Madison, we'll start with you. VICTOR you're gonna drag her over, show her off to Sloan, and then kill her.

JODY. Got it.

SHEENA. What about the scene where Victor tells Madison about Elise?

MARC. Nobody cares! Give me FEAR, give me TERROR, give me BLOOD. And no matter what happens, NO ONE STOPS. Everybody ready?

(*They nod.*)

And…ACTION.

(*Filming begins. Everyone tries to follow* MARC's *directions.*)

(JODY/VICTOR *holds* MADISON *around the neck, threatening her with a prop knife. She struggles to get away from him.*)

MADISON. (*In her movie voice.*) "Get off me, let me go!"

(JODY/VICTOR *drags her over in front of* SHEENA/SLOAN.)

MARC. Get her closer.

MADISON. "Help me, please, help me!"

MARC. Reach out to her, she's your only hope, that's it.

SHEENA/SLOAN. "Just let her go!"

MARC. Do it!

(JODY/VICTOR *slices* MADISON's *neck, blood shoots out like a geyser.*)

And Madison: death shake!

(MADISON *shimmies her shoulders and chest.*)

SHEENA/SLOAN. "NO!"

MARC. Madison, keep reaching for Sloan, keep reaching, try to speak—and Victor drop her!

(JODY/VICTOR *drops* MADISON *with a thud.*)

MADISON. Ow!

JODY. Sorry.

MARC. Keep going. Move in on Sloan.

(JODY/VICTOR *moves toward* SHEENA/SLOAN. *She tries to back away, but she's still handcuffed to the radiator.* FRANCES *watches intently.*)

SHEENA/SLOAN. "No, please, no—"

JODY/VICTOR. (*In his movie villain voice.*) "Now it's just us."

SHEENA/VICTOR. "Please, just let me go!"

(*He shows off the prop knife.*)

JODY/VICTOR. "You're all mine."

SHEENA/SLOAN. "No, please!"

MARC. Smear some blood on her chest.

SHEENA. Um—

(JODY *and* SHEENA *both look at* MARC. JODY *tentatively smears the blood on* SHEENA's *chest, being very careful to not touch her breasts.*)

JODY/VICTOR. "I can…do whatever I want."

MARC. Really rub it in.

(JODY/VICTOR *rubs more vigorously, but still in the "safe zone."*)

SHEENA/SLOAN. "Don't touch me!"

MARC. Now grab her by the hair.

JODY. (*Totally breaking from his* VICTOR *character.*) Um, what?

MARC. I said grab her!

SHEENA. You could grab my arm, and—

JODY. Like here?

MARC. Grab her hair and pull her up—

SHEENA. Just give us a second to figure this out—

MARC. Shut up and give me the mask!

SHEENA. What?

MARC. I said give me the mask!

JODY. Okay.

(MARC *takes the mask from* JODY, *puts it on.*)

SHEENA. I'm sorry, what are we doing?

MARC. (*To* JODY.) Just keep her in the frame.

JODY. Got it.

SHEENA. Marc—

MARC. And don't stop filming.

SHEENA. Wait, what are we doing?

MARC. Whatever we have to. (*To* JODY.) Ready!

JODY. Action.

> (MARC/VICTOR *moves in to* SHEENA/SLOAN *with the prop knife.* SHEENA *tries to resume acting, but as the threat of* MARC's *actions becomes more real, all artifice drops away.*)

SHEENA/SLOAN. "Please, no!"

MARC/VICTOR. Why didn't you listen to me?

SHEENA. "I should have—"

MARC/VICTOR. You should have stayed home with me instead of going off with that boy—

SHEENA. "I'm sorry!"

MARC/VICTOR. Liar!

> (MARC/VICTOR *grabs* SHEENA's *hair on the top of her head and pulls her up to her knees by her hair.*)

SHEENA. Ow! You're hurting me!

MARC/VICTOR. Just like you hurt me.

> (MARC/VICTOR *cranks her head back so she is looking up at him, he caresses her face.*)

MARC/VICTOR. You were the only one who understood me—

SHEENA. Please—

MARC/VICTOR. Who believed in me—

SHEENA. You're really hurting me—

MARC/VICTOR. And you left!

> (*He gives her head another rough jerk.*)

SHEENA. (*Screams.*) Stop!

> (MARC *has completely strayed from the script.*)

MARC/VICTOR. You're so beautiful.

SHEENA. Stop it, just stop—

MARC/VICTOR. Everyone telling me no, telling me it's not right—

SHEENA. Fucking let go of me!

MARC/VICTOR. Telling me I wasn't good enough—

SHEENA. You're really hurting me—

JODY. Um, okay—

MARC/VICTOR. But not this time—

SHEENA. Stop the camera, stop!

MARC/VICTOR. I SAY WHEN WE STOP.

(*He throws her down forcefully and straddles her, pinning her to the ground. He tosses the prop knife aside, takes out his knife from his belt.* SHEENA *is crying now.*)

SHEENA. No!

JODY. I don't think this is in the script—

SHEENA. What are you doing?

MARC/VICTOR. I just needed something a little, sharper.

SHEENA. No, stop—

JODY. Maybe we should stop for a second—

MARC/VICTOR. (*To* JODY.) KEEP FILMING. (*To* SHEENA.) Now you have to stay very still. I would hate for something bad to happen.

(MARC *runs the knife along* SHEENA*'s neck.*)

SHEENA. Okay, okay, I'll be still.

MARC/VICTOR. That's my girl.

(*He runs the knife between her breasts.*)

First we have to get you out of these clothes.

SHEENA. No, stop, Marc—Jody? Stop!

MARC/VICTOR. *Just react.*

(*He takes his knife, puts the point of it under the center of her bra, as though he's going to slice it open.* FRANCES *suddenly springs up from her chair. She has worked one of her hands free, and she runs, full-force, at* MARC. *They wrestle.* JODY *jumps in and tries to pull them apart.* FRANCES *fights fiercely.*)

MADISON. (*Whispers to* SHEENA.) Is this part of the movie?

SHEENA. No!

(FRANCES *knocks* JODY *out, turns her attention back to* MARC. MADISON *slowly moves toward the door.*)

MARC. I've had enough of you!

(MARC *knocks* FRANCES *to the ground. He grabs her ankle, pulls her toward him.*)

Oh no you don't!

SHEENA. JUST STOP!

MADISON. Someone let me know about the call time for tomorrow, 'k?

MARC. Madison get back here!

(FRANCES *grabs the cordless drill and attacks* MARC.)

MARC. (*To* FRANCES.) What the fuck!

MADISON. Okay, see ya!

(MADISON *exits.* MARC *and* FRANCES *struggle,* FRANCES *gets the drill very close to* MARC's *face.*)

MARC. No no no no no no—

SHEENA. Leave her alone!

(MARC *pushes* FRANCES *back. With his hands clasped over her own, he turns her hands so that the drill is now facing* FRANCES. *She tries to back away, but* MARC *is too strong. He pushes the drill dangerously close to her neck.*)

CALL THE POLICE!

MARC. What's the matter? Nothing to say now? I remember you! Screaming all over the news, trying to make it sound like I was the villain! Well nobody listened then, and nobody's gonna listen now, so just shut up!

(JODY *is finally able to get up. He sees* MARC, *rushes over to help* FRANCES, *but stumbles into* MARC, *which sends the drill plunging into* FRANCES' *neck.*)

What…

No…

(MARC *releases his hands,* FRANCES' *hands remain on the drill, which is still in her neck.* JODY *reaches over pulls it out of her.*)

JODY. Holy shit. We've gotta…

(JODY *takes the tape out of her mouth. A puddle of blood begins to appear all around* FRANCES' *head and neck. It is dark, different from the movie blood.* FRANCES *makes terrible gurgling noises.*)

MARC. I was just holding it over her—I wasn't—

SHEENA. Oh my God—

JODY. Give me something to put on it.

MARC. I didn't—

SHEENA. What's happening?

(MARC *hands him a T-shirt.*)

JODY. Call an ambulance.

SHEENA. Is she okay?

JODY. Call them, now!

(MARC *dials 911.* JODY *tapes the T-shirt to her neck with his gaff tape. The blood keeps coming.*)

MARC. I need an ambulance, there's been an accident.

SHEENA. What's happening—

JODY. (*To* FRANCES.) Just stay still, don't move. Holy shit, there's so much blood.

MARC. I think her neck is broken, she's bleeding—

SHEENA. SOMEBODY UNLOCK ME!

JODY. Oh my God, she's bleeding out.

SHEENA. SHE'S MY MOTHER! UNLOCK ME NOW!

(JODY *rushes to* SHEENA, *fumbles for the key.*)

MARC. 12695 Rancho Vista Way.

SHEENA. Oh my God, hang on, Mom. Just. I'm sorry, I'm sorry I said all those things the other night, I love you Mom, I do. I just want to be happy, that's all! I don't want be angry at everybody all the time. I never meant to hurt you, please—WHAT THE HELL IS TAKING YOU SO LONG!

JODY. The key won't work!

(FRANCES *looks at her watch. She sits, starts to stand. Blood has soaked through the T-shirt taped to* FRANCES' *neck and is pouring down her chest.*)

MARC. Jesus Christ! She's getting up!

JODY. No, don't move—you'll lose more blood—

FRANCES. Shhhhhh, Sheena—

SHEENA. Mom?

(FRANCES *is up, takes a few staggering steps towards* SHEENA, *who is still locked to the radiator.* FRANCES *tries to motion to* SHEENA *to get down.*)

MARC. Ma'am, just sit back down—

SHEENA. Don't touch her!

FRANCES. Sh Sh Sh Sh Sh Sheena—

JODY. Please sit back down—

SHEENA. Mom, please! You're gonna die if you don't sit down, please please—

(*With her last remaining strength,* FRANCES *throws her body over* SHEENA's. *A bright light flashes across the stage, along with the sound of a huge explosion.*)

(*Blackout.*)

(*Sound of sirens.*)

(*A* TV NEWS ANCHOR *appears in another area. She may be backed by video clips of* SHEENA *leaving a hospital in a wheelchair pushed by* HILDY, *surrounded by flashing cameras.*)

NEWS ANCHOR. Authorities are still baffled by a bombing last week that left several people injured and one presumed dead. Austin resident Frances McKinney is believed to have died when a bomb was detonated at a residence in Round Rock. No body was recovered from the scene, but police say it would be impossible for anyone to have survived both the explosion, and the ensuing fire that burned the structure to the ground. The home was being used as a location for the upcoming horror movie, *Bloodbath*. In a movie-worthy twist, police say the bomb was planted by McKinney, whose daughter, Sheena McKinney, stars in the forthcoming movie.

(*Perhaps another video clip of* PASTOR DAN, *speaking at a podium, with* CHRISTI GARCIA *behind him, nodding in agreement.*)

NEWS ANCHOR. Round Rock residents gathered last night for a prayer vigil to end violence organized by Holy Shepherd Church. Church leaders say they are planning to boycott the movie, but the movie's distributors don't appear to be worried. They've scheduled a press conference in town tomorrow, where they're expected to announce that the film will be released in August. For WTEX Channel Five News, I'm Belinda Chapman.

Scene 18

FRANCES' *house.* SHEENA *enters wearing a short, low-cut black dress, her hair in a towel. She walks with a lumbering thud—one foot is in a cast, the other foot is bare.*

SHEENA. I can't find my shoe.

HILDY. It's right here.

SHEENA. Not those, my black ones.

HILDY. The ones with the huge heels?

SHEENA. They're here somewhere—

HILDY. You can't wear those.

SHEENA. Watch me.

HILDY. You're not even supposed to be walking this much. The doctor said you're supposed to be taking it easy, not—

(SHEENA *has found the shoe and shoves her good foot into it. She stands teetering a little.*)

SHEENA. *I am perfectly fine.*

(*Beat.*)

HILDY. Are you seriously wearing that to the press conference.

SHEENA. What's wrong with it?

HILDY. Nothing, for Shakira.

(SHEENA *takes off the shoe, carries it as she lumbers around the living room. She goes to the front door, opens it to look for the limo, leaves it open.*)

SHEENA. Well what else am I supposed to wear? I can't get pants on over my cast! This is the only other black I have!

HILDY. Oh, right! You're in mourning. I forgot, what with all the interviews, and your agent—

SHEENA. What is your problem?

HILDY. Nothing, why would I have a problem with you promoting a movie that our mother killed herself trying to stop—

SHEENA. You don't need to remind me what happened, I'm the one she was trying to blow up, remember?

HILDY. She saved your life!

SHEENA. Only at the last minute!

Only because she tried to kill me in the first place—

> (SHEENA *starts to cry.*)

Crap.

HILDY. I'm sorry. I didn't mean to—

You know you don't have to do this.

SHEENA. I'm doing it, all right?

HILDY. They can still have their press conference without you, just—

SHEENA. *This is the biggest opportunity I'm ever gonna get.* This is gonna pay off the house, pay for your college. That agent says he's got three movie offers for me already because of all the publicity. So if this is what I have to do to take care of both of us, that's what I'm gonna do.

> (*Sound of a honk.*)

Crap. Tell them I'll be right there.

> (SHEENA *lumbers off.* JODY *appears in the doorway. He wears a large stabilizing neck brace, and carries a cactus.*)

JODY. Hey.

HILDY. Hey.

SHEENA. (*Offstage.*) I just need two seconds!

HILDY. Hair.

JODY. Right. I brought a cactus.

HILDY. Yeah.

JODY. Just to say, I'm sorry, for your loss.

> (*He gives it to* HILDY.)

HILDY. Thanks.

JODY. You coming to the press conference?

HILDY. I take the PSAT tomorrow?

JODY. Oh.

HILDY. I think it's a little more important.

JODY. Definitely.

MARC. (*Offstage.*) Hildy!

HILDY. Plus someone has to look after Sheena's charity case.

JODY. Right.

    (MARC *enters on* FRANCES' *scooter. He wears a bathrobe. He's got an awkward bandage over one eye and ear, and he's a little deaf from the blast.*)

MARC. (*To* HILDY.) The fridge is EMPTY. Don't you EAT anything in this house?

HILDY. I think we have pickles?

MARC. What?

HILDY. YOU WANT SOME PICKLES?

MARC. Jesus Christ, I want FOOD. What the hell is he doing here?

JODY. This is so weird.

    (SHEENA *appears. Her hair is done.*)

SHEENA. Hey Jody.

JODY. Sheena. You look amazing.

SHEENA. Really?

JODY. Definitely.

MARC. What's going on?

SHEENA. He can't hear you, just ignore him.

JODY. For real?

MARC. Why are you so dressed up?

JODY. Look, Sheena, I'm really sorry, about your mom, and everything—

SHEENA. Thanks.

JODY. Things got so crazy at the end, and—

    (*Sound of another honk.*)

SHEENA. It's okay. Let's do this.

MARC. You're doing something for the movie, aren't you?

JODY. He doesn't know about the press conference?

MARC. What are you doing, you're doing an interview?

SHEENA. Don't say anything.

MARC. HEY! Answer me!

SHEENA. (*Loudly, so he can hear.*) I am letting you stay here out of the kindness of my heart until your insurance settlement comes, but do not think for a second—

MARC. I wouldn't NEED to be here if YOUR MOTHER hadn't tried to BLOW US ALL UP!

SHEENA. (*To* HILDY.) Will you be okay here?

MARC. Fine, go. We'll see who's the big star after my interview next week on *Dateline NBC*. Oh, they're very interested in my side of the story.

SHEENA. What are you talking about?

MARC. It seems you forgot to tell everyone how you got the part. How you came to my hotel room. Spent the night with me—

HILDY. What?

SHEENA. Nothing happened!

MARC. Oh, that's not how I remember it, Sheena.

SHEENA. (*To* HILDY.) Hildy, get your stuff, you're coming with us.

HILDY. Good.

(JODY *helps* HILDY *gather her stuff.*)

MARC. They say you make it sound like a Lifetime movie. "Innocent co-ed trying to support her family gets exploited by evil director!" But nobody's gonna believe that when I'm done with you.

SHEENA. I'm through feeling sorry for you! I won't let you hurt me again.

(SHEENA *pulls out her phone, dials 911.*)

MARC. Hurt you? You got exactly what you wanted. Hell, you negotiated. You sold your tits and ass for fifteen grand.

(SHEENA *adjusts her dress, trying to make it more modest.*)

Look at you. You're still selling it. I think you'd better start learning Pilates.

SHEENA. (*On the phone.*) Hi, there's an intruder in my house? He keeps saying he lives here.

(SHEENA *waves* JODY *and* HILDY *out the door.* JODY *stops, grabs the cactus for good measure, then exits.*)

MARC. You can't leave me here, HEY!

SHEENA. Yes, he's a white, male, about 40?

(*They are gone.* MARC *shouts after them.*)

MARC. You fuckers! Oh, fine, get in your limo! Live it up! We'll see who gets the last laugh!

(*He slams the door.*)

This is not over. This was MY movie, MY comeback. I'm gonna get on *60 Minutes. 48 Hours. Doctor Phil.*

(*He zips back over to the door, to shout after them again.*)

I'll go to the *National* Fucking *Enquirer*—

(MARC *opens the door and sees:*)

(FRANCES. *She's covered in ash and dried blood, but she's strong and powerful. Lights shift.*)

(MARC *tries to back away, but his scooter won't work. She unsheathes a knife.*)

MARC. No. No no no no no—

FRANCES. *Oh yes.*

>(FRANCES *raises the knife.*)
>(*As* MARC *lets out a long girly scream:*)
>(*Blackout.*)

End of Play.

3:59AM:
A DRAG RACE FOR TWO ACTORS
by Marco Ramirez

BIOGRAPHY

Marco Ramirez has had plays produced at City Theatre, the Kennedy Center, the Mad Cat Theatre Company, The Naked Stage, The Yellow Tree Theatre, and Actors Theatre of Louisville's Humana Festival of New American Plays, where he has twice received the Heideman Award (in 2006 for *I am not Batman.* and in 2009 for *3:59am*). The *Miami New Times* gave him the Best Original Work Award for *Twenty-Six: a play About a Giant* and his collection of plays for young audiences titled *Mermaids, Monsters, and the World Painted Purple* was nominated for a Helen Hayes Award in 2008. Other honors include the Bryan Award for Drama from The Fellowship of Southern Writers and the Le Comte Du Nouy Prize from Lincoln Center. He's currently a Playwriting Fellow at The Juilliard School.

ACKNOWLEDGMENTS

3:59am: a drag race for two actors premiered at the Humana Festival of New American Plays in March 2009. It was directed by Amy Attaway with the following cast:

LAZ ....Daniel Reyes
HECTOR ....Matthew Baldiga

and the following production staff:

Scenic Designer .... Paul Owen
Costume Designer.................................Emily Ganfield
Lighting Designer...Nick Dent
Sound Designer ....Benjamin Marcum
Properties Designer................................ Mark Walston
Stage Manager.................................Paul Mills Holmes
Assistant Stage Manager............................Debra Anne Gasper
Dramaturg ....Julie Felise Dubiner
Assistant Dramaturg ....Sarah Lunnie

First production at the Mad Cat Theatre Company, Miami; Equity premiere at the 2009 Humana Festival.

CHARACTERS
LAZ, a teenager
HECTOR, mid-twenties

TIME
Later tonight.

PLACE
An apartment building, a parking lot, a Subaru and a Honda Civic.

Matthew Baldiga and Daniel Reyes
in *3:59am: a drag race for two actors*

33rd Annual Humana Festival of New American Plays
Actors Theatre of Louisville, 2009
Photo by Harlan Taylor

3:59AM:
A DRAG RACE FOR TWO ACTORS

Black.
Then a pin spot on LAZ, *nineteen,*
Direct address.

LAZ. It's like a hundred degrees outside
And the asshole downstairs is watching porn again with the volume all the
    way up
Like he wants everybody in the building to know,
And every time I close my eyes I feel the walls closing in on me in my room,
'Cause even though it's just *me* in there now,
(My sister moved out like two weeks ago
And we don't know where she is
And we don't talk about it),
Even though it's just *me* in there now,
I swear to god the place is getting smaller.
…
And my aunt is coloring her hair,
And my mom is smoking cigarettes in the kitchen,
Screaming some shit about how I'm just like my father
But I just *go.*
…
I leave the apartment in my flip-flops and my gym shorts and my Field Day
    T-shirt from the sixth grade that still fits me 'cause I was a fat little shit,
…
I just *go.*
…
And even though it's a hundred degrees outside I still gotta warm up my Civic,
'Cause this?
My "escape pod"?
Is old-school like Jesus and I bought it off a guy named Ray-Ray who
    works at Chicken Kitchen,
But I get in,
Keys in ignition.
…
And for a minute or two I just listen to that Honda engine put-put some
    shit in Japanese
…
And it comes to life,
…

The trunk smells like Chop-Chop curry mustard and Mr. Pibb but that doesn't
    even matter,
'Cause with the volume all the way up,
I sink into the driver's seat like shit was
Custom-made for my ass.
…
And I just start driving,
In my flip-flops and gym shorts and Field Day T-shirt from the sixth grade
    that still fits 'cause I was a fat little shit.
…
And I don't remember putting my foot to the pedal
Or first gear
Or second gear
Or stop lights
But they're all mine
And I'm gone.
…
I fly.
…
And next thing I know I'm down a half a tank of gas
And I look at the clock,
And bro,

HECTOR & LAZ. It's two o'clock—

LAZ. —In the fucking morning.

> (*Pin spot on* HECTOR,
> *Late twenties,*
> *A nametag,*
> *Direct address as well.*)

HECTOR. And my manager's being a dick.
And not just because all managers are dicks pretty much always,
I mean, tonight he's being like a *remarkable* dick,
So I wave to him all nice on my way out of my job
But my other hand's in my pocket and I'm totally flipping him off and hoping
    he lands headfirst on a fucking stapler.
And I take out my keys and I take out my cell phone on my way to the car—
Which is a long-ass walk but it's company policy unless you're a manager
    (don't even get me started)—
And I am SO tired
And I am SO hungry
And I didn't even wanna work a second shift today but my wife's three months
    pregnant
So that means I'm working a third and a fourth shift if I have to,

And I *just* wanna go home.

...

I know it's two o'clock in the morning but I call her anyway just to let her know
   I'm on my way,

...

And she picks up fast like the phone was already in her hand.

...

And the first thing she says is "How was work."
But she's not asking,

...

She's stalling.

...

She does that, especially when it's bad news—
So I ask her what's wrong,
And there's this silence.

...

There's this silence but I hear monitors and machines in the background.
And she's with her mom and my mom
And I'm like "What?"
And she tells me she didn't want me to worry.

...

Three months pregnant,
She didn't see the *point* in bothering me at work.

LAZ. But that doesn't even matter—

HECTOR. —And that's when she tells me we lost him.

...

...

And ten minutes later my sleeves are covered with tears and snot.
And twenty minutes later my knuckles are scraped and dented from punching
   the dashboard.
Window's fogged.
Empty parking lot.

LAZ. (*Quiet.*) It's just *me* in there now.

HECTOR. And I'm getting calls from the hospital but I can't pick up.

LAZ. (*Quiet.*) ...Just *me*.

HECTOR. And this is the point where I realize I've memorized the geography
   of my Subaru:

   (*He takes a quick inventory.*)

Crooked sun visor that fell months ago but I haven't fixed yet.
Scooby Doo steering wheel cover.
Empty pack of cigarettes,

Anthrax CD Freddie left in my car.

"Guardian Angel" card my wife insists I keep clipped to the rear-view.

…

It was familiar before, but now I got all of it memorized.

LAZ. Keys in ignition—

HECTOR. —It's *my* car,

Yeah,

But at this point these things've all been staring quietly at snot dripping outta my nose

And we've become friends.

And I know I *should*,

I know it should be the first thing I do,

But something tells me I can't see her.

I can't.

…

Not 'cause of *her*.

…

'Cause of *me*.

…

…

'Cause I'm just not strong enough.

LAZ. Keys in ignition,

HECTOR. So I start the car—

LAZ. —And I don't remember putting my foot to the pedal—

HECTOR. —I start that car—

LAZ. —I don't remember first gear or second gear

But by now I've driven *past* the places I know and now I'm driving *past* places where every streetlight is like something I never seen before—

HECTOR. —And I just go—

LAZ. —And I'm *not* thinking about my sister,

Or the look on her face when she left,

Or how weird it is to sleep in that room,

Or the fact that I prayed

—Me: the fucking loser of all losers—

To make sure she was all right.

And I'm *not* thinking about how I should call her

Even though my mom told me if I did I'd be a traitor and an embarrassment to the family

And I'm like "The Family"?

Like we're Elizabethan?

Like we're the Sopranos?—

HECTOR. —And the seatbelt light is still on with this annoying chime thing that goes ding-ding-ding-ding if you don't put it on and I'm normally real safe about everything but not tonight—

LAZ. —And I turn on the radio—

HECTOR. —Tonight I don't—

LAZ. —And it's the shitty late-night DJs that are like not good enough for regular radio so let's give them their own shitty late-night programs—

HECTOR. —And the streetlights are getting dimmer—

LAZ. —And it's one—

HECTOR. —After another—

LAZ. —After another—

HECTOR. —Streetlights—

LAZ. —And eventually I just settle on static—

HECTOR. —I don't even know where I'm going—

LAZ. —Static—

HECTOR. —I'm the kinda guy who makes his parents recycle and here I am just eating up gas streetlight after streetlight 'cause driving is just—

LAZ. —*Nice* with the static all up and—

HECTOR. —Loud—

LAZ. —So—

HECTOR. —LOUD—

LAZ. —Yeah—

HECTOR. —Clean—

LAZ. —Fuck yeah—

HECTOR. —*Blinding*—

LAZ. —And every streetlight is like something I never seen before!—

HECTOR. —And for no reason in particular at one point in my driving,
In my nothing,
In my *driving*,
I slam on the brakes,
…
Put it in park.

      (*A beat.*)

LAZ. And I put the car in park.

HECTOR. And I look at my watch.
And—

LAZ. —Jesus bro—

HECTOR. —At this point—

LAZ. —It's three fifty-eight am and I dunno where the hell I am.

HECTOR. But I don't care.

    (*A beat.*)

LAZ. And wherever it *is* I've driven, everything looks pretty much—

HECTOR. —pitch black—

LAZ. —Except a thin trail of moonlight tracing over a couple buildings in the background—

HECTOR. —And every building I look at isn't even like a building,
It's just a shell of a cube glowing from behind—

LAZ. —Like in the movie *Tron.*

HECTOR. And normally there's someone on the street
Even this late, right?
Normally there's at least a cop car or a crackhead
But right now there's—

LAZ. —Nothing.
…

Tron.

HECTOR. Nothing—that is—except this stupid put-put sound coming from a car next to me.

LAZ. And in the middle of all the dark I look up and there's this fucker I never seen before.

HECTOR. And it's just us and our steering wheels.

LAZ. And he looks me in the eyes like we're friends or some shit—

HECTOR. —Cowboys without horses—

LAZ. —In the eyes—

HECTOR. —Showdown—

LAZ. —Like we're friends.

HECTOR. …And I rev the engine—

LAZ. —Oh yeah?—

HECTOR. —And, you have to understand:
I've never "revved" the engine before,
I don't even know how you spell that—

LAZ. —Like he's some kinda hot shit in his Subaru—

HECTOR. —I got it at Carmax—

LAZ. —So I do the same—

    (—*Building*—)

HECTOR. —And it's just me and this guy I don't know—

LAZ. —And everything is pitch black except his headlights—

HECTOR. —And I have NO idea where we are,
We're in some part of the city they don't even put on maps—

LAZ. —Come on—

HECTOR. —And am I really about to race someone?—

LAZ. —Come on, yo—

HECTOR. —What is this, *Grease?*—

LAZ. —COME ON—

HECTOR. —And I dunno what the hell got into me but I just go—

LAZ. —And I don't even remember putting my foot to the pedal—

HECTOR. —Or first gear—

LAZ. —Or second gear—

HECTOR. —Or third gear—

LAZ. —Or fourth—

HECTOR. —Or stop lights—

LAZ. —But it's three fifty-nine am and we're gone—
          (*—Building—*)

HECTOR. —Holy shit—

LAZ. —And next thing I know I'm going eighty—

HECTOR. —Ninety—

LAZ. —Ninety-five miles an hour down a stretch of road that's empty, that nobody's been on for like a hundred years—

HECTOR. —I fly—

LAZ. —Hundred miles an hour, the road curves—

HECTOR. —I curve with it—

LAZ. —Hundred-ten he catches up—

HECTOR. —What the fuck am I doing—

LAZ. —And at a hundred-twenty I'm about to max out but I don't even care—

HECTOR. —I'm going a hundred-thirty miles an hour like some kind of ~~moron~~—

LAZ. —And the speedometer isn't even doing nothing no more—

HECTOR. —It's not registering—

LAZ. —COME ON DAWG—

HECTOR. —FIFTH GEAR SIXTH SEVENTH EIGHTH GEAR HOW MANY GEARS DO I HAVE?—

LAZ. —HOLY SHIT—

HECTOR. —THE SPEEDOMETER ISN'T EVEN REGISTERING HOW FAST I'M GOING ANYMORE WHAT THE HELL AM I DOING—

LAZ. —AND I AM *NOT* THINKING ABOUT MY SISTER—

HECTOR. —NINTH GEAR TENTH GEAR HOW FAST AM I GOING—

LAZ. —FLYING—

HECTOR. —AND SUDDENLY ALL THE DARKNESS AROUND US BECOMES LIKE SOMETHING ELSE—

LAZ. —WHAT?!—

HECTOR. —SOMETHING *ELSE*—

LAZ. —AND OUTTA NOWHERE THERE'S MAD STREAKS OF LIGHT JUST STREAMING ACROSS THE WINDSHIELD LIKE LIGHT WAS MADE INTO WATER AND IT'S RAINING BRO—

HECTOR. —I HAVE NO IDEA WHAT'S GOING ON—

LAZ. —LIKE *HYPERSPEED*—

HECTOR. —IT'S RAINING LIGHT BUT AT THIS POINT I'M EVEN SCARED TO SLOW DOWN—

LAZ. —HYPERSPEED HAN SOLO MILLENNIUM FALCON-STYLE—

HECTOR. —AND OUTTA NOWHERE THERE ARE THESE COLORS—

LAZ. —THERE'S STARS SCRAPING AGAINST MY WINDSHIELD AND I MOVE TO PUT THE WIPERS BUT I CAN'T 'CAUSE—

HECTOR. —THERE'S LIKE A G-FORCE HOLDING ME BACK AND I CAN'T MOVE—

LAZ. —LIKE ON A ROLLERCOASTER—

HECTOR. —LIKE IN SPACE—

LAZ. —*APOLLO THIRTEEN* DAWG!—

HECTOR. —AND AT THIS POINT WE'RE NOT EVEN RACING AGAINST EACH OTHER—

LAZ. —AT THIS POINT I'M LOOKIN' THROUGH THE WINDOW AND I COULD SEE THE SIDES OF THIS DUDE'S SUBARU ON FIRE BRO—

HECTOR. —WHAT?!—

LAZ. —ON *FIRE* BRO—

HECTOR. —AND THE STEERING WHEEL AND THE SCOOBY DOO COVER AND EVERYTHING START TO RATTLE—

LAZ. —AND MY "PUT-PUT" BECOMES LIKE SHAKING—

HECTOR. —AND EVERY HINGE AND EVERY SCREW IN MY CAR FEELS LIKE IT'S ABOUT TO COME APART—

LAZ. —BUT JUST BEFORE IT DOES—

HECTOR. (*To himself.*) —EVERYTHING'S ABOUT TO COME APART—

LAZ. —AAAAGH!—

HECTOR. —WHAT AM I DOING?!—

LAZ. —JUST BEFORE IT DOES—

HECTOR. (*To himself.*) —GROW UP YOU FUCKING COWARD—

LAZ. —JUST JUST JUST—

HECTOR. —*GROW UP!!*—

LAZ. —JUST BEFORE LIKE *ALL* OF IT—

HECTOR. —EXPLODES, I HEAR—

LAZ. —NOTHING.

> (*A beat. Silence.*)
>
> (*Just.*)
>
> (*Silence.*)

HECTOR. And there's this moment.

This moment of…

LAZ. …nothing.

> (*A beat.*
>
> *Then softer.*)

HECTOR. And through the flames and the light and the dark and the shaking and the speed and the confused mess I see—

LAZ. —This fucker's face I never even seen before—

HECTOR. —And wherever it is I've driven,

Everything looks pretty much—

LAZ. —Pitch black.

> (*Silence.*)

HECTOR. And when I wake up, my car is in the middle of an intersection.

LAZ. Streetlight, puddle, garbage cans, payphone, just…

HECTOR. An intersection.

…

And I'm in one piece.

LAZ. Yup.

HECTOR. And so's *he*.

LAZ. (*Shock.*) Whatthefuck, yo.

HECTOR. And somewhere a gutter drips,

LAZ. And you could hear a car a block or two away.

HECTOR. And now,

Everything's—

LAZ. —Normal.

HECTOR. …

My tank's almost empty,

LAZ. And my engine's back to put-putting,

HECTOR. And I lean out my window and I can see there's a streak like a burn-mark on the side of my car, but other than that—

LAZ. —We're *alive*.

> (*For the first time, they look at each other.*
> *A beat.*)

HECTOR. And I look at this guy and I dunno what to say—

LAZ. —And neither does he—

HECTOR. —But he shoots me this little head-nod like—

> (—*LAZ shoots him an alpha-male head-nod.*
> *A beat.*)

And that's enough.

> (*A beat.*
> *Something's changed.*)

And I turn the key in the ignition,

LAZ. Put-put. Put-put.

HECTOR. Scooby Doo steering wheel.

Crooked sun visor that I haven't fixed yet.

LAZ. Like normal.

HECTOR. And I put my seatbelt on.

LAZ. It's 3:59 in the morning.

Still.

And I don't know where the hell I am—

HECTOR. —But I got somewhere I need to go.

> (*Light out on* HECTOR.
> LAZ *looks around, taking inventory.*)

LAZ. Chop-Chop smell.

Streetlight.

Puddle.

Garbage can.

Pay phone.

…

Pay phone.

…

…

And now I'm outta my car.

And now I'm picking up the headset.

…

Now I'm outta my car,

…

And my sister gets a call.

(*Blackout.*)

End of Play.

AMERIVILLE

by UNIVERSES

271

BIOGRAPHIES

Gamal Abdel Chasten, a founding member of UNIVERSES, is a songwriter/poet/screenwriter. His work has toured more than 25 U.S. cities and 5 countries. Theatrical writing credits include *The Last Word*, *God Took Away His Poem* and the UNIVERSES shows *The Ride* and *Slanguage*. Directing credits include *The Last Word*, Full Circle's *Innerviews* (Dance Theater Workshop) and *Articulation*. Mr. Chasten is currently working on several screen projects, including *Red Moon*, *Joe Blow* and *North Borough*. He appeared with UNIVERSES on the cover of *American Theatre* magazine (2004) and *Source* magazine (2000). He was also part of the 2008 Jazz at Lincoln Center: The Rhythm Road and is a member of Network of Ensemble Theaters (NET) and New York Theatre Workshop's Usual Suspects. Publications include: *Writers Corp Teacher Anthology* (City Lights Books), *UNIVERSES—The Big Bang* (TCG) and *Slanguage* in *The Fire This Time* (TCG).

Mildred Ruiz, a UNIVERSES founding member, is a playwright/actor/vocalist. Credits include *The Denver Project* (Curious Theater; dir. Dee Covington), *One Shot in Lotus Position* (*The War Anthology*—Curious Theater; dir. Bonnie Metzgar), *Blue Suite* (dir. Chay Yew), *Rhythmicity* (Humana Festival 2003), *Slanguage* (New York Theatre Workshop; dir. Jo Bonney), *The Ride* (playwright/actor) and Alfred Jarry's *UBU: Enchained* (Teatre Polski in Poland; dir. Steven Sapp). Awards/affiliations include: 2008 Jazz at Lincoln Center: The Rhythm Road Tour; 2008 TCG Peter Zeisler Award; 2006 Career Advancement Fellowship (Ford Foundation) through Pregones Theater; 2002-2004 and 1999-2001 TCG National Theater Artist Residency Program Award; BRIO Awards (Bronx Recognizes Its Own); Co-Founder of The Point; board member of National Performance Network (NPN); former board member of Network of Ensemble Theaters (NET); New York Theatre Workshop Usual Suspect; Bard College, B.A. 1992. Publications include: *UNIVERSES—The Big Bang* (TCG) and *Slanguage* in *The Fire This Time* (TCG).

William Ruiz a.k.a **Ninja** was born and raised on the Lower East Side of Manhattan. Acting credits include UNIVERSES' *Slanguage* (dir. Jo Bonney), Jack Kerouac's *Ti Jean Blues* (adapt./dir. JoAnne Akalaitis), Nicole Quinn's *Tree Tails* (dir. Shelly Wyant), Oscar Wilde's *Salome* (dir. Nick Jones), Anthony Rivera's *Latin Howel* (dir. Todd A. Jackson) and Nicky Cruz's *Run Baby Run* (dir. Chris Fredricks, Houston Astrodome, Texas). He was both playwright and director of *Waiting for Gordo* (an adaptation of Samuel Beckett's play). Mr. Ruiz was also part of the 2008 Jazz at Lincoln Center: The Rhythm Road as Ambassador of Music and a member of

NET (Network of Ensemble Theatres). Mr. Ruiz received his B.A. in theatre from Bard College, where he studied under JoAnne Akalaitis and Elizabeth Smith and learned poetry under the tutelage of Bob Holman. Publications include: *UNIVERSES—The Big Bang* (TCG) and *Slanguage* in *The Fire This Time* (TCG).

Steven Sapp, a UNIVERSES founding member, has worked on the collaborations *The Denver Project* (Curious Theater, dir. Dee Covington) and *One Shot in Lotus Position* (The War Anthology—Curious Theater; dir. Bonnie Metzgar), *Blue Suite* (dir. Chay Yew), *Rhythmicity* (2003 Humana Festival) and *Slanguage* (New York Theatre Workshop). His directing credits include *The Ride* (assistant), *The Architecture of Loss*, Will Powers' *The Seven* (University of Iowa) and Alfred Jarry's *UBU: Enchained* (with Teatre Polski, Poland). He toured with Jazz at Lincoln Center: The Rhythm Road and was the recipient of TCG's Peter Zeisler Award (2008), National Directors Award (2002) and their National Theater Artist Residency Program Award (2002 to 2004 and 1999 to 2001). He also received a Van Lier Fellowship with New Dramatists and is a New York Theatre Workshop Usual Suspect. Mr. Sapp is co-founder of The Point and holds a B.A. from Bard College. Publications include: *UNIVERSES—The Big Bang* (TCG) and *Slanguage* in *The Fire This Time* (TCG).

ACKNOWLEDGMENTS

Ameriville premiered at the Humana Festival of New American Plays in March 2009. It was directed by Chay Yew with the following cast (in alphabetical order):

> Gamal Abdel Chasten
> Mildred Ruiz
> William Ruiz a.k.a. Ninja
> Steven Sapp

and the following production staff:

Scenic Designer... Paul Owen
Costume Designer .... Lorraine Venberg
Lighting Designer .... Russell Champa
Sound Designer... Benjamin Marcum
Properties Designer.. Alice Baldwin
Movement Supervisor..................................... Millicent Johnnie
Video Designer .... Jason Czaja
Stage Manager .... Megan Schwarz
Stage Management Intern .... Leslie Cobb
Dramaturg.. Morgan Jenness
Assistant Dramaturg... Brendan Pelsue
Assistant Director... Lila Neugebauer

This production was made possible in part by a grant from the Association of Performing Arts Presenters Ensemble Theatre Collaborations Grant Program, a component of the Doris Duke Charitable Foundation Theatre Initiative; and The National Performance Network (NPN) Creation Fund Project. Major contributors to NPN are the Doris Duke Charitable Foundation, Ford Foundation, Nathan Cumming Foundation, MetLife Foundation, the National Endowment for the Arts (a federal agency) and the Mid-Atlantic Arts Foundations and Mid-Atlantic Tours. Additional Development Lab Support was received from New World Theatre and New York Theatre Workshop.

UNIVERSES gives special thanks to: The National Performance Network, Theatre Communications Group (TCG), Chay Yew, Morgan Jenness, Harold Norris, Maya Sue, Ann Wager, H-Art Management, Marc Masterson, Actors Theatre of Louisville, New York Theatre Workshop, New World Theater, Wesley Montgomery, Teatro Pregones, Elis Finger & Lafayette College, The Sheldon Theater, Tanya Palmer & The Goodman Theatre, Fabian Obispo, NYU Skirball Center, Jazz at Lincoln Center (Rhythm Road), Network of Ensemble Theaters, Chip Walton & Curious Theater,

Nick Slie, Kathy Randels, Millicent Johnnie, Jose Torres Tama, Saddi Khali, Mrs. Herreast Harrison and The Guardians of the Flame, Kalamu Ya Salaam, Jim Randels, Students at the Center, Matt Schwartzman and John and Creative Forces (NOLA), Claudia Garofalo, Ashe Cultural Center, Tulane University, M.U.G.A.B.E.E., John O'Neil & Junebug Productions, Sunder Ganglani, Aimee Hayes and Southern Repertory, Miriam Weisfeld, Lisa Mount, Helena Presents, and Dance Place.

Ameriville was developed with Chay Yew and Morgan Jenness.

SETTING

New Orleans/Everywhere U.S.A.

Steven Sapp, William Ruiz a.k.a. Ninja (facing back),
Mildred Ruiz, and Gamal Abdel Chasten
in *Ameriville*

33rd Annual Humana Festival of New American Plays
Actors Theatre of Louisville, 2009
Photo by Harlan Taylor

AMERIVILLE

SUITE ONE

GAMAL. Said I[1]
Wonder what's the matter

ALL. Oh lord

GAMAL. Said I
Wonder what's the matter with my

ALL. Long time here

GAMAL. Won't you ring ol' hammer

ALL. Hammer ring

GAMAL. Won't you ring ol' hammer

ALL. Hammer ring

GAMAL. Won't you ring ol' hammer

ALL. Hammer ring

GAMAL. Won't you ring ol' hammer

ALL. Hammer ring

GAMAL. I said the sky fell down

ALL. Hammering

GAMAL. And I almost drowned

ALL. Hammering

GAMAL. Water so high

ALL. Hammering

GAMAL. I swam for my life

ALL. Hammering

GAMAL. I saved my wife and my kids

ALL. Hammering

GAMAL. First thing I did

ALL. Hammering

GAMAL. I sat on my house

ALL. Hammering

GAMAL. I needed help some how

ALL. Hammering

GAMAL. Won't you ring ol' hammer

ALL. Hammer ring

GAMAL. Won't you ring ol' hammer

ALL. Hammer ring

GAMAL. Won't you ring ol' hammer

ALL. Hammer ring

---

[1]   Adapted and sung in the style of an old work song.

GAMAL. Won't you ring ol' hammer

ALL. Hammer ring

GAMAL. Three days went by

ALL. Hammering

GAMAL. And I almost died

ALL. Hammering

GAMAL. Bodies floatin' by

ALL. Hammering

GAMAL. Held a sign to the sky

ALL. Hammering

GAMAL. Help! Help Me, Please!

ALL. Hammer ring

GAMAL. I lost everything

ALL. Hammer ring

GAMAL. Except your promises

ALL. Hammer ring

GAMAL. I needed help to live

ALL. Hammer ring

GAMAL. Won't you ring ol' hammer

ALL. Hammer ring

GAMAL. Won't you ring ol' hammer

ALL. Hammer ring

GAMAL. Won't you ring ol' hammer

ALL. Hammer ring

GAMAL. Won't, won't, won't you ring ol' hammer

ALL. Hammer ring

Mmhuhu
Mhu
Hammer ring
(*Continuous through* MILS' *piece.*)

MILS. The Lord
Told Noah
To build him
An arky arky
Lord
Told Noah
To build him an arky arky
Build it out of
Wood and barky barky

Children of the Lord[2]
But where was Noah
When the levees started breaking?
Where was Noah
When the levees started breaking?
Where was God
When the God-damned Dam
Was breakin'?
New Orleans is down

Zubadubadoo

        ALL. Duroom duroom
        Duroom doorum
        Zigizigi
        Hey
        (*Continuous through* MILS'
        piece.)

It's nobody's fault
That's what they say
It's nobody's fault
That's what they say
It's nobody's fault
But mine
Nobody's fault but mine
If I should die
And let my soul be lost
It's nobody's fault but[3]

        ALL. Cadoorum Doorum
        Hey
        Duroom duroom
        Duroom doorum
        Zigizigi
        MILS.
        Zubadubadooheyea/
        Hey/Eha Eha Eha ehey.
        (*Continuous through*
        STEVE's *piece.*)

STEVE. Has anybody seen my momma?
I said, has anybody seen my momma?
She didn't call me tonight,

---

[2]   Adapted from the Christian children's song "Rise and Shine."

[3]   Excerpt from "Nobody's Fault But Mine," Traditional Blues, referencing version by Nina Simone.

And it's late.
Gonna have myself a drink
At the bar
If that's all right?
See it's three o'clock in the morning
And I gotta be to work at six
See I work at the Post Office
It's good work
It's good pay
It keeps me on the good foot
On the straight and narrow
On the yellow brick road
But has anybody seen my momma?
'Cause she didn't call me tonight
'Cause everything I know and everything I've got
is sittin' underneath water
and we ain't sittin' 'round waiting
For the saints to come marching in
'Cause they're probably
They're probably at the FEMA office
Waiting for somebody else to make the first move
Or they're shoppin' for shoes with Condoleezza
And has anybody seen my momma?
'Cause she didn't call me tonight
Has anybody seen my country?
Has anybody seen my life?

Boom
Pa
Boom Boom
Papa Papa[4]

> **ALL.** Boom
> Papa
> Boom Boom
> Papa Papa
> **MILS.** Boom Boom
> Boom boom (*x4.*)
> **ALL.** Boom Boom
> Papa
> Boom Boom

---

[4]   Referencing "Papa" by Prince from the album *Come*, 1994.

Papa Papa
Boom

MILS. Papa was
Papa was
Papa was
Was Papa?

G, S, N. Yes,
Yes he was

MILS. Papa was
Now Papa isn't
Papa isn't the Papa that was

ALL. Boom Boom
(NINJA, *High Hat.*)
Booboom Boom Boom
(GAMAL, *Vocal guitar.*)

GAMAL. I never got a chance to see him[5]
Never heard nothing
But bad things about him
Momma I'm dependent on you
To tell me the truth
Momma hung her head
And she said son

MILS & GAMAL. Papa was a rollin' stone
Wherever he laid his hat was his home
Papa was a rollin' stone
Wherever he laid his hat was his home

ALL.
Papa was a rollin' stone
Wherever he laid his hat
was his home
Papa was a rollin' stone
Wherever he laid his hat
was his home
(*Continuous through* MILS'
Rollin'.)

MILS. He was "rollin', rollin'"[6]
Rollin'" down "the river"

---

[5] Excerpt from "Papa Was a Rollin' Stone," by Norman Whitfield and Barrett Strong, popularized by The Temptations.

[6] Referencing "Proud Mary," by John Fogerty, popularized by Ike and Tina Turner.

"Rollin', rollin'
Rollin'" down "the river"

He was "rollin', rollin'
Rollin'" down "the river"
"Rollin', rollin'
Rollin'" down "the river"

ALL. He was rollin'
Rollin'
Rollin'
Rollin'
I said he was rollin'
(*Continuous through*
NINJA's *piece.*)

NINJA. He went down like a rock
They were liars and thieves,
Heretics and heathens,
Worshipers of pagan gods
And he went down like a rock

He saved us all
Died
So that we could live to sin again
Clambering for more beads
Booze and weeds
Everything we could want
Much more than we could need

Like a rock
Sinking
Drinking lungfulls of ocean
After saving me and Mommy
He went back and did it all again
He saved the barber
The bartender
The locksmith down the block
Saved a sailor
Swimming from his sinking ship
Anchored at the dock
He saved a loan shark to square his debts
And a cop
Because well…why not
He used the copper's radio to signal choppers to the rooftop
After that Papa rested.

(Pace slows down and MILS *stagers "Rollin'.")*

(NINJA *pauses briefly.*)

Exhausted from his efforts
Papa couldn't move
But he heard a child let out a scream
And jumped back into the pool
Looking lifeless
Papa was half dead
After he handed me the child
I lost sight of Papa's head
He went down like a rock
Papa was brave
Was Papa?
Yes he was wasn't he?
Papa was
But now Papa isn't
Papa isn't the Papa that was

ALL. ...Rollin'
Rollin'
I said he was
Hu Ha
Hu Ha
(Continuous through STEVE's.)

STEVE. I got the law man[7]
The con man
The liquor store man
The man sippin' Jin and Juice at the bar man
I got the old man callin' on the young man
I got the soul man tryin' to keep a hold

I got the this is your land man
This is my land man
I got the blood on the tracks man
I got the guilty man
I got the innocent man

ALL. I got the buffalo soldier
Dreadlocked Rasta man

---

[7]   Referencing and adapted from "Fame," by Citizen Cope.

ALL. Hu Ha
Hu Ha
NINJA.
Misery's the river of the world
Misery's the river of the world
Everybody row
Everybody row
Everybody row
Everybody row.[8]

(ALL *&* NINJA *continuous through* MILS' *piece.*)

MILS. He was rollin' rollin' rollin'
And the waves
Kept rollin' rollin'
And the waves
Kept rollin' rollin'
Rollin' in
Just rollin' by

Rollin' rollin' rollin'
And the waves
Kept rollin' rollin'
And the waves
Kept rollin' rollin'
Rollin' in
Just rollin' by

And Air Force One
Flew by
A shot to the gut
Capturing images of death
From thirty thousand feet above sea level
Leveled by the sea
And we see it all on CNN and NBC
Well media
Woke up!
And found out that the sand man had been here for years
Roll the tape!
Roll the tape!
Roll the tape
Roll the tape

---

[8]   Referencing Tom Waits' "Misery Is the River of the World," from the album *Blood Money,* 2002.

Roll the tape
And roll and roll and roll
And roll and roll
And roll and roll
And roll and roll
And roll and roll
And roll and roll!

You can't tie beads to trees
And expect people to hold on long enough

To row
And row and row
And row and row
And row and row
And row and row
And row and row
And row and Row!
Inexistent boats

Flowers in the attic,
Broke their fingers
Breaking through rooftops

And as they looked up to the sky
As they looked up to the sky
All they see
All they see
Is Air Force One
Just flyin' by
Just flyin' by
Just flyin' by
Just flyin' by

As they looked up to the sky
All they see
All they see
Is Air Force One
Just flyin' by
Just flyin' by
Just flyin' by
Just flyin' by

And you can
Row and row and row

And row and row
And row and row

And row and row
And row and row
And row and Row!

Everybody row
Everybody row
Everybody row
Everybody row

(MILS *joins* NINJA *on "Misery."*
STEVE *sings "row, row, row your
boat."* [9]

ALL *fade out and* GAMAL *is
left gasping, till last breath.*)

GAMAL. Hu Ha
Hu ha
Hu ha
Hu

SUITE TWO
Black Like That

STEVE. Huh ha huh!
Can't we get over this already
Haven't they fixed the levees
(*Mockingly.*) I was hit by a storm…
I lost my home…
Whimper, cry, bitch and moan
I don't know about anyone else, but I'm done
I donated a trumpet to the musicians' relief fund
I've got a rubber bracelet to mark the occasion
I extended my hands to Creoles and Cajuns
It's been four years since
What about the rest of the country
You've got your health care, two wars, and a crumbling economy
FEMA, floods and fuck ups, I get it.
Now get over it already.

GAMAL. We've heard you say things
We've heard the whispers under your breaths
We can hear you screaming at us loud and clear

---
[9]   American children's song, "Row Your Boat."

We hear
Y'all have heard it more than you want to.
But you hear it, don't you
Call us lower class, lazy and shiftless
But we're still waiting for the shift
Don't you realize that after all this time
And it's been a long time
Recovery efforts haven't recovered
Basic services, doesn't serve us.
Aren't we neighbors, aren't we friends
Aren't we family, aren't we fellow citizens
Aren't we you.
Why is this story important
Why is any story about anybody important
Why is right and wrong important
Important to know how others live
Even if you don't live that way
Even if you don't know them
Know us
The same way we don't know you
But love you as us.
Before this and after this
We exist.

GAMAL. Before the storm hit I was Black.
I was black like I was neglected.

STEVE. Since the storm I'm black like, "forget about him" type Black

GAMAL. Black like "I go to a tuff school" type Black.

STEVE. Black like "they closed my school" type Black

GAMAL. Before the storm hit I was Black like
"every store in my parish sells liquor and cigarettes" Black.

STEVE. I'm black like "they closed my store" type Black

GAMAL. I was black, "from front to back" type Black

STEVE. Black like blue black, Black like that

STEVE. Since the storm I'm Black like, "I ain't got no job" type Black

GAMAL. I was black like broke black like "I lived in the projects" type Black

STEVE. Black like "they tore down my projects" type Black

GAMAL. Black like "I get arrested for being" Black,

STEVE. Black like "I get shot for being" Black

GAMAL. I was black like "my momma's momma and them" type Black

STEVE. Black like "where's my momma" type Black

GAMAL. I was black like that
STEVE. Now I'm black like this
GAMAL. Black like real, real Black
STEVE. Black like damn you Black
BOTH. But why it got to be like that
In my face and behind my back
No more whip-cracks
No more click-clack
Just trying to come back
I'm just like…that.

Ghost Tour #1

NINJA. Ha-ha all right, all right ladies and gents
Climb aboard the SS Arrr Bootleg
You can call me Captain Jean Lefitte
If you're looking for a ghost tour
Then I've got your treat
I'll take you where your cameras yearn to be
Where the stories are priceless
And photography is free
Just pass me a few bucks
And you can hop on the duck
For a tour
Down the might nine
Step up, step up
First stop
St. Louis Cemetery Number One
          (*Changes to somber.*)
Where we can find the final resting place
Of the one and only voodoo queen of New Orleans[10]
Legend has it
She had control over her entire population
Such is the power of the hairdresser
Matter of fact
I've plundered her favorite black comb
Like to buy it?
Ten bucks

---

[10]   One of the most popular women in New Orleans history, Marie Laveau, voodoo queen. People today still place flowers at the site of her tomb and mark X's in chalk on the vault as assurance of favors to be granted.

But you have to get them quick
I've only got five of them left
>   (*Changes to his more somber state.*)
Sea men and women
>   (*Face* MILS, *watch her.*)
I give to you
Marie Laveau 1827-1881
If you believe real hard
You might have your wishes granted
Approach me lady's crypt and mark upon it
Three X's
As you can see from all these other X's
She's been quite busy since the storm.

Marie Laveau

MILS. (*Sung.*) Who goes there?
Go away!

Got my own problems
Can't deal with you today

Couldn't stop the storm from comin'
Place no more X on me
Go away
Go away

The levees have broken but it's nothing new,
'Cause even then I could do nothin', as Hurricane winds blew.

Wanted to save them!
>   Marie save me
Wanted to save them!
>   Marie save me!
>   (BRIAN *throws up on the street.*)
NINJA. (*As* BRIAN.) Awww
Woohoo!
MartiGrawww
Been here two nights and I'm lovin' it
I had a blast at that bar on the corner
Got blasted and plastered
And woke up with no pants on
It was great
I guess I must have stayed up too late

'Cause this morning I woke up at night
Like half-past eight
Tonight I'll do it again
I'll be seeing titties on the streets
Girls gone wild
Just me and a couple of friends
I've got a week full of plans
This is a party with no end

I've booked a tour
I got a Jazz tour
Ghost Tour
Ninth Ward Tour
Marie Laveau's to make a wish
For more, more, more
Oh, give me some beads
You,
Look like Little Wayne
What are you drinking?
Hurricane?
Hey! I'd like a hurricane
That should help me bury the pain

Ooh, I found a Voodoo shop
Can we make a stop
You have a pin cushion man
How much for pin cushion man?
I'll take a keychain too.
Two for five?
Give me five, old man
Yeah that's COOL
Really cool
Give me this
Give me that
Give me paintings
Give me masks
Give me Seeds
Magic beans
Give me, give me New Orleans

MILS. *(Sung.)* It drives me crazy
All my people calling me
My body's aching
My womb's ripped right out of me

Catholic saints and martyrs,
Voodoo Gods and Goddesses
I begged them all to save you
But didn't hear what I said

There a child was drowning
There was nothing I could do
And there, another child was dying
And you turned your back on them too

SAVE ME

GAMAL/STEVE. Marie save me

MILS. SAVE ME

GAMAL/STEVE. Marie save me
NINJA. Have some reverence
You gotta be respectful when visiting the dead
You know?
This tomb is the second most visited tomb in the country
You are standing amidst history
Powerful forces from powerful people

That crazy Pirate didn't drop you off here, did he?
Hmmm, well
I'm Nick
I work for the State Historic Preservation Office
Marie's tomb is not on the register
But I showed up for a brush-up on my day off
Actually she doesn't look too bad
Most of these crypts
They've been through it all before
But this one here, she's special
A little piece of America's history
Like so much here in New Orleans
Our culture, freedom, arts, family
We left a lot for the world to remember us by
Feels like since the storm
We've got forgotten
And how do you neglect such vital history?
What if fire ravaged Boston?
Paul Revere's home would be in no danger of damage
What if D.C. suffered storm after storm?
I guarantee not a Lincoln head would be spared

To ensure the Tomb of the Unknown Soldier would still be there
But here,
Our own Queen Marie drowns in tears of despair
So please
Be respectful while you're here
With the Queen
Queen Marie

MILS. The water kept rising
And washed their life away
There's one dead in attic
He's the one I wanted to save

Someone tagged some X's
And I thought they were for me
But X's
Marked my city dead
One Thousand Eight Hundred Thirty Three

Wanted to save them!
                    Marie save me
Wanted to save them!
                    Marie save me
Wanted to save them!
                    Marie save me
Wanted to save them!
                    Marie save me
          (*Music fades,* MILS *ends on high note.*)
Wanted to save them!

MASKING INYAN

ALL. *(Sung.)*
Somebody's gotta sew sew sew
Somebody's gotta sew all night long
Somebody's gotta sew sew sew
Somebody's gotta sew all night long[11]

GAMAL. It's not the same anymore
The flavor changed
Sure, the clouds still puffy
And the water still imitates the color of the sky
But the jazz, not so jazzy anymore

---

[11] Referencing "Sew, Sew, Sew" form the Mardi Gras Indian song cycles.

And the citizens, well…we wrapped in cynicism
It's not the same
See, when I was a real young
For Mardi Gras I was a flag boy then a little chief
At first I liked the beads and feathers
But then I get older and I think my father
He look like a peacock
And I say I never want to strut like him
My father, he always stress the pride
He say you got to have pride when you mask Inyan
You got to remember the past, he say
My father had a good memory
But he took it with him when he die
I remember the pride
He had so much respect from his tribe, his friends.
But they don't see when he make my mother cry,
When he knock her down.
Nobody else see. But I remember.
Those feather suited
Beads and gemstones weigh me down
Making me think about yesterday
Beads and feathers that was my father's thing
I didn't have money or time for that
But when my father die
My mother she forgive, so I ask myself why can't I…
No sense in holding on to all those bad memories
The storm take away all Inyan costumes
They gone…washed away and faded
Beads and feathers caked with mud.
So who gonna preserve tradition
Gotta be flag boys and little chiefs
I wanna hold on
And I like it again
That's why this year for Mardi Gras
I mask Inyan
ALL. INYAN!

HEART HOUSE

GAMAL & OTHERS. Every house has a heart
And a home ain't just a house
In New Orleans
When the floorboards creak

They speak to a wife
To let her know that her husband cheats
And when a mamma gives birth
The walls contract with every
Cleansing breath she breathes
every house has a heart
And a home ain't just a house in New Orleans

Right there was a house
Big ole house
Right there was a house
Lovin house
And right there was a house
Screamin house
Right there was a house
Hard workin house

And the man worked hard
Like any man works hard
To keep his family fed and clothed
But when the Hurricane came
It washed away
any semblance of a home
Mmmhmmm

Cuttin' Heads (On top of Heart House)

STEVE. Yo Bobby!
I need you to do something with my hair real quick,
Give me a shape up or something,
You know just give me a line around the sides
You know make it look neat.
I gotta go see my momma today man
And you know she always got something to say about my hair.
Man I know when I see her,
The first thing she's gonna say is
When you gonna cut that off
I can't wait for you to get out that phase.
And I keep telling her I'm too old to be in a phase
This is me!
Then she tells me "Malcolm Jamal Warner cuts his off"
And I gotta tell her, "I don't know Malcolm Jamal Warner,
And you don't know Malcolm Jamal Warner
So why are we even talking about him"

Then she says,
"I'm not giving you my opinion, I'm telling you what to do,"
Like I'm some kid or something.
I remember when I got my first haircut
And my momma brought me in 'cause my father had to work
And she sat me down in Harold's chair,
You remember Harold right?
Harold was the guy who had one ear bigger than the other
And you had to tell him stuff in the big ear
'Cause if you told it to him in the small ear
He'd always get it wrong
And my momma didn't know it
And nobody told her
And he messed up my hair
And she punched him in the jaw
Reared back and punched him right on the jaw
And dared him to say something
My momma is crazy,
Man I love her for that
I ain't seen her since…
it got all crazy down here.
I'm looking for her…
And I don't know where she at…
Every day now, different people come down here looking
But all they do is look
I mean some have some good intentions
All type of people come down here
Christian groups
College kids
And them bleeding-hearted liberals
Trying to add their two's and fews
Tragedy Vultures
Already moved on to the next subject

I mean maybe I should just cut it all off, my hair
'Cause you know people hold a lot of energy in their hair
And I couldn't walk around with all this stuff inside me
If something happened to her
And I wasn't there…
I couldn't live with that.
Told me they found a body in my momma's house man
That ain't my momma man, my momma strong
She punched out Harold

I mean it's cool what you did with this extra room in your house
Since your old shop got flooded,
But I gotta bounce
Nah, nah, nah don't worry bout it man maybe I come back tomorrow
I gotta go find my momma

Heart House (continued)

GAMAL & OTHERS. Right there was a house
Big ole house
Right there was a house
Lovin house
And right there was a house
Screamin house
Right there was a house
Hard workin house

Right there was a house
Big ole house
Right there was a house
Lovin house
And right there was a house
Screamin house
Right there was a house
Hard workin house

And the con men came
laid down the con game
and bought up every stitch of land
and they gonna hold on till they break
that heart,
'cause nobody's coming back
Mmmhmmm

Eleven Eleven (The White Album)

GAMAL. It didn't just happen to black folk
Good hard working white folks lost their homes too
I'm 61 years old
I suffer, I got issues, I deserve to be seen too
Every night, at 11:11 I wake up, and I'm sweatin…I mean I'm soaked.
No disrespect doc, but ain't nothing post about it.
It's not post racial, post corruption, post anything,
It's right now, it's every night.

11:11 is like a bridge, and every night I get stuck in the same spot.
Wading in that muddy water.
Even with everything going on around,
you tried real hard to keep your head above it
No telling what you might swallow if you didn't.
For true, it stank, stank so bad you couldn't think straight.
And it's my job to think.
Smell worse than regular death.
And I smell that smell every night.
Maybe you got a name for that, a pill for that?
Let me ask you something
What would you call it when people,
black people and white people are trying to survive?
Holding on to anything.
Some were so desperate they clung to dead bodies.
I have no idea what to do with these dead little children I see floating by me
         every night.
Either I want to kill myself or I feel like I'm already dying.
The thing that kills me is not that I couldn't get an appointment,
or because I'm white and uptown, it's assumed that I'm okay.
It's none of that! What it is, is that I'm reduced to this.
I'm glad you got a nice pretty name for what I'm going through night after night.
I go to sleep at 10 p.m. I sleep for one hour and eleven minutes.
Wake up smelly and frightened in a lake of perspiration, thinking about killing
         myself
And here you are, wanting to give me a pamphlet to read on post-traumatic stress.

Heart House (continued)

GAMAL & OTHERS. Right there was a house
Big ole house
Right there was a house
Lovin house
And right there was a house
Screamin house
Right there was a house
Hard workin house

Right there was a house
Big ole house
Right there was a house
Lovin house
And right there was a house

Screamin house
Right there was a house
Hard workin house

And then the con men came
laid down the con game
and bought up every stitch of land
and they gonna hold on till they break
that heart,
'cause nobody's coming back
Mmmhmm

MILS. There is a house in New Orleans
Beneath the risin' sun
And it's been the ruin
Of many a poor girl
And me
Oh Lord I'm one

I'm goin' back
To New Orleans
My race is almost won
I'm goin' back to spend my life
Beneath the risin' sun[12]

In The Shadow of Jesus

MILS. I'm always here
Always at the white church
The one with the touchdown Jesus

Praise the Lord, Halleluiah, Amen!

The statue casts a shadow on me here.

So I'm always here
Every day
After school
Making palm tree art
Turning fallen palm tree leaves into African masks

And you know, tourists love New Orleans masks
So I make them out of fallen palm tree leaves
and give the peoples what they want

---

[12]   "House of the Rising Sun" (The Rising Sun Blues), American folk ballad.

I guess they think it's more exotic
So I like to add a little drama to the product

Sometimes
I add pieces of discarded splintered wood from houses...

Maybe wood from Katrina-damaged houses...

Maybe fallen palm tree leaves from the Ninth Ward...

Palm tree art from the remainders of the storm
A reminder of what happened

Like when they sold pieces of the World Trade Center
Coins made out of steel from the fallen towers

No one even knew,
if the steel was actually steel from the World Trade.
But they bought it
It's the sentiment of the thing!
Tourists wanna contribute to the economy
and I wanna help them do it...
The economy of my pocket

Hey,
good schoolin' comes at a high price
and my bills are stackin' up!

My mama never did get her FEMA check
Now she can't get me the things I need
And who gotta take care of house and home
and I may be poor but I gotta rep.
Gotta look my best
Gotta get the latest gear
Can't be rockin last year

I'm a get it with my art
Just gonna take a little artistic license that's all
Artistic license and make the peoples feel good

It's like a little white lie
Just a little white lie Jesus

A little lie for the little white folks
that wanna help the economy

They won't hate me too terrible
I'm in the shadow of Jesus
He knows what's up

He'll forgive me
He knows my truth

And just in case he don't
Cause you can't expect God
To do everything for ya.
Gotta do for self and God will help with the rest

That's right!
Let the tourists take home some palm tree arts
Have a Café au Lait and a little fried powdered sugar
Let them get a voodoo doll with pins at the voodoo shop

Let them go home happy
dreaming 'bout New Orleans
and remembering me…

In the Shadow of Jesus

Praise the Lord, Hallelujah, Amen!

Hey!
You wanna buy a little piece of New Orleans?

Lost Youth

This little piggy went to Houston[13]
This little piggy stayed home
This little piggy had gumbo
This little piggy had none
This little piggy cried all the way home/all the way home/all the way home
        (Notes: song collage includes: "If you want me to stay"; "I'll Stay.")

NINJA. My mother, she came from Vietnam
She moved here because war there killed so many of my people
So she decided to start all over again here
Where she had me.
She said this hurricane, it's nothing like living through the war
She said I got nothing to complain about
This is easy
So now we have to rebuild.
We have to rebuild and start all over again
This is one of the things my people can do best
And that's what we have to do here
Again.

---

[13] Adaptation of English language Nursery Rhyme, "This Little Piggy."

(*Music drops out.*)

TOGETHER. The theme park is a ghost town
The Ferris wheel stopped spinning
The Little League diamond's damaged
Muddy in every inning

MILS. Kids running round with no place to play
Gotta move on to a better day
Kids running round with no place to play
Gotta move on to a better day
    (*Music drops in.*)

GAMAL. My mom and dad, both, neither found
I bounce from house to house
'Cause nowhere is home now
I've got six months left before my graduation
Sometimes I feel torn
Between staying and leaving
I ain't gonna lie, it's real bad
But if everybody leaves, who's gonna bring
New Orleans back
People like me, you'll see
People like me
    (*Music shift: "Shallow Water Oh Momma" x4.*)[14]

STEVE. When I've got a book
Tucked under my arm
I feel strapped, a 44-gauge aimed at my brain
And I've read story after story, and book after book
And I've only seen glimpses of me
In those pages
So I've got to go live a little more
Go straight from my graduation
With my cap and gown still on
Straight into the car, not stopping to say goodbye
I'm gonna make books for those who want to understand
A story like mine
And I'll be Huck Finn and Jim
Floating up the Mississippi on a raft
And the whispers of Louisiana hitting me on my back
    (*Music shift: "How High is the Water Mama?"*)[15]

---

[14]   Adapted from the Mardi Gras Indian Folk song "Shallow Water."

[15]   Adapted from Johnny Cash's "Five Feet High and Rising" *Five Feet High and Rising*, 1974.

How high is the water Momma?
10 feet high and rising
How high is the water Papa?
10 feet high and rising
Now the floodwater's coming right up to the gutter
The rooftop's starting to tremble and shudder
Gonna get help hold on to your mother
The water's 10 feet high and rising
10 feet high and rising
How high is the water Momma?
12 feet high and rising
How high is the water Papa?
14 high and rising
How high is the water Momma?
16 high and rising

CRAWFISH

GAMAL. So I was at the bar wit my man,
and we was talkin' 'bout,
politics,
global warming,
gynecology.
You know deep shit.
So then I asked him…
what you think about Urban Renewal?
And he was like,
I don't know
I didn't listen to it yet.
And I'm like…
nah you stupid motherfucker,
Urban renewal.
You know, when they take a bunch of brown people
and replace 'em with a bunch of white people.
Otherwise known as Nigger Removal.
Just the other day,
this polite stranger knocked on my door
and knew everything about me.
NINJA. *Are you Mr. Crawfish?*
GAMAL. Yes!
NINJA. *The same Mr. Crawfish*
that does stand-up comedy at Larry's Stripper Spot?

GAMAL. That'd be me

NINJA. Well I'm Bucky Harris
with the chokeaniggerout investment group
and we would like to offer you $25,000 cash for your property.

GAMAL. And I'm like:
Any possibility of negotiating that price,
and he's like…

NINJA. *No sir!*

GAMAL. And I'm like…
how am I supposed to find a home in this market for $25,000.
And he's like…

NINJA. *That's not my concern,
my job is simply to chokeaniggerout.*

GAMAL. $25,000 sounds like a lot,
to a brother who can't keep $2 between paydays
$25,000 is enough to make a brother, pause…
They gonna give me $25,000 for this small-ass lot of land
we got a whole lot a vacant lots around here,
that's a whole lotta $25,000 checks
they must have a whole lotta money, maybe I should wait.
My little piece of property might be the future site of the new
Starbucks bathroom
I'll be able to skip the bathroom line anytime
Free Lattes!
Free Lattes!
That's right, chokeaniggerout!
Also known as gentrification,
See what they do is
They hike up the real estate
Store owners start bitchin
I can't afford this.
I got to pack up and find somewhere else to sell my shit.
Then the neighborhood becomes deserted,
trash only gets picked up on Martin Luther King's Birthday,
Grandmothers start carrying weapons and shit,
and here come Bucky & the chokeaniggerout investment group.

    (*Knock, knock, knock.*)

NINJA. *Think of what you and your family can do
with $15,000 and a fresh start*

GAMAL. Fifteen thousand dollars?
I thought you said $25,000

I can't even buy a FEMA trailer for $15,000
'Cause $15,000 is choice money,
which means you got to make a choice about what you spending it on.
Mmmm, maybe I can get me some bad-ass rims
but shit I ain't got no car.
I know, I'll fix that roof I've been meaning to fix,
but oh lord, I ain't got no house.
Call it what you want,
Gentrification,
Urban Renewal,
it's always planned.
But poor folk know how to make it anywhere.
Poor folks know how to struggle
Any time you can come up with 325 different ways to use a peanut
Now that's creative struggle
Let me see,
what can I do with this peanut…
I'll make some peanut oil, then
I'll make some peanut cake,
And I'll use the rest
To make some nitroglycerin,
to blow up the master's house
if he keep fucking with me.
Poor folk know how to struggle
and can make it anywhere…
but they shouldn't have to!
But they don't care.
So after all the fires,
floods and decay,
here come Bucky again.

        (*Knock knock knock.*)

NINJA. *We'd like to offer you $5,000 for your unfortunate loss*
                1,000 dollars

GAMAL.		*for all your years of struggle*
NINJA.	1,000 dollars	
GAMAL.		*for all you hopes and dreams*
NINJA.	*1,000 dollars*	
GAMAL.		to replace your childhood memories
NINJA.	1,000 dollars	
GAMAL.		to replace the missing punch line

NINJA.   *1,000 dollars*

GAMAL.   because that's what it cost to chokeaniggerout.

GUN CLUB

NINJA *plays all characters.*

ANNOUNCER. For a limited time only,
Your Friendly Neighborhood Gun Club has got an exclusive offer.
NRA-approved firearms licenses for you, and your family.
No gun necessary.
Just come on down to the *Hood Gat Society*
on the corner of Smith & Wesson.
Inquire within.
We have a large selection of Kalashnikov,
Remington 870's, Colt, Beretta, Desert Eagle.
AND THAT'S NOT ALL!
Given the nation's growing crime rate
This is the time to defend your home

MAC 10. Picture yourself and your family chillin' twenty deep,
with nines and AK's,
Just sittin' in the living room
watching *America's Funniest Home Videos*
When suddenly who kicks down yo mama's front door?

ANNOUNCER. Burglars, rapists, DEBT COLLECTORS

MAC 10. See how many buckshots you could bust off
when it's time to duck.

ANNOUNCER. The buck stops here!

PITO. My name's Pito.
I've been busting caps for a minute now,
you know,
tryin' to get good with the gat.
I figure, if crazy looking rednecks with green teeth
are allowed to own guns, why can't we?
At least I got my G.E.D.

ANNOUNCER. No more burglars breaking and entering.
No pesky bullies beating your children in school.
No baby momma screaming…

BABY MOMMA. Get yo' sorry ass back in the house, right now!

ANNOUNCER. Just you, and your boys,
In the hood,
WITH GUNS!

No bank, no credit, no problem.
Apply today.

MAC 10. 'Cause when you're armed to the teeth in your sleep,
your target's guaranteed to become Swiss cheese.

ANNOUNCER. Having problems with your math teacher?
Tired of Mom's new boyfriend touching your stuff?
Tired of Muslims, Christians, and Eskimos?
Are you done with teenagers running up in your school
shooting up the place, and you without a gun?
Arm yourself today!

PITO. It ain't right man.
These hooligans are running around, burglarizing my shit.
Well that's over!
I'm taking full advantage of my American rights
by defending my home.

ANNOUNCER. "It's better to have a gun and not need it,
than to need a gun and not have it."

MAC 10. It's time to exercise your constitutional right to bear arms,
and flare arms whenever you fear harm.

(*Gunshots ring out.*)

PITO. Yo, you saw that?
That dude was trying to steal my mail!
Ah, he's the mailman?

ANNOUNCER. Never be caught off-guard.
Call 1.800.jushoot.
That's 800.587.4668.
defend your home today!

PITO. Yeah. Be a patriot.

MAC 10. Come down to the Hood Gat Society first precinct.
Together we'll discover what murder weapon's right for you.
Ask for me, Mac Ten.
I'm not only a client,
I'm the buckin' president.

ANNOUNCER. Friendly Neighborhood Gun Club is not a licensed dealer
or manufacturer. Background check required. Some restrictions apply. See
local advertising.

(*Sung.*) We just want you to shoot.

BOYS IN THE HOOD

ALL. We are the original
Boys in the hood
We live our lives
Misunderstood
You think we're always
Up to no good
The original
Boys in the Hood

We stand on the steps
where great men have stood
all we need is a sheet
and a cross made of wood
in an all pure clean
white neighborhood
the original
Boys in the Hood

Where there's a whip, there's a way
Where there's a whip, there's a way

> (*Whip sounds, stomping & chanting "Where there's a whip, There's a way"
> throughout.*)[16]

MILS. We are the original
Boys in the hood
We live our lives
Misunderstood
You think we're always
Up to no good
The original
Boys in the Hood

ALL. We stand on the steps
where great men have stood
all we need is a sheet
and a cross made of wood
in an all pure clean
white neighborhood
the original
Boys in the Hood

---

[16]   Referencing "Where There's a Whip," from the 1980 animated *The Return of the King* movie,
music by Maury Laws.

(MILS, STEVE & NINJA *hum "Favorite Things" grotesquely throughout.*)[17]

GAMAL. Crackers hate niggers
Crackers hate niggers
That dance and sing
Crackers hate niggers
That dance and sing
On MTV with too much money
That's why Crackers hate Niggers
And Niggers hate Mexicans
Niggers hate Mexicans
That work, and work
And never stop working
'Cause Niggers hate to work
And Puerto Ricans hate Dominicans
Puerto Ricans hate Dominicans
Because if you ain't Puerto Rican or Dominican
You think they all the same
And Puerto Ricans and Dominicans hate that shit
And Jews hate Arabs
Jews hate Arabs
Because they stubborn
And they won't leave
Jews hate Arabs
Because they stubborn
And they won't leave
Because they throw rocks and shit
And Arabs hate Jews
Because they're stubborn
And they won't leave
And because they are cousins
That's right they cousins
And Christians hate Jews
Because Jesus was a Jew
But Jews don't talk about Jesus
Like Christians do
And Muslims hate Christians and the Jews
And Catholics hate the Protestants
And Pygmies hate tall people
Pygmies hate tall people
Who knock down tall trees

---

[17]   Referencing "My Favorite Things," lyrics by Richard Rodgers, music by Oscar Hammerstein II, from *The Sound of Music.*

Pygmies hate anybody who knock trees down
Because if they ain't got tall trees around
they don't feel like Pygmies anymore
And fat people hate skinny people
Well, because they ain't fat
And skinny people hate fat people
Because fat people eat what the fuck they want
And that makes skinny people jealous
And jealous motherfuckers hate everybody
Jealous people hate tall people
Because they can reach the top shelf
They hate short people because
When they drop shit,
they don't have to bend down to pick it up
Jealous people hate sick people
Because they get too much attention
And they hate rappers
Because rappers always talkin' 'bout
"you know what I'm sayin"
"you know what I'm sayin"
Jealous people hate deaf people
Because they good with their hands
And people who don't have hands
Hate people with hands
Because they can masturbate
And prudes hate sex fiends
Sex fiends hate religion
Because religion is always telling you
What you shalt not do
But there's one passage in the Bible that sex fiends love
Sex fiends love that passage that says, love thy neighbor
Sex fiends love to love thy neighbor
But you know what
I hate all them Motherfuckers

How high is the water momma?
17 high and rising
How high is the water Papa?
18 high and rising
How high is the water momma?
19 high and rising
How high is the water Papa?
20 high and rising

COUNTRY FIRST

ALL. Country first
Country first

MILS. I'm home,
My battalion just landed.
I drop my stuff off at Motel 6
It is raining,
Boots get muddy in an instant,
I haven't set foot here since the flood
I walked heavy, heavy hearted, locked in heavy stare,
I see faces,
See landmarks,
Hear the familiar rustling of corn.

And I almost feel like myself again
My schizophrenic self,
that sported both an American and Puerto Rican Flag
on the hood of my Toyota before I left for the war.
When the towers fell
I was the first to enlist

It continues to rain
I walk to where my house used to be

And there it is…

I find pieces of who I was here
My husband's Double-Six Domino…
Two of my son's LEGOs…

This is where we used to play *Castle Attack*…
Building LEGO fortresses that always looked like El Morro…
We would carve a moat around it in the shape of Puerto Rico and fill it with
          water…

My eyes dart around
Interpreting the blurry scene
Trying to see if my baby boy, Junito
runs out for me
But he doesn't

People salute me as they pass the concrete slab
where my house stood
The same people that talked a lot of mierda about me
When I chose to join the service
Called me a mala madre for leaving my son during my tour of duty

But they salute me now
I left my family here,
Safe!
So I that could fight
For home
And Country

ALL. Country first
Country first

MILS. I went to fight for freedom

Not for Halliburton

Not for Oil

Still,
I stayed
and fought the war
For Country

ALL. Country first
Country first

MILS. Home is Country and Country comes first
Now my home in this country,
flooded,
river flooded
My son,
gone.

And I stand
Paralyzed
Choking back salty tears
But the Commander in Chief says
Keep it moving soldier!
For Country

ALL. Country first
Country first

MILS. I was sent to fight
Fight
Fight
Against a country
Whose eyes look like mine
Run
Run
Run
I see them run and scatter like ants through the dry desert heat

Run for life and limb

Suddenly, I see the enemy
Through the dry desert heat
One with the landscape
he turns
and I hunt
and he runs
he stops

And there he is
Towelhead
Cowering in a dead-end corner
Nowhere to run
Screaming bullshit in my ears
holding onto his towelhead son
I close my eyes
And I shoot…

I check out of Motel 6,
They salute me
In the lobby
Down the street
Up the ramp
At the terminal
In the café
At the checkpoint
At the gate

They salute,
They smile,
Some look away
Someone calls me

GAMAL. "Hey spic"

MILS. And I keep on marching

I'm a Category 5 soldier
Who lost everything along the way
And I have nothing left at home
So I fight
For Country
ALL. Country first
Country first

SHOESHINE

ALL. Penny and a nickel and a dime and a quarter
Penny and a nickel and a dime and a quarter
Shoe shine

(*Continue underneath* STEVE.)

STEVE. If a turtle has no shell, is it naked or is it homeless?
Do you have any idea...
how much energy it takes...
to raise enough money, to feed yourself every day?
How much thought and planning goes into this complicated task?
See, I have found, after doing extensive research
that the best place to tap into my full earning potential
is on the corner of right here and right now
This is the perfect spot
because it is right in the middle of the everyday hustle and bustle.
And every now and then
you'll catch someone who wants to really talk to you...
Someone who acknowledges your presence.
Somebody who's not afraid that my homelessness is contagious...
'Cause that's everybody's worst nightmare right.
That you're going to wake up one day
and you can't take care of your shit,
and you're going to be out here with people like me.
Well I've embraced my nightmare
what else can I do,
I mean who really wants to be out here
not knowing what each day going to bring...
will some group of kids set me on fire just to watch me scream,
like it's some video game or something
and who's going to care?
I am not on anybody's radar
I'm an invisible man
Ellison right
ha ha ha...
yeah I can read you know
But I know who I am
Having people look at you like you're the garbage
they wish would go away
But I know it
But they don't know my story
That I don't fit your homeless profile.
I'm not mentally ill

or a drug addict
or an alcoholic
I've learned and played by the rules
I've gone to school
Got my credit score in order
Bought a house
Even had my own computer business
Before the Wal-Mart moved into the neighborhood
and all the hard work
and the promise of 401k
and health benefits are gone.
Downsized to nothing.
And your subprime mortgage doubles.
Because the economy is drowning.
And you can't provide for your family
and you feel ashamed
And you lose your house and your dignity
And you end up living in your mother-in-law's basement
With boxes and boxes of her memories
Mixed in with what's left of your stuff
that you couldn't sell or pawn for money
and you're cramped in with your wife and your three kids
all sleeping on an air mattress on a concrete floor
You'll be damned if you are gonna live like this
or have your family on the streets
so you leave
they'll be better without you
you leave
and they turn their backs on "you"
and start a new life without "you"
and before you know it
you're on the streets.
Learning a whole new set of rules
on the streets
trying to hustle up enough money just to get something to eat
maybe find someplace that'll let you take a shower
in one of them cheap ten dollars an hour fuck hotels
and the shelters are dangerous
They're some real crazy people in there
So you take your chance on the streets
doing things you never thought you'd end up doing
And now you're on your knees

trying to polish people shoes for change,
Spit Shine method
It's amazing how polished shoes make people feel…
Confident
full of themselves
important…I use to feel like that.
Now the white guys get real nervous
Scared 'cause they see their future when they look at me
Or you get the ones who look down at you
Half-smirk on their face like "yeah come on buddy just shine my shoes"
And the black guys try real hard to not even look at you
I guess I'm a painful reminder of what they use to be
I guess all I need is some blackface
to make this picture complete…
When all I am is somebody trying to make it to another day.
And believe me I'm not…
proud about this…
but damnit I'm still here…
you know?

God Created Everything

GAMAL and MILS. (*Sung.*) I know where my god is
He's inside my heart
He is where my love is
We will never part

MILS. I know where my god is
He's inside my heart
He is where my love is
We will never part

Okay class,
do you have your school papers ready?
Billy?
Let's start with you.

BILLY. God is Omnipotent
The creator
Without God, there would be nothing
God created the heavens and the earth
Created the sun and the moon
So that we could have light
All day and all night

God created the clouds
So that we could have rain
And fresh drinking water
God created everything

God created the sea
And all the living things within it
God made dolphins whales and tuna fish
Crabs, lobsters, sharks, and manatee
God created everything
That man can imagine
Bacteria, amoeba, algae
Shrimp and phytoplankton

And Animals
God created animals
God created mice, lice, rabbits, bats
Foxes, oxes, lemurs, rats
But his favorite thing of all he made
Was man
And God was proud

And then
God gave us gifts
He made clothes, spears, knives, and caves
And fire, and art
To decorate
He gave us horses to enslave with ropes
They won't complain
My dad said He made 'em that way
God's really great

God created Politics
He made the church
He made the state
First God created the church
Lifted its shirt
Crucified a rib
And then came the state
The church is the boy
The state is the girl
The girl does what the boy says
And it'll be a much better world

We shouldn't tamper with his blessings
That would be bad

Sometimes God makes mistakes
He created Democrats and gays
Mom says that's why God gave us miracles
Like poverty and AIDS

God made houses, buildings, wooden shacks
Bricks, metal, paper, glass
Canons, slingshots, poison darts,
Crossbows and tear gas
And camp
God made lots of spots to set up camp
Birkenau, Auschwitz,
Abu Ghraib, Guantanamo
He even made little camps for American Japs

God gave us shackles, and bars
Prison yards, and prison guards
Electric chairs and guillotines
And shots that make your heart stop

God inspired the Spanish Inquisition
God is wise
He knows what we need to protect our nations
So he invented coercive measures for collecting information

In God's name we invented torture
And slavery
And all forms of purity
God is always there for you and for me
God blessed America
Because God is an American

Jethro & Cleophus

GAMAL *plays* JETHRO; STEVE *plays* CLEOPHUS, *vaudevillian style.*

CLEOPHUS. Say you know what I do for my arthritis. I mix two cups of Quaker Oats and one cup of hot water, mix it together, rub it on the spot that ails ya. Instant relief.

JETHRO. I hear you, I got another one, if you ever get toenail fungus, you know what you do, you get a bottle of that Listerine Mouthwash.

CLEOPHUS. Listerine.

JETHRO. Yeah, you take the Listerine soak your feet in it, and it will clear everything right up, and then it works two ways, it takes away your fungus and then when your woman suck your toes, she'll walk away with clean breath.

CLEOPHUS. Ha Ha, see people don't think we know shit they think all we do is sit here, die slow and try to get into heaven.

JETHRO. Ain't nothing wrong with that, at least health insurance is free in heaven.

CLEOPHUS. Yeah, but you've got to die to get into heaven.

JETHRO. Now don't get me wrong, I'm all for everybody having some health care.

CLEOPHUS. But some people needs to die, and I gots me a looong list.

JETHRO. But lord knows there ain't a single government agency that runs right. Think about it. Post Office—

CLEOPHUS. Lost Mail.

JETHRO. Education—

CLEOPHUS. Dumb kids.

JETHRO. FEMA—

CLEOPHUS. No comment.

JETHRO. White House.

CLEOPHUS. Black man.

JETHRO. And you know if it ain't broke they'll break it. And it's already broke down so we've got a problem.

CLEOPHUS. Now if everybody gets health care, you know what that means.

JETHRO. The longest lines since the free cheese program.

CLEOPHUS. Now, I might not live to the next century but if I call now I might get an appointment.

JETHRO. My doctor told me to avoid unnecessary stress so I don't open his bill.

CLEOPHUS. Don't you know it. Remember when my older brother Pete found out he had prostate cancer, he lost all hope right there, 'cause Pete was a sonofabitch, and he knew he wasn't getting into heaven.

JETHRO. Yeah, but it scared us into going to get ours checked out, the only problem was they didn't tell us how they was gonna go about it until we walked in the room.

CLEOPHUS. It did catch me off guard, but I stopped him, just as the doctor was putting on the glove, and I said "wait a minute, how much is this gonna cost, 'cause I don't need to feel violated twice."

JETHRO. Yeah, at least they could give us a free Viagra coupon or something like that.

CLEOPHUS. See I get my free Viagra from the doctor on the side, said that the whole pharmaceutical industry was robbing everybody blind. But good lord knows that stuff is dangerous. 'Cause all I need is 20 minutes. I will work a woman out in 20 minutes but that stuff had me going for four hours. So me and my lady had done it once and did it again. And she starts screaming oh Cleophus Clareance Caldwell the third, oh Cleophus Clarence Caldwell the third, and I'm like oh lord you can't be screaming my name out like that, haven't you heard of identity theft, somebody will hear my whole name, and start running up my credit all over the place. 'Cause all you need is a name nowadays.

JETHRO. You damn right, 'cause when I did have insurance before my premiums, my co-pays, and my deductibles went up, they would constantly mess up my name, 'cause when I went down to the doctor office, I have to fill out way too many pieces of paper. And then somewhere between the intern, the nurse and the doctor, I went from Jethro Williams to Janet Wills. So when I try to go get it straightened out I have to fill out more paperforms, so they can then misplace my paperwork all together, which means somewhere Janet Wills is gonna have some health insurance and Jethro Williams don't. So HIP, HMO, is all S.H.I.T. to me.

CLEOPHUS. And what about COBRA, something to help you after you lose your job, but what is a COBRA?

JETHRO. A snake.

CLEOPHUS. A what is a snake gonna do?

JETHRO. Bite you.

CLEOPHUS. Right in your ass when you realize how much money you got to pay to keep the COBRA.

JETHRO. Now you know I was married to my wife Shirley for 35 years, and she worked in the public school system for twenty of them years. Twenty years she put in, and she got sick, had an aneurysm, and do you know that her insurance ran out in three months. The doctor wanted me to sign a paper to take her off life support…told me I was in denial, that I love her too hard, now how in the hell do you love your wife…too hard. I couldn't pay her bills and pay the mortgage, so I lost the house, and the kids moved out on their own. And she passed away, and I had to get my own place and start over.

CLEOPHUS. Now me and you go back twenty years, and it don't need to be this hard.

JETHRO. That's why you got to take care of yourself, 'cause the health care don't care.

CLEOPHUS. Took us a long time to get this old—

JETHRO. Mmmhmm.

CLEOPHUS. And if I got grey hair on my head, on my face and on my pubics—

JETHRO. Then that means I know a thing or two about a thing or two—

CLEOPHUS. that's why two glasses of Gatorade can get rid of headache pain,

JETHRO. Colgate toothpaste is good for burns,

CLEOPHUS. And red wine is suppose to help the blood flow.

JETHRO. But you know what they say—

TOGETHER. Wine is fine but liquor is quicker.

INeS

As MILS *sings, the lyrics are projected.*

MILS. *Vengo de tierra lejana…*[18]	I come from a faraway land,
El viaje fue inmenso	an immense journey,
Cruce mil desiertos…	I crossed a thousand deserts
Por venir aquí	From poverty,
Con ojos despierto	I arrived, disheveled,
De un hogar humilde	for a better life.
Llegue deshilada	
Por mejor vivir	
Tengo dos travajos	I have two jobs.
En un hotel limpio y lava	At sunrise,
Al subir el sol	I wash and clean rooms at a motel.
Y cuando oscurese	At sunset,
Me presento al otro jefe	I sew and fasten buttons on garments
A la fabrica e boton	in a factory outside of town.
Mis manos me duelen	I sew till my hands ache and bleed
Y aveses me sangran	I sew till my eyes can't see
Pero sigo cociendo hasta no poder ver	Sometimes, when no one is looking
Mientras mi hija duerme	I put a few buttons in my pocket
Le pego nuevos botones	Late at the night
Que escondi en mi bolsillo	When my daughter is sleeping
Pa su traje de ayer	I sew new buttons
	to her hand-me-down dress.
No la veo despierta	I work all the time
Y todo lo hago	I never get to see her awake
No la veo reir	Never to see her smile
	I have no rest

---

[18] Inspired by Lola Flores in the 1953 Mexican motion picture *Ay, Pena, Penita, Pena!* by Miguel Morayta.

Is this what I came here for?

Estan botando empleados	I hear they are firing people
Soy Ilegal	I am illegal
Y Reemplazable	Replaceable
Que importo yo aquí	Why should I matter?
	I am no one

Cuando estoy sola—	Sometimes when I'm alone
Me imagino—	I imagine
Que en esta tierra rica soy	that I am rich in this country.
Y estoy to el dia con mi niña	All day, I will play with my little girl
Ni un problema existe hoy	with no worries in the world.

Pero despierto de ese sueño	When I wake up from the dream,
Y no soy dueña yo de na	I'm still the maid
Soy esclaba de tu dinero	Still the worker
El cual tu votas como na	Back to slaving for that hard-earned dollar,
	Back to nothing.

Ya llego la madrugada	It's almost morning
Y tengo que trabajar	And I have to get ready for work
Un delantal	I put on my uniform
Y una sonrisa	Put on my smile
Y veo como mi nina duerme	And I see my daughter sleep
antes de la puerta cerra	as I walk out the door.

WATER SUITE

Stepping leads out of INeS.
(MIL's first then NINJA *(llamadas continue.)*
hands drop out when water rising starts
MILS *keeps clapping as* GUYS *pick up chair.*
One bar stomping
One bar water rising

NINJA. Soon as the rain come down,[19]
it's bottled up and sold.
Who wanna make a dollar?
Water's worth its weight in gold.

Soon as the rain come down,
it's bottled up and sold.
Who wanna make a dollar?
Water's worth its weight in gold.

---

[19] Inspired by the musical riff in Big Boi's "Kryptonite (I'm on It)" from *Got Purp? Vol. 2,* 2005.

(*Continues—*MILS *comes in on the second round.* STEVE *adds "I Can't Stand the Rain" riff.*)[20]

STEVE. Here comes the rain again.[21]
Here comes the rain again.
Here comes the rain again.
Here comes the rain again.

MILS. The other day I heard my mom tell my dad that she's retaining water
And I don't know what that means,
but I bet she's gonna make me drink it.
My mom says that I can not drink the water from the faucet.
And my mom says I can't water the flowers with the water
And that my dad had to stop smoking because one day,
he threw a match in the sink and the water got on fire.
My mom says the water has gas in it,
lots of gas,
like in the stove,
and it's bad for you.

My mom said they made a hole in the ground to get the gas
And they put chemicals in to push the gas out
And then it gets into the water
And now we have fire water
So I guess I gotta drink the water that my mom is retaining
'cause I bet it don't have gas in it.

Water,	
water	
rising water,	**GAMAL.** How high is the water momma?
water	twenty-four feet high and rising
water,	How high is the water Papa?
water	twenty-four feet high and rising
rising water.	

(*Clapping/water water continues under* GAMAL.)

GAMAL. The sun is shining once again for McCloud California,
as they rid themselves of the water bottling Giant called Nestle.
Can I get a Fi-Fi-Fo-Fum.
That's right;
score a victory for the little people.
In 2003, the giant called Nestle sealed a deal

---

[20]   Musical riff from "I Can't Stand the Rain", written and originally recorded by Ann Peebles. Inspired by Tina Turner's cover on *Private Dancer,* 1984.

[21]   Excerpt from "Here Comes the Rain Again," The Eurythmics, from *Touch,* 1984.

to open a new water bottling plant
in the once prosperous logging town of McCloud California.
Locals say the deal was sealed with a chocolate thumbprint
and a Kit Kat bar.
McCloud was promised increased revenue and over two hundred new jobs.
But those numbers were quickly reduced,
because the giant ate half the workers.
It was also reported that the big bad giant
was chased out of town before he could
make off with all the water from golden pond.
Reports are that the bottling giant for such products as
Arrowhead, Deer Park, Poland Springs and Perrier
no longer needed to build a plant in McCloud,
because they have now secured a site in [current city, state].
MILS/STEVE. There's a hole in the bucket, dear Liza.[22]
There's a hole in the bucket, dear Liza, dear Liza.
There's a hole in the bucket, dear Liza.
There's a hole in the bucket, dear Liza, dear Liza.

(All four start the step for one bar.)
STEVE. Imagine
walking a long way
To reach water.
Imagine
That it has not rained for months
And the land is dry and cracked,
A desert where there should not be one.
Imagine watching your mother and sister
Walk on unpaved roads/ carrying forty pounds of water
In a bucket/ that has a hole
It leaks/ and you need every drop
Imagine that water isn't totally clean
This is what you are forced to drink
And sometimes that you have to choose between food
Or water.
This is how I use to live.
But I never imagined
That I would come/ here
To this country/ on a student visa
To a land of paved roads

---

[22] "There's a hole in the bucket," traditional American children's song; inspired by Spearhead's version on *Home*, 1994.

Where something so precious as water
Is not seen as the gift it is.
One day I sat and watched a man
Use a water hose on a sidewalk he could have swept.
If I could have a glass of that, it would have saved a child
Where I'm from.
And no matter how many labels you put on water bottles
Everyone in the world should have it.
But I can imagine
Getting my education/become an engineer
So I can go back and help my people
And imagine a better world
Imagine that.

MILS/NINJA.

Water	Water
Water	Water
Rising	Rising
Water	Water
Water	Water
Water	Water
Water	Water
Rising	Rising
Water	Water
Water	Water

ALL. Soon as the rain come down
It's bottled up and sold
Who wanna make a dollar?
Water's worth its weight in gold.

NINJA. I used to have a farm
But now the thing is sold
I had to sell
Because the river in it wouldn't flow

And all my fish they died
Because of chemicals
They got the pesticides
PCBs and
Heavy metals

To think
That I had planned to do the daddy thing
Teach my son to fish and swim

Work the farm
Well think again.

I can't feed my family
They can't eat what I grow
Not tryin' to poison them
I know when it's my time to go

We gotta relocate	Uhuh
And find another place	Uhuh
Now we can start again	Uhuh
And take life at a faster pace.	

I'll get my hustle on
In any city son
Long as I got a tap
I'll drink that water
Free of charge.

Probably be good for me
And for my family
I'll be damned
If I gotta pay for water when it's free.

Soon as the rain come down
It's bottled up and sold
Who's wanna make a dollar?
Water's worth its weight in gold.

Soon as the rain come down
It's bottled up and sold
Who's wanna make a dollar?
Water's worth its weight in gold.

MILS/STEVE.

Water	Water
Water	Water
Rising	Rising
Water	Water
Water	Water

(GAMAL *begins to blend in "La La La LaLa LaLa" and all join in.*)

NEW WORLD WATER

NINJA. The whole world is drowning as the icebergs melt
Eskimos cope with the cards they're dealt

Polar bears swim and can't stop to rest
'Cause the planet's getting warmer, meltdown manifests.

Think about the Lower East Side of Manhattan
When the tide rise, what you think gone happen?
Folks in New York don't know how to swim
So we all going down when it fills to the brim.

The reason for the panic is the heat we created
Now we reminisce about the ice that we skated
With elevated temperature the ice evaporated
Became a hurricane, touched land and deflated.

Water saturated into muddy mountain sides
Now you lose your crib when terrain start to slide
Mosquitoes overpopulate the land with malaria
Diseases in the water stagnated in your area.

New Orleans is sinkin' in/ new world water
Iowa's sinkin' in/ new world water
New York is sinkin' in/ new world water
Florida's sinkin' in/ new world water

MILS. How high is the water?
How high is the water?
How high is the water?
How high?

EULOGY FOR AMERICA (Hostile Gospel)

STEVE. And the hunt is on
and there will be no mercy given tonight.
We chase you through the woods
the dogs are going crazy.
They are thirsty for blood.
When we caught you,
you were shaking like a leaf,
scared to death.
Ain't nothing like a good chase before killing
and sometimes some things just need to be killed.

MILS/NINJA. *(Sung.)*
Bum, bum, bum, bum
Bubum, bum bum burubu

(Repetitions throughout.)

STEVE. Dearly Beloved,
Ladies and Gentlemen,
Good people of this congregation,
We are gathered here to say goodbye to the dearly departed.
It was dearly and now it's departed,
in other words, it's dead.
And we have come to bury America not to praise it.
We took America out back and shot you like Old Yeller,
'cause you were foaming at the mouth and going crazy.

It's time to put to rest our arrogance,
our corporate greed,
our spin doctors,
our apathy,
That is the America we've come to bury.
This is a gospel for the confused and convinced,
for those who pray to God and that American Idol.
And I'm losing my religion on purpose.
Even Mother Teresa struggled with her faith,
sat and waited for God to answer,
not realizing that God was always there,
waiting for her to stop waiting.

And we've paid our tithes,
gave ten percent of our soul to the church of America
but we want it back
some spiritual reparations.
unless you pay me,
distract me with Lotto tickets,
March Madness
And the Super Bowl of bullshit and reality shows
and fifteen minutes of fame.
Is *Survivor* really teaching you how to survive?
Maybe you need a break from this mind state,
a mindfuck without the condom.
'Cause I've seen the best minds of my generation,
the best minds of my generation,
the best minds of my generation,
reduced to sound bites and YouTube
MyFace and SpaceBook pages,
while the people wait to be entertained,
have all necessities provided
all anxieties tranquilized

all boredom amused
escape from freedom.
Have all the answers without asking the questions.
Waiting for somebody else to make sense out of this nonsense.
It's time to take the "kick me" sign off America's back
Press the reset button.
leave the porch light on
so we can all find our way home.

So, we get on our knees to God.
Hello God!
And we raise your hands to the heavens.
Help me lord!
Hands,
Hands,
Hands running through your pockets.
The Government hands are running through your pockets.
Can't afford to be an American.
Can't give in to that recession depression.

But Steve Jobs got a job
and Bill's got the keys to the gates
and some think Donald Trump is a chump
and AIG says fuck it.
You better get hip to the game but know that the rules are fixed
And nobody gets out of this life alive.

At the funeral for America
the corpse was put into a Ford F-150
and driven through the streets until it reached the off-White House.
And all races, creeds and colors came to view the body.
The Bald Eagle flies high over the festivities wearing a wig.
The Statue of Liberty finally puts her torch down
'cause her arms are tired
and she needs some deodorant.

Andy Griffith is whistling in the corner
and Aunt Bee is making bean pies
At the cemetery,
it is bright sunshine but everybody has an umbrella.
Walt Disney is here
and so is Charlie Parker.
Superman,
Kunta Kinte,

and Geronimo,
and The Three Stooges
(Uncle Ben, Uncle Tom, and Uncle Sam)
are the pallbearers.
And all the countries in the world are all glued to their television sets
for this once-in-a-lifetime event.
So everybody,
let's put on our Sunday best,
have a twenty-one-gun salute,
pour out a little liquor,
take the ashes and sprinkle them from the Rockies to the ghettos.

And some will wonder if America was simply a dream,
a hallucination,
some thing that never was
but wanted to be,
a wish that was granted
and wishes should never be left unattended.
They can get out of control.
But out of death comes life,
a rebirth,
and we're gonna put a remix on the Constitution
And we will hold on to America's promise of
diversity,
tolerance,
free speech,
and democracy
even when it fights against itself.
So folks,
what else can I say,
America has become the number one game player
and can't figure out when the games end and reality begins.
And to you, the only reality is death,
so now,
for the final appearance on the great stage of life,
I give to you...
A new beginning.

FREEDOM CODA

GAMAL. Won't you ring ol' hammer

                                  ALL. Hu

GAMAL. Won't you ring ol' hammer

GAMAL. Won't you ring ol' hammer

ALL. Hu

GAMAL. Won't you ring ol' hammer

ALL. Hu

GAMAL. Built my house up right,

ALL. Hu

GAMAL. Work day and night,

ALL. Hammering

GAMAL. Build a big skylight,

ALL. Hammering

GAMAL. So I can see the sky,

ALL. Hammering

GAMAL. You got to lend a hand,

ALL. Hammering

GAMAL. to do what we can,

ALL. Hammering

GAMAL. take a hammer and a nail,

ALL. Hammering

GAMAL. and let's blaze a trail,

ALL. Hammering

GAMAL. Won't you ring ol' hammer

ALL. Hammering

GAMAL. Won't you ring ol' hammer

ALL. Hammer ring

GAMAL. Won't you ring ol' hammer

ALL. Hammer ring

ALL. Hammer ring

GAMAL. Won't, won't, won't you ring ol' hammer
This here is tough but we've seen tough before[23]
Do you remember the ricochet pop of a gunshot
That checked into the Lorraine Motel
Do you remember the ho chi man
Carrying your buddy's body through mosquitoes and swamp

Do you remember the virus and plaque called AIDS
Did you wash your hands after shaking a skinny person's hands
Do you remember crack cocaine, and Nancy Reagan
Did you just say "no"
Do you remember Exxon Valdez,
Chernobyl and the San Francisco Earthquakes
Do you remember Tower One falling

---

[23] Inspired by Louis Reyes Rivera's poem "Bullet Cry."

Then Tower Two
Did you hear the cries? Was you there, in the Superdome
I was there on a Thursday, on a rainy hot hopeless Thursday
I was there and so were you
This here is tough, but we've seen tough before

> **ALL.** Hammer ring
> Think about it /
> Think about it (*Repeat.*)

STEVE. All right people looka here…
Don't make no diff/er/ence what side of the fence
you standing on…uh-huh.
'Cause we all in same boat baby
and we got to get our paddle on. Uh-huh.
Got to/ come together/ in this stormy weather
Times are hard/ and it's tougher than leather.
Come a long way baby/ from *Driving Miss Daisy*
And you gotta learn to how never say never.

> (*Chorus.*)

Think about it/ Think about it (*Repeat eight times.*)
Okay hold on
We're gonna chop down the trees
That our great-great grands/ understand
Hung from in the sun
Here it come. (*Bang.*)
Hit it again (*Bang.*)
Hit it again (*Bang.*)
Again (*Bang.*)
Again (*Bang.*)

> (*Bang, Bang, Bang, Bang, Bang.*)

MILS. Freedom
STEVE. Beatbox, come on!

> (NINJA *hold beat repetitive;* GAMAL *hums House toon.*)

MILS. Just rang this mornin'
Freedom
Knockin' at my door
Oh, Freedom
Please come in
Please come in
I'm glad you finally got here
You're what I've waited for.

> (*Beatbox and House beat.*)

If I'm Dreamin'
I must be sleep
Somebody wake me up
If I'm dreamin' I must be sleep
Somebody wake me up
If I'm Dreamin'
I must be sleep
Somebody wake me up
If I'm dreamin' I must be sleep
Somebody wake me up.

                                        (MILS, NINJA, GAMAL *collage of*
                                        If I'm dreamin' I'm
                                        If I'm dreamin' I'm
                                        If I'm dreamin' I'm.)

NINJA. wake me up. (*Repeatedly.*)

MILS. If I'm dreamin' I'm
If I'm dreamin' I'm
If I'm dreamin' I'm

NINJA. What's freedom worth?
Is freedom worth the dedication?
Is it worth paying my taxes
To ensure your child's education
Am I willing to let a bigot speak,
Just to respect his freedom of speech?
Am I willing to give up my cell phone?
I heard it's killing all the bees
Without bees we won't have plants
Which means no more food for me
And I love to eat food
Especially my rice and beans
Wanna protect the sanctity of marriage?
Why not protest divorce?
Allow everybody the freedom of love
A ring and certificate from the courts
Wanna find freedom in immigration,
Read the writing in Lady Liberty's hand
They're coming in search of freedom
To the world famous freedom land
No one said freedom is pretty
And it damn sure ain't free
You know you're free to pay the price for freedom
So what's it gonna be…

EL VELORIO

MILS. Albizu Campos meets Cantinflas on a dark rainy night.
In a back room of a bodega in el barrio.
The conversation is intense.
They speak in Spicanese to throw off any asesinos
who may have infiltrated.
The time is at hand.

Lorca will give the opening speech,
and the Rev. Pedro Pietri will give the holy blessing

The Fania All-Stars is the house band
playing that salsa boogaloo, Baby.
Hector Lavoe smiles from his throne,
while Charo, Rita Moreno and Carmen Miranda
talk about how to destroy the objectification of the Latina woman.

"Oh, we're going to the party,
we're going to the fair,
to see the señoritas with flowers in their hairs,
don't shake it señorita,
don't shake it if you can,
so all the boys around the block
don't see your underwear, oh."[24]

Lolita Lebrón is passing around how-to manuals
Just in case the government can't get it together.

And Che Guevara arrives
wearing a Che Guevara T-shirt.

Speedy Gonzales is wearing a zoot suit,
smoking a joint with Cheech and Chong and Zorro,
planning on how to shut down all the damn Taco Bells in the world.
In the back room Antonio Banderas is teaching R-rolling classes,
Frida Kahlo is giving tattoos.
Ricky Ricardo
tells them the secret of the Babalu.
How to truly infiltrate the system.
Using a three-camera shot to change the world.

Pablo Neruda
is in charge of writing the mission statement, and all the proposals.

---

[24] "I'm going to Kentucky," traditional American children's song.

They have a plan
on how to add their voice to the national agenda.

'Cause things are different now.
As the nation takes its coffee black
With a side of half-half
And we prepare
And become more visible.

As Sotomayor holds court
And Supreme Justice is served
And as Don Quixote climbs back on his horse
And our next president,
She stands in wait
With a cup of Café con leche
'Cause we're next on the menu.

She tells Quixote to get off that horse,
And she climbs on instead
And as Quixote draws his sword
And she draws her machete

And they charge at the White House singing

"To dream the impossible dream."

MILS. And row and row and row and row and row and row and row and row and row and row and row and row and row.

> **GUYS.** Everybody Row
> Everybody Row
>
> Hu Ha
> Hu ha
> Hu ha
> Hu

HOME

STEVE. Just the other day
I woke up early from a deep sleep
And took a long look at the day ahead
And thought,
there is a chance to get it right.
Redemption
To be better
To be that
Which you hoped to be

Intention
But forgot a long time ago
A country with no direction.
And then there is today
Tomorrow
Something that isn't promised
But holds promise
And what does tomorrow have that is different than yesterday
Will tomorrow love me
Love any of us
Or are we on a long walk to the slaughter?
The Fire Next Time
Ain't that what the good book says?
Well I say tomorrow is coming
And I'm gonna bring yesterday with me.
But here we all are
A work-in-progress
A byproduct of genius and insanity
Love and insecurity
With a chance to write a new chapter
To the greatest story
Ever stole, bought and sold
Let's start the long painful journey
Together.

Welcome to Ameriville!

GUYS. Everybody row
Everybody row
Everybody row
Everybody row

MILS. And row and row
And row and row
And row and Row!

ALL. Everybody row
Everybody row
Everybody row
Everybody row
(*Unison.*) Everybody row

End of Play.

THE HARD WEATHER BOATING PARTY

by Naomi Wallace

BIOGRAPHY

Naomi Wallace's work has been produced in the United Kingdom, Europe, the Middle East and the United States. Her major plays include *One Flea Spare* (1996 Humana Festival), *In the Heart of America*, *The Trestle at Pope Lick Creek* (1998 Humana Festival), *Things of Dry Hours* and *The Fever Chart: Three Visions of the Middle East*. Ms. Wallace received the Susan Smith Blackburn Prize, the Kesselring Prize, Fellowship of Southern Writers Drama Award and an Obie Award. She was also a recipient of the MacArthur Fellows Program Award. Her award-winning film *Lawn Dogs* is available on DVD and her new film, *The War Boys* (co-written with Bruce McLeod), will be released in 2010. Ms. Wallace is presently under commission from Oregon Shakespeare Festival, The Public Theater and Clean Break of London.

ACKNOWLEDGMENTS

The Hard Weather Boating Party premiered at the Humana Festival of New American Plays in March 2009. It was directed by Jo Bonney with the following cast:

STADDON VANCE	Michael Cullen
LEX NADAL	Jesse J. Perez
COYLE FORESTER	Kevin Jackson

and the following production staff:

Scenic Designer	Paul Owen
Costume Designer	Jennifer Caprio
Lighting Designer	Russell Champa
Sound Designer	Matt Callahan
Properties Designer	Doc Manning
Movement Consultant	Delilah Smyth
Fight Director	k. Jenny Jones
Stage Manager	Kathy Preher
Production Assistant	Mary Spadoni
Dramaturg	Adrien-Alice Hansel
Assistant Dramaturg	Brendan Pelsue
Casting	Vince Liebhart Casting
Assistant Director	Lila Neugebauer

Naomi Wallace and Actors Theatre of Louisville are participants in the Theatre Residency Program for Playwrights, a project of the National Endowment for the Arts and Theatre Communications Group.

This play was developed with the support of The Ensemble Studio Theatre/Alfred P. Sloan Foundation Science & Technology Project.

CHARACTERS

STADDON VANCE, fifty years old, white male.

COYLE FORESTER, late forties, African-American.

LEX NADAL, early twenties, Latino.

TIME

Some time now in the United States.

PLACE

Rubbertown, U.S.A.

SET

A sparse, simple Motel 6 room, or a dream a Motel 6 room had about itself. Two single beds, small desk, lamps.

Jesse J. Perez, Kevin Jackson, and Michael Cullen
in *The Hard Weather Boating Party*

33rd Annual Humana Festival of New American Plays
Actors Theatre of Louisville, 2009
Photo by Harlan Taylor

THE HARD WEATHER
BOATING PARTY

ACT I

Hard rain is heard on the roof of the motel room. No lightning, but steady, hard rain.

Lights up on STADDON VANCE standing in the center of a cheap, sparsely furnished motel room, staring intently at the floor. He carries a brown paper bag with a bottle and cups inside it. There are two single beds.

STADDON stares for some moments at a small, perhaps foot-long, crack in the hotel floor. After some moments, he carefully gets on his knees and tries to see inside it. He looks and looks but he can't really see anything.

Suddenly LEX bursts into the room. STADDON gets to his feet. LEX is dripping wet with rain, but he takes no notice of it.

STADDON. You're supposed to do a knock.

LEX. We didn't discuss a knock.

STADDON. You still could have done a type of knock.

LEX. What type of knock?

STADDON. You know. Tap ti tap, tap ti tap ti tap. That kind.

LEX. If you want a tap ti tap ti tap ti fuckin tap type knock I can go back out and try it again?

STADDON. I was just expecting a knock.

(LEX's *boots leave damp prints as he walks around the room.*)

Lex Nadal, right?

(LEX *ignores him.*)

Mr. Nadal, glad to meet you. In person.

(STADDON *holds out his hand, and moves towards* LEX.)

LEX. Didn't I tell you to keep your fucking distance?

(STADDON *watches* LEX.)

STADDON. Would you like a towel?

LEX. No thanks.

STADDON. You're making the floor wet.

LEX. Well if the floor's got a problem with it, it'll let me know, right?

(*Checking out the room.*)

I've stayed in worse. I've stayed in better. This is OK, isn't it?

STADDON. Yeah.

LEX. When do we start?

STADDON. There's no hurry.

LEX. I'm ready now.

STADDON. That's good. But we have to wait until midnight, at the least.

LEX. I'm ready now. *Estoy listo.*

STADDON. Well. I appreciate that you have arrived ready.

LEX. Where's the other guy?

STADDON. He should be here any minute.

LEX. You better hope so.

> (LEX *now takes off his cap and wrings it out over the trash can, then puts it back on.*)

You ever wondered 'bout the bed covers?

STADDON. They're in every motel, no.

LEX. Sort of quilted, slippery and ugly.

STADDON. Your point?

LEX. They're made to withstand staining. Rubs right off. Lot of staining in motels. And there's always a big mirror so that you can…. Hey, where's the mirror?

STADDON. Room service took it away.

LEX. Why?

STADDON. You like mirrors?

LEX. No.

STADDON. Neither do I. (*Beat.*) You look pretty good, Lex.

LEX. Yeah?

STADDON. Yeah.

LEX. Thanks. You look okay yourself.

STADDON. Made an effort. It's a special night tonight.

LEX. Like you said. On the phone. Tonight, right?

STADDON. Tonight.

LEX. You don't sound excited.

STADDON. Yes, I am.

> (LEX *clears his throat and spits on the floor. Then he lightly touches his hand to his stomach for just a second, as though it hurts him, but then he's fine.*)

LEX. You're sure you want to do this, right?

STADDON. Of course.

LEX. 'Cause, it was your idea—

STADDON. We're going to do it.

LEX. Because you called me. Yeah. You dialed my number.

(STADDON *now notices the spit on the floor.*)

STADDON. Is that yours?

LEX. Not anymore.

STADDON. Please. Clean it up.

(LEX *just stares at* STADDON, *then he steps on the spit and slowly drags his foot across the floor, smearing it away.*)

LEX. Done, boss.

STADDON. Tonight we're equals.

LEX. Said the zookeeper in his crisp new suit.

(*They are silent some moments.*)

What's your first name (*Beat.*) Mr. Staddon?

STADDON. Staddon is my first name. Vance is my last name.

LEX. Vance. That's kind of a loser name. Like Nance. Anything that rhymes with chance hasn't got one.

STADDON. Have a seat, Mr. Nadal. Relax.

LEX. No thanks. But you can call me Lex. If you don't overdo it.

(LEX *sees the crack in the floor.*)

Mierda. You bust the floor?

STADDON. No. No, I did not.

LEX. Motel guy is gonna be pissed.

STADDON. It was like that when I arrived.

LEX. They make you pay for stuff when you break it. I'm not paying.

STADDON. We didn't do it so let's forget about it.

LEX. You hear that?

STADDON. What?

LEX. Shhhh.

(LEX *puts his ear to the crack and listens. A rhythmic knock on the door.* LEX *jumps up.* STADDON *walks to the door. The knock comes again.* STADDON *opens the door, and lets* COYLE *in.*)

STADDON. (*To* LEX.) He did a knock.

COYLE. Vance?

STADDON. Yes, Staddon Vance. Come in.

(COYLE *comes in warily. He looks around the room, then at* LEX. COYLE *has a raincoat on that is dripping wet.*)

COYLE. This is the other guy?

STADDON. Lex Nadal.

COYLE. Looks like a kid.

(LEX *gives* COYLE *the finger.*)

COYLE. So the party has arrived.

(COYLE *looks at both the men, then removes his raincoat.*)

Damn. I'm feelin' better tonight than I have in months. Blood's movin', muscles jumpin'. Hey, something's not right about this room…. Where's the mirror?

STADDON. The Motel took it back.

COYLE. But I might want to have a look. Before we start.

STADDON. You look just fine, Mr. Forester. I can tell you that. Mirror won't.

COYLE. Only two beds. We're not sleeping here, right?

STADDON. No, we're not.

LEX. Motel guy doesn't know that.

COYLE. Yeah. Three men, two beds. I mean. You know.

LEX. We can share, old man. I always like meat in my bed, no matter the grind.

COYLE. Hey. You watch your step.

(STADDON *opens the paper bag and takes out a pint of whiskey and three plastic cups.*)

STADDON. Motels make me shiver. No one sleeps in them, they just close their eyes. Mr. Nadal, Mr. Forester. Party of three. That's us. Let's toast.

(STADDON *parcels out the cups, pouring a little whiskey into each one. The men make a toast, using the plastic cups. But no one knows what to say. After an awkward silence,* LEX *speaks.*)

LEX. Here's to this "bang" changing our lives—

COYLE. Here's to gut-rot courage, and no cop-outs—

STADDON. Here's to us. Amen.

LEX. I don't do Amen.

COYLE. I don't either. Most of the time.

STADDON. Well. All right. Why don't we just say "Hurrah"?

(*The men nod at one another.*)

LEX/COYLE/STADDON. Hurrah!

(*They are now silent for some time. They drink and look into their cups.* LEX *dives onto the bed to try it out.*)

LEX. Not bad. New springs. I can feel it.

COYLE. So what did you bring?

STADDON. A turn of phrase. Or two.

COYLE. That won't cut it.

STADDON. You'd be surprised. Properly placed it can bring a man to his knees and melt his caps. I also brought a gun.

LEX. A gun. Cool.

COYLE. And a bullet, I hope.

LEX. Very cool. Like January. February.

STADDON. Of course.

LEX. Winter's best 'cause it hurts less in the cold.

COYLE. That's for sure. Summers are a bitch. And August the hottest bitch of all.

STADDON. You're from Algonquin Parkway?

COYLE. Yeah. Born there too.

STADDON. (*To* LEX.) And you?

LEX. Wilmouth Ave.

COYLE. I know you don't live in Rubbertown.

STADDON. No. Across the river. In Clarksville.

LEX. Of course. Like to keep your distance.

COYLE. From people like us. What's it like in your neighborhood? In (*Emphasizing.*) Clarks-ville?

STADDON. It's—

COYLE. clean.

STADDON. It's—

LEX. quiet.

STADDON. It's—

COYLE. Safe.

STADDON. I was going to say it's got trees.

LEX. Big ones?

STADDON. Tall.

LEX. Used to be like a forest in Rubbertown.

COYLE. It was never a forest.

LEX. Trees up and down the streets. You could swing from one branch to another and make it all the way round the block.

COYLE. Managers always live across the river in Clarksville.

LEX. You work at Amalgamated?

STADDON. There's nine industries in Rubbertown. I've worked at six.

COYLE. Why you move around so much?

STADDON. Restless.

LEX. You don't seem like the restless type.

COYLE. Started at Amalgamated when I was 19. Still there. Take my eyes out I could walk every room backwards in that building and not touch the walls.

LEX. I started at D-Chem. Switched to Amalgamated five years ago.

STADDON. Why?

LEX. Piss breaks. You get piss breaks at Amalgamated. Not at D-Chem.

STADDON. Do you have a bladder problem?

LEX. If I did it would be none of your business. You don't know me so don't even think about my bladder.

COYLE. Then why you love the piss breaks?

LEX. There's other things you can do on a break.

STADDON. Smoke?

LEX. Fuck.

STADDON. No one fornicates at our plant, on our time.

LEX. How would you know? There's 64 tanks at Amalgamated, at any one time half of those are empty.

COYLE. Like rooms, yeah. Empty rooms.

LEX. What do you think people do with empty rooms?

STADDON. I don't like it when people lie.

LEX. And the tanks are soundproof.

STADDON. We're not stupid.

LEX. Yeah?

COYLE. Okay. Okay. Let's focus here. (*To* STADDON.) You've got the information, time, place?

STADDON. Yes.

COYLE. One man.

STADDON. One man.

LEX. Then the money.

COYLE. What if his family gets in the way?

STADDON. One at a time then.

LEX. I'm ready.

COYLE. So am I. (*To* STADDON.) But why tonight?

STADDON. What do you mean?

COYLE. I mean why tonight? Why not yesterday, or the day before?

STADDON. Well. They've forecast snow. It should be a beautiful night. The kind of night to take your breath away.

LEX. To take someone's breath away.

COYLE. But why'd you call me?

STADDON. Because you've got it in you.

COYLE. Bullshit me and I'll take your teeth. You don't even know me.

STADDON. I knew you'd say yes.

COYLE. How?

STADDON. I don't know. Perhaps a look. A way of walking.

COYLE. We never met.

STADDON. I've seen you at work. You don't hesitate when you walk, Mr. Forester. Once you put your foot down you commit to the direction. No matter what that direction is.

COYLE. And him? (*About* LEX.) Why'd you bring him in?

LEX. Hey. He called me cause he needed me. (*To* STADDON.) Didn't you? You needed me.

STADDON. Yes. Yes I needed you. Both of you. There are some things you can't do alone. You need. The company of other men.

LEX. Zookeeper needs the seals.

COYLE. You be careful; I'm not a seal.

> (LEX *barks like a seal. Then* COYLE *barks like a seal, and it's believable, and much better than* LEX's *seal. And he's aggressive with his bark. Even scary.* COYLE's *seal shuts* LEX *up.*)

LEX. (*To* STADDON.) What about my walk?

STADDON. I didn't notice your walk.

LEX. Then why am I here?

STADDON. Mr. Nadal. It was in April. Just after lunch break. I saw you hit your locker. With your fists.

COYLE. So the boy's got a temper. Girlfriend burn you?

STADDON. Twenty-nine times you hit that locker.

COYLE. Damn.

STADDON. Twenty-nine times. It's a wonder you can still use your hands. I saw in you, Mr. Nadal, a man who doesn't quit 'til he's broke.

LEX. I wasn't broke, the locker was.

STADDON. Exactly what we need.

COYLE. Hey. Cut the sweet talk. You know what sticks in my throat? Lex and me. Okay. We work the same floors. But you. Why?

LEX. Yeah. Why?

STADDON. It happened to all of us.

COYLE. You were always at a distance.

STADDON. Not lately. Actually, I tried speaking with a couple of co-workers.

COYLE. White folks.

STADDON. Managers.

COYLE. That's what I mean.

STADDON. Not all of them are.

COYLE. Ugly. Right. But most of them are.

LEX. (*To* COYLE.) He's kind of ugly too.

STADDON. Most of the managers are

COYLE. ugly and white.

STADDON. But some of them are

LEX. just ugly.

STADDON. Not all of them are white.

COYLE. But most of them are ugly.

STADDON. I don't care about ugliness.

LEX. Well, you wouldn't, would you?

STADDON. Not all of your co-workers are

COYLE. ugly. No, they're not. And some of them are white, too. But none of them live in Clarksville.

STADDON. But the point is that some of the managers are black. Asian, even.

COYLE. How many?

STADDON. At Amalgamated?

COYLE. That's it.

STADDON. One.

LEX. Black. Or Asian?

STADDON. Portuguese, I think. With a mix of Asian. But at the other plants, there are

COYLE. more ugly managers. Can we quit on this now?

STADDON. The point is. With the managers, I couldn't even get the conversation going. So I asked both of you, you said yes.

COYLE. The lower depths…. They're an easy lay, right?

STADDON. We don't have to like one another to work together towards a common goal. As a unit.

COYLE. We are not a unit.

STADDON. What I mean is that liking one another is not a necessary ingredient. What we need is agreement as to the basics. So, let's talk about the plan.

LEX. I'm ready.

STADDON. Yes, Lex. What are your thoughts?

LEX. I think we need to bust right in there. Because I know how to bust, I volunteer.

(LEX *acts this out.*)

I'll run at the door with my shoulder. I'll do a power run the last few steps and then Bang. Ker-pow. Smash, splinter, splinter. The door breaks open and we're in.

STADDON. I have a key.

LEX. Oh.

COYLE. You ever killed anyone, Lex?

LEX. I don't think so.

COYLE. What the hell does that mean?

STADDON. I have not.

LEX. (*To* COYLE.) Have you?

COYLE. I'm a fucking vegetarian. No.

STADDON. So that is why we must talk about it. This is an extraordinary endeavor. It's not "I'll have a burger and fries." It's not "Cash or credit." It's not "Have a good day."

LEX. I'm ready.

STADDON. This is a curve in the road. A detour.

COYLE. A one-way street.

STADDON. Lex, what's your proposal once we're in?

LEX. I'm going to kick him. *Lo voy a patiar y patiar.* Just like the door. Kick, kick, kickaroo.

COYLE. He might kick back.

LEX. Not after my kick.

COYLE. A man's head is hard. Thick.

LEX. I'll put velocity behind it.

COYLE. You sound eager, Lex?

LEX. I'm tired. That's a kind of eager without the sleep.

STADDON. Kicking is a possibility. Absolutely a possibility. But it takes too long.

COYLE. I could choke him. I got the grip.

STADDON. Choking is more focused than kicking.

LEX. *¡Chingao!* You're favoring Coyle.

STADDON. I'm not favoring anyone. We're trying to decide, together, what's most efficient. We could use the gun. Unfortunately we don't have a silencer.

COYLE. Then it will be loud.

LEX. Loud but quick.

STADDON. Perhaps here is where I should repeat myself: I made it very clear on the phone. Whatever we do, we do together. This is not the act of a lone assailant. This is the act of a mob.

COYLE. Mob yourself, buddy. We go in there together and whoever does the job, does the job.

STADDON. No. We need something more synchronized. In concert.

COYLE. What the fuck's it matter how we do it? I don't trust you.

STADDON. You can trust me completely.

COYLE. Said the manager. Huh.

LEX. Okay. Here's a plan: I'll kick him while Coyle, you choke him and Staddon you put the bullet in his head. Then we get the cash.

STADDON. Hmmm. Yes. That might be the only way that we can do this together, in the actual moment. But we must also speak to him before he dies. Each one of us. One at a time. And then we must give him a chance to speak.

COYLE. What the hell is this? A fucking twelve-step murder program? Hello. My name's Coyle Forester and I'm going to choke you one minute at a time.

STADDON. Don't you dare.

(*For the first time* STADDON *loses his cool, but regains it quickly.*)

COYLE. What?

STADDON. Say that word among us.

(COYLE *eyes* STADDON, *unsure.*)

COYLE. Hell?

STADDON. No.

LEX. Fucking?

STADDON. No.

COYLE. Murder?

STADDON. Not again. Not among us. It's a degrading word. It degrades us.

COYLE. The 'M' word?

STADDON. It's godforsaken. We are not.

COYLE. Right…sure.

LEX. Chill Vance.

COYLE. But why do we have to let him talk?

LEX. The man's had years to talk. His talking is done. When I'm spending his money, that'll be his chat.

STADDON. It's important that a man knows why he's to die, exactly. To die without this knowledge would be…murder. We are not committing…murder.

COYLE. So you can say it but I can't?

STADDON. (*Continuing.*) We are allowing a man to gather his thoughts before he dies. And I want the last thing that goes through his mind to be us.

COYLE. Yeah. All of us.

STADDON. Thank you. Thank you both.

LEX. (*Casually*.) I'm going to be sick.

COYLE. (*Casually*.) Don't do it on the floor.

(LEX *sits on the bed and dry heaves into his open hands, as though he might catch whatever comes up. But nothing comes up and he recovers. The others pay little attention.*)

STADDON.
"But thou wilt sinne and grief destroy;
That so the broken bones may joy,
And tune together in a well-set song,"

LEX. Huh.

COYLE.
"Full of his praises,
Who dead men raises.
Fractures well cur'd make us more strong."

LEX. Double fuckin huh.

COYLE. George Herbert.

STADDON. I'm impressed.

COYLE. Shit. You disappoint me, Staddon. You can't picture a black man reading nothing but a summons, can you? Bedside reading. Like most of us, I don't sleep. So I read in the night.

LEX. I don't read at night. I pretend I'm asleep.

STADDON. Well Chelton Steff will not be asleep, though he'll surely be a-dying. And after we've allowed his last thought to pass in and out of his mind, we'll shoot a tiny round window straight through it.

COYLE. And then get the hell out.

COYLE/LEX/STADDON. Right.

LEX. I hear it's a rush, killing a man. Like a water cannon pumping through you, *te levanta*, lifts you right off the ground. That's what I heard.

COYLE. Bullshit. You're making it into something it's not: magic show, pick a card. Fuck that. It's flushing the toilet. It'll feel good after you let it out.

LEX. You know, we're talking about doing it together, this. Thing, this killing thing, and I hardly know you guys. You're almost strangers. Coyle, I've seen you at work. I think we've sat next to each other in the cafeteria. Staddon, I know your face cause we got to know the zookeeper's face.

STADDON. Here I'm no manager.

COYLE. (*To* LEX.) You did a chicken and peel at lunch. You wrapped your piece of chicken in a banana peel.

LEX. Yeah. That's me. Chick 'n' Nana. My invention. You should see how it works in the bedroom.

COYLE. Yeah. But we never sat with you. You eat in your office.

STADDON. I share a…cubby with three other people. I don't do lunch. I munch on saltines when I'm hungry.

> *(Some moments of silence.* LEX *and* COYLE *stare at* STADDON. *He gets uncomfortable.)*

What?

LEX. *(To* COYLE.) Did he say "munch"?

COYLE. Yeah. I think he did.

LEX. Munch.

COYLE. I knew we should have had this conversation earlier.

STADDON. What do you mean?

COYLE. I can't work with a man who uses that word.

STADDON. What's wrong with it?

COYLE. Sounds like an office desk.

LEX. Yeah. Office desk/Munch. Hear the rhyme?

COYLE. Munch is not to be associated with food.

LEX. Yeah. It's something you do to clean your nose.

COYLE. We don't munch. We swallow our food. We go in deep.

LEX. We open up the craw and—

STADDON. *(Interrupts.)* All right then. Let me rephrase it: I…snack on saltines …when I'm hungry.

COYLE. Snack.

LEX. He did it again.

COYLE. *(To* LEX.) Should we go on home?

LEX. Snack? That sounds like something pathetic you make on the toilet.

STADDON. Listen. I don't care about these words. Snack. Munch. We are planning a mur—

COYLE. Ah ah! Don't say it.

STADDON. I will say what I like. We are planning a m—

LEX. —a munch.

COYLE. —a snack.

LEX. We are planning a munchy snack.

COYLE. Shut up, Lex. It's a snacky munch. And we'll put our feet up on his desk while we eat it—

STADDON. Stop it. You are disrespecting me. We cannot work together if there's disrespect. We need to be a unit.

COYLE. I don't do units.

LEX. Neither the fuck do I.

COYLE. Solo. That's me.

LEX. Me too.

STADDON. Fine. Not a unit then. But we have to coordinate this. Like a team.

LEX. I don't do teams.

COYLE. Me either. Their uniforms are always ugly. I like to dress nice.

STADDON. Fine. Okay. Then what shall we call our efforts?

(LEX *and* COYLE *both think it over.*)

COYLE. How about C.M.S.D?

LEX. Huh?

COYLE. Circumstantial Movement in the Same Direction.

STADDON. That's a mouthful.

COYLE. Yeah. Munch on it.

LEX. I like it.

STADDON. Okay.

LEX. But I won't snack on it. What's it mean?

COYLE. It means let's get this bastard of a night over so I never have to see either of your ugly duck walking faces again.

LEX. Hey. You like me.

COYLE. Don't kid yourself. Just cause we sat together doesn't mean I'd slap your back if you were choking.

STADDON. I'd slap your back, Lex.

LEX. Yeah? Thanks. I could make you a Nana and Peel.

STADDON. I'd love to try one.

(LEX *smirks at* COYLE.)

COYLE. Look. I just want to get home. So let's get started.

LEX. Well I'm ready.

COYLE. So am I.

STADDON. No. It's too early. We have to be sure he's in bed. Asleep. We need to relax.

LEX. I don't want to relax. I want to move.

COYLE. Let's watch some TV then. Nothing else to talk about. Where's the TV?

STADDON. It's a distraction. I had it removed.

COYLE. There you go, Lex. Already making decisions without us.

LEX. Yeah. Maybe I need some entertainment.

STADDON. We need to focus. We need some quiet before the noise.

COYLE. That's not the point. Point is you didn't ask us if we wanted it removed.

LEX. Yeah. You didn't count us in.

STADDON. You're right. I should've asked you. I will now. Coyle, do you want me to call room service and order another TV?

COYLE. I don't watch TV. I just like the weight of it in the room. (*Beat.*) But I can do without it.

STADDON. Lex?

LEX. I don't care. But if we got to wait here, I might get bored. You don't want to see me bored.

STADDON. What happens when you're bored?

LEX. Let's just say it smells bad.

STADDON. Alright, then it's decided, we're okay without the TV.

COYLE. And the mirror. You decided that one too.

LEX. Yeah. Without us.

STADDON. Do either of you want me to retrieve the mirror?

COYLE. No. Long as you didn't break it.

LEX. Long as you're not hiding any bad luck.

STADDON. I'm not hiding anything.

COYLE. I'm not so sure. Something 'bout this whole night don't feel right.

STADDON. You said you were feeling better than you have in months.

COYLE. That's my point exactly.

(COYLE *approaches* STADDON *menacingly.*)

LEX. Hey. Hey. No mirror, no TV. We all agree. Party of three. Right?

STADDON. That's right, Lex.

COYLE. Sure. But if we got time to spare, just leave me alone. Call me when it's time.

(COYLE *throws himself on the bed with a small book and begins to read.*)

STADDON. I get the distinct feeling you don't like people.

COYLE. Like people? "Like" people? I wouldn't do people that kind of harm.

STADDON. But don't you like company?

COYLE. What, a chorus like you? Or Lex? No chance.

(LEX *shrugs, then takes off his jacket, finds a pack of Twizzlers and a hand exerciser in his pocket and sits down. Then he sticks a Twizzler in his mouth and begins to exercise one of his hands. The exerciser makes a squeaking noise in the quiet room.* STADDON *watches the other men for some moments.*)

STADDON. I didn't choose you because of your stride, Mr. Forester.

COYLE. (*Continues reading.*) Hear that, Lex? He lied. Knew we couldn't trust him.

STADDON. I saw you reading in the canteen. You got up from the table to get an extra helping of peas.

COYLE. See how they watch us, Lex? Tabs on our peas. Tabs on our piss.

LEX. Tabs when we jerk off in the bathroom.

STADDON. You do that at work?

LEX. Come and have a look-see at noon. Stalls are full.

STADDON. I didn't know that. You see, I don't know everything. But I did see Coyle get up from the table to get that extra helping of peas.

LEX. I fucking hate peas. Little green sneaky bastards travel in a crowd.

STADDON. (*To* LEX.) He used a knife for a bookmark. I opened to the page he was reading:

LEX. Hey. I got an idea. So there's no TV.

STADDON. "Hard as hurdle arms, with a broth of goldish flue/ Breathed round; the rack of ribs—"

LEX. But that don't mean we can't make some entertainment. Coyle. Truth or dare.

STADDON. Deeply religious, he was.

COYLE. Nah. That was his mist. He's all about "Amansstrength," or lack of it.

STADDON. A strange and brutal style. He forced the disparate together.

LEX. Staddon. Truth or dare?

STADDON. That day I thought: a man who can read Hopkins without sentimentality, that's the man we need.

COYLE. I'm as sentimental as a butterfly. Asshole. Why do you think I'm here?

LEX. I'll say this one more time, then I'm going to hit someone:

(COYLE *just looks at* LEX.)

Truth or dare. (*Beat.*) We'll pass the time. Break the ice.

COYLE. There is no ice.

LEX. Yes there is. I'm cold just standing next to you two frozen motherfuckers.

COYLE. No.

LEX. Why not?

COYLE. Leave me alone.

(COYLE *continues reading.*)

STADDON. Wait a minute. Just a minute…. Should we play his game? Yes. Let's play Lex's game. It's an old bonding exercise, really. It builds trust. We'll need that tonight. We'll need that tonight more than anything else.

COYLE. More than the gun?

STADDON. Yes. More than the gun.

COYLE. I forgot how to play.

LEX. (*Delighted.*) Okay. I say "truth or dare," let's say, to Staddon here. Then he has to pick. If he says "truth," he's got to answer any question I ask him.

Honestly and in detail. If he says "dare," he's got to do what I ask, no cop-outs.

COYLE. What if he refuses?

LEX. Then we…kill him?

(*They are silent, then* COYLE *laughs.*)

But he can't refuse. That's the trust part. That's the core.

COYLE. Huh.

LEX. I go first?

(*No one objects.*)

Coyle. Truth or dare.

COYLE. Ask Staddon first. He wants to play.

LEX. Yeah. Staddon?

STADDON. Fire away.

LEX. Truth or dare.

STADDON. (*Eager.*) Truth!

LEX. Truth. Truth. Let's try and make these questions—

STADDON. Constructive.

LEX. Bonding.

STADDON. Bonding.

LEX. All that. Check.

COYLE. Right.

LEX. Okay…. Okay…. Okay. (*Beat.*) Staddon. Staddon. Staddon.

COYLE. That's his fucking name, Lex.

LEX. Have you ever, at any time, in any place, inserted a hard or narrow instrument into the hole at the end of your dick?

(STADDON *is frozen some moments.* COYLE *slowly puts his book away and gets interested. Then.*)

STADDON. How dare you!

LEX. Hold it. Hold it. Just answer the question. Honestly and in your own time.

COYLE. I'm not playing this game.

LEX. Hey. I didn't ask you I asked Staddon. Staddon, should I repeat the question?

STADDON. Yes. Certainly not. I heard you. I heard you. And my answer is no. I did not insert a hard instrument into the hole. No.

LEX. Hard or narrow. What about narrow?

STADDON. I no longer see the benefit to this exercise.

COYLE. Answer the damn question.

LEX. Answer or you break the trust. Break the trust and we could be three dead men tonight.

> (*After some moments.*)

STADDON. Yes. Narrow. Yes.

> (LEX *and* COYLE *burst out laughing. When they subside,* STADDON *continues steadily.*)

But that was many years ago. I just wanted to see if it would be painful.

COYLE. Was it?

LEX. Hey. This is my question. You stay out of it. (*Beat.*) Was it painful?

STADDON. At first. But then something interesting happened—

COYLE. That's enough detail.

LEX. What happened?

COYLE. Stop. And if you think you're going to get a chance to ask me about blunt instruments, you're dead wrong.

STADDON. (*To* COYLE.) Truth or dare.

COYLE. Dare, motherfuckers. Ha!

STADDON. Oh. Dare. I'd rather you say truth?

LEX. No. He can't change it now. You have to make Coyle do something.

STADDON. Do something.

LEX. Yeah. Anything. Just not. Life threatening.

STADDON. All right. Coyle. Coyle Forester. What can I make you do?

COYLE. Whatever it is, yours'll be worse, bud.

STADDON. Dance for us.

> (COYLE *laughs.* LEX *and* STADDON *don't.*)

Ballet. Yes. Dance some ballet.

LEX. Cool.

COYLE. Out of luck. I can't dance.

STADDON. Ballet. The best you can do will be acceptable, right Lex?

LEX. But it's got to be ballet.

COYLE. I don't know ballet.

STADDON. Do the damn ballet. Now!

> (COYLE *lifts his arm as though he'll begin. He makes one motion, then quits.*)

COYLE. No fucking way.

STADDON. Keep the trust, Coyle.

LEX. Yeah, keep the trust.

> (COYLE *just glares at the men. He stands in silence some moments. Then he readies himself, doing some boxing moves. Then* COYLE *does a couple of*

awkward, stiff poses. Then, he begins to move, slowly, into a kind of ballet, working to make the simple moves, then the more advanced moves professional dancers make. COYLE *moves slowly, and somehow painfully. He looks ridiculous. He begins to hum classical music for himself now. The other men watch. After some moments, they hum with him.* COYLE *is really putting his all into the effect. He even attempts a couple of small leaps. The cumulative effect of his dance now loses its ridiculousness, and becomes somehow impressive, moving.* COYLE *lastly holds a pose. Then quits.* STADDON *and* LEX *clap.*)

COYLE. Triple fuck you both. Hey. I keep the trust. Let no man ever say I don't. Ever. (*Beat.*) Staddon. Truth or dare.

STADDON. Ask Lex. It's his turn.

COYLE. I can ask who the hell I want to ask. Right, Lex?

LEX. Right.

STADDON. I won't answer any more questions about my penis.

COYLE. Truth or dare.

STADDON. Dare.

COYLE. (*Right into it.*) Show me how your old man hit you when you were a kid. (COYLE *clicks his fingers once.*)

LEX. Smack.

(STADDON *does not react. He holds* COYLE's *gaze.*)

STADDON. (*Calmly.*) How did you know he hit me?

COYLE. I didn't.

(STADDON *just nods. He walks over to* COYLE. *He circles him slowly. Once. Twice.*)

Took his time did he?

STADDON. Yes. He took his time.

(*Suddenly* STADDON *throws a quick, hard punch into* COYLE's *kidney. It hurts* COYLE, *but he takes it.*)

COYLE. Son of a bitch.

STADDON. He was. But when I got scarlet fever, nine years old, I shook so hard the bed shook too, he held me 'til my fever broke.

LEX. My turn. Someone ask me.

COYLE. Nah. I quit.

LEX. We all get a turn.

STADDON. (*To* COYLE.) Do you feel closer to me now?

COYLE. Nope.

STADDON. Bonded?

COYLE. No way.

STADDON. Don't think I do either…. (*Beat.*) Coyle. Lend me your Hopkins. We'll wait 'til midnight, then we'll go.

LEX. Just one fucking minute. We quit when we're done. We're not done. We're not done! Ask me, Staddon. Truth or dare. Ask me. Ask me.

STADDON. Can't you see we've lost interest?

LEX. Ask me. *¡Pregúnteme horita!* Ask me or I walk out of here.

COYLE. You better ask him, Staddon.

STADDON. Okay, Mr. Nadal. Truth or Dare.

LEX. Both.

STADDON. Both?

COYLE. You can't say both, you have to choose. You're an idiot, Lex.

LEX. I say both. I'm bending the rules. Bending the rules doubles the trust.

COYLE. Shit. Maybe he's right.

STADDON. Okay, my young friend. Double the trust.

> (STADDON *winks at* COYLE.)

I dare you to…sing us a song, while…answering this question: If you were ever to grow up, what would you be?

> (COYLE *laughs with* STADDON. LEX *ignores them, taking it very seriously.*)

LEX. Damn. That's tough.

COYLE. Keep the trust.

LEX. Can I have a minute to plan it out?

STADDON. We'd like it to be spontaneous.

COYLE. Yeah. Shoot from the hip, baby.

LEX. Let me clear my throat.

> (LEX *clears his throat, a number of times.*)

COYLE. (*To* LEX.) You're stalling. (*To* STADDON.) He's stalling.

> (LEX *sings his song hesitantly, but with real intent and effort. The tune is original and he makes it up as he goes.*)

LEX. (*Sings.*)

> If I could grow up, you know what I'd be?
> Not a tailor, nor a tinker, but a…wolf of the sea.
> If I could grow up,
> If I could grow up,
> I know this much for sure,
> I'd never…wake up.
>
> Because all of these years have been
> pickled in tears.

My mother is old, my father in beers….

(*Whispers.*)

Drunk ass.

(*Sings.*)

My sister, my twin: alike, bone to bone.
But she died—fuck you God—and now I'm ever alone.
So if I could grow up, you know what I'd be?
In a grave right beside her
with the cold dirt over me.

(LEX *finishes his song.* COYLE *and* STADDON *are silent for some moments.*)

COYLE. I'm sorry about your sister. I didn't know.

LEX. (*Casually.*) A few months back. End of April. We were twins.

COYLE. I met her at the company picnic last summer. Nice looking. Laughed a lot. She didn't look like you.

LEX. We weren't identical.

COYLE. She sick a long time?

LEX. I don't know. She wasn't the complaining type.

STADDON. That was a nice song, Lex. You should write it down.

LEX. You think so?

STADDON. Folks live all their lives and never write a song.

COYLE. I never did.

STADDON. Certainly not a song that rhymes.

LEX. I can rhyme. I can do that. Always could. Anybody got a pen?

(STADDON *and* COYLE *search their clothes half-heartedly for a pen. But no pen.*)

I'll write it down when I get home.

COYLE. We might not make it home.

STADDON. You'll have forgotten the song by then. Spontaneous song, it just disappears back where it came from.

LEX. Where'd it come from?

STADDON. God.

LEX. I don't believe in God.

STADDON. But he gave you a song just now, didn't he? (LEX *considers this.*) You mean that, about being a man of the sea?

LEX. Always liked water. My mother says as a little kid I used to hide a lot. One day she can't find me upstairs. Downstairs. Then she hears the water, splashing. It's coming from the bathroom. Two years old and I'm sitting in the toilet. Not on it but in it. Our toilet had one of those old pull-chains and I'm pulling it and flushing myself over and over and it's spilling out of the toilet and onto the floor 'cause my butt's stuck way down in the hole like a plug. Happy as a bee. Happy as a bee. Yeah I like the water. Always wanted a boat. Not a big fancy one, just big enough to float the Ohio River.

STADDON. I know how to sail. Used to go with a couple of friends from work on the weekends. Friends.

COYLE. Where you want to go, Lex?

STADDON. About the only thing we had in common was our height.

LEX. (*Shrugs.*) You can get in a boat and it doesn't matter. Every direction is straight ahead clear.

> (*Suddenly there is a low rumbling, as though something were moving beneath the floor, as though a tremor passed through the room. It lasts only a couple of seconds, then is gone.*)

COYLE. What the fuck?

> (LEX *jumps out of the way onto the bed.*)

LEX. The floor's moving.

STADDON. Shhh. Shhh. Listen. (*They all listen. Its quiet again.*) Probably a bad pipe.

LEX. Big fucking pipe.

COYLE. I don't like it.

STADDON. Well, it's gone now. And we've got more important things to think about.

LEX. Yeah. Like mu...mu...mu...

> (LEX *is pretending he's going to say* "*murder.*")

STADDON. Don't say it, Lex.

LEX. Mu.... Mu.... Money.

COYLE. Yeah. Money. I'm gonna buy me a....

LEX. What?

COYLE. I don't know.

LEX. What are you gonna buy, Vance?

STADDON. I'm not sure.

LEX. You don't know? You're not sure? You're both dead in the head. I can't stop thinking about it 'cause I'm sure: I'm going to buy a boat. And if you two don't know where to put your bucks, how about we go in on it together? Three times the cash will get us three times the boat. (*Beat.*) Staddon, you in?

STADDON. (*Shrugs.*) Why not?

LEX. Yessss. (*Beat.*) Coyle? You want in?

COYLE. With the two of you?

STADDON. Three's company.

COYLE. I don't like it.

LEX. You could be the Captain. We'd take your orders. Right, Staddon?

STADDON. (*Playing along.*) Ay, Ay, Sir. We'll scrub the deck. While you steer us under the stars to another land, where it never rains and people

LEX. Never munch

STADDON. or snack but open up their bellows and take it all in, 'cause it's so plentiful

LEX. and there is no sickness.

STADDON. Never any sickness. The only fever around is the heat of the day.

    (COYLE *considers.*)

COYLE. Why not?

    (LEX *lets out a shriek of celebration, which then brings on a coughing fit.* LEX *coughs hard and short, and as he does so, he brings something up from his chest. It lands on the floor between the men. The three men silently look at what* LEX *has coughed up. Miraculously, the phlegm begins to smoke. The men watch the trickle of smoke rise.*)

But we're not going to invest in those buy one get one free pieces of shit that floats on water cause you begged it to. We'll buy us a classic, with craft, chrome hardware, mahogany sides. How 'bout a Cesilde, 1956, from Italy? They put the double "e" in speed boat.

STADDON. So you know boats.

COYLE. Shit yeah. Ohio River's just about in our backyard. Ever since I was a kid I watched them pass by. Money in motion on water, those classics. Herring Gull. Zamora. Panther.

LEX. I don't care what it is, long as it's got the speed so no one can catch us.

COYLE. I'm at the wheel, no one ever will catch us.

STADDON. No one would come after me anyway. I don't have any family. Not even a sister. Or a brother. It's just me. Not married. So no children. I would have liked to have children.

COYLE. Girlfriend?

STADDON. Had one. But I lost her.

COYLE. That's bad. They aren't like a glove or a key. They don't come back. I never lost my wife. Almost, but no. Twenty-three years together. One girl, grown up now. Florist in Tennessee. I get flowers on my birthday. Bouquet so big I can't see when I walk, so much in my arms.

LEX. What's her name? Your daughter.

COYLE. Angela.

LEX. She single?

COYLE. Don't think about it.

(The phlegm has stopped smoking now.)

LEX. I bet her hands smell like flowers from arranging all day. My hands. I come home from work. I wash. They still smell like

COYLE/STADDON/LEX. Eggs.

LEX. But if I had Angela's flowers on top of my eggs.... When's she home from Tennessee?

COYLE. Leave it.

STADDON. I had a girl a few years ago. Girl? She was my age. She had this way of clicking her teeth together when she was happy. I first met her I called her "Clicker." And let me tell you men, I had her clicking all night some nights. I could satisfy her, yes I could. But time passes.

(LEX and COYLE wait for STADDON to continue but he doesn't.)

COYLE. But time passes?

LEX. The Clicker?

STADDON. I've always hated that expression: time passes. So why do I use it? There are sayings I've hated all my life and I don't know how they just climb on in my mouth and sit there. Shit there, really.

COYLE. What happened to your woman?

STADDON. She clicked less and less as time. Went on. I heard her last click one night while I was working her hard below the belt to give her some extra fireworks. She'd already had one orgasm.

COYLE. No, no, no, man. Don't say that word.

STADDON. Fireworks?

LEX. Orgasm.

COYLE. I hate that word. Why they give something so sweet such an ugly name I never understood.

LEX. Orgasm. Yeah. It's ugly.

COYLE. Like a cross between an organ and a spasm. Or an oyster passing gas.

STADDON. May I finish with the orgasm now?

COYLE. Say "come." That's dignified. To the point. So your woman "comes".... Yeah I love that. Women coming. And I like it all over my face, that's my beauty mask. I walk around all day wearing it, smelling her, hearing her sounds.

STADDON. Her clicks.

COYLE. That too.

STADDON. The next morning she said, "Staddon. I'm not in love with you. Never have been, never will be." Then she left.

LEX. Damn. After all the work you put into it?

COYLE. You use your tongue wrong you can kill her love that quick. You got to use the tongue like a bird. And I don't mean some delicate little tweeter—I mean a powerful bird, a crow or a hawk, and you call to her, sing. Flutter that tongue. Flutter it and flutter it and when she gets close you add a hum.

> (COYLE *demonstrates a hum. The others try a hum until it matches* COYLE's *in pitch and tone.*)

That'll put a sputter on your flutter and send your woman straight to Mars.

STADDON. Your wife is a lucky woman.

COYLE. Luck's all mine. She's some woman.

LEX. The flutter, huh? I'll give it a try, Coyle. When's your daughter get home?

COYLE. Don't do that.

LEX. Hey. Just a joke.

COYLE. I never made a joke about your sister.

LEX. That's why you're still alive.

STADDON. If I'd known, Coyle. If I'd only known.

LEX. (*Dreamily.*) I've always liked the taste of cunt.

STADDON. I never call it that. You shouldn't either.

LEX. It's a good word. I respect it.

COYLE. Yeah. But it's only good in the dark. In the dark, even the devil's words sound sweet.

LEX. First I ever had, I was thirteen. My sister had a sleepover, five screaming girls in sleeping bags all over the living room floor. There was this one girl named Dallas. Funny name. She could talk about the weather like a bioengineer. Sexy. Middle of the night I crawl on my fours into the living room. All the girls are asleep. Dallas has this zipper sleeping bag and the zipper goes all the way round. I start at her neck and I zip down, slow, slow. Must have taken me an hour to get to her waist, on down to her ankles. I crawl up into the bag from her feet. She was asleep. I pushed up her nightgown and touched her with my tongue. Wild and sweet. Knocked the breath right out of me. I didn't stay long, only a couple seconds. *Todavia me hago la pregunta.* I still ask myself now: was she asleep? Couldn't she feel it in her dream?

STADDON. I'd say you violated that girl. Without her consent it's violation.

LEX. I was a kid.

COYLE. You're still a fucking kid.

LEX. After we kill Chelton Steff, you won't say that again.

STADDON. That's right, Lex. That's right. (STADDON *glances at his watch.*) But before we head out, I suggest a little practice, so that when we arrive, it will be more manageable. Coyle, you pull him out of bed.

LEX. He's got a wife. What about her?

STADDON. We'll improvise on her. But the power is Chelton Steff. We go for him first. I'll be Chelton. (LEX *laughs.*) Is it such a stretch?

(STADDON *unbuttons his shirt a couple of buttons, undoes his cuffs. Then lies down on the bed, and closes his eyes. The other men just stare at him.*)

LEX. But you don't look like Steff.

COYLE. Though Chelton Steff is

LEX. ugly.

STADDON. I wouldn't say he's ugly. Though he is somewhat

COYLE. white.

LEX. How old is Chelton Steff?

COYLE. Who cares?

LEX. The more info we have, the smarter the choices.

STADDON. Lex has got a point. (*Beat.*) I'm fifty-six years old.

LEX. How long's he been in Rubbertown?

STADDON. Seventeen years. Came in as top manager, fresh out of Princeton. In six years I, Chelton Steff, was running the show. That's how good I am.

COYLE. Yeah, what makes you so good?

STADDON. I make the shareholders money. I keep—

COYLE. —Wages capped.

STADDON. I keep—

COYLE. Unions out.

STADDON. I keep the shareholders happy. I do what needs to be done.

LEX. But Steff gives us pee breaks.

STADDON. Because I care about my workforce.

COYLE. Yeah, you love us.

LEX. But if we can't keep up. If we fall behind.

COYLE. If we get sick enough that we can't work.

STADDON. Then I send you home.

COYLE. You fire us.

LEX. Never fired me.

COYLE. I keep up. I don't fall behind.

STADDON. I'm at the top. Look up. You can see the soles of my shoes. I'm floating over your heads. I never come down.... Even when I have to make a ...bowel movement.

COYLE. Jesus. He can't even say it.

STADDON. Even when I have to make a

LEX. Shit. But you "take" a shit. You don't "make" a shit.

STADDON. Even then I don't come down. I just…let it fall on your heads.

COYLE. I thought you were asleep, you son of a bitch.

STADDON. I am asleep. I'm Chelton Steff, in bed, asleep. You've just entered my home. And you're leaning down over me…. And now you pull me out of bed.

COYLE. I'm not going to touch you. No matter what you say.

STADDON. Please. We have to practice.

LEX. Why do we need to practice? We know what to do.

STADDON. If you want to play piano, you practice. If you want to kill a man, you practice. Both of you. Trust me.

> (COYLE *and* LEX *eye one another.*)

COYLE. Trust you? Trust you? Sure. All right. You're in bed. You're asleep…. Deep asleep.

> (*Suddenly* COYLE *jerks the bed into the center of the room between him and* LEX. STADDON *does not move.*)

LEX. Are you dreaming?

STADDON. Yes. Yes, I'm dreaming.

LEX. What are you dreaming?

COYLE. It doesn't matter.

STADDON. Yes. It does.

> (LEX *smirks at* COYLE.)

LEX. Ha.

STADDON. I'm dreaming I'm just a boy again and I'm—

COYLE. What?

STADDON. fishing.

COYLE. Predictable.

STADDON. But with my hands. And I'm in Harrods Creek and it's a summer day and I'm wading in my shorts, looking for crayfish and turtles. And I reach under this bank and I grab hold and I think it's a rock but its moving. I pull it out and it's a water turtle. A little buddy.

LEX. Aw.

STADDON. Not much bigger than a half dollar.

COYLE. I found one of those once when I was a kid.

STADDON. And it's swimming in my hand. There's no water in my hand but that doesn't keep it from trying. And I've never seen anything so strange and alive and. Spectacular.

> (*Suddenly* COYLE *lunges at* STADDON *and drags him violently out of bed and onto the floor.*)

COYLE. And that's when I drag that bastard out of bed. He drops the turtle and the creek smacks him right in the face.

(COYLE *slaps* STADDON *a few hard, quick times.*)

STADDON. Yes. Okay. Yes. Just like that. Just like that. And now you, Lex. You start kicking. Kicking and stomping. Stomping and kicking. Come on! Come on!

LEX. I don't want to hurt you, Vance.

(STADDON *suddenly jumps up and grabs a chair. He uses it against* LEX, *as a Lion Tamer would.*)

STADDON. I'm not your amigo, kid. I'm Chelton Steff and I don't give a shit about you.

(STADDON *uses the chair to poke at* LEX. LEX *runs away, circling the bed.*) I thought you were ready. Are you ready, Lex? Are you ready?

(LEX *finally reacts and attacks the chair. He kicks it and stomps it and breaks it into pieces. He's out of breath. He coughs once, checks himself.*)

LEX. Where's your turtle now motherfucker? (*Suddenly* LEX *looks around the floor.*) Shit. I didn't step on it, did I?

COYLE. Nah. It crawled up under the bed. It's safe.

STADDON. By now I'm almost done for. Coyle is still choking me and Lex has stomped me into pieces. (*The men surround the broken chair, as though it were Chelton Steff.*) My arm's broken in three different places.

LEX. And your shoulder's popped.

STADDON. Yes.

COYLE. And you haven't had a breath in almost three minutes and you're beginning to fade. You're turning blue.

LEX. Grey. You're turning grey.

COYLE. And slobber's coming out of your mouth.

STADDON. Like cottage cheese.

COYLE. Nah, not cottage cheese.... Like porridge. Yeah, porridge.

LEX. With hot little raisins

COYLE. on top.

STADDON. Exactly. And that's when I, Staddon Vance, step up and say, "Mr. Chelton Steff. You know why you're about to die?" And he's an intelligent man so he says "Yes."

COYLE. He even tells us why, hoping that might soften us up.

(LEX *stomps on a piece of chair.*)

LEX. But we don't soften up.

STADDON. We say, "Make your last thought a good one 'cause you'll be living with it for eternity." And then

LEX/COYLE/STADDON. Bang!

COYLE. You really think we should give a man like him time to prepare a last thought?

STADDON. It's standard decency. No need to be bastards.

(*The men move away from the chair.*)

LEX. What'll it be, huh? His last thought.

COYLE. Mine would be…I don't know. My daughter. My wife.

LEX. Ah, ain't he cute? (*Beat.*) So hey, what are our chances?

STADDON. That we get away with it?

LEX. I don't want to die in his home.

COYLE. Me neither.

STADDON. I'd say maybe a seventy/thirty chance.

COYLE. Let me guess: the seventy isn't the percentage for our escape with the loot.

STADDON. I'm sorry.

LEX. Thirty percent chance we make it out of this night alive, that's good enough for me.

COYLE. We stick to our plan, I'd say fifty/fifty.

STADDON. I appreciate your optimism.

COYLE. They won't get me.

LEX. Yeah. Me either.

(STADDON *studies the men.*)

STADDON. Good. (*Beat.*) Good. I knew I chose right…. Gentlemen, are you ready? Coyle, you brought the rags?

COYLE. Yep.

(COYLE *takes a crumpled paper bag out of his coat. He throws a mask to* LEX *and* STADDON. *Easily, surely, the men put the stockings on their heads.* STADDON *pulls his stocking completely over his face. They stand in a row, and they no longer look uncertain, but professional and frightening.*)

STADDON. This is the kind of moment where prayer comes in handy.

COYLE/LEX. We don't pray.

STADDON. Then let's just…think…how we want it to be. Tonight.

LEX. If you think hard enough on a thing, it will happen.

COYLE. Thinking hard is a kind of

STADDON. prayer.

LEX. Three men thinking hard together is a kind of

COYLE. pact. So that's what we are now? (COYLE *considers this, then makes up his mind.*) Yeah. A pact.

STADDON. Lex?

(LEX *pulls his stocking down over his face.*)

LEX. *Estoy listo.*

STADDON. Coyle?

(COYLE *pulls the stocking down over his face.*)

COYLE. Yep.

LEX/COYLE. Staddon?

(STADDON *shows the gun.*)

STADDON. Gotcha.

LEX. With that son of a bitch's cash, we'll buy us that boat. Rush the Ohio, glide the Mississippi and shoot right on out Hell's asshole, and on to new land—

(*The room seems to shake, hard, once, twice. Then there is a tearing sound and a crack appears, perhaps three or four feet long, in the floor in front of the men. It is in a different place from the first crack. Then it's quiet. The men are motionless, stunned, looking down at the crack in the floor.*)

COYLE. That's no broken pipe.

LEX. Shit.

STADDON. It's just a crack in the floor.

COYLE. Right.

STADDON. It's time to go.

LEX. Yeah, let's fuckin' start. (*Beat.*) Let's vamoose.

COYLE. Okay. Here's to a quick kill and keeping the trust.

(COYLE *puts his hand out, then* LEX *puts his on top of it, then* STADDON *puts his hand on top of* LEX's.)

STADDON/COYLE/LEX. Hurrah!

(*Blackout. In the dark the crack in the floor glows blue like water. Again we hear the sound of rain.*)

End of Act One

ACT II

Same motel room. LEX *is standing poised with the oar over his head. It is a long, beautiful, wooden oar.* LEX *is performing impressive, though original, martial arts moves.*

A rhythmic knock comes at the door. LEX *freezes at the sound of the knock. The knock comes again. Then* STADDON *opens the door and enters. Now* LEX *continues his moves.* STADDON *stands and watches* LEX *perform with the oar. He says nothing for some moments.*

STADDON. (*Slowly.*) You have an oar. (LEX *concentrates further on his moves.*) You look good with that oar, Lex. Not every man looks good with an oar. (*Beat.*) Where's Coyle? (LEX *doesn't respond.*) There's blood on your face.

(STADDON *moves to clean the blood off* LEX's *face.* LEX *brandishes his oar to protect himself, but continues his moves.*)

It's different now, Lex. Everything is different. (LEX *ignores him.*) Coyle was out of the house before the both of us…. He'll be here. He'll be here. Did you see that dining room? Wow. You could park a half-dozen fire trucks in that room and still have a ball. Water taps like chandeliers. How is it possible for a man to get a bathroom like that? Rooms like that? 'Cause he's Top Dog for seven chem plants in the neighborhood. King of Rubbertown. Chelton Steff.

(*On hearing Chelton Steff's name,* LEX *quits his moves.*)

LEX. I never even saw him before tonight. Slept with his socks on. (LEX *begins to laugh.* STADDON *approaches him and spits on his hand. Now* LEX *lets him clean the blood off his face.*) Fucking idiot. Slept with his socks on!

(STADDON *quits cleaning* LEX's *face.*)

STADDON. I sleep with my socks on.

LEX. You ever meet him before tonight?

STADDON. Not personally. Once or twice a year they'd bring a dozen of us to the office, pep talk, saltine, glass of juice.

LEX. When he bled, I felt nothing. When I saw his socks I felt. His socks had little trees on them. We're not close to Christmas.

(LEX *gets a sudden sharp pain in his stomach, but hardly shows it.* STADDON *studies* LEX.)

STADDON. How many times?

LEX. We said we wouldn't talk about it. Before we got here tonight we agreed. You breaking the trust, Vance?

STADDON. I'm just asking.

LEX. You mean how many times at work?

STADDON. Yes. At work.

LEX. Five times.

STADDON. More than that. I'm certain.

LEX. No. I'm certain. *Estoy seguro.*

STADDON. All right. But I'd still say seven…. No. I'd say eight times. That you know of.

(LEX *stares at him, surprised.*)

LEX. Huh. *Hijo de puta.* You're pretty good. Yeah. Eight times. How'd you know? (STADDON *shrugs.*) What about you?

STADDON. Guess.

LEX. I'm no good at it. No way I could guess.

STADDON. Try.

LEX. I'd say three. Maybe even just. Two.

STADDON. Wrong! Twice early on. Eleven times in the past eighteen months. That's a total of thirteen contamination episodes.

LEX. No way, no way.

STADDON. I got you beat.

LEX. But you're a manager. You don't wash and rinse reactors. Don't regulate exhaust. Don't do valves or agitator tanks. Don't do storage drums or neutralizer tanks. You just count our peas.

STADDON. Thirteen.

LEX. Really?

STADDON. Cross my heart. (*Beat.*) They'll come for us, you know. In a little while they'll have it figured out and they'll come for us.

LEX. (*Quietly.*) Days?

STADDON. No. Hours. Maybe less.

(*Suddenly* COYLE *bursts into the room, out of breath, but excited.*)

COYLE. We did it. Jesus, we did it!

LEX. I tied him to the chair. Oh yes I did.

COYLE. I hit him—bang—so he'd stop jumping.

LEX. Did I kick him before I tied him to the chair or afterwards?

COYLE. Both. You did both, Lex.

(LEX *barks like a seal.* COYLE *matches it.*)

LEX. His nose bled when I slapped him. He was sweating. Like he'd been in an onion shower.

COYLE. When I gave him my fist, you heard that air go out of him, just like a tire.

(COYLE *makes the sound of air going out of a tire.*)

LEX. You got a punch, Coyle. Jesus, you weren't lying.

COYLE. And you got the kick, brother. Just like you said.

LEX. (*Hopefully.*) I think I broke my foot.

COYLE. The wife was more calm.

LEX. I like lines on a woman's face.

COYLE. But he wouldn't open the goddamn safe.

LEX. No fucking money to take home. I'd counted on that.

COYLE. And that damn alarm. My ears are still ringing.

LEX. I thought we disabled it.

COYLE. There must have been two.

LEX. But that didn't stop us. Nothing could've stopped us.

COYLE. I'm running and I'm running and I'm hearing the sirens and the cops are getting close and my chest's about to burst. Damn. I feel like I'm seventeen again.

> (COYLE *shadow boxes with* LEX. LEX *responds. They go at it hard, almost hitting each other but not quite. They feel exhilarated.*)

STADDON. I'd just like to point out to you both that I'm the one who actually pulled the trigger. (*The men stop shadow boxing.*) Not you, or you.

COYLE. Yeah. But we did it together. Just like we said.

LEX. Just like we said.

> (COYLE *pours them each a drink.*)

COYLE. Here's to a job well done.

LEX. I second that.

STADDON. Here's to both of you. For showing up in the first place. For keeping the trust.

COYLE. And. Reluctant as I am to say it: Here's to Staddon Vance—

LEX. Ex-zookeeper—

COYLE. —for calling us here together. For making this night the only night in a fucking long line of nights that finally matters.

LEX. I second that too.

STADDON. Well then, to all of us. Men in hard weather stick together. To our Party of Three.

LEX. To the Boating Party.

COYLE. To the Hard Weather Boating Party.

STADDON. There's nothing else like it!

LEX/COYLE/STADDON. Hurrah!

> (*The three men drink. Silence. Alone with their thoughts.* COYLE *goes for another drink but trips over one of the cracks in the floor.*)

COYLE. Shit. It's worse. We broke it worse.

> (COYLE *examines the crack.*)

LEX. No we didn't. We had nothing to do with that.

COYLE. Motel guy won't believe us. He'll make us pay.

(COYLE *rolls up his sleeve and starts to put his hand down inside the first crack.*)

STADDON. You shouldn't do that, Coyle.

LEX. You could get electrocuted.

(COYLE *puts his hand in the crack, then squeezes his arm in. It's deep.* COYLE *pulls out his arm; his arm and sleeve are wet.*)

COYLE. Must be bad pipes. Maybe the basement's flooded.

(LEX *observes the water dripping from* COYLE's *arm.*)

STADDON. A motel room has a basement?

COYLE. Fuck if I know.

LEX. Oh God. We killed a man.

(LEX *vomits into his hands but nothing comes up. Dry heaves.*)

COYLE. Yep. We killed a man. So don't call on God, Kid. 'Cause God just stopped coming.

STADDON. You said you quit God.

COYLE. Yeah, but sometimes on a Tuesday or maybe a Thursday something comes back into me, maybe it's God, I don't know. But I do know this: when you take a motherfucker out, God steps back and you hear that yawn between the two of you. Nothing can cross that divide.

LEX. The Chair. We'll get the Chair.

STADDON. Yes, we will.

LEX. Well I'm going to stay in this room. Fuckin' cops'll have to kill me.

COYLE. I never been shot before.

STADDON. If they call my name. If they say "Staddon Vance. Come out with your hands in the air," I'll do it. If they call my name I'll have to. (*Beat.*) Coyle, you with me?

COYLE. Bullshit. I step outside with you, it's me that's dead.

STADDON. I wouldn't let that happen.

COYLE. Cops take one look at us and think—

LEX. You're both ugly.

COYLE. But we both ain't white. Guess which one they're gonna think killed Steff?

STADDON. We're still in this together.

COYLE. Right.

STADDON. Coyle. There's something I'd like to know.

COYLE. Don't ask me.

STADDON. You don't know what I'm going to ask—

COYLE. (*Interrupts.*) Yeah I do.

LEX. He asked me too.

STADDON. (*To* COYLE.) How many times?

COYLE. We said we wouldn't talk about it. (*Beat.*) Why do you want to know?

STADDON. Because it happened to all of us.

COYLE. What difference does it make?

STADDON. How many times? Please.

COYLE. Shit. That I know of?

STADDON. It is always. Only ever. What we know of.

COYLE. At work? Or at home? 'Cause I have no idea how many times it happened when I was at home. I stopped counting.

LEX. At work.

COYLE. Guess.

LEX. Seven.

STADDON. No. Give me a minute. You have no feeling in your hands, right?

COYLE. How'd you know that?

STADDON. The whites of your eyes. Have a hint of blue. Almost.

LEX. You can figure out his hands by his whites?

STADDON. Yes.

LEX. How?

STADDON. Just something you pick up on after a while. (*To* COYLE.) And your feet are hot.

COYLE. As a son of a bitch.

STADDON. I oversaw the workforce on level three through seven for years…. I'd say you were exposed to general concentrated chemical contamination at the workplace…nine times. Exactly.

(COYLE *eyes* STADDON *a moment.*)

COYLE. I started in the warehouse, loading, unloading tanks. Then moved on to flushing pipes, mixing gas, cleaning stacks. Last couple of years I replace damaged equipment, gauge tank levels. When that's not enough of a kick I regulate the speed of chemical reactions, quality and yields. (*Beat.*) You're right. Nine times of "accidental" exposure. That I know of.

LEX. I never got out of flushing pipes. Six years and still flushing pipes.

STADDON. (*To* COYLE.) But you don't cough.

COYLE. No I don't.

STADDON. But that strange. It's a typical symptom.

COYLE. What is this? Fucking doc time? Because I made it clear from the start, that I don't like to talk about the symptoms—

LEX. (*Interrupts.*) Hey! Hey! They're coming for us. Any minute now they'll break through that door.

STADDON. Lex. They don't know we're here.

LEX. (*Ignoring* STADDON.) We just going to stand here? Run! Should we run?

STADDON. We wouldn't get far. You know that.

LEX. Then it's any minute now. Any minute. *Cualquier minuto, cualquier minuto.*

(LEX *points the oar at the "door," chanting "any minute."*)

COYLE. Where'd you get the oar, Lex? Nice-looking oar. But we'll need two oars to row.

(LEX *quits chanting.*)

LEX. Steff had only one on his wall. So I took it. Didn't get the money. But we got an oar.

STADDON. That's a museum piece.

LEX. Yeah?

COYLE. There's a plaque on it.

(LEX *looks on the oar and finds the plaque.*)

COYLE. What's it say?

LEX. (*Reads.*)

"I want to be a cavalryman
And with John Hunt Morgan ride,
A colt revolver in my belt
A saber by my side.
I want a pair of

LEX/STADDON. epaulets

(STADDON *finishes the quote for* LEX.)

STADDON.

to match my suit of gray,
The uniform my mother made
And lettered 'CSA'."

COYLE. Huh. C.S.A. Confederate State Army. Glad we wasted the asshole.

LEX. Who's John Hunt Morgan?

STADDON. Confederate Army general who led his army a thousand miles to cross the Ohio as he tried to invade the North. Oar belongs to the Morgan's Men Association.

COYLE. Yeah, but Morgan failed, the slave-owning snake, took his sorry ass back through Kentucky to Bardstown. (*To* STADDON.) How do you know about the Morgan Association?

STADDON. I was their secretary.

(COYLE *moves in on* STADDON.)

COYLE. You Confederate bastard.

STADDON. No. A few hundred dollars a year to keep their papers in order. I was a good paper keeper. There were only three members listed. But there were hundreds of associate members. Of course, folks like that, they want their names kept out.

COYLE. My old Kentucky home.

LEX. I'm going to kill some cops with this oar if they get close enough.

COYLE. I don't think Morgan would appreciate that. Now take a whack at me and the old gizzard might show his ghost!

STADDON. I couldn't stand the chanting. They would stand in a circle and chant that song. Bank men, real-estate men, company men. (*Chants.*) John Hunt Morgan. John Hunt Morgan.

LEX/STADDON. John Hunt Morgan. John Hunt Morgan.

(STADDON *breaks off the chant while* LEX *continues quietly to chant the name, using it as music with his oar moves.*)

STADDON. It crawled into my ears like an earwig and it wouldn't let go. I couldn't sleep at night so after a few months, I quit.

COYLE. Good for you. (*To* LEX.) Lex. Shut the fuck up. (LEX *goes quiet. To* STADDON.) Or I'd have to suspect you of being part of something worse.

STADDON. What could be worse than what's acceptable?

LEX. What are we going to do? What the fuck are we going to do?

STADDON. I'd say we have two choices: we can wait for the cops to find us here, or try and get home to say good-bye to our families.

COYLE. We'd never make it. They'll be combing the streets. You take out one of the most prominent citizens of Louisville and no cop sleeps.

STADDON. Might be worth the risk to say goodbye. Coyle? (COYLE *doesn't answer.*) Lex?

LEX. I'm staying here. I'll fight it out. (*To* COYLE.) What about you? You gonna say goodbye to your wife?

COYLE. We did that almost two years ago. When she left. When it started.

STADDON. You said you never lost her. You lied.

COYLE. Yeah. I lied.

LEX. What, she didn't want to stay around and change your diapers?

COYLE. I asked her to leave. Then I told her. I gave her no choice.

LEX. Hard man. Hard. Or had you gone soft? That happens too. I can pump mine for hours and it just sleeps.

(STADDON *looks towards the window and speaks slowly.*)

STADDON. In a few hours it will be morning. I'm sorry we're going to die today. It's snowed most of the night.

COYLE. You know that's not snow.

(*A moment of silence.*)

STADDON. A clear sky would be a more kindly day to die in. I'd have liked a son to say good-bye to. "Son. I've got to say goodbye." "Son. Son." How beautiful it sounds.

LEX. I'll be your son. If you want to say goodbye to someone.

COYLE. Shit.

STADDON. No. That's not right.

LEX. Why?

STADDON. You're not my son.

LEX. So? You chose me. Out of all the other sick bastards that work at the plant, you chose me. I owe you one.

STADDON. But it's a lie. I don't lie.

LEX. I do. All the time. But at least I'm honest to myself about it.

STADDON. Lying is wrong.

LEX. Lying is a tool. If a screwdriver won't work, try a hammer. If a hammer won't work, try a lie. If it works, use it. (*Beat.*) Hi Pops!

STADDON. I wouldn't know how, really, to speak to a son.

LEX. I'll show you how.

STADDON. Why?

(LEX *ignores the question and plays a* "son.")

LEX. Hi Pops! You wanted to see me?

(*After a moment.*)

STADDON. Yes.

COYLE. Jesus.

LEX. What's up, Pops?

STADDON. Pops.

LEX. Yeah, Pops. What's up, Pops?

STADDON. You know I've asked you not to use that name: Pops. I don't like it.

LEX. Why not, Pops?

STADDON. It sounds. Insignificant. I'd prefer it…Son…if you'd call me: Father.

COYLE. No one says Father anymore. These days it's Dad, Daddy, Poppa, hey you, or Asshole.

LEX. So what's up (*Beat.*) Father?

(*A slight tremor of joy goes through* STADDON.)

STADDON. Well. Son. I know we haven't had a lot of time lately, me being at work so often, late home at nights. And I know we haven't always seen eye to eye. But—

LEX. (*Interrupts.*) Father. My buddies are waiting outside. I gotta go.

STADDON. Wait. I need to tell you something.

LEX. And I need to ask you something.

STADDON. Yes. Ask me. By all means. What do you want to ask?

LEX. Fifty bucks. You promised me fifty bucks for my birthday.

STADDON. When was your birthday, Son?

LEX. You always forget. You always forget.

(STADDON *gets out his wallet.*)

STADDON. I'm sorry. I'll give you seventy.

(LEX *takes the money and pockets* it.)

LEX. Thanks, Dad.

STADDON. Dad. Dad. Yes, Dad is all right. But Son.

LEX. Yes, Dad.

STADDON. We may not see each other again. We need to say good-bye. Son.

LEX. (*Matter-of-factly.*) Shit. You in trouble again, Dad? You been hitting Mom again?

STADDON. Of course not. I never hit your mother.

LEX. You hit me.

STADDON. I never hit you.

LEX. (*Calmly.*) You fucking did, Dad. Yeah, for years. Sometimes I'd be asleep and you'd smack me in the head while I lay on my pillow. You hit Chrissy too.

STADDON. Chrissy…I have a daughter too! A daughter!

LEX. Had. Had. Chrissy's dead. Or did you forget.

STADDON. No. No. I didn't forget. My son, my daughter. My darlings.

LEX. Ah. You never loved us.

STADDON. How dare you! I loved you all my life.

LEX. Bullshit.

(LEX *starts to turn away.*)

STADDON. Don't go yet. Son. I'm sorry if I hit you. I'm sorry for Chrissy too. Fathers should cherish their children.

(LEX *just stares at* STADDON. *Some moments of stillness. Then* COYLE *bursts out laughing. The laughter is a release for him.* LEX *is silent.* STADDON *seems wounded and retreats.*)

COYLE. (*To* LEX.) That was good. Yeah, you're good.

LEX. Who you need to say goodbye to, Coyle?

COYLE. I done my goodbyes.

LEX. You touch your wife with those hands? Those dead hands? She like that?

COYLE. Lex. I'm not Staddon. I got a limit.

LEX. A limit. Yeah. I got eight exposures. You got nine. Hot feet. Check. Dick's dead. Check. Numb hands. Check. I figure your back teeth are gone. Gum rot. Can't keep food down anymore. Your ears bleed at night? You should see my fucking pillow. Strawberry jam with the pulp. But what's the worst for you, Coyle? What was it that made you send your woman packing?

COYLE. I'll hit you.

LEX. Let me guess. She wouldn't let you touch her anymore 'cause your fingers were that cold. No blood in the tips anymore.

COYLE. Shut your mouth, Lex.

LEX. No blood then no touch. Winter.

STADDON. Lex. Don't.

LEX. Your wife lay down every night next to winter. Winter. (*Beat.*) With hot feet. (COYLE *just stares at* LEX. LEX *moves closer to* COYLE, *now speaking gently.*) What was her name, your wife?

(For some moments COYLE *is silent.)*

COYLE. First I lost the memory of my feet. As though grass never happened or dirt, or fuckin' wool socks. Then I lost the memory in my hands. The feel of water. Gone. The weight of a glass. Gone. A few weeks ago, it was my mouth. (*Beat.*) Coralee. (*Beat.*) Know what I regret? That I didn't kiss her goodbye. If I'd touched that mouth again, I wouldn't of let her go. First time I met this woman was like doin' 90.5 on the freeway, rolling down the window she just pours all over me. That kind of rush makes you go from little bitty breeze inside you to a cataclysmic storm. That strong. (*Beat.*) But now I can't remember kissing her. Can't remember the feeling. The memory of her kiss is wiped out. (*To* STADDON.) You say Hopkins forced the disparate together. You're wrong about him, Staddon. The right word is fused. Hopkins fused the disparate together, like they were meant to be together. Belonged together. Like my woman and me.

STADDON. Like the three of us?

(The men eye one another for some moments.)

LEX. She used to fall asleep on her feet, my sister. Rocking back and forth. When I was a kid and pissed off at Dad or Mom, I'd go to my room and I wouldn't come out. Chrissy, she'd put little notes under my door that said stuff like "There's a turtle in your head," or "Why can't you stop thinking about groundhogs?" And soon as I read her note, sure enough I'd have a turtle in my head or I couldn't get the groundhogs out of my skull. Chrissy wouldn't go to the hospital. She knew they couldn't save her. She lay dying five days. I held her hand. Then she said, "*Mátame.*" She could hardly speak. "*Mátame.*" I said no. She kept saying "Kill me." She was in.

COYLE. Unimaginable pain. So you killed her.

LEX. I didn't kill my sister, the fuckin' industry did. We never closed the windows in our house. We knew it did no good. The sirens. The release. The sirens. The release. Seems like something's always getting loose in Rubbertown. Getting broke. Getting spilled. Into the air. How many times did it happen and we didn't know?

COYLE. How'd you kill her?

LEX. Her fingernails had fallen off. She wept at how her hands looked. She'd always been proud of her hands. And it hurt when I held her hand but she wanted me to hold her hand. I'd put applesauce on her tongue. The only thing she'd stomach in the end. In the end. That's a stupid fucking phrase 'cause the end doesn't come when it's. Love.

COYLE. How did you kill her, Lex?

LEX. Shut up.

COYLE. How'd you kill her?

LEX. *Mi mejor amiga.* She was my best friend. My twin.

COYLE. Lex.

LEX. (*Explodes.*) Shut the fuck up. *¡Cállate el pinche osico!* You don't know. You don't fucking know— (*Now* LEX *is quiet again.*) —what happened. If I'd killed her she wouldn't have died. If I'd killed her she wouldn't have died. Like that. Her mouth full of. Her lungs full of. Blood. She didn't blame me. For what I couldn't do. And all I could do was sit beside her. They killed her. Then I killed her again by not killing her. So twice. Twice she had to die. 'Cause I was too scared to do it.

(*The men are silent.*)

COYLE. You know what I thank God for Staddon? I thank God he let us kill Chelton Steff. Motherfucker fought and won every lawsuit we brought against him. For every scientist our neighborhood brought in to fight him, and let me tell you it cost us, he had three brought in to do a ring dance 'round our graves. He said we're dying 'cause we use too much barbecue sauce on our ribs, that we don't get enough exercise, that we're just a sick people. But little by little spring doesn't come anymore to Rubbertown, summer neither. No leaves on the trees so autumn don't bother. Even the calendar's sick. No more seasons. Just night.

(*After some moments.*)

STADDON. I didn't kill Chelton Steff.

(LEX *and* COYLE *just stare, stunned, at* STADDON.)

I put the gun to his head. I said: Hello. My name is Staddon Vance.

COYLE. You didn't kill him?

STADDON. I work for you.

LEX. You didn't fuckin' kill him?

STADDON. I'm your third submanager at Amalgamated Synthetics.

COYLE. But I heard the shot.

STADDON. I can take you for a tour of your site.

LEX. I heard it too.

STADDON. As you very well know, we run a tip-top ship.

COYLE. I don't believe you.

STADDON. He didn't speak.

LEX. He's lying, Coyle.

STADDON. Then I said, "Think your last thought now Mr. Chelton Steff because you are going to die."

COYLE. Staddon.

STADDON. I thought he'd say, "Eat me, Mr. Vance." I thought he'd say, "Go to hell, you loser."

COYLE. (*Louder.*) Staddon!

STADDON. I thought he'd say, "You're a dead man, Staddon, just like me."

COYLE. (*Still disbelieving.*) Tell me you're lying.

STADDON. But you know what he said? He said.

LEX. Tell us you're fucking lying!

STADDON. Chelton Steff said. (*Beat.*) "Please please please please please…. (STADDON *says "please" about twenty-three times, deadpan, counting, slowly, steadily, then cuts off.*) Exactly that many times. He deserved to die. But in that moment I hated him too much. Killing a man with that kind of hate inside you is a kind of touching. I didn't want to touch him. So I shot him in the leg.

LEX. Jesus. Jesus.

STADDON. He passed out. I ran.

(COYLE *grabs* STADDON *by the collar.*)

COYLE. We should kill you right now, Staddon.

STADDON. Go ahead. I'll be dead in a few weeks anyhow. It's been blood for a month now.

COYLE. We really should kill you.

STADDON. I'm a manager. I work for Chelton Steff.

(COYLE *pushes* STADDON *away, otherwise he'd hit him.*)

COYLE. So do I.

LEX. Not anymore we don't. Now we don't even have a job. (*Resigned.*) Never count on the fucking zookeeper.

(*Suddenly, seemingly out of the blue,* LEX *strikes* STADDON *with the oar.* STADDON *crumples to the floor.* LEX *stands over him.*)

He promised me. He said it was payback.

(LEX *begins to beat* STADDON *with the oar as he speaks.* COYLE *turns away.* STADDON *hardly struggles but attempts to curl up and ward off the blows. Then* LEX *pounds the bed.*)

This was your fucking plan. You called me! You called me and told me it was a good plan. Now everything is fucked and I've got nothing. Nothing. *Nada. Nada. Nada.*

(*Then* LEX *quits.*)

COYLE. You know what's almost funny? The end didn't seem so bad anymore, not after tonight. For years, months, you see that end coming. You see your neighbors die around you. (*To* LEX.) You see your family die too. (*To* STADDON.) And then you finally do something that your gut's telling you is wrong but feels so damn right. And all those dead places inside you, the numb places, they wake up. Even if only for a minute. Everything inside me woke up tonight. And now? Just like Lex says. We got nothing. And worse, we've done nothing. I'd wipe my feet on you, Staddon Vance. I'd wipe my feet on you right now but there's a doormat just outside I'd rather use.

(STADDON *composes himself before he speaks.*)

STADDON. Well, I can't blame you for drawing that conclusion that it's my fault. (*Beat.*) But you walked away, both of you. I was alone.

COYLE. (*To* LEX.) I knew I should've looked when he did him.

STADDON. But you didn't look, did you Mr. Forester. You walked away. I understand that.

COYLE. So my stomach was flipping. I just stepped outside.

STADDON. And you, Lex Nadal, you ran out to the yard.

LEX. I had to shit. I didn't want to. Not in his house.

STADDON. We went in there. Me, you and Lex. But then you left me to do it alone. Both of you.

COYLE. All you had to do was pull the trigger.

STADDON. Then why didn't you do it? (*To* LEX.) Or you? I offered the gun to both of you but you wouldn't take it. Neither of you would take it.

COYLE. It was your gun.

STADDON. But it was our pact!

LEX. I kicked him. It was your job to shoot him.

COYLE. I tied him up. I hit him. That's what we agreed.

STADDON. No. We agreed to do it together.

COYLE. And we did it together. We each had our part.

LEX. Yeah. We each had our part.

STADDON. We practiced. Before we went we practiced. To kill him together.

We built the trust. We built the trust and you broke it.

COYLE. No.

LEX. You broke it. You broke it.

STADDON. Both of you walked away. I was left alone. (*Beat.*) The fact is, you're both cowards. And there's nothing worse than cowa—

COYLE. Don't you dare or I'll kill you where you stand.

LEX. Hit him, Coyle. Hit him. He didn't do the job. He broke the trust. He broke the trust. He broke the trust. Hit him. *Pégale. Pégale.*

> (COYLE *moves in on* STADDON. LEX *continues saying "Hit him" in Spanish, over and over. Suddenly* COYLE *turns on* LEX.)

COYLE. (*To* LEX.) Shut the fuck up. You kicked him? You kicked Chelton Steff? Like a fucking ten-year-old kicks his bedroom door.

LEX. Coyle?

COYLE. You're a bad joke, Lex. You're just a kid.

LEX. *¿Soy un pinche niño?* I'm just a kid. Yeah. Then what do you call what you did to him? Your hands were shakin' so hard you couldn't even tie the ropes. I had to do it for you. Pathetic.

COYLE. Shut your mouth.

LEX. Fucking pathetic. Knock the wind out of him? He didn't even have to catch his breath when you punched him.

> (COYLE *gut-punches* LEX *and it's hard.* LEX *shuts up. The men are silent now for some moments.*)

STADDON. Well. (*Beat.*) He did get a bullet in his leg.

LEX. Yeah. Maybe he bled to death.

COYLE. He'll probably limp for the rest of his life.

LEX. He'll always have a hobble.

STADDON. He won't ever forget us.

COYLE. No. He won't ever forget us. (*To* STADDON.) But you had the gun. You had the key to get inside. Why'd you drag us into this?

STADDON. It would have been meaningless to do it alone. You gave it meaning. Both of you.

COYLE. Why?

STADDON. Because the industry was killing you with the exposures.

LEX. But you said you wanted to kill him because of your exposures. Eleven times in eighteen months. That's more than us. Or were you lying? He was lying.

STADDON. No. I wasn't lying. Twice it was an accident when I was on the floor. Then nine times more. I climbed into the tanks. Over a period of months I climbed into the tanks and just. Breathed.

COYLE. You mother fucker. You did it on purpose? On purpose? We spend years dodging and ducking what can never be dodged and ducked and you do it on purpose? Why?

STADDON. I saw. I saw your faces over the years. You went into those buildings and you went in whole. You went in strong like a thousand blocks of ice, hard and clear and useful. Whole crowds of you. Whole crowds. I was outside that crowd. I was outside that. Power.

LEX. Because you're the god damn zookeeper. You count our peas.

COYLE. You wanted to join us?

STADDON. Yes.

LEX. So you'd be like us?

STADDON. Yes.

COYLE. Well if that isn't the most distorted, disgusting, sentimental piece of solidarity bullshit I have ever heard. Well. I got news for you Staddon Vance. You are not like us.

STADDON. Now I am.

COYLE. No, buddy. You'll never be like us. 'Cause you had a choice about the exposures.

STADDON. But it brought us together. Like tonight.

COYLE. It won't ever be the three of us.

LEX. Hey. If Chelton's not dead, maybe the cops won't kill us.

COYLE. Don't count on their grace.

STADDON. I'm sorry. You're both right. I broke the trust.

(*The men refuse to look at* STADDON. STADDON *coughs into his hand. He coughs and coughs and it's an ugly cough, as though his insides were coming up. Blood pours into his hand.* LEX *and* COYLE *now look at* STADDON. STADDON *wipes the blood from his lungs on his shirt. There's a lot of it.* STADDON *composes himself.*)

It's all the excitement.

COYLE. Well, well, well.

(COYLE *slowly begins to remove his shoes.*)

So he's not dead. Chelton Steff's not dead. Chelton Steff lives on!

(COYLE *reclines on the bed. Then his feet begin to smoke.*)

LEX. Fucking Jesus Christ.

(STADDON *and* LEX *examine* COYLE's *smoking feet.* STADDON *whistles with admiration.*)

STADDON. I've never seen that symptom before.

LEX. Wow. Anyone got some marshmallows?

(COYLE *gives* LEX *a warning look.*)

LEX. Hell. I'm hot inside too. Like now, if I swallowed an egg whole it'd be hard boiled in three minutes. But I never been as hot as you, Coyle. But you ain't all that. You ain't all that! Watch this. Now it'll take a minute 'cause I got to go in deep....

(LEX *readies himself to cough up something deep. He works and works at it. Finally he spits something up. It's larger than before. It glows florescent on the floor.*)

STADDON. Now if that doesn't make you believe in the existence of God....

COYLE. Looks like water from our lake. Same glow. So damn glorious, that lake in the dark. Incandescent, just like Rubbertown is at night, in the dark, like some blow-back acropolis. Smoke, steam, pouring out the stacks—

STADDON. —like God's mind on overflow.

LEX. And that whole complex lit up with a thousand lights like some kind of

STADDON. heaven on earth.

COYLE. Yeah. But poisonous. Deadly.

LEX. Just like our lake. And I still swim in that lake. So thick with chemicals you can scoop the water up and pour it like sand. And if I'm not dead tonight I'll swim it tomorrow 'cause it's our fuckin lake. Swimming in that lake I feel alive even when it's killing me 'cause its my way of saying fuck you to Chelton Steff.

STADDON. They'll still come for us. Even though we didn't kill him. Attempted murder. They'll still come.

COYLE. Attempted murder. Huh. I'd call it willful, what they've done to us.

STADDON. I'm finished, Coyle. I had one real job in my life to do, and I couldn't do it. I just couldn't do it. And what's worse, maybe I'm glad.

COYLE. Yeah. Maybe we're all glad.

(LEX *nods in agreement.*)

STADDON. Mr. Forester. I'm dying every minute.

COYLE. Well so am I. So is Lex. It's only weeks we got left.

STADDON. I need you to kill me. (*Beat.*) I can't do the rest of the minutes.

LEX. How come you ask him to do it, not me?

STADDON. (*Not looking at* LEX.) I can't ask you. You're my son.

(LEX *doesn't answer but nods, almost imperceptibly.* STADDON *puts the gun on the bed but* COYLE *won't take it.* STADDON *kneels beside the bed.*)

LEX. Shit.

STADDON. I always wondered what would be my last thought when I died? A thought about God? About my baby's clicker? Something bigger than them both?

COYLE. Don't think I can do it.

STADDON. Yes you can.

COYLE. (*To* STADDON.) No. Shoot your own damn self.

(COYLE *walks away.*)

STADDON. But I'm asking you to do it.

LEX. Well don't fucking ask him.

STADDON. But we're friends. After tonight.

COYLE. We're not friends.

LEX. We don't even like you.

STADDON. (*To* COYLE.) I need your kindness.

COYLE. That's not the kind of feeling you can force.

STADDON. Just try.

LEX. Stop it old man. Just quit.

(COYLE *turns away.*)

STADDON. I don't want to die alone. I will if you don't help me. (COYLE *just shakes his head "no," turns away.*) But what if I can help you. Remember. Your wife.

COYLE. What?

LEX. Jesus, he's lost it.

STADDON. Coralee. What if I can help you remember her the way you want to remember her?

COYLE. No. You can't do that. It's gone.

STADDON. Yes I can.

COYLE. You can make me remember?

(COYLE *only now turns to face* STADDON *again.*)

LEX. No, he can't. He can't.

STADDON. Yes I can. But if you remember, Coyle, you owe me. That's the deal. Keep the trust. Agreed?

COYLE. You broke our trust already.

STADDON. Give me a chance to restore it. Please. (*Beat.*) Now close your eyes.

COYLE. Fuck off.

LEX. Yeah, fuck off.

COYLE. You're out of your mind.

STADDON. Go on. I can make you remember.

LEX. No one can do that.

STADDON. (*To* COYLE.) I can. One chance.

COYLE. No.

STADDON. Just one chance. Close your eyes, Coyle. (*Beat.*) Go on.

(COYLE *closes his eyes.* STADDON *steps towards* COYLE *and takes* COYLE'*s face in his hands.* STADDON *kisses him. For a second* COYLE *resists strongly but then for a moment gives in to the kiss.* STADDON *steps back.* COYLE *turns away, but is suddenly calm.*)

COYLE. No way, no way. Jesus.

LEX. Can't you see he's fucking with you?

COYLE. No, Lex. I felt it.

LEX. He's fucking with you!

COYLE. (*To* LEX.) It was her.

LEX. *Por favor, párale.* (*To* STADDON.) How?

STADDON. I don't know.

LEX. Coyle. This is bullshit.

COYLE. It was Coralee.

LEX. No. No.

STADDON. You think you two are the only ones who can do things or feel things that you couldn't do or feel before? Smoking feet. Blue phlegm. That's nothing. I knew a man at Carbide. He defrosted valves. He died from the exposures last month. After the last contamination, he could whistle "Skip to My Lou."

LEX. So?

STADDON. From his ear.

LEX. How did you make Coyle remember?

STADDON. (*Shrugs.*) Maybe…. Maybe this kind of poisoning, it leaves behind in us….

COYLE. An opening.

LEX. An opening?

COYLE. Capacity where there wasn't before.

LEX. So? So? Shit. You going to kiss Chelton Steff then? Will that make him remember us? (*To* COYLE.) You gonna set his plant on fire with your feet? (*Beat.*) Jesus fucking Christ. An opening? Capacity? It's just cheap tricks. Cheap party tricks. And then we die.

COYLE. What if it were more than that?

STADDON. What if we could—

LEX. (*To* STADDON.) Shut up. After what you pulled tonight you better shut the fuck up. (*To both men.*) Because what does it matter? What does it fucking matter when we can't save our lives?

(*The men are silent some moments.*)

STADDON. Well (*Beat.*) Coyle. We had an agreement. I helped you remember. Now be a man of your word.

(COYLE *walks away.*)

LEX. No. (*To* STADDON.) This stops here. This stops right here.

STADDON. (*To* LEX.) Lex. My lungs are filling with blood. Don't make me die twice. (LEX *turns away. To* COYLE.) Coyle. Kill me.

COYLE. What do you think, Lex?

(LEX *doesn't answer.*)

I think it's truth or dare.

LEX. Yeah. Truth or dare.

(*Long beat.*)

COYLE. Choose.

STADDON. Truth.

LEX. Make it good, Coyle. Make it good.

COYLE. Ok. Now. (*Beat.*) Would you do the same for me, right now? (*Beat.*) Would you do the same for Lex?

STADDON. I don't want to continue—

LEX. (*Interrupts.*) Just answer the question, Mr. Vance.

STADDON. (*Beat.*) No. I couldn't do the same for you. (*To* LEX.) Or you. I wouldn't have the courage.

LEX. Right.

COYLE. But you ask it of us?

STADDON. Yes.

(STADDON *and* COYLE *now look at one another, eye to eye, a moment.*)

COYLE. Well, at least you're not bullshittin' us. For that, we thank you.

LEX. Yeah. Thanks.

(COYLE *picks up the gun.*)

COYLE. (*Quietly.*) Son of a bitch. We work for you, Staddon Vance. We get sick for you. And now we've got to put you out of the misery you've made. All right. Get on your knees.

(STADDON *hesitates.*)

LEX. (*To* STADDON.) It's okay. It's okay.

(STADDON *gets on his knees.* COYLE *is behind him.*)

STADDON. Yes. (*To* COYLE.) Thank you.

(COYLE *pulls the trigger. There's a "click" but no bullet.*)

COYLE. Damn it.

(COYLE *fires again. Another click.* LEX *urges* COYLE *on.*)

LEX. If you stop now it'll be worse. Don't stop.

STADDON. Yes. Keep going. I'll think about math.

LEX. Yes, think about math.

STADDON. That's not a bad last thought.

> (LEX *kneels in front of* STADDON.)

LEX. Math is a good last thought. Now, Coyle!

> (COYLE *fires again, just as* LEX *dives out of the way.*)

COYLE. Shit.

STADDON. Or that one I learned in grade school:
> (*Recites.*)
> "Long since I hate the night,
> more hate the morning."

LEX. Again!

STADDON.
> "Long since my thoughts chase me"

COYLE. (*Click.*) Fuck.

STADDON.
> "Like beasts in forests."

(*Beat.*) Sir Philip Sydney.

COYLE. No.

LEX. (*To* COYLE.) Concentrate.

STADDON. Yes, concentrate. We're in Motel 6. In the middle of the world.

COYLE. I won't do it.

> (COYLE *puts down the gun.*)

STADDON. We're at the center of the earth.

COYLE. 'Cause we're still here. We're still alive.

STADDON. But what ever happened…I ask you, what ever happened to Motel 5?

> (*Suddenly* LEX *picks up the gun and fires at* STADDON*; this time the gun shoots.* STADDON *slumps over. After a long silence,* LEX *stands over* STADDON *and sings.*)

LEX. (*Sings.*)
> If I could grow up, you know what I'd be?
> Not a tailor, nor a tinker, but a wolf of the sea.

(*To* COYLE.) He liked this song.

> (*Sings.*) If I could grow up.
> If I could wake up.

> (*A storm begins outside again. A crash of thunder, a flash of lighting. The lamps in the room flicker.* LEX *speaks to* COYLE.)

Coyle. We'll be dead soon. Real soon. By the cops or by the sickness. (*Beat.*) So let's pray. I don't pray anymore. But./ Let's pray.

COYLE. (*Overlapping at /.*) No. (*Beat.*) All right. But to who?

LEX. I don't know. To whoever.

COYLE. To whatever. To whatever's got an ear wide enough to take us in.

> (COYLE *gets to his knees beside* LEX. *They begin to pray some moments beside* STADDON's *body.*)

You know, Staddon woulda loved this.

LEX. Yeah.

> (*They pray. Then at the same moment, they look at one another and* COYLE *nods.* LEX *and* COYLE *reach over and pull* STADDON *between them.* LEX *and* COYLE *prop up* STADDON's *dead body between them.*)

Okay. Party of three.

COYLE. Let's pray.

> (*They bow their heads and pray again. Thunder rolls harder outside. Loud. Louder. Then there is an ear-splitting burst of lightning and crash of thunder and suddenly the floor of the motel room cracks open and the hull of a boat breaks up through the floor behind the praying men.* LEX *and* COYLE *begin to slowly turn around as the rest of the boat appears and comes to rest/land in the motel room. It is a beautiful, classic 1960s speedboat, with wood sides. It seems timeless.* COYLE *and* LEX *are frozen, staring at it. We can now hear water lapping. The hull of the boat is wet and streaming with water. As though a lake were below the floor, or water surrounding the hotel.*)

LEX. Are we dead, Coyle?

COYLE. Not yet.

LEX. We do that?

> (LEX *slowly gets off his knees and moves towards the boat.*)

COYLE. Looks like it.

> (*The boat seems to glow.*)

LEX. Motel guy's gonna kill us.

> (LEX *tentatively touches the boat, then runs his hands along the hull, caressing it.*)

I think it's our boat.

COYLE. Yeah. (*Beat.*) It's our boat.

> (LEX*, in one easy, smooth motion, sits on the hull.* COYLE *watches* LEX*, nods to him.* LEX *looks off in the distance, as though he can see the Ohio. Another crash of thunder, just a little farther off now.* COYLE *looks up at the thunder. Then darkness.*)

End of Play

BRINK!

A RITES OF PASSAGE ANTHOLOGY

by Lydia R. Diamond, Kristoffer Diaz, Greg Kotis, Deborah Zoe Laufer, Peter Sinn Nachtrieb, and Deborah Stein

BIOGRAPHIES

Lydia R. Diamond's plays include: *Voyeurs de Venus* (2006 Joseph Jefferson Award for best new work, 2006 Black Theater Alliance Award for best writing), *The Bluest Eye* (2006 Black Arts Alliance Image Award for best new play and 2008 AATE Distinguished Play Award), *The Gift Horse* (Theodore Ward Prize, Kesselring Prize 2nd Place), *Stick Fly* (2008 Susan Smith Blackburn Finalist, 2006 Black Theatre Alliance Award for best play), *Lizzie Stranton*, and *Harriet Jacobs*. Producing Theatres include: Arena Stage, The Huntington, New Vic, Goodman, Steppenwolf, Long Wharf, Hartford Stage, McCarter, Playmakers Rep, Providence Black Rep, Chicago Dramatists, Congo Square, TrueColors, The Matrix, and Company One. Commissions include: Steppenwolf, Actors Theatre of Louisville/Victory Gardens, McCarter, Huntington, and The Roundabout. *Stick Fly* is published by Northwestern University Press. Ms. Diamond is a 2009 NEA/Arena Stage New Play Development Grant Finalist, an 2006-2007 Huntington Playwright Fellow, a current TCG Board Member, and is on faculty at Boston University.

Kristoffer Diaz's plays include *The Elaborate Entrance of Chad Deity* (produced by Victory Gardens/Teatro Vista, InterAct, and Mixed Blood), *Welcome to Arroyo's* (developed/presented by American Theater Company, Donmar Warehouse, Summer Play Festival, Lark Play Development Center, Hip-Hop Theatre Festival, Queens Theatre in the Park, South Coast Repertory, The Tank and New York University), and *The Trophy Thieves: A High School Love Story* (New York University and The Gallery Players; published by Playscripts). *Welcome to Arroyo's* will be published in 2009 as part of the first major anthology of hip-hop theater. Awards include the Jerome Fellowship (The Playwrights' Center), the Van Lier Fellowship (New Dramatists), a Donmar Warehouse Playwright Residency and the 2008 National Latino Playwriting Award.

Greg Kotis is the author of many plays and musicals including *Yeast Nation* (Book/Lyrics), *The Truth About Santa*, *Pig Farm*, *Eat the Taste*, *Urinetown* (Book/Lyrics, for which he won an Obie Award and two Tony Awards), and *Jobey and Katherine*. His work has been produced and developed in theatres across the country and around the world, including Actors Theatre of Louisville, American Conservatory Theater, American Theater Company, Henry Miller's Theatre, Manhattan Theatre Club, New York Stage and Film, Perseverance Theatre, Roundabout Theatre Company, Soho Rep, South Coast Repertory, and The Old Globe, among others. Greg is a member of the Neo-Futurists, the Cardiff Giant Theater Company, ASCAP, and the Dramatists Guild. He grew up in Wellfleet, Massachusetts, and now lives in Brooklyn with his wife Ayun Halliday, his daughter India, and his son Milo.

Deborah Zoe Laufer's play *End Days* received the 2007 ATCA/Steinberg New Play Citation. It premiered at Florida Stage, as did *The Last Schwartz* and *The Gulf of Westchester*. Samuel French published *End Days*, *The Last Schwartz* and *Out of Sterno*. *The Last Schwartz* appeared in *Women Playwrights: The Best Plays of 2003* and recently enjoyed a six-month run at Zephyr Theatre in Los Angeles. *Out of Sterno* is receiving its world premiere at Portland Stage Company, Maine. Her other plays, *Fortune*, *Random Acts* and *Miniatures*, have received productions and workshops around the country. Ms. Laufer is a Juilliard graduate, a two-time recipient of the LeCompte du Nouy Award from The Lincoln Center Foundation and a Dramatists Guild member.

Peter Sinn Nachtrieb is a San Francisco-based playwright whose works include *boom* (TCG's most-produced play 2009-10), *T.I.C. (Trenchcoat In Common)*, *Hunter Gatherers* (2007 ATCA/Steinberg New Play Award, 2007 Will Glickman Prize), *Colorado*, and *Multiplex*. His work has been seen Off-Broadway and at theatres across the country including at Ars Nova, SPF, Woolly Mammoth Theatre, Seattle Repertory, Actors Theatre of Louisville, Cleveland Public Theatre, Brown/Trinity Playwrights Rep, Wellfleet Harbor Actor's Theatre, Dad's Garage, and in the Bay Area at Encore Theatre, Killing My Lobster, Marin Theatre Company, Impact Theatre, and The Bay Area Playwrights Festival. He is under commission from South Coast Repertory and American Conservatory Theater, and is a Resident Playwright at the Playwrights Foundation, San Francisco. Peter holds a degree in Theater and Biology from Brown and an M.F.A. in Creative Writing from San Francisco State University. He likes to promote himself online at www.peternachtrieb.com.

Deborah Stein's plays have been produced/developed at Seattle Repertory Theatre, Guthrie Theater, Women's Project & Productions, The Wilma Theater, The Playwrights' Center, Red Eye Theater, Live Girls Theater, Dance Theater Workshop and Project Artaud Theater; and internationally in Poland, Ireland, Edinburgh (Traverse Theatre) and Prague. She collaborated with Pig Iron Theatre Company on six new works, including *Shut Eye* (dir. Joseph Chaikin), and was twice nominated for the Barrymore Award for best new play. Her writing is published in *TheatreForum*, *Play: A Journal of Plays* and *The Best American Poetry of 1996*. Commissions include the Guthrie Theater, The Children's Theatre Company and the EST/Sloan Project. Ms. Stein holds an M.F.A. from Brown University and is a two-time Jerome Fellow at The Playwrights' Center and member of New Dramatists. Recent productions include *Wallflower* (Stages Repertory Theatre) and *God Save Gertrude* (The Theatre @ Boston Court).

ACKNOWLEDGMENTS

Brink! premiered at the Humana Festival of New American Plays in March 2009. It was directed by Sean Daniels with the following cast:

Big Birth Opening Number, by All
Ensemble .... The Company

Grandpa's Cologne: One, by Kristoffer Diaz
Danny ....Daniel Reyes
His Boys .... Matthew Baldiga, Michael Dalto,
Steven Rausch, Jacob Wilhelmi

Today I am a Woman, by Deborah Zoe Laufer
DJ ....Aaron Matteson
Sarah .... Anna Kull
Mr. Kotler .... Andy Nogasky
Mrs. Kotler.. Anne Veal
Auntie Susie .... Allison Moy
Uncle Hershie...Jon Riddleberger
Aunt Mary...Julia Bentz
Barry Kotler.. Chris Moore
Spandex Dancers .... Alison Clayton, LaKeisha Randle
Photographer.. Matthew Baldiga
Ensemble ....Company

New Rite, by Kristoffer Diaz
Big Momma.. Alison Clayton
Lil' Daddy ....Jon Riddleberger
Sweet Darlin' ....Nancy Noto
Tall!..Chris Moore
Fire! .... Andy Nogasky
Jumper! ....LaKeisha Randle
Guitar!..Ami Jhaveri
Dancer! ....Steven Rausch

The White Bread Ballet,
by Peter Sinn Nachtrieb and Deborah Stein
Karma.. Katharine Moeller
Security Guard ....Steven Rausch
Dad/Boss/Husband .... Eric Eteuati
Mom .... Anne Veal
Ensemble .... The Company

First Job, by Lydia R. Diamond
Corrine ....Claudine Mboligikpelani Nako
Carol ....LaKeisha Randle

My First Trojan, by Peter Sinn Nachtrieb
Ramses.. Eric Eteuati
Durex..Jon Riddleberger

Grandpa's Cologne: Two,
book by Kristoffer Diaz, music and lyrics by Greg Kotis

Danny ....Daniel Reyes
Jolie ....Julia Bentz
Backup Girls...............Alison Clayton, Ami Jhaveri, Anna Kull,
                        Katharine Moeller, Allison Moy,
                        Claudine Mboligikpelani Nako,
                    Nancy Noto, LaKeisha Randle, Anne Veal

Evolution, by Deborah Zoe Laufer
Cuttle .... Alison Clayton
Lizzie...Allison Moy
Mama .... Eric Eteuati
Paw .... Chris Moore

Losing Your Virginity with Anne and David, by All
Anne .... Anne Veal
David ....David Michael Brown

An Actor Arrives, by Greg Kotis
Actor...Jacob Wilhelmi
God of Fortune ....Aaron Matteson
God of Good Regard .... Andy Nogasky
God of Fame.. Anne Veal
Agent ....Michael Dalto
Assistant Casting Agent..........................David Michael Brown
Playwright ....Nancy Noto

Internal Audit, by Peter Sinn Nachtrieb
1 ....Steven Rausch
2...Ami Jhaveri
3...David Michael Brown
4...Jon Riddleberger
Professor .... Andy Nogasky

Never a Bride, by Deborah Zoe Laufer
Amy .... Anna Kull
Shelley .... Allison Moy
Mick .... Michael Dalto
Dexter .... Steven Rausch

Losing Your Foreskin with Anne and David, by All
Anne .... Anne Veal
David .... David Michael Brown

First Baby, by Lydia R. Diamond
Noah .... Aaron Matteson
Becky .... Claudine Mboligikpelani Nako

American Dream, by Greg Kotis
Father .... Jacob Wilhelmi
Mother .... Ami Jhaveri
Son .... Jon Riddleberger
Daughter .... Julia Bentz
Banker .... Chris Moore
Cops .... David Michael Brown,
Claudine Mboligikpelani Nako,
LaKeisha Randle, Daniel Reyes
Ensemble .... The Company

Instructions to My Future Life Partner re: what to do in the event of my (sudden, heartbreaking, heroic and/or dramatic) death.
by Deborah Stein
Matthew .... Matthew Baldiga
Ensemble .... Julia Bentz, Ami Jhaveri,
Anna Kull, Nancy Noto

Losing Your Life with Anne and David, by All
Anne .... Anne Veal
David .... David Michael Brown

Trojans–Time to Go, by Peter Sinn Nachtrieb
Ramses .... Eric Eteuati
Durex .... Jon Riddleberger

Grandpa's Cologne: Three, book by Kristoffer Diaz, music and lyrics by Greg Kotis, with additional music by Kristoffer Diaz

Danny	Daniel Reyes
Jolie's Grandma	Anne Veal
Jolie	Julia Bentz
Ensemble	The Company

and the following production staff:

Scenic Designer	Paul Owen
Costume Designer	Emily Ganfield
Lighting Designer	Brian J. Lilienthal
Sound Designer	Benjamin Marcum
Properties Designer	Alice Baldwin
Wig Designer	Heather Fleming
Orchestrations and Vocal Arranger	David Keeton
Music Supervisor	Margret Fenske
Movement Director	Delilah Smyth
Fight Director	Lee Look
Stage Manager	Mary Spadoni
Stage Management Interns	Leslie Cobb, Kelsey Daye Lutz
Dramaturg	Julie Felise Dubiner
Assistant Dramaturgs	Rachel Lerner-Ley, Brendan Pelsue

Commissioned by Actors Theatre of Louisville.

The Ensemble
in *Brink!*

33rd Annual Humana Festival of New American Plays
Actors Theatre of Louisville, 2009
Photo by Michael Brosilow

BRINK!

BIG BIRTHING NUMBER

Actors are "born" onto the stage.

1.) *Look around/try to go back down/come back out*
2.) *Feet first*
3.) *Water birth*
4.) *Ramses*
5.) *Septuplets*
6.) *Scream and run*
7.) *Silver spoon*
8.) *Smooth baby*
9.) *Stork and baby*
10.) *Hard Weather Boating Party Boat*
11.) *Durex*
12.) *C-section*
13.) *Umbilical Cord*
Leading into: Busby Berkeley-style dance number

GRANDPA'S COLOGNE: ONE
by Kristoffer Diaz

Lights on DANNY.

DANNY. Her name was Jolie. (*Lights on* JOLIE.) She was in seventh grade. Me and my friends were in fifth. She was a newcomer to the communal pool in the Miami condos where we spent our summers. We may have been young, but as soon as we saw her, we all knew what had to be done. (DANNY *joins the guys.*) Did you guys see the new girl?

GUY 4. You mean Jolie?

ALL GUYS. (*Ad-lib.*) Yeah! Wow! She's so hot!

GUY 2. I heard she's in seventh grade.

GUY 3. I heard she only dates younger guys.

GUY 4. Like fifth-graders?

(*Pause. They all look to each other.*)

ALL GUYS. (*Ad-lib.*) I'm asking her out!

GUY 4. You wouldn't even know how to ask a grown woman like that out.

GUY 2. She's got braces!

GUY 3. And a bra!

ALL GUYS. (*Ad-lib.*) Ooooh.

GUY 4. I know exactly how to ask her out. And I *am* going to ask her out!

GUY 2. Oh yeah? What are you going to say?

(GUY 4 *looks to* GUY 1. GUY 1 *starts to beatbox. Everyone joins in.*)

GUY 4.

EXCUSE ME JOLIE, LISTEN
BUT THAT GLISTEN ON YOUR SHOULDER
AS THE WATER'S GETTING COLDER
'CAUSE THE NIGHT IS DRAWING NEAR

MAKES ME MISS MY MOMMA'S KITCHEN
AND HER COOKING 'CAUSE YOU'RE LOOKING
EVEN FINER THAN THERE'S TIME
FOR ALL MY RHYMES TO HIT YOUR EAR

GUY 2. (*Pushing* GUY 4 *out of the way.*)

SEE MY BOYS ARE FILLED WITH FEAR
STEADY STARING JUST PREPARING
EVEN IF THEY AIN'T AWARE
THEY'RE TRYING TO COVER UP THEIR DOUBT

BUT ME, I'M CALM AND COOLER
THAN THE WATER IN THIS POOL AND
WHILE THESE FOOLS JUST FLOAT AND DROOL
I'LL BE THE ONE TO ASK YOU OUT.

GUY 3.

HERE'S WHAT I'M ALL ABOUT
IT'S JOLIE FIRST AND JOLIE SECOND
IF YOU RECKON THAT I'M CHECKIN' FOR YOU
YOU WORKED OUT MY PLAN

AND THOUGH MY GRADE IS ONLY FIVE
AND I'M NOT OLD ENOUGH TO DRIVE
BUT STILL AS SURE AS I'M ALIVE
JOLIE I WANT TO BE YOUR MAN

(*Music out.*)

DANNY. You guys are so stupid.

You really need to do all that?

Why don't you just go up to her and ask her out?

(GUYS *laugh.*)

GUY 2. You can't just go up to a girl and ask her out.

You gotta talk nice to her.

GUY 4. You gotta tell her that you and her fit together.

GUY 1. Like Bert and Ernie!

GUY 3. Well, maybe not like Bert and Ernie. (*Thinks.*) Well maybe yeah, like Bert and Ernie.

GUY 1. 2, 3, 4…

    (*Beatboxing.*)

GUY 3. (*To* Sesame Street *theme song.*)
    YO JOLIE, GO ON A, DATE WITH ME
    YOU CAN SEE, THAT I THINK YOU'RE SWEET

    HEY THERE JOLIE, I COULD BE YOUR ROLLEY POLLEY
    LITTLE SIDEKICK, YOUR FLY KICKS, AND YOU COULD
        BE THE FEET
    OR YOU COULD BE THE PUPPETEER, AND I COULD BE
        YOUR MUPPET, DEAR

ALL GUYS EXCEPT 3. And *tell you how to get*

GUY 3.
    TO SESAME STREET

GUY 4.
    HERE'S MY NUMBER, JOLIE, WHEN YOU'RE READY, YOU
        COULD CALL ME
    YOU COULD BE EVE
    I COULD BE WALL-E

GUY 2.
    YOU COULD BE THE CHEERIOS
    I'LL BE THE BANANA

GUY 1.
    YOU COULD BE HANNAH
    I'LL BE MONTANA

    (*Music stops. Everyone stares.*)

What? I'm in fifth grade.

    (*Music back.*)

GUY 4.
    WHAT I'M SAYING IS I COULD BE ANYTHING YOU CHOOSE
    YOU COULD BE BLUE
    I COULD BE YOUR CLUES

GUY 2.
    YOU BE SENIOR CITIZENS
    I CAN BE THE CRUISE

GUY 3.
    YOU CAN BE REPUBLICAN

I CAN BE FOX NEWS

ALL GUYS. (*Echo.*)
(NEWS.)
(NEWS.)
(NEWS.)
(FAIR AND BALANCED.)

GUY 4.
THAT'S NOT WHAT I WANT TO DO, BUT I'M SET TO DO IT STILL

GUY 1.
YOU COULD BE MY SLUGGER
I COULD BE YOUR LOUISVILLE.

(JOLIE *enters. Everyone goes quiet and shy. They're all afraid of her. They try to push each other to go talk to her.*)

DANNY. What's wrong with you guys?
Forget you. I'm doing it.

(*He slowly goes to her.*)

Umhijoliedoyouwanttogoooutwithmetonight?

JOLIE. What?

DANNY. Um. Hi Jolie. Do you want to go out with me tonight?

(*Silence.*)

JOLIE. Yeah. Sure.

(*She exits. DANNY acts cool until she exits. The GUYS are silent.*)

DANNY. I got a date I got a date I got a date!

(*He runs through the house, high-fiving audience members. He exits.*)

GUY 1. He didn't even rap.

End of Scene

TODAY I AM A WOMAN
by Deborah Zoe Laufer

There are disco lights and the pounding sound of "Celebration" by Kool and the Gang. The DJ, too loud and very cheesy, leads us through the ceremony.

DJ. (*Singing.*) "Celebration! We're gonna celebrate and have a good time." Oh MAN! We are celebrating tonight peoples. We are celebrating this very, very special night on this very, very special occasion. Is everybody having a GOOD TIME? (*He holds out his mike to the audience.*) What??? What was that??? I can't heaaaar yoooou. Are we having a GOOD TIME???? (*He holds out his mike to the audience.*) That's more like it boys and girls. The fun never ends here at Sarah Kotler's big day!! Now I want to hear from all the men folk—that's you too boys. Let's show Sarah how much we love her. Come on and give me a—HEY HEY! (*Holds mike out to audience.*) WHAT??? That's the best you men can do??? Girls. Laaadies. Let's show them how it's done! Come on and give me a—HEY HEY! (*Holds out the mike to the audience.*) Now girls. Babes. Chicas. I know you can do better than that. I want you to reach down to the bottom of your…. (MRS. KOTLER *hurries over to the* DJ *anxiously and whispers to him.*) All righty then! Let's get this show on the rooooad!

It's my favorite time of the night peoples. It's that time of night when our beautiful Bat Mitzvah girl gets to honor each and every one of the very special people in her life who got her here to this special day. That's right peoples. It's time for Sarah Kotler's Bat Mitzvah CANDLE LIGHTING CEREMONY!

> (*Loud rock music comes up, and spandex-attired dancers enter rolling in either a cake or a fourteen-candle menorah. Or maybe it rises up from the ground and the dancers just dance around to make it even more super-special.*)

And here to introduce the birthday girl is her mom, this beautiful lady, Dr. Miriam Kotler!

> (MRS. KOTLER *takes the mike.*)

MRS. KOTLER. Thank you. Thanks. Honey? Stuart? (*Looking around through the audience.*) Honey, come up here please. (MR. KOTLER, *excruciatingly shy in front of so many people, joins her.*) First of all, thank you all so much for being here to celebrate with us on this very special day. Friends and family have come from all corners of the map, from as far away as Denver! (*There is obligatory applause from the crowd.*) Thank you. Stuart and I have been blessed with two beautiful, smart children, our beautiful, smart son Barry—many of you were here to celebrate his Bar Mitzvah two years ago. (*A smattering of applause.*) Thank you. Thanks. And now our beautiful, smart daughter Sarah. Thanks. (*To* MR. KOTLER.) Did you want to say anything, Honey? (*She hands him the mike.*)

MR. KOTLER. (*Very nervous. Completely incomprehensible.*) As…Miriam said…. We are proud. Very much…so. And….

> (MRS. KOTLER *reminds him.*)

Thank you.

> (*He hands the mike back to* MRS. KOTLER.)

MRS. KOTLER. And now, without further ado, we present to you, our sweet angel, the light of our lives, besides Barry of course, our Bat Mitzvah, Miss Sarah Kotler!

DJ. Miss Sarah Kotler!!!

(*"Isn't She Lovely"* is piped in loudly. *The two spandexed dancers escort* SARAH *in. All in black, dour, humorless, perhaps Goth, certainly Emo. Maybe smoking a cigarette.*)

MRS. KOTLER. We couldn't be prouder of you, Honey. Here you go.

(*She hands her the mike.*)

SARAH. As the great French existentialist philosopher Jean Paul Sartre said, "Every existing thing is born without reason, prolongs itself out of weakness, and dies by chance." (MRS. KOTLER *whispers in her ear.*) And… thanks for coming. (SARAH *takes out her list.*) Mother requested that these acknowledgements be presented in the form of poems. As many of you will remember, two years ago my brother Barry made seemingly endless dips into the rhyming dictionary. I found it somewhat distasteful and depressing. But as she is the woman who birthed me, raised me, and saw me through the myriad illnesses and anguishes that are childhood, I will honor her wishes partly in rhyme, while fulfilling the rest of my obligations with quotes. (*Reading.*)

> Here's for my cousins, you know who you are.
> You live down the street, so you came in a car.
> We're so close in age you would think we'd be close.
> But we've nothing in common. Come light a candle.

DJ. Jamie, Julie, Jeffrey, and Jerry Gotlieb. It's your big moment with the birthday girl! Come on down!

(*"We are Family"* plays loudly. *The* COUSINS *come up. They each light a candle. Pose for the* PHOTOGRAPHER *who madly shoots flash pics. All but* SARAH *smile brightly. They are led off by the spandexed dancers.*)

SARAH. Mother insisted I include "friends." So…I invited the JV debate team. Two of whom came. As the great Algerian-born French author, philosopher, and journalist Albert Camus said, "I shall tell you a great secret, my friend. Do not wait for the last judgment, it takes place every day."

DJ. Jake and Stephanie come on down!

(*"You Gotta Have Friends"* plays as they come down and together light one candle. *Pose for the pic.*)

SARAH. (*She reads.*)

> This one's for Aunt Susie, and for Uncle Joe.
> You broke up last week, so he didn't show.
> It never would last, my mom always claimed
> His boozing and whoring are clearly to blame.
> Come light a candle.

DJ. Aunt Susie Fineman, come on down!

(*"Pretty Woman"* or something better plays as AUNT SUSIE *comes up. She has clearly been crying. Lights the candle, smiles brightly for the pics, and slinks away.*)

SARAH.

> Here's for Uncle Hershie who once was a Jew
> He married Aunt Mary—to give you a clue.
> Their children are named John, Joseph, and Chris
> They won't be Bar Mitzvahed, oh look what they'll miss.
> Come light a candle.

DJ. Could we have Hershie, Mary, John, Joseph and Chris! Come on Dooooown!

> (*"How Sweet it is To Be Loved By You" or something actually funny plays as they come up and light their candle.*)

SARAH. And now, for my brother Barry, who has embraced every societal norm needed to receive the approbation of the earthbound and secure the future of a dentist, a quote from the German-born Swiss novelist and poet, Hermann Hesse, "The bourgeois prefers comfort to pleasure, convenience to liberty, and a pleasant temperature to the deathly inner consuming fire." Come light a candle.

DJ. Barry Kotler, come on down!!!

> (*"Can't Smile Without You" comes up as* BARRY *lights his candle.*)

SARAH. And at last, we come to my parents. Stuart and Miriam née Farber Kotler.

> It all means nothing, and yet you both wed
> It all means nothing, and yet you both bred
> It all means nothing, and yet here I stand
> You are my parents, please give them a hand.

DJ. Let's hear it for the great couple, Drs. Miram and Stuart Kotler!!!

> (*"The Greatest Love of All" comes up as* MIRIAM *and* STUART *pose with their daughter for candle lighting and pics.*)

And now, that beautiful moment peoples, that moment when the Bat Mitzvah and her father dance that special dance! Let's hear it for Stuart and Sarah Kotler!

> (*"Sunrise, Sunset" plays.* STUART *and* SARAH *look horrified. But at everyone's urging and then insistence, they approach each other with terror. Eventually, they touch, and awkwardly dance, at arms' length. Little by little, they draw in closer, until they are in each other's arms.* SARAH *steps back, takes off her shoes and, like a little kid, steps on her dad's feet as he dances with her as they did when she was five, and still full of hope. The music swells as the lights come down.*)

End of Scene

NEW RITE

by Kristoffer Diaz

CHARACTERS:
> BIG MOMMA and LIL' DADDY, parents.
> SWEET DARLIN', daughter.

BIG MOMMA. Happy birthday, Sweetie!

LIL' DADDY. Pumpkin, there comes a time in every girl's life when she officially becomes a woman.

SWEET DARLIN'. I already get my period, Dad.

BIG MOMMA. Oh no, Honey. Your father is referring to a rite of passage— a formal event where we celebrate your official maturation.

LIL' DADDY. Our Jewish friends have Bar and Bat Mitzvahs. The Latinos celebrate *quinceñeras*. The Amish family down the block has *rumspringa*…

SWEET DARLIN'. I know. I've been waiting for this for so long! I'm going to have the best Sweet 16 ever.

LIL' DADDY. Yes you are. You're going to have the best…what now?

BIG MOMMA. A sweet…what?

SWEET DARLIN'. Sweet 16.
My sixteenth birthday party.
'Cause I'm turning 16.

LIL' DADDY. What the—God's green earth!

BIG MOMMA. Where your father and I come from, a young woman doesn't celebrate her impending womanhood with some kind of party.

LIL' DADDY. We've got a more sophisticated approach to the occasion.

SWEET DARLIN'. You guys didn't arrange a marriage for me, did you?

LIL' DADDY. No, silly. This is far more important than that.

BIG MOMMA. Guitar!

> (GUITAR! *appears, playing dramatic guitar. She plays continuously under the scene unless otherwise noted.*)

SWEET DARLIN'. Oh sweet! It is a party—

BIG MOMMA. Dancer!

> (DANCER! *enters, dancing dramatically.*)

SWEET DARLIN'. Oh, it's some kind of performance thing. Well, I—

BIG MOMMA. ASSASSINS!

> (TALL!, FIRE!, *and* JUMPER! *appear, looking intimidating.*)

SWEET DARLIN'. Really, Mom and Dad? Really?

JUMPER!. Behold the power of my Jump Rope of Pain!

(*She jumps rope impressively.*)

FIRE!. Behold my mastery of flame!

(*He eats fire impressively.*)

TALL!. Behold my tall…ness or I'm scary or something I don't know.

(*He kind of stands there.*)

BIG MOMMA. Honey, if you defeat them, you'll be a woman.

LIL' DADDY. And if you don't, well…we'll love you anyway. And miss you.

(*The* ASSASSINS *descend on* SWEET DARLIN'.)

SWEET DARLIN'. WAIT!

(*The* ASSASSINS *wait. The music waits. The* DANCER *waits.*)

This is crazy. Defeating assassins doesn't make you a real woman. What about love? What about understanding? What about a sense of responsibility towards every little creature on this earth?

TALL!. Oh my God that's what I was trying to tell you guys!

SWEET DARLIN'. Mom, Dad, I know you want to test me. I know our society is sorely lacking in formal rites of passage with real meaning and clear stakes, but this isn't the way. You've raised me well, and… AAAAAAAHHHHHHH!

(*She flips out and kills the* ASSASSINS. *The music plays as she kills them.*)

LIL' DADDY. Our little girl!

(*The music continues.* SWEET DARLIN' *kills the* MUSICIAN. *And the* DANCER. *She feasts on their blood.*)

BIG MOMMA. Ah, our little girl.

End of Scene

THE WHITE BREAD BALLET
by Peter Sinn Nachtrieb and Deborah Stein

CHARACTERS:
KARMA
SECURITY GUARD / BOSS / HUSBAND
DANCE CHORUS

SCENE.

The airport. Two circus clowns hugging their conservatively dressed daughter (KARMA) *goodbye.*

KARMA *gets on line to go through security. The parents wait and wave, but* KARMA *pointedly ignores them.*

The line inches forward, taking KARMA *slowly closer to the threshold that will take her to a new life. Very mundane, very ordinary.*

Finally she puts her bags through. The alarm goes off.

SECURITY GUARD. Ma'am? Come with me.

KARMA. Is something wrong?

(*They go to the security table and he unpacks her bag. He takes out all sorts of circus trick paraphernalia—juggling pins/balls/rings, rainbow-colored ballet shoes, sparkly hats, clown makeup.*)

SECURITY. You can't take these on the plane.

KARMA. Throw 'em away. I didn't even realize those were in there. You see, my parents are in the circus, and that's the only life I've ever known.

(*Behind her, we begin to see the circus scene of her childhood, with* BABY KARMA *[either a puppet or a live actor] counting everything in sight, as described.*)

My father was the juggler, he would juggle three, five, seven, fifteen balls of fire —but all I wanted to do was count them in the air. My mother was the contortionist, but all I wanted to do was measure the angles she put her body in, sine, cosine, tangent, cotangent! The only thing that excited me about the circus was the number of rings. The only thing I was good at was counting the tickets and adding up the money. But they can't keep me away from numbers forever. Today, I am finally leaving all that behind. Today, I am starting a new life. When I get on that plane and finally land in Cincinnati, I will be…an accountant!

(KARMA *looks out dreamily. The world goes all wiggidy, like the cheesy transitions in* Wayne's World *[do do do, do do do….]*)

The Dream Ballet Begins.

(*The TSA employees and other waiting passengers play all the characters.*)

1. ARRIVAL (Welcome to Cincinnati!)

A big cardboard sign held up by two actors: "WELCOME TO CINCINNATI!"

KARMA *steps off the plane, stands beneath the banner. She is in heaven. Like Gene Kelly arriving in Paris.*

At the airport, a row of dancers holding signs for various jobs—Donut Maker, Bus Driver, Bible Salesgirl, Drag Queen, Accountant. KARMA *approaches the person in the accountant gear, they shake hands ["making a deal" style] and off they go to Main Street.*

Main Street Cincinnati: tableaux of Wonderful Conservative Conventional Cincinnati. A "Main Street" promenade of tableaux that KARMA *interacts with—a Starbucks where she orders something iced, a Sbarro where she gets a calzone, etc.*

Last stop: Target! A dance of costuming herself, reinvention, shedding her circus duds for the Uniform of the Accountant. Maybe a series of tableaux of various choices of uniform: Painter, Soccer Mom, Police Girl, College Professor. Until she comes upon: The Power Suit.

Transition: putting on the suit jacket…and an office environment forms around her.

2. THE BIG JOB (Love, Conformity, and Foreclosure)

KARMA's big job interview. OFFICE WORKERS enter in lockstep, unison dancing. They hold up cardboard signs with houses, and KARMA has to say how many houses are on each sign. [Repetition of the counting scene with her dad.]

She gets every question right! She's hired!

A big cardboard sign that says "BANK."

Dance of making copies, sending her first email, printing her first spreadsheet. Clacking on the keyboard makes a drumbeat, a dance of the office. Unison dance of an army of OFFICE WORKERS, identically clad, all doing the same office-y things.

A CO-WORKER offers her a flyer that says "Circus Coming to Town!" She pushes it away.

Dance of Foreclosures. KARMA hands out "Foreclosure" cards to a series of characters stationed around the perimeter of the stage, each of whom crumple to the floor upon getting their foreclosure notice: a FARMER, a YOUNG COUPLE, a SMALL CHILD, and then finally…her PARENTS and the group of circus PERFORMERS.

A moment of pause, but she does it. She forecloses her parents. As she turns around, she is handed—a rose!

Her BOSS from the Bank is congratulating her, taking her out on a date. Dancers bring in chairs and set up the dinner scene around them. Glass of champagne. BOSS talks and talks and talks and KARMA listens, listens, listens. Dinner is brought out, one piece of white bread on a platter. They share it, each eating from one side until they meet in the middle (Lady and the Tramp).

From the kiss, someone runs on and with a veil and a bow tie and all of a sudden it's their wedding. The PRIEST has clown shoes. Moment of recognition between KARMA and the PRIEST but she chooses to go ahead with the wedding.

Suddenly a bed flies in and they're in their new home! Missionary position sex! Two babies fall from the balcony—twins! Bliss! Happy ever after!

They go to bed happy.

3. NIGHTMARE (The White Bread Attacks)

Nighttime. KARMA *and her* HUSBAND *sleeping.*

The FORECLOSED-UPON *start to rise like zombies. Are all bent at weird angles and begin to move towards the bed.* KARMA *wakes, tries to protect her babies as the* ZOMBIES *approach.*

She tries to use the material objects of her new life to defend herself: money, perfume, computers, Starbucks cups—but they continue to move scarily towards her.

She wakes her HUSBAND, *who is also a scary twisted zombie. He starts juggling the babies, who multiply—triplets! quadruplets! quints! A creepy carnival sideshow.*

KARMA *tries to run away but the exits are blocked—*

KARMA *needs to call upon her long-forgotten circus skills to protect herself. Tumbling! Trapeze! Ninja juggling!*

The bed turns into giant slice of white bread and starts to attack her. The zombies are joined by human-sized white bread puppets…

KARMA *explodes into a feast of fierce, fearsome, expert circus skills, battling back the zombies one by one and two by two until—*

—she is all alone, standing on her head—

A voice in the dark: "Ma'am? Ma'am?"

End of ballet.

Return to the airport security line.

SECURITY. Miss? Are you okay?

(*It's* KARMA's *turn to go through security.*)

KARMA. Sorry, what?

SECURITY. Are you coming, or what?

KARMA. Sorry, I—I'm not going to Cincinnati. I don't think I belong there.

SECURITY. Let me see your ticket.

KARMA. Sorry, sir. I'm going back where I belong—back to the Circus.

(*And she steps out of her staid black shoes, revealing brightly colored mismatched rainbow-patterned socks, and cartwheels into her future.*)

End of Scene

FIRST JOB

by Lydia R. Diamond

CORRINE *and* CAROL *face out. Lights out on one when the other's speaking.* CORRINE *always speaks to an imagined* CAROL. CAROL *always speaks to the audience.*

CORRINE. Morning Carol. Pretty dress. I have an extra croissant if you'd like…. OK so, I should just get started where I left off then? (*Beat.*) I um, I had a stack of cards, input data, that I had problems with yesterday, so I could just…or if it's better, I could…I, I, I'll, I'll just…. OK Yeah.

CAROL. Look. I went to college. I got my degree, and all I'm sayin' is that's no reason to think you better than someone else. I've been workin' here, supporting my little girl, goin' on ten years now. And you think these people care about me?

CORRINE. Quick question.

CAROL. No. It's been all I can do to teach them not to take the Lord's name in vain and wash out their coffee mugs.

CORRINE. I'm noticing an anomaly…an inconsistency with the…

CAROL. And she comes in here, like, I'm so great, got a degree from Yale, got a play gone happen at some big downtown theatre, and they all like, oooo, she so smart, she so well-spoken…

CORRINE. Another quick question. Well, I see you're busy…I'll just continue, with my work then, but if I could, grab a couple of seconds of your time, I have a thing…a thing that's come up…I just, well, when you have a second.

CAROL. So, I'm sitting here, tryin' to sort out the same problem that happens with payroll every month…all she got to do is input the incoming and outgoing and alphabetize the files. It's not rocket science. But she coming to me, every half hour…

CORRINE. "Are we supposed to have two active files on the same person?"

CAROL. And

CORRINE. "The numbers in this column don't add up."

CAROL. And

CORRINE and CAROL. "The date over here doesn't match the date over here."

CAROL. Did I ask her to add the numbers or check the date? No. And Harold's office is right there, so he hears her…and he's like, "Carol, why aren't the numbers adding up?" and I'm like, that's not my job, and he's like, "It's not hers either but she found it…" and I'm like, she don' have anything else to do…. I'm running up after all ya'll tryin' to collect your reimbursements, chasing down payroll, fighting with HR and she in there sittin' on her degree, making trouble for me. If she so smart, why she ain't got a job with benefits, thas what

I like to know? How you sposed to be smarter than me an' you a temp? So, yesterday, she brings in this little radio right, an' she comes to me…

CORRINE. Carol, I'm running to Starbucks, can I bring you something?

CAROL. This the other thing I don' like about her. She too nice. Always complimenting my clothes. Always tryin' to do me a favor. I don't trust it. An', how she got money for Starbucks and don't have a job? Sure…. I'll have a Venti-Mocha-Whatever-the-hell. But what was I saying? Oh, yeah…she brings in this little radio, 'cause they gone do a thing about her show on talk radio an' can she listen to it while she type? An' I'm like, no. No you can't listen to the radio. They won't let me play my music, how she think she can listen to talk radio?

CORRINE. If you would rather, I can just put the cards that don't make sense aside, or highlight things or something…. I feel like, I'm um, maybe getting on your nerves, and well, it's just that, Harold told me to track the problems, and I can stop doing that, but I thought, I mean, if you would rather…well, I thought that…

CAROL. An' that shoulda been it, right? I say, "No you can't listen to the radio," she should say "Oh, OK" 'Cause I'm supposed to be her supervisor, right?…but no, her eyes well all up an' she's like, I couldn't get anyone to tape it, an' they don' know what time it comes on, an' maybe she could wear earphones, it's not talk radio, an' I'm like, "Do they play music?" an, she's like "No" an' I'm like, so there's no music? An' she's like "No." An' I'm like, well that's talk radio…an' seriously, I'm startin' not to care, really I don' care that much, an' I'm just about to say, "sure but keep the earphones on or I'll get in trouble,"

CORRINE. I've devised a way to keep moving forward without bothering you so much, but you know, to keep track of the inconsistencies, the things that are different from the other things…yeah. If you see here, I put the net figures in pink, when they don't add up I leave the recorded amount there, in yellow, and I've inserted a separate column for the adjustments. That's in um, blue. I know you're doing important things and I just hate bothering you so much…

CAROL. And I know she means well, she's just annoying. So yeah, I'm about to tell her she can wear her earphones when she says…

CORRINE and CAROL. I'm a playwright by profession.

CORRINE. I'm just doing this to pay the rent. And, well, I really need to hear it,

CORRINE and CAROL. for my work,

CORRINE. for my career…

CAROL. and then she says,

CORRINE. It's not talk radio. NPR stands for National Public Radio.

CAROL. An' I say, "Please don't forget to wash your mug out at the end of the day, you left it on your desk last night and I had to wash it." And I go to my office and call her agency and I say, send me another girl. And that was that.

End of Scene

MY FIRST TROJAN
by Peter Sinn Nachtrieb

The deck of a Grecian ship. RAMSES and DUREX, two soldiers, stand next to each other. They are on the deck of a ship, eating some pita bread. They are actively trying to not look at each other. Nervous. Furtive glances. DUREX seems to be building up the courage.

DUREX. Can you believe this lack of wind?

RAMSES. It's so crazy.

DUREX. Gods.

RAMSES. Seriously.

DUREX. Yeah.

RAMSES. Yeah.

DUREX. Yeah.

(Awkward beat, a look away.)

At least we've gotten some free time to…

RAMSES. Eat?

DUREX. Yeah. I love eating. Do you love eating?

RAMSES. Sure.

DUREX. I'll eat anything.

(DUREX looks off in inward frustration. Both mount energy to introduce themselves.)

I'm Durex.

RAMSES. Ramses. Like the sheep.

(They shake hands; the touch of the hands has a profound effect.)

DUREX. It's nice to meet you. Officially.

RAMSES. You too.

DUREX. I've seen you around.

RAMSES. We're on a boat.

DUREX. And you're near me in the rowing area.

RAMSES. Yeah.

DUREX. I watch you all the time.

(Awkward beat. DUREX *slaps head in private. They eat.* RAMSES *smiles to himself.)*

So…. Is this your first time fighting in a Trojan War?

RAMSES. First time on a ship.

DUREX. The first time I ever rowed was at the training session.

RAMSES. I hate rowing.

DUREX. Not too excited about the killing part either.

RAMSES. I'm not much of a killer.

DUREX. I don't know about that. You stabbed very well in the training.

RAMSES. You saw that?

DUREX. Oh my god, I can't get you out of my head. (DUREX *realizes the overshare.) It.* It out of my head. I mean it was a very skillful stabbing. The technique. I just hope I can stab like that.

RAMSES. I'm sure you will when a big Trojan comes running at you.

DUREX. I'm a wheat farmer. I don't really get to kill a lot.

RAMSES. I make ceramics.

DUREX. Really?

RAMSES. My parents were not happy about that career choice.

DUREX. I love ceramics.

RAMSES. I love wheat.

DUREX. We should barter sometime.

(Beat.)

RAMSES. You row different than everyone else.

DUREX. You've seen me row?

RAMSES. Yeah.

DUREX. Am I that bad?

RAMSES. Everyone else seems so dour, staring forward and chanting along to that drum. But you…. You smile. It's comforting to know that there's someone who can smile in the middle of all this…

DUREX. I didn't notice you noticing me.

(A look at each other, a look away.)

DUREX and RAMSES. How's your Pita?

(They laugh. Silence. A horn goes off or drum beats.)

DUREX. Oh man, back to rowing in circles.

RAMSES. Yep.

DUREX. Shoot.

RAMSES. Well…. It was nice meeting you.

DUREX. OK.

RAMSES. Bye.

DUREX. Bye.

RAMSES. Bye.

DUREX. Bye.

RAMSES. Bye.

DUREX. Bye.

    (RAMSES *and* DUREX *walk in opposite directions.* DUREX *stops, turns around.*)

Hey…

    (RAMSES *stops, turns.*)

RAMSES. Yes?

DUREX. I don't even know if you're at all…I don't know if you…. OK I'm just going to ask it and it's fine if you say no and I'll totally understand and I won't be devastated or anything but I just have to ask…

RAMSES. What?

DUREX. I was wondering…

RAMSES. What?

DUREX. If you'd be interested in going to the bow of the ship with me sometime.

RAMSES. You want to go to the bow of the ship. With me?

DUREX. I know I don't really know you. We just row together.

RAMSES. No one's ever asked me before.

DUREX. Here we are, surrounded by men from everywhere on a ship next to a thousand ships…we're on our way to fight *Troy* and it's a pretty good chance we're going to die in a horrible slow disgusting way, and I'm a wheat farmer, you're a ceramicist, and everything feels so…

RAMSES. Epic.

    (*Beat.*)

DUREX. I'm scared.

    (RAMSES *walks back to* DUREX *and takes his hand.*
    The boat rocks.
    They hold hands.)

End of Scene

GRANDPA'S COLOGNE: TWO
by Kristoffer Diaz
Music & Lyrics by Greg Kotis

DANNY *runs onstage.*

DANNY. I got a date I got a date I got a date… (DANNY *notices the audience and composes himself.*) After Jolie said she'd go out with me, I ran straight home. I had to make everything perfect for our date. First, I had to make sure I looked nice, which meant I needed to take care of my hair. (*He grabs a bottle of hairspray.*) Grandma's hairspray took care of that. (*He sprays an enormous amount of hairspray.*) Next: plan the night's entertainment. Luckily, I have ten dollars in saved up allowance and permission to walk down to the McDonald's on the corner without parental supervision. So that was under control.

Now I just had to make sure I smelled good. And for that…I knew just the thing.

(*He pulls out his grandfather's cologne.*)

SONG: GRANDPA'S COLOGNE

GIRL ONE.
> THERE'S NOTHING QUITE LIKE A MAN
> WHO WOULD WEAR HIS GRANDFATHER'S COLOGNE
> TO MELT THE HEART OF ANY WOMAN,
> AND LET HER SEE THAT AS A MAN
> YOU STAND ALONE!

GIRLS.
> GRANDPA'S COLOGNE IS NICE AND STRONG
> JUST LIKE A MAN'S SUPPOSED TO BE.
> GRANDPA'S COLOGNE IS LIKE A CLOUD OF LOVE,
> ON THIS WE GIRLS AGREE.
>
> AND WHEN SHE SMELLS YOU,
> ALL THE WORLD WILL SMILE,
> SHE'LL TAKE YOUR HAND IN HERS
> AND WALK WITH YOU AWHILE.

GIRL TWO.
> THERE'S NOTHING QUITE LIKE A MAN
> WHO'S GOT TEN DOLLARS IN HIS HAND—
> A MAN WHO WOULD TAKE HIS WOMAN TO A MC-
> DONALD'S RESTAURANT AND BUY HER A TWO
> CHEESEBURGER VALUE MEAL WITHOUT EVEN
> ASKING WHAT SHE WANTS—
> THIS IS A GIFT WE GIRLS UNDERSTAND!

DANNY. (*Spoken.*) And if that doesn't work.

GIRLS.

> GRANDPA'S COLOGNE IS NICE AND STRONG
> JUST LIKE A MAN'S SUPPOSED TO BE.
> GRANDPA'S COLOGNE IS LIKE A CLOUD OF LOVE,
> ON THIS WE GIRLS AGREE.
>
> AND WHEN SHE SMELLS YOU
> ALL THE WORLD WILL SIGH.
> SHE'LL BE YOUR GIRLFRIEND THEN,
> AND YOU WILL BE HER—!
>
> GRANDPA'S COLOGNE IS NICE AND STRONG
> JUST LIKE A MAN'S SUPPOSED TO BE.
> GRANDPA'S COLOGNE IS LIKE A CLOUD OF LOVE,
> ON THIS WE GIRLS AGREE.
>
> AND WHEN SHE SMELLS YOU
> ALL THE WORLD WILL SIGH.
> SHE'LL BE YOUR GIRLFRIEND THEN,
> AND YOU WILL BE HER GUY!

End of Scene

EVOLUTION
by Deborah Zoe Laufer

All the action takes place beneath the ocean. The stage is lit with blue flickering movement, maybe the reflection of a cloud. The fish may move about with their arms flat against their bodies, while LIZZIE has tiny little doggie paddle hands. She is treading water. She comes to a rock, looks around to make sure there is no one watching, and begins trying to hoist herself onto it. Her sister CUTTLE swims up.

CUTTLE. Oooh, Lizzie! I'm telling Mama!

(*LIZZIE hurriedly gets off the rock.*)

LIZZIE. Tell Mama what?

CUTTLE. I saw you climbin' up there on that rock again.

LIZZIE. So? Mama don't care.

CUTTLE. Are you joshin' me? That's how Uncle Eft died. He had them little nubs like you. Pulled himself up on that there rock and couldn't get back.

LIZZIE. He only had one.

CUTTLE. So?

LIZZIE. So, I have two. I can pull myself back in.

CUTTLE. You are so durn full of yourself with them little nubs of yours. I think it makes you look like a freak. Everybody thinks so.

LIZZIE. They do?

CUTTLE. That's what they all say when you're not around. Makes me near die of shame.

LIZZIE. Jeepers. Really?

CUTTLE. None of the boys want to swim with you with your freaky little nubs.

LIZZIE. Iggy is nice to me—he doesn't have nubs exactly, but he's got those kind of bumps.

CUTTLE. Makes me sick. You wind up with Iggie and I bet your kids'll have four little nubs stickin' out. Ewwww.

LIZZIE. Yeah. But Cuttle, don't you ever wonder what's up there? Don't you ever want to see for yourself?

CUTTLE. No, I do not. You get up on that rock and you're not gonna be able to breathe and there won't be nary a thing none of us can do to help you. And it'll be your own durn fault.

LIZZIE. I don't know Cuttle. Last time I got up there, something weird happened. I felt my insides get real big, and I opened my mouth, and my gills went flat and…. I felt like…well…

CUTTLE. What?

LIZZIE. I felt like I didn't need the water.

CUTTLE. Didn't need the water. You think you're soooo special. I'm telling Mama. Just wait. You're gonna catch it but good.

> (*She swims off. Left alone,* LIZZIE *tries again to hoist herself up on the rock. Gets quite far.* MAMA, PAW, CUTTLE *and possibly some of her brothers and sisters quickly swim in.*)

MAMA. Lizzie! What in the ocean do you think yer doin??? Get down offa there!

LIZZIE. It's okay Mama…. I'm okay.

MAMA. Yer gonna plum kill yurself. What were you thinking of, crazy girl? Don't scare me like that.

LIZZIE. I can't help it Mama. I feel this strange yearning. It's calling to me. I want to know what's out there. I want to see for myself. I think I can do it Mama. I think I can climb this rock and see.

MAMA. There is plenty in this here ocean for you to see. I have had 638 childurn, and every one of them has been perfectly happy here where your parents and our parents and their parents and their parents and their parents have lived. It's been good enough for them and it's good enough for you.

LIZZIE. I think I have a calling Mama. A calling for something different.

MAMA. I don't want to hear about your strange…urges. Every one of my yungins has been happy here. Some have been slow and some have been fast, and some were odd shapes or colors. But every one has been happy to stay put and live like we've lived for billions of years.

LIZZIE. I'm different Mama.

(*She holds up her nubs.*)

MAMA. Just because you're a little…deformed, doesn't mean you can't fit in just fine here, Babygirl. We all have special needs, some are just more… obvious than others.

LIZZIE. I have a dream Mama. I have a dream that if I do this, if I climb this rock and keep on going, someday there will be unimaginable things. Critters that move up and down, and objects that soar through the sky, and a large strange shape called an Xbox. But none of that can happen if I don't do this. If I don't make the first move onward.

MAMA. But why you? Why my child??? No! I won't allow it. You stay here with us.

PAW. Now Maw…. Wait a gosh durn minute now. Lizzie has a dream. She's special. We can't hold her back.

LIZZIE. Thank you Paw.

MAMA. If she wanted to swim into an ocean volcano and get burnt to a fishstick would you say we can't hold her back?

PAW. Lizzie is a pioneer. An explorer. I can only hope if I had her…extra… somethin's…. I can only hope that I would also have her courage.

LIZZIE. Why…thank you Paw. That means a lot. Thanks.

PAW. We can't hold her back. I think we must let her go.

CUTTLE. Can I have her room?

MAMA. What will she breathe? What will she eat? Who knows if there's enough plankton up there.

PAW. She'll make her way, Honey. That's all we can hope for any of our yungin. That they find their own way.

MAMA. I just hate this. I hate all this change. Why, when my great-great-great-great-great-great-great-great-great-great-great-great Grandmaw was alive, there weren't even no rocks stickin up atall. It was just ocean. I wish we could go back to then. It was a simpler time. It shur was.

LIZZIE. But we can't go back Mama. And we'll never any of us know what's out there unless I try. I want to feel the sun on my face Mama. I want to feel…dry.

(*They all gasp.*)

MAMA. Oh, Baby girl.

(*They all watch as* LIZZIE *makes her way to the rock and hoists herself up on it. Little by little. Maybe they sink into the ground as she rises.*)
(*We hear their gurgly water voices as she rises.*)

PAW. Goooood Byyye Sweetheart. Goooood Luuuuck…

MAMA. I looooove you Babygiiiiirrrlllll.

(*As* LIZZIE *rises, the sun gets brighter and brighter and the blue vanishes to a rainbow of colors.* LIZZIE *lifts her face to the sun to feel it on her skin for the first time.*)
(*Lights out.*)

End of Scene

LOSING YOUR VIRGINITY WITH ANNE AND DAVID
by All

Lights up.

DAVID. Wow.

ANNE. Wow.

(*Lights down.*)

End of Scene

AN ACTOR ARRIVES
by Greg Kotis

A dark stage except for a single spot. Three God-like figures stand across from each other in three separate points in the house.

THE GOD OF FORTUNE. I am the God of Fortune!

THE GOD OF FAME. I am the God of Fame!

THE GOD OF GOOD REGARD. And I am the God of Good Regard!

ALL GODS. Actor—come!

(*An* ACTOR, *disoriented, frightened, walks on stage and finds his light under the spot.*)

ALL GODS. And welcome.

(*The* ACTOR *peers into the darkness, seeking the voices that are speaking to him.*)

ACTOR. I…I've arrived?

THE GOD OF FAME. Your audition went well.

ACTOR. My audition? Oh, right, my audition! Scorsese!

THE GOD OF FORTUNE. Scorsese!

ALL GODS. Martin Scorsese!

THE GOD OF FAME. You've been auditioning for months.

THE GOD OF FORTUNE. Years, even.

THE GOD OF GOOD REGARD. A few nibbles here.

THE GOD OF FAME. There.

THE GOD OF FORTUNE. Off-Broadway.

THE GOD OF GOOD REGARD. Off-OFF-Broadway.

ALL GODS. And then THIS!

(*An* ASSISTANT CASTING AGENT *appears at one edge of the stage.*)

THE GOD OF FORTUNE. Out of the blue.

THE GOD OF GOOD REGARD. A call from your cousin.

THE GOD OF FORTUNE. An assistant casting agent.

ALL GODS. And he says:

ASSISTANT CASTING AGENT. I may have something for you. We had a cancellation. It's small, five lines, but it's funny—you need to MAKE it funny. Can you be here in, I don't know—FIFTEEN MINUTES?!

(*The* COUSIN *disappears back into the darkness.*)

ACTOR. Right, yes, I remember now. The prescreen.

THE GOD OF FAME. With the camera and the casting agent.

THE GOD OF FORTUNE. And then getting into the room with the great man himself.

ACTOR. I made him laugh.

THE GOD OF GOOD REGARD. Not an easy task.

ACTOR. He said "Do it again, but do it funny." And I did it funny! Ha! Ha-ha-ha-ha-!

(*The* ACTOR *laughs, the Gods join in. Then.*)

THE GOD OF FAME. But silence!

ACTOR. So…um…I guess I got the part, huh?

THE GOD OF FORTUNE. Not so fast.

THE GOD OF GOOD REGARD. We didn't say that.

THE GOD OF FAME. Only that the audition went well.

ACTOR. I can do funny. Scorsese, he sucks at funny. I mean, name one funny Scorsese film!

THE GOD OF FORTUNE. *The King of Comedy.*

ACTOR. Okay, name two.

THE GOD OF GOOD REGARD. *Taxi Driver.*

ACTOR. *Taxi Driver* wasn't funny!

THE GOD OF FAME. It was VERY funny.

ACTOR. It wasn't even a comedy!

THE GOD OF FORTUNE. It was a GREAT comedy!

THE GOD OF GOOD REGARD. A very great, MISUNDERSTOOD comedy!

ALL GODS. But silence!

THE GOD OF FAME. We're not here to talk about Scorsese!

THE GOD OF FORTUNE. We're here to talk about you!

THE GOD OF GOOD REGARD. For you, actor—!

ALL GODS. Actor!

THE GOD OF FAME. —Stand at a crossroads!

THE GOD OF FORTUNE. Every actor comes to a point like this at least once in his or her career.

THE GOD OF GOOD REGARD. Not this exact point. You're at an ideal-*idealized* point.

THE GOD OF FAME. But a point LIKE this.

THE GOD OF GOOD REGARD. Your first big, professional role.

THE GOD OF FAME. The first time a playwright fights for you.

THE GOD OF FORTUNE. A moment when you are confronted with the value of who you are and what you do.

ACTOR. So…I got the part?

ALL GODS. Not so fast!

THE GOD OF GOOD REGARD. First, a question:

>   (*An* AGENT *appears at the lip of the stage.*)

THE GOD OF FAME. You will get a call from your agent.

AGENT. Heard you knocked the Scorsese thing out of the park today!

ACTOR. I did, I really did! I made him laugh! Ha-ha-ha-ha—!

>   (*The* ACTOR *laughs. The* AGENT *joins in, until.*)

AGENT. GOOD—for you! No easy feat.

ACTOR. He's not really a funny guy, is he.

AGENT. Oh, he's funny. *Raging Bull.* So listen, I got you booked for the Snackwell's spot.

ACTOR. The bite and smile?

AGENT. Told them about the Scorsese thing, told them they'd better jump or they'd lose you.

ACTOR. What do you mean?

AGENT. Callbacks for the Scorsese thing are tomorrow.

ACTOR. Right, I should be here for that!

AGENT. For five lines? Forget about it, you'll be on a plane.

ACTOR. But can't the Snackwell's people reschedule—?!

AGENT. HEY! No one keeps the Snackwell's people waiting! Not you! Not nobody! This is a national spot we're talking about!

(*The* AGENT *storms off.*)

ALL GODS. And then!

(*A* YOUNG WOMAN *appears elsewhere at the edge of the stage.*)

PLAYWRIGHT. Hey, it's me. I know you've been locking horns with the director, and as the playwright I'm not supposed to give notes or anything— even for a small, downtown thing like what we're doing. But still, I wanted you to know…you're the first actor I've worked with who really understands my stuff. You help *ME* understand my stuff. So…thanks. We're going to have a great opening tomorrow.

(*The* WOMAN *disappears back into the darkness.*)

THE GOD OF FORTUNE. I am the God of Fortune.

THE GOD OF FAME. I am the God of Fame.

THE GOD OF GOOD REGARD. And I am the God of Good Regard.

(*The* ACTOR *peers into the darkness.*)

ACTOR. I'm sorry, what was the question? You said there was a question.

(*The* ACTOR *waits, no answer. Lights dim.*)

End of Scene

INTERNAL AUDIT
by Peter Sinn Nachtrieb

It starts as a scene at the IRS.

Four actors. 1, 2, and 3 of them are dressed in IRS outfits, behind desks.

4 is a civilian who sits at the desk of 1, nervously. 1 scrutinizes a file. 2 and 3 work on other files at their desks. 1 squints at a detail.

1. So, Mr. Shamlife, I see here that you're a virgin.

4. Excuse me?

1. This your first time?

4. Oh…yes. I never thought I made enough money to be audited.

(*2 and 3 laugh at their desks.*)

I don't know why it's worth auditing—

1. Hush now, Mr. Shamlife. Breathe. Relax. Bear down. We're the IRS. There's nothing to be nervous about.

       (*2 and 3 laugh at their desks.*)

4. OK.

1. So. You. Tell me about yourself.

4. Well, I work part-time as a freelance barber and—

1. Shhh.

4. What?

1. We don't care about your "job." Your "income." Who are *you*? Deep down? Beneath that freelance barber shell, there is a soft tender elf that's screaming to come out and be seen. Who is that little guy? *Come out already.*

       (*2 and 3 look up at 4, pencils ready. A pause that's not supposed to happen. 4 blanks…1 tries to help.*)

Come out already. Come out right now.

4. Yes. Well, okay, uh, well, when I was a child I used to play…I mean I used to play at this… (*Beat.*) When I was a child I… (*4 is forgetting his line. 1, 2, 3 exchange nervous furtive glances as actors.*) I was…I am…I…

2. (*As an actor adlibbing to help someone who's forgetting their line.*) Were there any *creeks* where something significant happened when you were a child?

4. Yes. Yes, when I was a child I would play at a creek with my friend…and there was one day…one day when there was this…this really big…. Lie.

       (*Beat. 4 stands up. 1, 2, 3 look at each other.*)

2. [Actor 4's name]?

4. I'm living a lie.

       (*1, 2, 3 look at each other, uncertain.*)

3. [Actor 4's name].

4. I AM LIVING A LIE.

1. OK. OK.

4. I'm sorry. There's something I need to tell you guys.

1. Now?

4. I can't hide this any longer.

3. We're in the middle of a scene.

2. Dude, every single theater professional in America is watching—

4. When I was a child I *would* play at a creek. Every day, with my best friend, [first name of the actor playing the PROFESSOR]. There was a granite cliff along the bank where we would giggle and wrestle and roleplay for hours. 'Twas a special place: The mighty trees, the rippling water, and [actor playing PROFESSOR's name]…

There was one day, one crazy awful magical day when my life would transform in an instant…

> (1, 2, and 3 *maybe a little irritated.*)

1. You kissed him.

2. And then he hated you and he then fell in love but it was too late.

3. So you killed him.

4. He was standing at the edge of the cliff doing his Britney Spears impression. It was so funny and so accurate. But then, as he transitioned to the mental breakdown portion of the routine, [actor playing PROFESSOR's name] lost his balance, slid towards the edge of the cliff and fell off, plummeting towards the jagged rocks below. And…

> (*It gets really hard to go on.*)

1. You watched him die?

2. You never called for help?

3. And then you ate him?

4. I…flew down below [actor playing PROFESSOR's name], caught him in my arms, and gently brought him back to the top of the cliff.

> (*Beat.*)

1, 2 and 3. What?

4. I'd never known that I could fly before and then I just did. It was so natural, so easy, so right. All of a sudden, woosh, I knew who I was. I need to tell you who I really am.

2. Who are you?

> (*Beat.*)

4. A superhero. I am a superhero.

> (*Maybe a longish beat where they all take that in.* 1, 2, 3.)

3. A superhero.

4. I can carry heavy things with ease, hear a cry for help from miles away, and freeze things with my eyes.

2. Jesus, [Actor 4's name].

4. And I can't stop using my powers for good! Every time I say I'm "going to the movies," "loitering in a badly lit park," or "working on my solo show," I'm actually protecting the innocent.

2. Jesus Jesus, [Actor 4's name].

1. He's doing this right now. Is he doing this right now?

3. So why don't you show us one of your powers?

4. I can't.

3. Why not?

4. I can only do it when there's danger.

3. Oh how convenient.

2. Jesus and all his friends, [Actor 4's name].

1. He always pulls shit like this.

4. I'm telling you the truth.

3. I suppose you have a superhero name.

4. Captain Awesome.

2. And a costume? You have a "supercostume"?

> (4 *rips off his quick release costume to reveal an skin-tight superhero outfit with tights.*)

That is threatening my marriage.

1. (*To the booth.*) Michael? Amy? Can someone mediate this?

3. You disgust me.

4. I don't have a choice! I have to wear this! [Current city] is under threat from a great evil.

2. Who?

4. Professor Vicious. He's been stealing all the Bourbon from Kentucky[1] and keeping it all for himself. And I'm the only man who can stop him.

I don't want this to come between us. Please. I'm still the same guy. I want to go to New York, get that place in Williamsburg, and bring new energy to the American Theatre just like you. Please, accept me for who I am.

3. I don't think so.

1. Sorry, [Actor 4's name]. this is…

2. Bullshit.

1. You are not super! You're are [Actor 4's name]! You're [Actor 4's full name] from [Actor 4's state] and you act pretty good, and you're sick, and you've ruined this moment for all of us. This was our moment. Thanks, thanks a lot.

2. My parents are here tonight. My nana. They don't need to see that.

3. C'mon guys, let's go get a drink!

> (PROFESSOR VICIOUS *enters from an aisle holding several bottles of bourbon and some sort of weapon.*)

PROFESSOR. Ohhh I'm sorry, little 'prenties but the bar is dry!

4. Professor Vicious!

> (PROFESSOR *circles around* 1, 2, 3.)

PROFESSOR. Some "friends" you have, Señor Capitan. A real friend would accept you for who you are. When you tell a real friend "I'm destined to live

---

[1] Feel free to substitute a popular regional item here and throughout the play.

a life of crime and hoard the tastiest regional liquor in America" they would say "That's OK, because you're my buddy and I love you!" But that's not how people really are. They only care about their own hides. They're scared of people like us and our special skills. What do you say we teach them a little lesson?

(3 *intervenes.*)

3. Hey you can't just run in here and—

(PROFESSOR VICIOUS *shoots bourbon into* 3's *mouth with his supersoaker.*)

PROFESSOR. Pedagogy!

3. Ah! Ahh! SO DELICIOUS GETTING SLEEPY!

(3 *passes out.*)

PROFESSOR. Who's thirsty now?

1 and 2. Oh no!

PROFESSOR. Say "ah"!

(4 *stands in the way.*)

4. I don't think you really understand, Professor. I believe in a world where everyone, no matter how amazing they are, is treated equally, without prejudice! Free to pursue our dreams, our loves, our happiness we all so desperately need. We all deserve happiness! Even you Professor.

PROFESSOR. Oh what an "Awesome" speech, I almost want to weep...I guess the Professor will have to teach them himself!

4. Noo!

(*Music*, PROFESSOR *and* 4 *fight.*)

PROFESSOR. The Professor doesn't grade on a curve!

Pop quiz!

Watch me drop this course!

I call this one my tenure track!

Pencils down!

(PROFESSOR *gets* 4 *pinned down, wielding bourbon bottle.*)

Oh, I'm sorry Captain but this is your last drink!

4. We'll *see* about that, Professor!

(4 *freezes* PROFESSOR *with his eyes.*)

PROFESSOR. Ohhh! Ohh! You've frozen me with your eyes!

(PROFESSOR *falls to the ground frozen.*)

4. Class dismissed!

(3 *wakes up.*)

1. You saved us.

2. I just said mean hurtful things and still you saved us.

3. Where the fuck am I?

2. [Actor 4's name], I'm…we're—

4. Don't be sorry. Just be my friends. Help me proud of who I am. And I'll be proud of you.

PROFESSOR. (*Through semi-frozen lips.*) Ohhhhh, [Actor 4's name], why? Why? Why have you saved me again?

> (*4 runs over.*)

4. [Actor playing PROFESSOR's name]?

> (*Suspenseful Button Music. BLACKOUT.*)

End of Scene

NEVER A BRIDE
by Deborah Zoe Laufer

The hallway outside the wedding chapel. MICK, AMY, DEXTER *and* SHELLEY *are all waiting for their entrance as bridesmaids and groomsmen.*

AMY. She stood there like she'd been frozen. Like someone had used a stun gun or something.

SHELLEY. I was like, umm…. Shouldn't you be DOING something?

AMY. Karen is balling her eyes out.

MICK. God babe. Would you let it go? I mean what's the big deal?

AMY. I'm not saying that it's a huge deal, Mick. I'm just saying, I DID something. OK? I didn't just stand there…

SHELLEY. Janet just stood there doing NOTHING. It was un-believable.

DEXTER. (*Looking through the curtains to the chapel.*) Guys, keep it down.

AMY. You keep it down, Dexter.

SHELLEY. While Amy totally knew what to do.

AMY. I knew what to do. I mean, Janet thought we should use Wite-Out.

SHELLEY. Can you imagine? On a bridal veil?

AMY. The mascara would have spread all over. It would have been like a total disaster.

SHELLEY. Un-believable.

AMY. It would have ruined the whole wedding.

MICK. Mascara on her dress would have ruined the whole wedding.

AMY. It was the veil.

SHELLEY. The point is, Amy should have been maid of honor. That's all.

AMY. That's all I'm saying.

DEXTER. Guys. Shhhh.

AMY. You "Shhhhh," Dexter. You shhhhhhh.

MICK. Come on Baby. She chose her sister. You can understand that.

AMY. Oh God. Why do I even talk to you?

SHELLEY. Amy's only been her best friend since freshman year.

AMY. Since freshman ORIENTATION.

SHELLEY. Since orientation. I mean, I didn't know them till sophomore year, so of course it wouldn't be me.

AMY. I'm her freakin' BEST FRIEND!

SHELLEY. Well, we're all really close. I mean, the three of us…

AMY. Right. But I've known her since freshman orientation.

SHELLEY. That's what I'm saying.

AMY. So of course it should have been me.

SHELLEY. That's my point, Amy. I'm saying it should have been you.

AMY. I mean, who will I pick now?

MICK. For what?

AMY. For my maid of honor. Does Karen think I'll pick her now? No way.

SHELLEY. Why would you? When she didn't pick you.

AMY. Right.

MICK. Oh, are you getting married? I didn't know. Congratulations.

AMY. When I DO, Mick. Is what I mean.

SHELLEY. She means when she does get married, she'd probably pick me now.

MICK. Did somebody ask you to marry him? How exciting.

AMY. Shut up.

DEXTER. Guys, they're getting ready to start. You really need to keep it down.

SHELLEY. I'm never getting married.

AMY. What?

SHELLEY. I hate this. It changes everything.

AMY. Well…yeah. That's the point.

SHELLEY. What was so bad with the way things were? We were all so great. Now it's going to be them and us.

AMY. It will not. We'll still all be together.

SHELLEY. No we won't. You'll see. It will never be the same. Soon they'll have kids, and then they'll be tired and cranky and fighting all the time and "Oh, we can't get a babysitter" and all that. And it will never just be the six of us again.

MICK. That's bogus. Dex and I are still going to play hoops with Ryan every week. We'll still all have movie night. What's going to change? This is just a few words and a big party. That's all.

SHELLEY. You'll see. Soon they'll be meeting with other married couples on movie night. Soon Karen won't want Ryan to be playing basketball on Saturdays.

DEXTER. Who cares what she wants? He'll do what HE wants.

SHELLEY. You'll see.

> (*The all stand soberly for a minute.*)

AMY. Don't you think you should have been Ryan's best man. It's bogus that he chose Peter.

MICK. (*Grinning over at* DEXTER.) Oh, I don't know. I think Peter's done a kick-ass job.

DEXTER. You said that Dude. All hail Peter. He's my freakin' hero.

> (*They laugh.*)

AMY. What is that supposed to mean?

DEXTER. Nothing. Just think he's done a man's job like a man.

MICK. And then some.

> (*They high five and chest butt each other and grunt.*)

AMY. What?

SHELLEY. You didn't hear? About last night?

AMY. What about it?

SHELLEY. Oh. Never mind.

MICK. Nothin' Babe. It was just a good time. A nice sendoff to marital bliss for our good buddy Ryan.

DEXTER. And Mick was best man last night. Ask anyone.

AMY. What? What did you do?

DEXTER. What didn't he do? That is the question.

AMY. You said there weren't going to be girls.

DEXTER. (*Cracking up.*) You did?

MICK. Hey, I wasn't the best man Babe. It wasn't up to me.

AMY. You swore to me.

DEXTER. And you believed him?

AMY. Oh my God.

MICK. Come on Baby. (*Going to put his arm around her.*) It was a bachelor party.

AMY. Get away from me.

MICK. (*Going in for a kiss, she pushes him away.*) Come on Pooker Bear.

AMY. Don't touch me. Again. Ever again. Don't even look at me.

DEXTER. (*Over this.*) Pooker Bear. Ewwwwww.

SHELLEY. Shut up Dexter. Just leave her alone, you guys.

AMY. I am through with you. I don't even want to know what you did. I am through.

MICK. Are you joking?

AMY. I would NEVER marry you. Karen should just call the whole thing off. I would never marry someone who was with cheap girls the night before my wedding.

MICK. Who asked you? Who asked you to marry him?

SHELLEY. You're a total ass, Mick.

DEXTER. Oooooooo.

AMY. Just get away from me. Leave me alone.

> (*They all stand silent for a moment. Then there is the groom's music from the chapel.*)

DEXTER. Oh shit. There goes Ryan. To his doom.

SHELLEY. Get in line you guys.

> (*She and* DEXTER *stand together facing the curtain, waiting for their turn to go out. She hooks her arms through his.*)

> (MICK *gets in line behind* DEXTER. *He grins at* SHELLEY *and offers his elbow. She just glares at him. He kisses at her. She comes and stands beside him but won't take his arm.*)

> (SHELLEY *and* DEXTER *get their cue and step hold, step hold through the curtain.*)

MICK. (*Now alone, with her, much softer.*) Come on Baby. You know I love you.

AMY. Whatever.

> (AMY *coldly takes his arm, but she has melted a bit.*)

> (*They look through the curtains, then at each other. He kisses her head. They take a deep breath and march through.*)

End of Scene

LOSING YOUR FORESKIN WITH ANNE AND DAVID
by All

> *Lights up.*
> JACOB *reads from Mohel text.*

ANNE. Wow.

DAVID. Ow.

> (*Lights out.*)

End of Scene

FIRST BABY
by Lydia R. Diamond

BECKY and NOAH sit in a car, NOAH drives. A rear-facing baby car seat sits in the middle of the backseat. Raffi's theme song to Arthur *plays. NOAH and BECKY sing along.*

NOAH. So?

BECKY. Oh…don't make me…

NOAH. Just one…

BECKY. I can't. They're my relatives too, now, huh?

NOAH. Exactly why you can.

BECKY. It's mean.

NOAH. Just once, for me. Seriously, it's the best impression I've ever seen.

BECKY. I just can't believe she said it right after the prayer.

NOAH. She couldn't take it any more.

BECKY. Do you think she's jealous because Allison gets all of the attention now?

NOAH. No…she's not that insecure.

BECKY. What about Bob…

NOAH. Bob is, but he didn't say anything…

BECKY. Seriously, I understand. I wouldn't have three months ago, but now, I understand. Your family's so hard on that little boy.

NOAH. Jimmy's a brat…

BECKY. He's been diagnosed…

NOAH. As clinically a brat…

BECKY. No…ADHD is real.

NOAH. He climbed up the bookshelf, put the cranberry mold in the toilet, he's out of control.

BECKY. He can't help it.

NOAH. Please. Just do it…

BECKY. OK. (*She affects the slanted shoulders and drawn face of one who is beaten down by a challenging motherhood and a critical family.*) …Amen. I just want to say, before we eat, that if anyone else has something to say about Jimmy's paci [pacifier], they can kiss my ass. Because, Aunt Rachel could stand to lose forty pounds, Uncle Walter is on his fourth Vodka Gimlet, and Susie has always been, a bitch. And I don't comment on any of those things.

NOAH. You do it so well.

BECKY. I didn't know she had it in her and I really liked it.

(*They laugh. The baby begins to cry….*)

Oh shit. (*Instantly panicked.*)

NOAH. What?

BECKY. What? Allison's crying…pull over.

NOAH. We're on the highway…

BECKY. She's crying…

NOAH. She's a baby. That's what they do…

BECKY. Just pull over. She may need to nurse.

NOAH. I'll pull off at the first exit, but not the shoulder, it's dangerous. She's fine.

BECKY. That could be another thirty minutes.

NOAH. Or five…just hold on.

BECKY. Fine…. Fine…

(*She unbuckles her seatbelt and begins to climb into the backseat.*)

NOAH. What are you…oh my God…Becky…Beck…OK fine, but don't take her out.

BECKY. She's hungry…. She needs to nurse.

NOAH. Try your finger.

BECKY. I haven't learned how to make my finger lactate NOAH.

(NOAH *begins to sing…*)

NOAH. "Just what makes that little old ant, think he can move that rubber tree plant…"

(BECKY *is settled in next to the baby,* ALLISON *continues to cry,* NOAH *sings….*)

"Anyone knows an ant can't…" Come on Beck, sing with me…

(*Baby cries.*)

NOAH and BECKY. "Move a rubber tree plant. But they've got, high hopes, they've got, high hopes, they've got, high apple pie in the—sky hopes. So any time you're feeling low, 'stead of lettin' go, just remember that ant. Oops there goes another rubber tree, oops there goes another rubber tree, oops there goes another rubber tree plant."

(*There is silence.* BECKY *looks at baby,* NOAH *drives. Lots and lots of silence. Finally….*)

BECKY. I forgot to put on breast pads…

NOAH. I'm sorry.

BECKY. It's OK. I'll change at the rest stop.

NOAH. Did you have any idea?

BECKY. None.

NOAH. What were we doing before?

BECKY. I can't remember…it seemed very important though. I should have pumped for the car.

NOAH. Look…exit, two miles.

    (*Lights fade.*)

End of Scene

AMERICAN DREAM
by Greg Kotis

A family sits in deep, gloomy thought. Then:

FATHER. I want a house.

MOTHER. (*Disbelieving, appalled, not this again.*) What did you just say?

FATHER. I said I want to buy a house, a home.

SON. (*Frightened.*) Dad?

MOTHER. What are you talking about?! We can't afford a house!

DAUGHTER. Mom?!

FATHER. My dad owned his own house, as did his dad, and his!

MOTHER. You're a Ph.D. student, for God's sake, and I'm a, whatever, a truck driver or something! We're in debt as it is!

FATHER. Then we'll get into *more* debt!

MOTHER. You're out of your ever-loving *mind!*

    (FATHER *sings.*)

FATHER.
    AMERICAN DREAM!
    I WANT TO LIVE IT!
    WHO'S GONNA GIVE IT
    TO ME—AND MY FAMILY?!
    AMERICAN DREAMIN'!
    DON'T SIMPLY DREAM IT!
    GO AND REDEEM IT
    RIGHT NOW! I'M GONNA TELL YOU HOW!

    (MOTHER *runs off with the kids;* FATHER *turns to the audience.*)

FATHER.
    I WANT THE AMERICAN DREAM!
    A YARD FOR MY KIDS TO RAMBLE AND ROAM,
    A TWO-CAR GARAGE—AN AMERICAN HOME.
    TALKIN' 'BOUT—AMERICAN DREAM!
    YOU MAY CALL IT A PONZI SCHEME,
    BUT I WANT IN—ON THE AMERICAN DREAM.

    (FATHER *crosses to sit across from a banker who's looking over* FATHER's *mortgage application.*)

BANKER. I see on your mortgage application that you're a Ph.D. student and your wife is a, whatever, a truck driver or something.

FATHER. That's right.

BANKER. Any collateral? Your wife's truck, maybe?

FATHER. Still making payments on it.

BANKER. How about twenty percent down?

FATHER. How about zero percent down and interest-only payments for the first three years, huh?! How about that?!

BANKER. I think you better leave!

(FATHER *pulls a knife.*)

FATHER. And I think you better write me a check for, I don't know, what do you need to buy a house?! A million dollars!

BANKER. You are out of your ever-loving MIND!

FATHER.

AMERICAN BANKER!
FREE UP YOUR CREDIT
AND MAKE SURE YOU SPREAD IT
TO ME—AND MY FAMILY!

AMERICAN TAXES,
FAVOR THE OWNER
SO THROW ME A LOANER,
GIVE ME CASH—FROM YOUR BANK CASH STASH.

FINANCE MY AMERICAN DREAM,
A MORTGAGE WITH AN ADJUSTABLE RATE,
A HOME FOR MYSELF, MY KIDS, AND MY MATE, YEAH!

INVEST IN AN AMERICAN HOUSE,
SELLING IT LATER WON'T BE NO TROUBLE
IF YOU DON'T B'LIEVE IN NO HOUSING BUBBLE!
NO NO NO-NO!

(*As he sings, cops rush the stage to drag* FATHER *off to prison.*)

FATHER.	COPS.
'CAUSE THERE ARE THREE STEPS	
TO AMERICAN MANHOOD!	THREE STEPS!
THREE TRIPS EV'RY MAN HAS	
TO TAKE!	THREE TRIPS!

FATHER.

THE FIRST LEADS TO CAREER POTENTIAL.
THE SECOND ENDS WITH KIDS AND A WIFE.
THE THIRD LEG IS THE MOST ESSENTIAL:

FATHER and COPS.

    THE JOURNEY
    TO THE HOUSE
    HE LIVES HIS LIFE!

    (*The* COPS *throw* FATHER *behind bars.* MOTHER *and the* BANKER *meet him in his cell.*)

FATHER. All I wanted was to buy a house.

MOTHER. This is goodbye, Baby. Oh, and this is my fiancé.

FATHER. My banker?!

BANKER. My wealth makes me desirable.

MOTHER. He made a bundle during the bailout fiasco.

BANKER. The Bush years were more corrupt then anyone realized.

    (MOTHER *and the* BANKER *leave.* FATHER *turns to the audience.*)

FATHER. Looks like I missed the boat on all that easy money that was sloshing around the country a few years ago. But that doesn't mean you have to miss out! So, would those here who rent or don't own please raise your hand! Now, if you would, stand up, all of you! Great, and I want you to start clapping in time to the music, just like that.

    (FATHER *sings as audience claps.*)

    AMERICAN MAN!
    DON'T BE INCREMENTAL!
    DON'T LIVE IN NO RENTAL!
    SEIZE A HOUSE
    FOR YOURSELF AND YOUR SPOUSE!

That's right, I said seize! As in "confiscate," or "take possession of!" 'Cause what I think we could use right now is a violent, popular uprising culminating in me getting a house! And maybe you, too!·

    AMERICAN NATION
    GOT HIT BY SOME FINANCIAL TSUNAMIS!
    LET'S DO LIKE THE COMMIES,
    DO AWAY WITH PROPRIETY
    AND START A PEOPLE'S REVOLUTIONARY
    HOME-OWNERSHIP SOCIETY!

By just giving us all homes! For free! Instead of taking bailout money from the people and giving it to the banks, the government could take foreclosed homes from the banks and give them to the people! You can't or would rather not pay your mortgage?! Don't pay it! We're in a post-mortgage paradigm, people! Get used to it! You want a weekend home, a vacation home?! Just take one, by force of arms if necessary! What could be wrong with that?! I don't know! I don't care! And neither should you, because—!

(The CAST *chants "revolution" as* FATHER *sings.)*

FATHER.	CAST.
WE WANT THE AMERICAN DREAM!	REVOLUTION!
DON'T CARE 'BOUT NO FINANCIAL	
DISASTER	REVOLUTION!
WE WANT A HOUSE WHERE WE'RE	
OUR OWN MASTER!	REVOLUTION!
SUBJECT IS—AMERICAN DREAM!	REVOLUTION!
NATIONALIZE HOME-OWNERSHIP	
AS A MEANS	REVOLUTION!
TO REALIZING THE END OF	
SOME AMERICAN DREAMS, YEAH!	REVOLUTION!

(Cast also sings "American Dream" with FATHER.*)*

FATHER.	CAST.
COMING TO YOU FOR—	
AMERICAN DREAM!	AMERICAN DREAM!
A YARD FOR OUR KIDS TO RAMBLE	
AND ROAM!	REVOLUTION!
A TWO-CAR GARAGE—	
AN AMERICAN HOME!	REVOLUTION!
GONNA CLAIM OUR	REVOLUTION!
AMERICAN DREAM!	AMERICAN DREAM!

FATHER.
DON'T YOU CALL IT A PONZI SCHEME,
WE WANT IN—ON THAT AMERICAN…

ALL. DREAM!

End of Scene

INSTRUCTIONS TO MY FUTURE LIFE PARTNER RE: WHAT TO DO IN THE EVENT OF MY (SUDDEN, HEARTBREAKING, HEROIC AND/OR DRAMATIC) DEATH.

by Deborah Stein

SCENE.

A PowerPoint presentation. [Note: In the production at Actors Theatre, the text from slides was written on flip-chart paper. Productions are encouraged to use whatever form works best for them.]

SLIDE:

Instructions to my future life partner re: what to do in the event of my (sudden, heartbreaking, heroic and/or dramatic) death.

SLIDE:

Wherein I lay out the main points:

- A last hello.
- One day I will die.
- Goodbye and thank you.
- What to do with my body/ashes/organs/other (?)
- What NOT to do with my body in the event of &c &c.
- The event/party/ceremony/nothing at all (?)
- Last Will and Conclusion

SLIDE: A last hello.

(PERFORMER *speaks.*)

PERFORMER. Hello.

(*Beat.*)

SLIDE: One day I will die.

(*Beat.*)

SLIDE: Goodbye and thank you.

Thank you for looking hot today, even though I am dead, and that must be sad for you. I hope you are happy thinking of the many awesome years of travel, adventure, hard work, and great sex that we will hopefully share before the day you watch this.

I hope there are still computers, and that we haven't had to repurpose the parts for fuel, and that there is enough electricity to watch this in full.

I hate to think of you all alone, and in the dark.

SLIDE: What to do with my body/ashes/organs/other (?)

- Shoot my body out of a cannon.
- Donate my organs to science.
- Use me to fertilize the floral jungle in the Gorilla Exhibit at the Zoo.
- Preserve me cryogenically.
- Send my body into space.
- Shoot my <u>ashes</u> out of a cannon.
- Cast me in a TV procedural as the corpse character.

To start. One option is to shoot my body out of a cannon. You can do this while also simultaneously donating my organs to science.

Alternately, number three, using my body to fertilize the—

Wait.

Are there still zoos, when you are watching this?

Are there gorillas?

(*Beat.*)

By the time you watch this, it is quite possible that there are no more zoos in the world, and any remaining gorillas now roam freely in the cities and suburbs. That we have been encapsulated—taken over—by an exurban jungle—

I hope we meet each other before things change too much. So we can experience the major events of our lifetime together.

To share such things as glaciers melting, oceans boiling, the deserts spontaneously combusting, the continent shelf of California severed at its fault lines, ripped from the mainland and floating as an isolated cluster of islands 40 times the size of Hawaii, governments toppling and reforming into self-selecting bands of tribes—

Or will that be too sad? Should I hope instead that we meet after the major catastrophic changes of our lifetimes have occurred, so we don't have to endure the melancholy of remembering a life we once had but to which we can never return?

(*Beat.*)

Where was I?

SLIDE: What NOT to do with my body in the event of &c &c.
- **Do not scatter my ashes in the ocean(s).**

Oh yes.

Under no circumstances do I want to be scattered in the ocean.

By the time I die, it is quite likely that the oceans will be taking over the earth, due to the melting of glaciers, and we will have spent so many years battling the dangers posed by their roiling currents that I will be sick and tired of the oceans and I won't want anything to do with any of them in the afterlife.

I know you disagree with me. This is one of the things we fought about. Will fight about. Will have fought about.

But you should know that I really loved you when you said that we should become pirates. And I always regretted not taking you up on that. Because, really, if you want to be a pirate, and that's really important to you, I could get into that.

When things get bad it will be important to form a tribe. You can be the leader if you want, I'll trust you. I'll believe in you. We'll teach each other and our children how to kill prey with our bare hands and how to make a fire and how to fashion tools from slate and bark—how to make leather and mill flour—

and if the ocean thing happens, which it might, we'll build a raft, a really sturdy raft of repurposed materials like stainless steel pots and plastic toilet seats, and we'll stay afloat on whatever body of water washes us away. We will be prepared. We will survive the wet wilderness. We will thrive.

And even if I'm wrong about all this, thank you for believing in me enough to go along with it.

SLIDE: The event/party/ceremony/nothing at all (?)

I want wailing at my funeral. And dancing. And really good music.

Yellow tuxedo with green velvet trim. I want to be sexy one last time.

I want to be cooked and prepared by the best chef in Paris, and then served with a really good wine. I want a thousand paper cranes falling from the rafters. A thousand butterflies. A motorcycle parade. Shoot my ashes into the sky in a wide rainbow arc, spell my name in the stars. Spell your name! Freddie Mercury! David Bowie! BARACK OBAMA!

SLIDE: Last Will and Conclusion.

No. I don't want any kind of scene at all. I want to be grateful that I lived a good life, and to go with grace.

Most of all, after I am gone, I want you to feel able to move on into the world alone and without me, that I am gone and it's okay. Because you are strong and beautiful. And even though the glaciers have melted and wild gorillas have taken over large swaths of what remains of the North American continent, you know that we built that raft together and it's safe and sturdy and well equipped with salted meats and iodine for purifying the drinking water, and you have mad pirate skills, and you're going to be okay, because I love you.

End of Scene

LOSING YOUR LIFE WITH ANNE AND DAVID
by All

     Lights up.

DAVID. Now.

ANNE. Ciao.

     (*They embrace. Heavenly light beams down. Lights down.*)

End of Scene

TROJANS—TIME TO GO
by Peter Sinn Nachtrieb

DUREX *and* RAMSES, *extremely extremely old, both enter, each carrying ceramic vaces filled with wheat. They meet in the center of the stage, put their vases down. They stare at each other, smile.*

RAMSES. I still can't believe we survived the Trojan War.

DUREX. Best stabber ever. I told you.

RAMSES. Still can't believe we made it back to Greece.

DUREX. Still can't believe you went to the bow of the ship with me.

(*They smile again.*)

RAMSES. So many years.

DUREX. So many journeys.

RAMSES. Ups and Downs.

DUREX. Famines, Feasts.

RAMSES. Tragedies, Surprises.

DUREX. Joy and Pain.

RAMSES. So many vases.

DUREX. So much wheat.

(*Beat.*)

RAMSES. I'm going to miss this world.

DUREX. Me too.

RAMSES. I'm glad you're here.

DUREX. For eternity.

RAMSES. Maybe we'll become a constellation.

DUREX. Our names remembered and honored forever.

RAMSES. Ramses and Durex.

(*They chuckle.*)

DUREX. Ready?

RAMSES. It's time.

(DUREX *and* RAMSES *take coins or coin glasses out of their pockets and place them on each others eyes.*)
(*They take each other's hands.*)
(*Together, they descend into the Underworld.*)

End of Scene

GRANDPA'S COLOGNE: THREE
by Kristoffer Diaz
Music & Lyrics by Greg Kotis

DANNY *enters, ready for his date.*

DANNY. Jolie lived on the other side of the condo complex, so I made my way over there as soon as I was ready. I looked good, I smelled good, and I had a pocket full of cash. I had a plan. Tonight was the night I'd become a man…and maybe even get a kiss on the cheek.

(*He walks to* JOLIE's *door.*)

In our condo complex, each apartment door had a gate. I got to her door, I knocked, her grandmother answered.

(JOLIE'S GRANDMOTHER *comes to the door.*)

(*She reacts to the smell of the cologne.*)

JOLIE'S GRANDMOTHER. Can I help you?

DANNY. I'm here to pick up Jolie. For our date.

JOLIE'S GRANDMOTHER. Your date.
Really.
Hold on.

(JOLIE'S GRANDMOTHER *goes into the condo.*)

DANNY. And it was that simple. I was seconds away from adulthood. Any minute now, the girl of my dreams would come to the door, dressed up, smelling good, ready for the time of her life. The guys all talked so much, but I was the only one gutsy enough to just ask her out, and now I was going to be rewarded. (JOLIE *comes to the door. She is in her pajamas. She doesn't open the gate.*) Hi Jolie, ready for our date? (*To audience.*) She clearly wasn't ready, but I was so excited I didn't notice.

JOLIE. Our date?

DANNY. Yeah. I asked you out a few hours ago, you said yes. We're going to McDonald's. You ready? (*To audience.*) She wasn't ready, but I didn't notice.

JOLIE. A date?

DANNY. Yeah. A date.

JOLIE. You were serious about that? (*No response.*) I mean, you're very sweet, but you're not my type. I'm too old for you. I have braces. And a bra. (*No response.*) But it is very sweet. You're brave. And you smell good. (*No response.*) You okay?

DANNY. Me? Yeah. I'm fine. (*Pause.*) Can I get a little kiss on the cheek at least?

(JOLIE *laughs sweetly.*)

JOLIE. No. See you around, Danny.

(JOLIE *closes the door.*

DANNY *walks away.*
DANNY *returns to his friends.*
DANNY *hangs his head. A guitarist appears and plays one dramatic chord.*
MATTHEW *appears in the audience and sings.*)

SONG: GRANDPA'S COLOGNE REPRISE

MATTHEW.

THERE'S NOTHING QUITE LIKE A MAN
WHO WOULD WEAR HIS GRANDFATHER'S COLOGNE
TO MELT THE HEART OF ANY WOMAN,
AND LET HER SEE THAT AS A MAN
YOU STAND ALONE!

DANNY.

SO JOLIE WON'T GO ON A DATE WITH ME
THAT'S OK
'CAUSE I'M ONLY IN THE FIFTH GRADE ANYWAY, LET
      ME SAY
FIRST DATE TO HEARTBREAK, AT LEAST IT MAKES YOU
      THINK
AND LIFE'S NOT OVER YET
I'M ON THE BRINK!

(*As the last chord sounds, men enter from the voms and begin beatboxing; women appear in the house. After sixteen beats, the women sing over continuing percussion. Additional instruments join in throughout.*)

WOMEN.

GRANDPA'S COLOGNE IS NICE AND STRONG
JUST LIKE A MAN'S SUPPOSED TO BE.
GRANDPA'S COLOGNE IS LIKE A CLOUD OF LOVE,
ON THIS WE GIRLS AGREE.

AND WHEN SHE SMELLS YOU,
ALL THE WORLD WILL SIGH,
SHE'LL BE YOUR GIRLFRIEND THEN,
AND YOU WILL BE HER—

(*Instruments off; women add percussion; men sing.*)

MEN.

GRANDPA'S COLOGNE IS NICE AND STRONG
JUST LIKE A MAN'S SUPPOSED TO BE.
GRANDPA'S COLOGNE IS LIKE A CLOUD OF LOVE,
ON THIS WE BOYS AGREE.

AND WHEN SHE SMELLS YOU,
ALL THE WORLD WILL SIGH,

SHE'LL BE YOUR GIRLFRIEND THEN,
AND YOU WILL BE HER—
(*Women sing with men, instruments play.*)

ALL.

GRANDPA'S COLOGNE IS NICE AND STRONG
JUST LIKE A MAN'S SUPPOSED TO BE.
GRANDPA'S COLOGNE IS LIKE A CLOUD OF LOVE,
ON THIS WE GIRLS/BOYS AGREE.

AND WHEN SHE SMELLS YOU
ALL THE WORLD WILL SIGH.
SHE'LL BE YOUR GIRLFRIEND THEN,
AND YOU WILL BE HER GUY!
AND YOU WILL BE HER GUY!

End of Play